Praise for the first edition

"Ed Stetzer has written the new standard in church planting books. He has a story to tell, and he tells it with both precision and passion. Those who are already sold on the kingdom activity of church planting will be encouraged by this. But this book reads like a recruiting manual. It will charge up those who haven't yet gotten the bug."

Steve Sjogren
Launching Pastor, Vineyard Community Church Cincinnati, Ohio
Author, *Community of Kindness: A Refreshing New Approach to Planting and Growing a Church*

"Church planting has truly come of age. Ed Stetzer has masterfully engaged the priority of church multiplication with the Church's need to be culturally relevant. This work is comprehensive and, more importantly, it is integrative. Drawing from hundreds of sources, he has helped us all step into a new era that decompartmentalizes the sodalic work of the Church. He deals realistically with common obstacles for planting churches and gives leaders a compelling motivation for the highly focused mission of expanding the witness of Christ through church planting."

Kevin W. Mannoia
Dean, Haggard School of Theology
Azusa Pacific University
Author, *Church Planting: The Next Generation*

"Stetzer helps the new church developer think missionally, theologically, and practically about the process of starting new churches. I encourage you to read carefully, glean insights, and prayerfully apply the principles to your unique situation."

Bob Logan
Executive Director, CoachNet International Ministries
Co-developer, *The Church Planter's Toolkit*

"I give Ed Stetzer's Planting New Churches in a Postmodern Age a five-star rating. His treatment of the topic is theologically grounded, mission focused, well researched, richly referenced, and bears the mark of authenticity from someone who writes out of his own experience. If

I could buy only one book on church planting this would be my first choice."

Eddie Gibbs
Donald A. McGavran Professor of Church Growth
Fuller Theological Seminary
Author, *ChurchNext*

"I like this book! In *Planting New Churches in a Postmodern Age*, Ed Stetzer provides us with a fresh mind-set as he tackles church planting from a postmodern perspective. He blends well Scripture and theology in what is an extremely practical hands-on approach to church planting."

Aubrey Malphurs
Pastoral Ministries Department
Dallas Theological Seminary
Author, *Planting Growing Churches in the Twenty-first Century*

"Ed Stetzer is a wonderful theologian-practitioner, and he has provided a blueprint for church planting that is at once faithful to the message we proclaim and relevant to its proclamation in our fragile, changing world. This book is a timely gift to the church of Jesus Christ. No one should try to plant a church without it!"

Timothy George
Dean, Beeson Divinity School of Samford University
Executive editor, *Christianity Today*

"Ed Stetzer has done a great service for the churches of North America. In this book he has laid out a practical strategy for evangelizing North America by planting new churches. Stetzer's book successfully integrates biblical revelation, theology, postmodern philosophy, and sound, practical application. He explains why new churches are needed, and he teaches the reader how to start these churches. All those with a passion to see North America come to Christ would do well to read and heed this book."

John Mark Terry
Missionary and Professor
Malaysia Baptist Theological Seminary

"In this one book, Ed Stetzer has taken the complex issue of postmodernity and given church leaders a handle to address the need and opportunity. This book gives the reader basic how-to's of planting a church which will effectively evangelize and congregationalize. It addresses why and how church leaders should be planting churches. Ed Stetzer leads the reader through all the steps and issues which must be addressed to plant a church that can thrive in the twenty-first century."

Richard H. Harris
Vice President, Church Planting
North American Mission Board

"For long years we have had few books on church planting. Then, beginning in the 1970s, various helpful titles began to appear. Now we have one of the very best of them. Ed Stetzer's book grows out of extensive experience, thoroughgoing research, and the kind of dynamic involvement that has been evidenced by many evangelical groups in recent years. For solid preparation and step-by-step know-how, read this book before undertaking a church plant. For in course correction and direction, keep it close at hand from start to finish."

David Hesselgrave
Emeritus Professor of Missions
Trinity International University
Author, *Cross-Cultural Church Planting*

"Ed Stetzer has written a church planting book that will be effective in reaching the postmodern, i.e., the new emerging generation in America. Look carefully; he does not instruct us how to build "the church of yesterday," nor does he instruct us how to plant "the church of yesterday," nor does he instruct us how to plant "the church of today;" but Stetzer's focus is on "the church of tomorrow." He does not give us the principles that worked in the 50s; but with careful research into statistics, case studies, and from the vast field of authority, the author has given us practical steps in planting a church that will reach Generation-Next."

Elmer L. Towns
Dean, School of Religion, Liberty University
Author, *Starting a New Church*

"*Planting New Churches in a Postmodern Age* is comprehensive and practical, deals with both strategy and tactics, and is relevant, addressing this age between modernity and postmodernity most helpfully. It sets church planting in biblical and historical perspective, seeing North America and Europe as genuine mission fields demanding that Christ's followers make disciples and gather new congregations.

Church planters, denominational executives, mission administrators, and missiologists should read and reread this book."

Charles L. Chaney
Author, *Church Planting at the End of the Twentieth Century*

"*Planting New Churches in a Postmodern Age* by Ed Stetzer simultaneously blends the information of a theoretician with the insight of a practitioner while stressing both the content of Scripture and context of ministry. This book is the best to date on the subject of church planting in our emerging culture and is invaluable to all concerned with the mission of God and ministry of new churches."

Mark Driscoll
Pastor, Mars Hill Church, Seattle WA
Co-founder, Acts 29 Church Planting Network

"Ed Stetzer has done an important service to the church by 'breaking the code' in terms of how to evangelize people and people groups in today's world. The implications of this work move us one step closer to impacting effectively the North American mission field. *Planting New Churches in a Postmodern Age* moves beyond simply teaching church planters how to plant churches. It teaches them how to be missionaries, an absolute must in today's context. This work forces us to rethink how we approach our mission and gives us both practical and missional insights into achieving it."

David Putman
Founder of churchplanters.com
Co-author of *Breaking the Missional Code*

"As both a seasoned church planter and a respected scholar, Ed Stetzer delivers an exceptionally practical and well-integrated approach to the vast challenge of planting healthy, reproducing churches. Drawing insights from theology, culture and his years of experience in the church planting trenches, Stetzer shares helpful and innovative ways to communicate the gospel in a postmodern age without falling prey to compromise. This book is now required reading in all my seminary courses on church planting. I highly recommend it!"

Steve Childers
Professor of Practical Theology
Reformed Theological Seminary-Orlando
Director of U.S. Center for Church Planting, Inc.
www.churchplantingcenter.com

ED STETZER

PLANTING MISSIONAL CHURCHES

BROADMAN & HOLMAN PUBLISHERS
NASHVILLE, TENNESSEE

Printed in the United States of America

Ten-Digit ISBN: 0-8054-4370-3
Thirteen-Digit ISBN: 978-0-8054-4370-7

Published by Broadman & Holman Publishers
Nashville, Tennessee

This book revises *Planting New Churches in a Postmodern Age* (Broadman & Holman, 2003).

Dewey Decimal Classification: 254.1
Subject Heading: CHURCH PLANTING \
EVANGELISTIC WORK \ CHRCH GROWTH

1 2 3 4 5 6 7 8 9 10 11 12 15 14 13 12 11 10 09 08 07 06
D

Dedication

To my co-pastors at Lake Ridge Church, Philip Nation and Travis Vaughn, with whom I have the joy of planting the gospel in North Georgia.

Thanks to Carolyn Curtis, Pat Gillen, Dino Senesi, Andy Williams, Jeff Farmer, and Lizette Beard for their help on this book.

Contents

Preface

I believe in church planting. More to the point for this book, I believe in church planters. (This morning at 6:30 a.m. we started to set up, and I was reminded of the challenge.) Many examples and insights come from the three churches I've planted. And I've invested myself personally and professionally in folks who are following God's call into this much-needed endeavor. Oddly enough, the last month has been a church-planting month for me. I had the privilege of planting a new church where I currently live in Cumming, Georgia (Lake Ridge Church), speaking at the tenth anniversary of a church I planted in Erie, Pennsylvania (Millcreek Community Church), and speaking to the new pastor of a church I planted in Buffalo, New York (Calvary Christian Church), who helped start the church as a layperson eighteen years ago. It is a humbling experience to see the failures and successes of the churches you have planted, all while writing an updated book on church planting.

I have done church planting perhaps more than anything else in my ministry life. When I was not planting, I was working with planters. While teaching at a major seminary, I spent thousands of hours recruiting, teaching, training, and encouraging potential church planters. Later I recruited planters in a denominational capacity, not only finding people but pouring myself into them. Now my denominational responsibilities have changed. From my vantage point as Research Team Director and Missiologist, I see the need for effective church planting even more clearly. Today I combine our research work with the real-life effort of planting a church. In short, church planting is my passion—involving people and equipping them for the process. And I'm committed to excellence in the effort.

Which brings me to you, my reader and perhaps a church planter like me. God bless you and your work. You're headed into the adventure of a lifetime, and I pray this book helps. And, if experience is the great teacher, it will. It's jam-packed with wisdom, insights, and ideas from people as passionate about church planting as I am.

Since the book's first publication, much has changed in church planting. I have tried to reflect that here. Sources range from people who've studied the subject to people who've learned by doing and were willing to share their blunders as well as their successes. And what I couldn't fit into the volume you're holding spills onto my Web site at www.newchurches.com. Between the book and the Web site, you have a toolbox of much more than what you'll need. And that's the point. Because, as you'll soon see, there's no magic formula. (If there were, this would be a really thin book!) Effective church planting requires using tools that work in the context of the environment. And today no two environments are the same.

More info can be found at www.newchurches.com.

That's because church planting is a fast-changing field and one reason it's so exciting. For example, you will note the name change of the book. The first edition was called *Planting New Churches in a Postmodern Age*. The term *postmodern* has tended to lose much of its meaning, and I am not sure that the meaning was clear even in 2003.

I believe it is better to focus on *missional*, a broader term which emphasizes the approach rather than the population. Here's what I mean. Missional implies taking the approach of a missionary—being indigenous to the culture, seeking to understand and learn, adapting methods to the mission field—but winding up in the biblical form of a church. And, although the form is highly flexible, the purpose is the same: to see a biblical church planted in a local culture.

Chapter 1

Basics of Church Planting

The first major message of this book is to understand *missional*. Establishing a missional church means that you plant a church that's part of the culture you're seeking to reach. Since, in some cases, many will be hard-core emerging postmodern communities, this doesn't mean that the term postmodern can never be used. Thus, the mind-set of your mission field may be postmodern, but your methodology is still missional. Because we've heard so much about planting postmodern churches, we've come to think that's the goal. It's not. The goal of church planting is to reach people. They may be postmodern in their thinking, or they may be Korean or African American or young families or established professionals or counter-cultural or baby boomers or combinations of the above.

In most cases they will be combinations. In North America today, we have such a rapidly growing and changing population that church planters can't afford to target such a specific niche that we miss one part of a mission field in favor of another. And that's the tricky part, understanding the complicated fabric our society is weaving without becoming overwhelmed. For no church planter can do it all. You may gain a better understanding of families than singles. You may adapt methods that appeal more to young professionals than to retirees. But by *learning* about the components of the mission field around you, *reaching* at least some of them as effectively as you can, *adapting* your approaches while remaining faithful to the gospel—all of this is missional.

So, congratulations, reader, you're not only a church planter but a missionary! And can you see how we've come to this? At the same time we're experiencing rapid population shifts, we're seeing enormous changes in attitudes, in worldviews. It's possible to be a missionary without ever leaving your zip code. And that's a good thing because it helps you understand better than ever the second major message of this book, which is how the incarnation relates to church planting.

Missional is the posture—the way in church we approach people in culture—but *incarnational* describes what's actually happening. Just as Christ came to live among us, we dwell with the people around us. In many ways, we're like them. But we're changed, transformed; and because of that, we seek to change and transform. The concept of being incarnational as it relates to church planting emphasizes the importance of relationships in effective church planting. It's not about establishing a location for worship; it's about establishing a basis for coming together in the first place. Good church planting depends on good relationships.

It also depends on solid *theology*, which is the third major message. Relevance to the culture should never clash with the power of the gospel. There is much theological revisioning right now; some people are, in the name of missional thinking, abandoning basic theological messages. However, this book is not that book. Bible-based theology is the foundation for a successful church plant. No apologies for that!

The fourth major message is expressed in the word *ecclesiological*; the church matters. We know this because the New Testament is full of descriptions of how to transform the culture. The examples are all based on churches. Believers come together in churches, becoming stronger as individuals and as a body, with the goal of becoming the body, which in turn can transform the culture. That does not mean that the goal of a church is a brick building, large group, or incorporation. Yet the biblical idea and model of church *does* matter and *is* the goal of church planting. Church matters.

Fifth, today's successful church planter is *spiritual*—focused on spiritual formation. This may sound like a no-brainer (and perhaps it should be). But to be realistic about the state of church planting in North America, let's admit something: many church planters are by nature entrepreneurs, mavericks, free spirits, sometimes even misfits. (Thank God he can use cracked pots.) That energy can be harnessed and focused to be used for God's glory but only if the church planter is Christ-centered and transformed by the power of the gospel. In other words, a newcomer needs to leave the church being amazed by the awesome God the church planter serves, not what a cool preacher the church has.

I can relate to all these messages and more. I've come a long way myself and am still learning.

My own experience in church planting began in June 1988. I'd just graduated from college with an undergraduate degree in natural sciences. I arrived in Buffalo, New York, ready to start my first church. I was twenty-one years old and had a vision to reach the entire city but little experience and no training. I didn't know it then, but desire wasn't enough. The church was not the great success I thought it would be. Although the church grew and we saw people changed by the power of the gospel, I could have avoided countless mistakes with proper training.

TODAY'S CHURCH PLANTER SHOULD BE

- Missional
- Incarnational
- Theological
- Ecclesiological
- Spiritual

When I was planting this church, our district association was strategizing to plant seven new churches within three years. The church I started in inner-city Buffalo, Calvary Christian, continues to this day with a faithful part-time pastor who was a layman at Calvary when the church started eighteen years ago. It is not a large church, but it is a faithful church in an area known for drugs and prostitution, and it is now planting a French-speaking African church in its facility.

Only one other district church plant from that time is still alive. It is a small church that took over the property of another church to survive. (One other church started, died, then restarted with a different name and location.) So an ambitious church-planting effort that began with great enthusiasm dwindled to a whimper. Discouraged and demoralized, our church planting supervisor left the area and then the ministry. Untrained and discouraged pastors left the field for better salaries and better possibilities in established churches elsewhere.

My first attempt at church planting did not struggle because of lack of effort. I wore out my knuckles knocking on doors. With the help of partnership churches, we contacted tens of thousands of residents to start Calvary, canvassing neighborhoods, ringing doorbells, talking to people on their front stoops and porches. When Calvary decided to sponsor a new congregation, Lancaster Bible Church, we did so with what we assumed was an innovative strategy, using billboards. The team generated many ideas and worked hard hours, but little success followed. (That church later died and was restarted.)

At this time in western New York and across North America, some strategies had succeeded. Successful church plants had shared their methods of success with others. Practices such as direct mail, telemarketing campaigns, and large grand openings had appeared infrequently but had become hot topics of discussion. At the first church I started, we began a direct-mail campaign and experienced some success. This piqued my interest in new techniques. However, many of these early methods no longer work as well as they once did, as I discovered in my next church plant (Millcreek Community Church, Erie, Pennsylvania) and the one I'm currently involved in planting (Lake Ridge Church, Cumming, Georgia). The rapidly changing cultural landscape requires that we use different methods to reach different communities.

More important, many of us in church planting have begun to realize that some things need to change in our field of work. When I think about the churches I planted, I have to say that I missed a lot of the key values discussed in this book. When I planted Calvary Christian Church at the age of twenty-one, I must confess that the church was more about me than it was missional and spiritual. When I planted Millcreek Community Church and its daughter churches, we were more attractional than incarnational and not particularly theological or ecclesiological. Simply put, much of this book is birthed out of the struggle and failure of church planting. Hopefully, we have learned enough that Lake Ridge will reflect more of the character of Christ than the character of our planting team.

Today much more material on church planting is available, and it's catching the interest of evangelicals. Church planting conferences meet regularly with hundreds in attendance. Thousands of Web sites are devoted to church planting. (Only two years ago, a Google search produced 244,000; now I find 940,000 entries.) My own church planting Web site received more than six thousand hits per month. Many evangelical denominations have placed a renewed emphasis on the subject. My employer, the North American Mission Board of the Southern Baptist Convention, has committed to plant eleven thousand new churches by the year 2010. Other denominations have adopted similarly aggressive strategies. That's good news, particularly when it's partnered with better biblical foundations than in years past.

Objections to Church Planting

In spite of this, some people in church circles are not enthusiastic about this new emphasis on church planting. They misunderstand the purposes and intentions of church planters and new church starts. Perhaps they don't realize that God calls ordinary people to reach the lost among them, mistakenly thinking church planting is a task only for great visionary pastors who can go where no one has gone before. To others church planting is an alternative so that problem pastors can start their own churches without meddlesome lay leaders. And still others see church planting as a waste of valuable time and money, resources that could be used to revitalize declining churches. Finally, some see church planting as merely a way of stealing members from nearby churches.

While these problems may be true in some instances, the goal of missional church planting is glorifying God, growing his kingdom, and developing healthy churches with new converts. It's a godly, even respectable, goal; and the respect should go both directions. Nearby churches may be older, smaller, and more traditional; but they've paved the way for new churches to move ahead. And missional church planters focus on the Great Commission by reaching the unchurched, not by seeking to attract area Christians.

Church planting is essential. Without it Christianity will continue to decline in North America. According to easumbandy.com: "Studies show that if a denomination wishes to reach more people, the number of new churches it begins each year must equal at least 3% of the denomination's existing churches. Based on this formula, mainline denominations are failing to plant enough churches to offset their decline."[1] Without church planting, denominations will decline; but more important, the number of Christians will continue to decline. In fact, the few denominations that are growing attribute their growth to the increase in ethnic church plants. This shows that new populations to North America are being reached, which we celebrate, but established populations are not.

For denominations (or any partnership of churches) church planting is essential. The Reformed Church in America commissioned a study to find why some denominations grew and others did not. They studied nine evangelical denominations. Their first observation on the list explained that:

Church Planting Is Given High Priority

> All denominations surveyed placed church planting as a very important, if not the number one, strategy for evangelism.... The fact is, starting a new ethnic congregation or focusing on a particular generation in a new start is much easier than trying to change the culture of an established congregation.[2]

As for the objection about using resources to revitalize dying churches versus planting new ones, my belief is that both emphases are necessary. We want to see dying churches revitalized. God has allowed me the privilege of leading four churches through the process of revisioning, and it's a wonderful experience. But we must also start new churches.

Objections to church planting? Let's dig deeper, and find out what's really going on.

***

How did Christianity change from a faith spread primarily through church planting to a faith in which church planting is rare, sometimes even controversial?

One answer is that, as congregations become established and mature, the people who've invested themselves in those churches become protective, even wary of new ideas that might threaten the status quo. A new church plant—with all its excitement, attention, and buzz—seems like a competitor instead of a welcome newcomer. And why not? It's nice to be comfortable, isn't it? Protection and security are natural human tendencies. (Does your mother want her hard-earned retirement money invested in secure bonds and CDs or in a high-tech start-up company run by a bunch of twenty-somethings?)

But many pastors understand the need for, let's say, a charismatic, Presbyterian, and Baptist church in each community to serve the needs of members in these denominations. Yet many of those same pastors are hesitant to plant another church similar to their own in the same geography even though a different music style or congregational approach might reach an entirely different population segment. *It could be competition*, they reason. *Worse, it might make the older church seem tired and out-of-date by comparison.*

That attitude can spread like the flu. Laypeople in established and perhaps traditional churches who genuinely have a heart for reaching the lost in, for example, Asia or Africa sense that their pastor or other powers-that-be are uncomfortable and suspicious of the neighboring church start. So they become wary as well. *What can those people be doing over there? The music is loud, and, well, they don't even meet in a proper church with an organ or a steeple.* The reason for the change, engaging in mission among a new people, is missed. Ironically, they're completely on board with sharing the gospel in the language of a tribe of people in a faraway land, but they don't realize that same missionary tactic would be useful right there in Anytown, North America. And they certainly don't drop in just to see what's going on—like you might try that new restaurant your brother-in-law recommended—because that could be seen as disloyal to the church where they've invested so much of themselves. So the more they circle the wagons, the less they learn about missional church planting. And the cycle continues.

***

Critics of church planting usually don't voice their objections in such a straightforward manner. They typically raise a predictable series of objections. Here are a few.

1. Large-church mentality. For many the idea of one large church is more attractive than multiple churches. Large churches have the resources and programs to be full-service congregations. Thus, many leaders think the most efficient denominational strategy is to help medium churches become large churches.

Despite this bigger-is-better mentality, statistics do not support the assumption that size is necessarily the best way to reach people. Though large churches are often more cost effective than small churches, new churches are more effective than large churches, particularly in evangelism. On a per-capita basis, new churches win more people to Christ than established churches. Bruce McNichol explained the findings of his research in *Interest* magazine:

- Churches under three years of age win an average of ten people to Christ per year for every hundred church members.
- Churches three to fifteen years of age win an average of five people per year for every hundred church members.
- Churches over fifteen years of age win an average of three people per year for every hundred church members.[3]

Clearly, the newer a congregation, the more effective that church is in reaching those who don't know Christ.

If we know new churches reach more people per capita and if we value reaching the unchurched, we must conclude that the most effective method of evangelism is planting. And it's gaining new attention because it's a biblical method that works.

2. Parish-church mind-set. Both the large-church mentality and the parish-church mind-set limit the number of churches possible in an area. The large-church mentality focuses on developing larger congregations for a region. As described earlier, the parish-church mind-set advocates the presence of only one denominational church for a region.

A parish is simply a geographical region (Louisiana still calls its counties "parishes"). A denominational parish has historically been defined as a region needing only one church to meet the spiritual or congregational needs of its people in that area. This has its roots in Europe. Roman Catholics, Lutherans, and Episcopalians formally follow the parish model when planning the placement of new churches, and most other denominations follow it informally. They expect one church to meet the denominational and spiritual needs of a specific area. Proposals for new churches meet resistance because a church already exists in the area proposed for a new congregation. That resistance shows the parish-church mind-set: if a denomination has one church in a "community," the denomination has sufficiently reached that community, or so the thinking goes.

Parish mentality is a primary reason the church-to-population ratio is declining. Churches often die because people move out of rural areas to urban and suburban settings. Yet new churches may not be started in the new urban and suburban area because they're too close to other established churches of the same denomination. This and other factors have caused a decline in the church-to-population ratio.

Our Research Team at the North American Mission Board recently recalcuated the church-to-population ratio based on statistics from the U.S. Census.

- In 1900, there were 28 churches for every 10,000 Americans.
- In 1950, there were 17 churches for every 10,000 Americans.
- In 2000, there were 12 churches for every 10,000 Americans.
- In 2004, the latest year available, there are 11 churches for every 10,000 Americans.[4]

In 1900, the Census Bureau counted 212,000 churches. In 2000, the number of churches that existed in the United States was 349,506. In other words, the number of churches increased just over 50 percent while the population of the country has almost quadrupled. This decline in church-to-population ratio helps to explain the decline of the North American church during the past century. It's frustrating to evangelicals. At a minimum we should attempt to keep up with the population, but if we are truly to reach people in culture, we should want to do much more!

3. **Professional-church syndrome.** One of the greatest hindrances to church planting in North America is the notion that all churches must have seminary-trained pastors to be legitimate. My personal belief is that seminary education is important in helping provide doctrinal stability, ministry skills, and spiritual depth. My point, however, is that years of academic training are not necessary to start a church. In fact, waiting for a seminary-trained pastor in many cases delays God-called people from starting a church. (Now that I've said this, I'll point out that I take a high view of education, having taught at seminary and having personally earned two masters degrees and two doctorates. However, I stick to my guns on this. My educational choices are my own. Many well-qualified and highly successful church planters I know—in fact, most of them—made different educational choices.)

Roland Allen concluded that evangelistic growth in new churches is often inversely proportional to educational attainment.[5] Allen believed the more education a pastor had, the less effective he likely he would be in the evangelistic task.

With the increased professionalization (education) of the clergy, church planting has suffered. Seminary-trained pastors often expect full-time salaries provided by established churches. During their years of education, seminarians sometimes accumulate significant debt that makes impossible either (1) bivocationalism (having two jobs, one ministry and one secular) or (2) volunteer ministry. On the other hand denominational leaders often consider pastoral candidates without seminary training to be ineligible or unprepared to plant new churches. These biases hurt church planting.

However, both history and present-day practices of several faith groups tell another story. American history records that lay preachers effectively planted many Baptist and Methodist churches along the American frontier.[6] Today charismatic and Pentecostal churches encourage "anointed" persons, regardless of their level of theological training, to start churches. It's not surprising that Calvary Chapel, Vineyard, and Open Bible Standard churches are some of the most effective church-planting denominations in North America today. This is specifically because of their openness to using God-called, though not formally trained, leaders in founding new churches. (I caution that doctrinal error easily emerges in movements that don't provide adequate basic theological training. Wise denominations provide a middle option: offering training by extension for interested lay leaders and bivocational pastors.)

If we limit ourselves by assuming that pastors and church planters must be seminary graduates in order to plant new churches, we may never reach some areas of North America, such as expansive apartment complexes, mobile home villages, marinas, townhouse communities, and sparsely populated rural areas. Because of conditions such as poverty, transience, size, etc., many of these areas cannot support a "professional" seminary-trained pastor expecting a full-time salary. However, let's look more closely at the opportunities for evangelism and church planting in settings such as these, which experts call "multihousing" communities. By even conservative estimates, approximately 40 percent of United States residents (more in Canada) live in multihousing communities, yet only 5 percent of them (in the U.S. that's an estimated 5,000,000 of 100,000,000 persons!) *have any significant connection with any kind of church*. This population segment constitutes the largest unreached people group in North America. According to www.onmission.com, 60 percent of the unchurched in North America live in multihousing communities. Most of the people who will go into such communities and plant churches will not have spent seven years in college and seminary.

Obviously, the professional-church syndrome is a difficulty which denominations must overcome while simultaneously providing theologically sound and practical training for church planters.

4. **Rescue-the-perishing syndrome.** This is the idealistic assumption that denominations should first rescue dying churches before planting new ones. Every church planter has heard the objection: Why should we start new churches when so many struggle and die? However, saving dead and dying churches is much more difficult and ultimately more costly than starting new ones. Some authorities even argue that changing a rigid, tradition-bound congregation is almost impossible. As Lyle Schaller has indicated, even if it is possible, nobody knows how to do it on a large-scale basis.[7] Starting new churches is much easier and, perhaps, a better overall stewardship of kingdom resources, just as it's sometimes more cost-effective to purchase a new vehicle, rather than pouring money into an old one to keep it running like new. (Embracing a church's history and legacy is important, but the church cannot lose its mission and direction without developing some serious oil leaks and knocks under the hood.)

The ideal strategy, of course, is to do both—help revitalize dying churches and simultaneously plant new churches. Stuart Murray addresses the issue well: "Current initiatives to plant thousands of new churches are ill-conceived unless these are accompanied by a significant reversal of the decades of decline. . . . There is no empirical evidence to support such an expectation at present."[8]

Murray proposes, and I agree, that we need a strategy to revitalize established churches and, at the same time, to plant thousands of new churches. He explains: "Churches have been leaking hundreds of members each week for many years. Planting more of these churches is not a mission strategy worth pursuing. But planting new kinds of churches may be a key to effective missions and a catalyst for the renewal of existing churches."[9]

Church revitalization does not happen much, but it does happen sometimes. I have been struck by how infrequently it actually occurs. During a recent breakfast conversation with Len Sweet, Len explained to me that recent studies show that nine of ten people who are told by doctors to "change or die" cannot do so. In other words, they are told to stop smoking, lose weight, or quit drinking in order to survive, and nine of ten die rather than change. Churches are similar; they often choose their traditions over their future. But some can and do change.

Let's look at an example—Summit Church in Durham, North Carolina, formerly named Homestead Heights Baptist Church. HHBC was an older church in Durham that fit the description of many Baptist churches in the area. Under Pastor J. D. Greear the church has seen some major revitalization. It had always been a large church, but as the Durham community changed around it, coupled with some internal issues, the church rapidly declined in attendance. J. D. began as the youth pastor at this church, but a few years ago they called him to lead in a fresh direction as pastor.

Changing the church's name to Summit, they did much more than change their marquee. They started becoming intentionally missional in how they operated. In fact, the church recently sold its large, historic building to start meeting in a high school. This approach may seem backward to many traditional churches, but Summit Church considers it a great opportunity to become mobile and look for a location that will better suit their mission. As a church that's developed an intensely missional mindset, they're not only involved in starting and partnering with new churches and ministries overseas; they're also taking the same missional approach at home. Their once-dwindling attendance is now more than fifteen hundred and growing.

Summit is just one example. The point, of course, is that both revitalization and new church planting are needed. Unfortunately, many who call for the revitalization of dying churches do so while also finding "convincing" objections to church planting. We need strategies to revitalize those churches which desire change. We also need to plant thousands of new churches throughout North America. If growing the kingdom is our ultimate objective, we must admit that one can't be accomplished without the other.

5. **Already-reached myth.** Among the strongest myths that discourage church planting is the flawed understanding that the United States and Canada are already evangelized. Certainly North American Christians have access to abundant resources of information. Evangelicals have been reading Larry Burkett for financial information, listening to James Dobson for advice on raising children, singing along with Third Day, and purchasing fiction by Tim LaHaye and Jerry Jenkins. But unchurched persons in North America remain generally untouched by this evangelical subculture and abide in darkness because we aren't drawing them in with a culturally relevant gospel witness.

While there are many Christian resources in North America, unchurched North Americans no longer have a biblical worldview or understanding. (Some experts question whether they ever did.) Instead, their religious ideas tend to be distorted reflections of biblical truth. In other words, secular people may be familiar with certain religious terminology or ideas, but their familiarity is often a distortion of its original meaning. For example, the most-quoted Bible verse by secular North Americans consists of two words, "Judge not." Though they know the verse, their understanding of its meaning is skewed. They believe it's wrong to judge another person's choices as wrong or immoral, as long as those choices hurt no one. (In fact, intolerance is becoming the unforgivable sin in North America.)

Unchurched North Americans know Jesus said not to judge, but they seriously misunderstand biblical teachings on morals. For example, they have no understanding of the teaching on church purity in 1 Corinthians and the command that the church should judge in a redemptive spirit. When secular culture moves farther and farther from biblical norms, perceptions develop shadows—even corruptions—of biblical reality.

George Hunter believes:

- There are 120 million secular undiscipled people in the United States.
- The U.S. is the largest mission field in the Western hemisphere.
- The U.S. is the fifth largest mission field on earth.[10]

The spiritual deadness of North America appears not only in its culture but in its churches as well. Churches in the first decade of the twenty-first century are closing at a phenomenal rate. Eighty to 85 percent of American churches are on the downside of their life cycle.[11] Win Arn reports thirty-five hundred to four thousand churches close each year.[12] The percentage of Christians in the U.S. population dropped 9 percent from 1990 to 2001.[13] The number of unchurched has almost doubled from 1991 to 2004.[14] Gallup provides further insight in a January 2002 poll—50 percent of Americans described themselves as "religious," while another 33 percent said that they are "spiritual but not religious" (11 percent said neither, and 4 percent said both).[15] A recent book, *Spiritual but Not Religious*, chronicles this growing trend.[16]

Our churches are dying, and our culture is changing. We know new churches can make a difference. Church planting is not easy, but without it the church will continue to decline in North America.

Conclusion

Obviously powerful ideas and mistaken attitudes work against church planting. Most of the North American church has not caught a vision for church planting and New Testament reproduction—at least not yet. Most Americans and Canadians are not connected to any local church. The North American church is in trouble. We need to plant new churches, or the church will continue to decline.

Even though some people oppose the idea of church planting, we must do it anyway—because it's biblical. In the following pages, you'll discover three compelling reasons to enact the biblical mandate for church planting: the command of Jesus, the need for new churches to reach North Americans, and the ineffectiveness of our present methodologies. Without church planting, we will not fulfill the Great Commission. Detailed explanations of the practical how-tos of church planting also will be included in this book.

Church planting is slowly regaining its biblical prominence in evangelical life. Between 1980 and 2000, more than fifty thousand churches were planted in North America. Christians are beginning to realize, once again, the need to place an emphasis on church planting in North America. And, even though there's some resistance to church planting, evangelicals are realizing its value and priority. This book is written to inform, to clarify, to encourage, and to persuade evangelicals to embrace church planting. May your passion for planting churches and growing the kingdom of God be enhanced as you read.

Questions for Reflection or Dialogue among Church Planters

1. Which objection to church planting did you have to personally overcome before you took the plunge?
2. What did planting a church cost you? Your family?
3. Which objections have you faced the most in your own ministry efforts?

4. What's the most important thing you'd want to share with a new church planter?

Resources for Further Reading

In addition to referenced material, below are some recommended resources. At www.newchurches.com, I have an annotated bibliography of the major church planting books with a focus on application in North America.

Childers, Steve L. *Gospel-Centered Church Planting Manual*. Orlando, Fla.: U.S. Center for Church Planting, Inc., 2002.

Hesselgrave, David J. *Planting Churches Cross-culturally*. Grand Rapids: Baker Book House, 2000.

Logan, Robert E., and Steven L. Ogne. *Church Planter's Toolkit* (tapes and workbook). St. Charles, Ill.: ChurchSmart Resources, 1991.

Malphurs, Aubrey. *Planting Growing Churches for the 21st Century: A Comprehensive Guide for New Churches and Those Desiring Renewal*, 2d edition. Grand Rapids: Baker Book House, 1998.

Murray, Stuart. *Church Planting: Laying Foundations*. Scottsdale, Pa.: Herald Press, 2001.

Wagner, C. Peter. *Church Planting for a Greater Harvest*. Ventura, Calif.: Regal Books, 1990.

http://www.churchplanting.com.
http://www.coachnet.org.
http://www.churchplantingvillage.com.
http://www.dcpi.org.

Chapter 2

Redeveloping a Missional Mind-set for North America

A seismic shift is beginning to rumble in the North American church, especially in church planting. For about twenty years church planting has moved from "suspicious activity" at best to "in vogue" in the body of Christ. Thanks to the dynamic unfolding of stories such as Saddleback Community Church and Rick Warren, Willow Creek Community Church and Bill Hybels, and others who were planting churches before church planting was "cool," becoming a church planter is no longer viewed as a profession you would need to hide from your mother.

Alongside that growing credibility in birthing fledgling faith communities has come another phenomenon in American Christianity, the megachurch. With a storied church history that affirmed the average size of U.S. churches to be seventy-five members, these 1980s church-starting pioneers also achieved an unprecedented level of success in attracting and assimilating disenfranchised, disconnected and spiritually disoriented people. The church of more than one thousand people, an anomaly in America before this recent wave, has become normal and accepted. In fact, new research by the Hartford (Seminary) Institute for Religion Research uncovered at least twelve thousand Protestant churches in the U.S. with more than two thousand weekly worship attenders, nearly 50 percent more than the figure of 850 commonly assumed and quoted by researchers (see http:fact.hartsem.edu/megachurchnews.html, posted May 5, 2005).

But after ten to fifteen years of massive effort by churches to reach megachurch status, George Barna reported some disturbing trends in his book *The Second Coming of the Church,* and in subsequent studies. With more megachurches than anytime in our history, and more people attending church than ever before in America, the culture has not for the most part been changed.

Barna's research indicates that attitudes *inside* the church are much the same as they are *outside* the church. The divorce rate is the same inside the church, and sometimes higher, than among the pagan pool outside of our ever-expanding walls. Beliefs and values were found to be similar among the churched and the still unchurched. Some religious observers would say that in our desire to *attract* people to fill our freshly padded seats, something went awry.

In becoming highly attraction-oriented bodies, some would say we lost some of our transformational edge along the way. We got the idea of contextual ministry—the missional mind-set and attitude that calls a missionary into a cross cultural setting; compels them to eat, drink, and talk like the natives, and love and serve them in Jesus' name. But often we have not seen the transformational aspect in people's lives. For many churches and church plants, becoming attractive to its neighbors *is* part of their missional strategy. They recognize that it is worthwhile to tell of the exalted Christ and to bring others to hear about him. By offering culturally relevant, needs-oriented ministry, these churches are being missionaries to their communities. But that is not enough to be a biblically faithful church.

Current rumblings seem to be moving the church beyond mere attraction to attraction with an outward-focused mission as part of their culture. These churches are moving beyond a "come and see" mentality, shifting more into "go and tell." Those of us who believe all church plants should be *missional* church plants see this as a healthy trend. This does not mean there is no place for attractional ministry, but it does mean that attraction is not enough.

Beginning with Missions

Any book on church planting must be a book about missions. Church planting is effective when leaders make a decision to engage an unchurched world with a radical message: the gospel. Good missionaries always study the culture as they develop their strategy.

Christian leaders are recognizing this shift. A few examples:

- "Today North America needs to be treated as a mission field in the same way that we in the West have approached much of the rest of the world for the past several centuries."[1]
- "Christians living in modern culture face a fundamental challenge. That challenge is to learn to think about their culture in Missional terms."[2]
- "Just as God is a missionary God, so the church is to be a missionary church."[3]

An Emerging Movement

In the last two decades of the twentieth century, the development of a North American missiology (the study of missions) caught the attention of the Christian community. New models of church appeared on the scene and were tried with varying degrees of success. They forced the church to address issues not considered in previous decades, asking, "*How can the church relate to contemporary culture and contextualize the gospel in that setting?*"

A church planting movement is gathering energy. Charismatic and Pentecostal groups plant the majority of new churches. Baptists continue to plant a significant number of churches, with the Southern Baptist Convention planting the most churches of any evangelical denomination and stepping up the effort every year through methods such as multiplication.[4] Even outside the free-church tradition, mainline denominations are beginning to reemphasize church planting. Christians are realizing, once again, the need to place an emphasis on church planting in North America.

Theologian Richard Mouw says we're in a missionary "location," that North America needs to be considered a mission field in the same way we once considered the underdeveloped world.[5] We shouldn't be discouraged by this view; it presents us with a missiological challenge and opportunity.

And we shouldn't be surprised when we consider the population shifts that have occurred even in the last few years. Today, one in ten Americans was born in another country. It's true that the world has come to our doorstep. And, for that matter, the world at our doorstep is not the same as it was a few decades ago.

"Christendom," that realm or time when Christianity was the assumed religion of the West, has come to an end. No longer is Christianity the "chaplain" to the broader culture. Until the last several years in the history of the United States, Christianity was thought to be the "American religion" even though it was not embraced by everyone or practiced with the devotion that committed Christians would like. It once was perceived as part of America's national ethos. No longer can that claim be made. This "humiliation" of Christendom has been underway for two centuries.[6]

But here's an advantage: The end of Christendom allows the church to recognize that the gospel is distinct from Western culture. So the gospel must be addressed in fresh ways to the ever-changing population that's disassociated itself from "pseudo-Christian" roots. In other words, being missional is not just the task of taking the gospel to the "primitives" outside our borders. The new challenge is to bring the gospel to Western culture, including right here in North America, since it's become so resistant to the gospel.[7]

Mission-Minded Versus Missional

As I established in chapter 1, planting churches should be about planting missional churches. But don't confuse the terms *mission-minded* and *missional*. The first refers more to an attitude of *caring* about missions, particularly overseas. *Missional* means actually *doing mission* right where you are. *Missional* means adopting the *posture of a missionary*, learning and adapting to the culture around you while remaining biblically sound. Think of it this way: *missional* means being a missionary without ever leaving your zip code. You can see how a particular congregation or denomination can be *mission-minded* without being *missional*.

A missional church is "on mission." Time for another definition: *on mission* means being intentional and deliberate about reaching others. For example, *on-mission* Christians might look like these people: She establishes a Bible study in her home for neighbors who are unchurched. He finds opportunities to share Christ with coworkers. A couple's family vacations are mission trips, not only to share evangelism experiences but also to teach their children the value of sharing Christ as an ongoing lifestyle. An *on-mission* congregation might be one that sponsors events to bring into the church those people who usually avoid church, thinking it's irrelevant. To counter that notion, the church sponsors a Super Bowl party, a seminar on family finances, or a concert.

By the same token, a church or church planter who is missional is focused on God's mission *(missio Dei),* being aware of what God is doing in the culture and joining him in his work. A missional church is willing and eager to engage the culture with the truths of the gospel. We need to be about the business of applying the lens of mission to the field of North America. Christendom is dead, and missionaries are needed.

But its demise is not all bad news according to Hall: "Our Lord's metaphors for his community of witness were all of them modest ones: a little salt, a little yeast, a little light. Christendom tried to be great, large, magnificent. It thought itself the object of God's expansive grace; it forgot the meaning of its election to worldly responsibility."[8]

Christian leaders are beginning to understand that the church must not rework its programs; it must rediscover its mission. In short, it must become missional.

Obstacles to Missional Thinking

The gospel never fits properly within a culture.[9] As such, persons within the church will always find reasons to criticize (or polemicize) those who try to contextualize the gospel. For the church, it's always easier to adopt church-culture norms rather than prevailing-culture norms.

Lesslie Newbigin explains:

> Everyone with the experience of cross-cultural mission knows that there are always two opposite dangers, the Scylla and Charybdis, between which one must steer. On the one side there is the danger that one finds no point of contact for the message as the missionary preaches it, to the people of the local culture the message appears irrelevant and meaningless. On the other side is the danger that the point of contact determines entirely the way that the message is received, and the result is syncretism. Every missionary path has to find the way between these

> two dangers: irrelevance and syncretism. And if one is more afraid of one danger than the other, one will certainly fall into the opposite.[10]

There have always been people who stood in opposition to the church's being culturally relevant. And, when you think about it, that's not an unexpected response. When we see religious symbols and traditions recast in a manner that strikes us as disrespectful, it's normal to respond negatively. That sort of reflex may be the cause of some Christians' inability to recognize that high content (being biblically sound) and high culture (being culturally relevant) aren't mutually exclusive.

The gospel doesn't spread in a cultural vacuum, but it's always incarnated in a specific cultural context.[11] However, many Christians have been unable to distinguish churches that are culturally relevant and biblically based from those that are compromised by the culture. For them, anything culturally relevant seems worldly and therefore unspiritual.

Consider the following illustration known as The Hughes Scale.[12] The goal of the missional church plant is to be securely in Quad B—committed to cultural relevance and to biblical authority. Instead, churches tend to polarize around two axes of the scale. (Quad A churches are Bible-focused but unable to relate to the lost world around them. Quad D churches can relate to the world but have abandoned the basic tenets of the faith.)

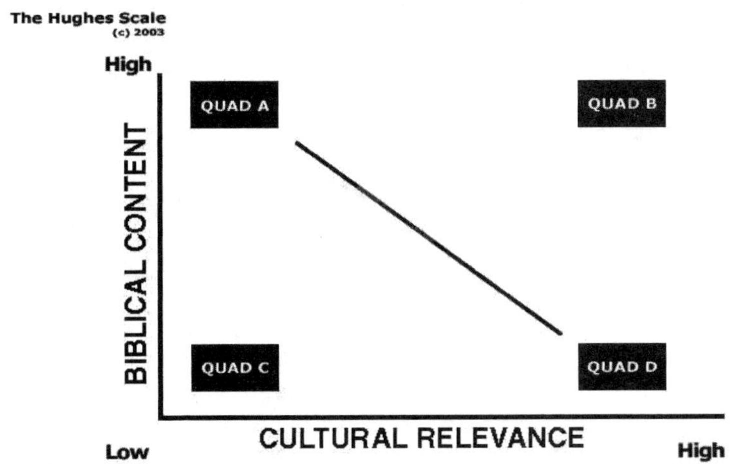

The New Testament church recognizes that we're never permitted to stop thinking missiologically.[13] But the church that considers itself committed to biblical authority and opposed to cultural compromise (represented in Quad A), often is unable to understand a biblically faithful, culturally relevant, missional church. Quad D churches are rightly labeled as "liberal"—compromised by the world and co-opted by the culture. But the conservative Christian church is often unable to distinguish the Quad B (missional church) and Quad D churches (the trendy or faddish church). Furthermore, the Quad A church is unable to see that contextualization is not necessarily the slippery slope to compromise. (By the way, Quad C churches tend to focus on their traditions without any commitment to biblical fidelity.)

Instead of engaging in missional thinking, churches tend to fall back to one of two positions. Two responses are common: an appeal to tradition or an appeal to technique. Neither is the response of the missional congregation.

The missional church rejects the false hopes of tradition and technique, repositioning itself as a body of people sent *on mission*. The Reformation provided the concept of the church where right things happen—correct preaching, administration of the sacraments, and other practices. A "correct" church understood and administered these things correctly. Contemporary methodologies provide the concept of the church as a vendor of religious goods and services. The church with the correct management structure to deliver said goods is the most successful.[14] Both methodologies are unsatisfactory ways to plant New Testament churches in our current age—missional churches.

Tradition—to the Extreme

For most people a vision for the future tends to involve revisiting an effective past experience. The difficulty seems obvious, but often it's not. To which preferred past do we return? Do we return to the Reformation and use it as the touchstone of revival? Some seem to think so. Why wouldn't returning to the early church be a better option?

New churches have an opportunity that established churches often do not. They have the opportunity to contextualize the unchanging message of the gospel without any preexisting patterns to copy. They don't return to a romanticized past, but they incarnate the gospel in a biblical present.

The unmet challenge is to separate ourselves from any unnecessary and traditional cultural wrappings.[15] Many among conservative evangelical churches retreat to a preferred past in order to maintain a sense of spiritual nostalgia. Yet the church must never become too comfortable with any culture,[16] whether it existed five, fifty, or five hundred years ago. What the church must be comfortable with is becoming missional, always looking for the best way to reach the culture it lives in at that point in time. If anything, the church should err on the side of becoming futurists (rather than historians) in regard to culture. Staying biblically relevant means we'll have to look beyond the present to perceive what's best for the church in the future, moving forward in God's kingdom.

Technique—to the Extreme

Hunsberger claims that the greatest indicator of the inadequacy of our current missiology is its lack of theological depth.[17] Malphurs says that an "accurate criticism of (the church growth) movement" is its overemphasis on the practical.[18]

Van Gelder explains:

> The continued drift toward the development of large, independent community churches, with their focus on user-friendly, needs oriented, market-driven models described by George Barna in *User Friendly Churches*, is in need of careful critique. While celebrating their contextual relevance, we need to be careful that we are committed in using these approaches to maintaining the integrity of both the gospel and the Christian community. These churches may just be the last version of the Christian success story within the collapsing paradigm of modernity and Christian-shaped culture.[19]

McKaughan warns that, if we don't have a missional strategy driven by solid theological and ecclesiological principles, we simply perpetuate culture-driven models of church and mission.[20]

So the false hope of technique continues to undermine solid missiological thinking. Bottom line: There's a lack of theological depth in many contemporary church-planting and church-growth movements because they emphasize technique, paradigms, and methodologies rather than genuine biblical and missiological principles.

Denominations are attracted to such methodologies. Denominations and churches want growth. These techniques have produced results, so they're often seen as solutions. It's not surprising that denominations and churches flounder under the influence of myths, unable to think missiologically in their setting.[21] Pastors often look for the latest technique and fad to make their church grow. Before, they ran to Southern California and came back with Hawaiian shirts and no socks—thinking that was what it took to engage their community. Lately they rush off to venues with candles and incense but still have not grasped that such expressions may not be right in their context.

Technique may be the more dangerous of the extremes. The church bound by tradition often recognizes its problem. The tradition-bound church may even bemoan its condition, even if it's unable to break out of its negative patterns. On the other hand, the church absorbed in technique is convinced that it's missional—that its techniques are actually expressions of mission, while they are actually methods that replace missional thinking.

Churches mistakenly conclude this because of their increasing attendance. Their trendy techniques cause a rapid rise in attendance, giving them a false sense that what they're doing is "working." As a result, they may be more willing to throw discipleship out the window as a goal if that helps them retain more warm bodies in their services. That's a compromise a biblical church won't make.

Ultimately our goal is much more than creating a large attendance; it's making disciples. Many church planters, especially those who depend heavily on technique, are afraid that by teaching theology they will be introducing subjects that won't interest seekers, thus driving them away. However, both statistically and anecdotally, I've found that a church which correctly applies the concept of true discipleship will accomplish both goals: growth and depth. In fact, studies show that the higher the standards of biblical teaching, the longer people remain engaged. Today's seekers are seeking depth. They won't interrupt a fine Sunday morning of sleeping in to attend a church that serves up shallowness, at least not for long.

A Healthy Balance

There's always a need for balance. We can't abandon tradition simply because it's traditional. Many traditional church expressions are finding new life in church plants reaching emerging cultures. But tradition or denominational distinctives must never take the place of being missional.

Overcoming the obstacles of tradition and technique requires an openness that's often absent among believers mired in cultural expressions of Christianity. Developing missional thinking requires us to have our own cultural presuppositions challenged, regardless of the era from which they are derived.

Cal Guy wrote some profound words that describe a balance between theology and contextualization: "We apply the pragmatic test to the work of the theologian. Does his theology motivate men to go into all the world and make disciples? Does it so undergird them that they, thus motivated, succeed in this primary purpose? Theology must stand the test of being known by its fruit."[22] I agree with Guy that if theology doesn't lead to mission it's an incomplete theology. The fact that a theology leads to conversion is not the only factor in its faithfulness, but it should be an important one.

As a counterbalance, Murray cautions: "In some recent church planting literature, the scope and level of theological discussion and engagement with biblical teaching has been disappointing. Responding to the objection we are considering here requires advocates of church planting to move beyond selected proof texts and develop a hermeneutically responsible and theologically coherent framework for the practice they are advocating."[23]

There is a New Testament balance. We need new churches not because they're trendy or because they provide places to try all the "cutting edge" techniques. Instead we need new churches that are fresh expressions of the unchanging gospel, new missional contextualized churches in every setting across the globe. This is balance.

Embracing a Missional Theology

A church becomes missional when it remains faithful to the gospel and simultaneously seeks to contextualize the gospel (to the degree it can) so the gospel engages the hearers and transforms their worldview.

The most obvious example is Paul and his encounter with the Greeks at Mars Hill. Paul attempted to connect with the worldview of his hearers.[24]

"Paul then stood up in the meeting of the Areopagus and said: 'Men of Athens! I see that in every way *you are [already]* very religious. For as I walked around and looked carefully at your objects of worship, I even found an altar with this inscription: TO AN UNKNOWN GOD. Now what you worship as something unknown I am going to proclaim to you'" (Acts 17:22–23, emphasis added).

This passage demonstrates what it means to be a missionary. Paul sought to understand the people he was reaching and relate to them in their cultural context. His approach was controversial then, and it still is.

Paul did four things in his effort to be culturally relevant:

- He understood the Athenians' position on reality.
- He understood the Athenians' underlying spiritual interest.
- He looked for positive points within their worldview.
- He encouraged them to find true fulfillment in Christ.[25]

Acts indicates that Paul approached Jews and Gentiles differently. He engaged them based on their culture and preunderstanding of gospel truths. With the Jews, Paul reasoned about the saving role of the Messiah and his resurrection (17:1–4). With the Gentiles, Paul's reasoning was more foundational—addressing issues of resurrection, morality, and judgment.[26] In all cases the culture of the hearer impacted Paul's evangelistic methods.

Culturally appropriate evangelism answers the *actual* questions being asked by a given culture rather than those questions the church *believes* the culture should ask. The *sine qua non* is found in 1 Peter: "But in your hearts set apart Christ as Lord. Always be prepared to give an answer to everyone who asks you to give the reason for the hope that you have. But do this with gentleness and respect" (1 Pet. 3:15). The world's questions, in fact, should help determine the evangelistic methodologies and expressions of the indigenous church.

My friend and former student, Daniel Montgomery, sought to apply these principles when he planted Sojourn Church in Louisville, Kentucky. Daniel explained:

> The gospel is God's; God is unchanging and so is his gospel. As a pastor I am not given the freedom to play around with the simple truths: "God you are Holy," "I am a sinner," and "Jesus is my Savior." But the culture we inhabit is constantly changing, and so the missional challenge is to take the unchanging Gospel and communicate it to an ever-changing culture.
>
> It means using culturally appropriate language and metaphors so that the words and ideas we're communicating are already

familiar to our audience. For example, when speaking about the deep sinfulness of sin in North America, we have to clarify and continually reemphasize that sin is more than "nobody being perfect" but rather evil that has ruined the human soul and society.

Musically this means we have tremendous amount of freedom to express the gospel in various sounds and styles. For example, the majesty and glory that was once communicated through the roar of an organ can now be communicated through the roar of a Marshal Half Stack.[27]

Understanding Missiological Thinking

Missiological thinking is not the same as missionary support. Many churches will support cross cultural missions yet oppose missiological thinking within their own context. They will send money to missionaries in South America but make no attempt to become a Hispanic congregation when their community has transitioned to all Latinos around their church.

Missiological thinking requires an understanding of the church's biblical identity, its loss of that identity, and its need to rediscover an indigenous expression of that identity in each culture.

The Church's Missional Identity

A century ago Martin Kähler stated, "Mission is the mother of theology."[28] I believe that in order to live out a missional mandate the church must rediscover that part of its nature. The church will not play its proper role in the new missional movement until it understands the biblical and theological basis for such.[29] God is a missionary God in this culture and in every culture. His nature does not change with location. Therefore, a missionary posture should be the normal expression of the church in all times and places.[30]

The church needs to realize that mission is its fundamental identity.[31] Paul's letters contain instructions for the churches he helped start. These churches struggled with the issues that all new churches face, yet they were challenged to be *on mission*. The text defines the mission, and the church must live that mission at all costs. A nonmissional church misrepresents the true nature of the church.[32] As Schenk points out, "The Great

Commission institutionalizes mission as the *raison d'être*, the controlling norm, of the church. To be a disciple of Jesus Christ and a member of his body is to live a missionary experience in the world. There is no doubt that this was how the earliest Christians understood their calling."[33]

Missionary identity is rooted in the triune and "sending" God. The fact that God is a sender is connected with the very existence of the church. The fact that Jesus was the "sent one" is the most fundamental identification of Jesus.[34] Jesus said, "As the Father has sent me, I am sending you" (John 20:21). Because of our identity in Christ, we are to continue the mission of Jesus:[35] "There is no participation in Christ without participation in His mission to the world. That by which the Church receives its existence is that by which it is also given its world mission."[36]

The concept of *missio Dei,* the mission of God, is recognition that God is a sending God, and the church is sent. It is the most important mission in the Scriptures.[37] Jesus Christ is the embodiment of that mission; the Holy Spirit is the power of that mission; the church is the instrument of that mission; and the culture is the context in which that mission occurs.[38]

Scripture identifies the elect as being chosen for "declaring the praises," a missional task carried over from the unfulfilled (and unappreciated) task of missionary Israel. The apostle Peter explains, "But you are a chosen people, a royal priesthood, a holy nation, a people belonging to God, that you may declare the praises of him who called you out of darkness into his wonderful light" (1 Pet. 2:9).

What Went Wrong?

How did the church lose its missional focus? The church of Western European Christendom was a church without mission.[39] After the Reformation took hold, the evangelistic mission of the church was often neglected. Roman Catholics were energized by "new lands" to reach. But Protestants lost this missionary passion. This loss did not go unnoticed. Counter-Reformation Catholics pointed to the lack of missionary participation among Protestants as evidence of a defective Protestant movement.

This loss of missionary focus was evident in both Protestant belief systems and practice. Although the Reformation restored much of primitive Christianity, it also lost much—particularly in areas of mission. The consequences of this loss of missional focus continue today.

There has been substantial debate regarding the nature of the Reformation church: Was it a missionary church? Did it value missions? These are valid questions with regard to whether the Reformation church engaged in the task of missions. They are, unfortunately, the wrong questions. The Reformers were trapped within geographic Christendom while their Catholic counterparts were engaged in colonial expansion. Protestant "mission" became missions to Catholics.[40] While Protestants focused on Catholics, Catholic missions flourished. So instead of asking, "Was the Reformation church a mission movement?" it's better to recognize that it was weak in its mission focus, and ask, "Why?"

Pre-Reformation confessions referred to the church as "one holy, apostolic church." Words like these aren't frequently found in the confessions of the Reformation. Instead the Reformation confessions reacted to the errors of "apostolic succession" (the idea that the popes and bishops held their power because of being appointed by subsequent bishops/popes back to Peter). By deemphasizing the "apostolic" nature of church, the Reformers were trying to say that the church did not derive its legitimacy from succession of leaders. However, apostolic is more than a "position"; it's a "posture." Although the word is often misunderstood, the root of the word *apostle* is "one sent... with a message." So we should be an *apostolic* church.

When the Reformers (and later evangelicals) started to deemphasize the apostolic nature of the church, they inadvertently lessened the sending nature of that apostolic church. The church that "reformed" lost touch with the God who sends, and the mission of the church suffered. "Lost in this deletion was an emphasis on the church's 'being authoritatively sent' by God into the world to participate fully in God's mission."[41]

This loss of missional focus also led to a loss of missional thinking. Evangelicals continue to struggle with presenting the unchanging gospel in an ever-changing cultural setting. Churches must parallel, in some ways, their host cultures. This process is called "indigenization."

The Process of Indigenization

Most church planters start the church in their head and not in their community. They come with preconceived notions, things they have always wanted to try, and strategies they were never allowed to use. This may make the planter relate better to the church, but the planter is called to reach the community. That requires planting a church *into* community, a church that is indigenous.

According to Beyerhaus, "To be indigenous means that a church, in obedience to the apostolic message that has been entrusted to it and to the living guidance of the Holy Spirit, is able in its own particular historical situation, to make the gospel intelligible and relevant in word and deed to the eyes and ears of men."[42]

Being indigenous was not the standard practice of the church from the fourth century until the seventeenth. The imperial church of the Middle Ages was accustomed to conquest by the sword, not by mission and evangelism. But a truly indigenous church seeks to become incarnate within the culture in which it finds itself.

Every culture is imperfect, and by definition that means it's sometimes hostile to the gospel. But we live within cultures. Cultures are part of who we are. And, the gospel comes to us as people within culture. So, if the gospel is to be understood, we must exegete (analyze) the culture to proclaim faithfully a biblical gospel.

Roland Allen (1868–1947) was an Anglican priest and a missionary to China. His *Missionary Methods: St. Paul's or Ours?* played a significant role in challenging paternalistic approaches to indigenization. Allen promoted the idea (radical at the time) that we must learn to trust the Spirit's work in and through new believers. This idea requires a mutual trust between missionaries and new converts as well as confidence in the Holy Spirit to guide both.[43]

The church always struggles with the need to take the gospel into culture without compromising that message. Today we need to be exegeting our culture as Paul did his in Acts 17. We need to understand people in order to reach them. "We need to exegete that culture in the same way that missionaries have been so good at doing with the diverse tribal cultures of previously unreached people."[44] But evangelicals have generally forbidden North American churches from doing the very thing we require international churches to do. While engaging in this struggle, there will always be antimissional forces who cannot separate their own culture (or the culture they pine for) from the church of the Scriptures.

> An indigenous church, young or old, in the East or in the West, is a church which, rooted in obedience to Christ, spon-

> taneously uses forms of thought and modes of action natural and familiar in its own environment. Such a church arises in response to Christ's own call. The younger churches will not be unmindful of the experiences and teachings which the older churches have recorded in their confessions and liturgy. But every younger church will seek further to bear witness to the same Gospel with new tongues. [45]

Indigenous churches look different from culture to culture. You expect a biblically faithful, indigenous church to look different in Senegal from an indigenous church in Singapore. You also expect an indigenous church in high-tech and blue-state Seattle to look different from one in apple-pie Sellersburg, Indiana. Indigenous churches look different from location to location. Further, they look different from generation to generation. Faithful indigenous churches take their teaching from the unchanging biblical text and apply it to the ever-changing cultural milieu.

Ecclesia Semper Reformanda

The Reformation was rooted in the concept that the church would continuously reform. The reformers expressed that as *ecclesia semper reformada,* the church always reforming. It would never arrive. That remains true today. As the culture changes, the church is compelled to change. But individual congregations often face sociological and institutional pressures that hinder such reform. Local churches often struggle just to change the color of the carpet in the worship center! They aren't dealing with cultural shifts (and the resulting dialogue on subjects like communication) that are going on in North America today. For example, they aren't grappling with the nuances of how epistemology (the theory of knowledge) is changing among missiologists (and others) to allow for subjective sources such as emotions to inform a person's overall perceptions. And yet understanding this is a part of how the church must continually reform.

Even cross-cultural missionaries struggle with the task of contextualization. At their best, most cross-cultural evangelists are not noted for their contextual successes.[46] Thus, it's no wonder that North American evangelicals, with a genuine love for missions and the lost, find it difficult to contextualize in a changing culture at home.

Add to this the challenge that change brings uncertainty, and uncertainty is a primary source of fear, which happens to be one of the vehicles God uses to move us forward! So embracing cultural change, while not embracing all of culture, can put us in a new environment; however, many people are simply uncomfortable with things being different. If they can overcome this challenge, the possibilities are wonderful, even biblical, because it's this environment that God uses to stretch us and remind us of our mission.

Unfortunately, most established churches are unwilling, or at least unable, to overcome this challenge and therefore to change. As a result, they're unable to become and remain indigenous as culture changes. How can we establish churches that are faithful to biblical teaching and also indigenous? In other words, where can we find solid missiological churches? Church planting is, and should be, the locus for missiological thinking in North America. New churches can indigenize in ways that established churches rarely can accomplish.

The reason for this inability to reach a changing culture should be clear. Many churches die because they make choices and adopt patterns of tradition that cause them to decline. Traditions and patterns which were meaningful years ago become contextually outdated, yet churches continue to practice those same traditions for sentimental reasons. These traditions and patterns can create barriers to surrounding neighbors who don't understand the traditions and who feel alienated by them.

Conclusions

The Christendom model of church kept the church from interacting in a missional manner.[47] In other words, at that time Christendom was commonly acknowledged as the preferred spiritual path within its geographical boundaries. So the church was handicapped because it did not have to be missional; its mission muscles did not have to be flexed.

But that's no longer true. We're not on "home turf." Instead, we're in a missionary setting, and we need to focus on reaching the unchurched around us. We've seen that church planting is the most effective way to reach those outside the faith.

Thus, a North American missiological movement is, and should be, engaged in planting new churches. New churches can engage the Bible and culture in their setting because they are required to think missiologically; they are missional entities.

C. Peter Wagner asserts, "The single most effective evangelistic methodology under heaven is planting new churches."[48] That's because church plants can often engage persons within the lost culture in a way that established churches cannot or will not.

There is no basis, biblically or theologically, for the territorial distinction of missions and evangelism.[49] The separation has more to do with centuries-old academic tradition than biblical missiology. On the contrary, their separation has caused harm to the church. While missions became the task of reaching those outside of Christendom, evangelism became the task of reaching those within its boundaries.[50] Like a bear fed by the tourists, the church was unable to fend for itself when the food was removed and Christendom was lost. Thus, in an attempt to promote the importance of missions, missiologists have often undermined the church by removing missional thinking from its rightful place.

Instead, the church must learn to exegete its culture and reflect on the culture from a biblical perspective.[51] If we take seriously theology of mission, the Word must become flesh in every new context.[52] "Solid, disciplined, and prolonged intellectual work in the context of missionary encounter between the gospel and contemporary cultures is an essential part of the mission of theology."[53]

"True theology is the attempt on the part of the church to explain and interpret the meaning of the gospel for its own life and to answer questions raised by the Christian faith, using the thought, values, and categories of truth which are authentic to that place and time."[54]

Church planting is always on the cutting edge of North American missiology because it has no emotional investment in the patterns of tradition. But it is also in danger of unspiritual pragmatism. In its attempt to become culturally relevant, it can often become culturally bound. Van Gelder observes:

> We need to exegete . . . culture in the same way that missionaries have been so good at doing with diverse tribal cultures of previously unreached people. We need to exegete . . . the themes of the Rolling Stones . . . , Dennis Rodman, Madonna, (and) David Letterman. . . . We need to comprehend that the Spirit of the Living God is at work in these cultural expressions,

> preparing the hearts of men and women to receive the gospel of Jesus Christ. We have to find, in good missionary fashion, those motifs and themes that connect with the truths of the gospel. We need to learn how to proclaim, "That which you worship as unknown, I now proclaim to you." This is the missionary vision at its best.[55]

We do this by taking risks. We risk condemnation of those who are comfortable within the crumbling walls of Christendom. They may never understand the necessity of taking these risks because they choose to equate contextualization with compromise. They cannot understand because they love their churched culture too much.

Theology and theologians need to reengage missional thinking by asking questions such as, "How can the gospel best become incarnate in this setting?" and "What cultural values and symbols can be used to illustrate gospel truth?" Steffen provides a detailed list of questions to be used when entering every culture:

- What is the worldview of the target audience?
- What is the culture's decision-making pattern?
- What does it cost a person in this culture to become a Christian?
- What redemptive analogy is best for this culture?
- How does this culture view Christianity?
- What does this culture understand about the basic components of the gospel story?
- Is this culture based on shame or guilt?
- How will this culture understand Christian rituals?
- What is the best delivery system for exposing the people of this culture to the gospel?[56]

Questions such as these force the church to analyze biblical truth in the light of culture and vice versa. The alternative is to lose the correct focus of the church. As Bosch declares, "Just as the church ceases to be the church if it is not missionary, theology ceases to be theology if it loses its missionary character."[57]

New churches approach evangelization in a way that tends to be more culturally indigenous than established churches. If new churches can avoid the trap of technique, they can engage the changing culture effectively with the unchanging gospel of Jesus.

North America desperately needs a true spiritual awakening. This can come, in part, from the planting of new churches. Misinformed and fearful people will always resist what they do not understand. But without church planting, we will not fulfill the Great Commission. The sending nature of God has not changed. He sends us to new and emerging cultures even here in North America. We are most like Christ when we join him in the mission of reaching the unchurched by planting new churches.

There is always risk, and many churches are unwilling to take those risks. Gilliland observes:

> Contextualization [is] a delicate enterprise if ever there was one . . . the evangelist and mission strategist stand on a razor's edge, aware that to fall off on either side has terrible consequences . . . Fall to the right and you end in obscurantism, so attached to your conventional ways of practicing and teaching the faith that you veil its truth and power from those who are trying to see it through very different eyes. Slip to the left and you tumble into syncretism, so vulnerable to the impact of paganism in its multiplicity of forms that you compromise the uniqueness of Christ and concoct "another gospel which is not a gospel."[58]

The end result, at least for our purposes, is to establish biblical new churches that are culturally relevant. If the church is willing to be missional and its theologians and thinkers are willing to assist in this process, the potential is unlimited. As the church rediscovers its missional nature, it will acquire a renewed passion to be a people *on mission*. Effective, missional, and biblically sound churches can be planted. These churches will engage the culture while remaining faithful to the "faith once delivered to the saints." The result may look different to us but not to God. From his perspective, the word has become flesh in a new setting. We will truly become missionaries in our communities.

Questions for Reflection or Dialogue among Church Planters

1. What risks have been required of you, or what risks do you anticipate, to follow the vision God has laid on your heart?
2. What keeps churches or leaders from being bigger risk takers?
3. In what ways do you think a church—and its theology—can lose "missionary character," as Bosch described?
4. Describe the dangerous ditches of contextualization of the gospel—the conventional, unbending right and the syncretistic left.
5. How do you stay out of those ditches?
6. How important is "cultural relevance" in church planting? Why or why not?
7. What is at the heart of a church that is "missional in nature"?
8. What are some ways you see that missional nature playing itself out practically in the life and ministry of a church?

Resources for Further Reading

Below are resources focusing on emerging North American missiology. You can find a longer bibliography at www.newchurches.com under resources/reading.

Bosch, David J. *Transforming Mission.* Maryknoll: Orbis Books, 1998.

Hunsberger, George R., and Craig Van Gelder, eds. *The Church Between Gospel & Culture.* Grand Rapids: Wm. B. Eerdmans Publishing Co., 1996.

McNeal, Reggie. *The Present Future.* San Francisco: Jossey-Bass, 2003.

Newbigin, Lesslie. *The Gospel in a Pluralist Society.* Grand Rapids: Eerdmans, 1990.

Roberts, Bob. *Transformation: How Global Churches Transform Lives and the World.* Grand Rapids, Zondervan, 2006.

Van Gelder, Craig, ed. *Confident Witness—Changing World.* Grand Rapids: Eerdmans, 1999.

Chapter 3

The Biblical Basis of Church Planting

Before anything else, we start with the Bible to understand and build on the clear New Testament patterns of church planting. We'd be wrong to send out planters with organizational, strategic, and marketing tools but not the fundamental truths of God's Word and the principles of Scripture from which to work. The book of Acts is the most important book ever written on the subject. And the rest of the New Testament was written to new churches in their respective life situations, warts and all. In fact, the New Testament is an anthology of church plants!

Church planting—how did the New Testament churches do it, and how can we rediscover their passion? Amberson observes:

> We, today, need to recapture the note of spontaneity which existed in the New Testament and, therefore, produced churches as the believers witnessed to the Lord Jesus Christ. Church planting does involve specific and deliberate intent to start new churches, but the New Testament points to the fact that new churches and church planting are the direct and inevitable consequences of believer's involvement in witnessing and proclamation.[1]

The Four Commissionings of Jesus

To regain our passion, let's see how the early church responded to the commands of Jesus. We'll begin with the best known, the Great Commission, which many consider to be laying the foundation specifically for church planting by listing vital tasks assigned to congregations—making disciples, baptizing, and teaching them to obey.

Then Jesus came to them and said, "All authority in heaven and on earth has been given to me. Therefore go and make disciples of all nations, baptizing them in the name of the Father and of the Son and of the Holy Spirit, and teaching them to obey everything I have commanded you. And surely I am with you always, to the very end of the age" (Matt. 28:18–20).

The earliest churches obeyed the Great Commission by planting new congregations to carry out the assignments of discipling, baptizing, and teaching that would begin the multiplication process of planting more and more churches. You notice that the process begins and ends with obedience. Jesus' command instructed his listeners to evangelize and to gather the new believers into local congregations where they could be discipled, baptized, and taught. In that setting the process of their growth would occur. And then the cycle would repeat itself as the believers learned that obeying the Great Commission meant they too were to go out and disciple, baptize, and teach.

The Great Commission is one of Jesus' four sending commands. In this chapter we'll look at each one in greater depth.[2]

1. "I am sending you..."

Each command provides details relating to the central tasks of discipling, baptizing, and teaching in a congregational setting. In John 20:21, Jesus explained, "As the Father has sent me, I am sending you" (John 20:21). Since the Father had sent Jesus "to seek and to save what was lost" (Luke 19:10), we are sent in the same manner as Jesus—by the Father—to seek and save the lost. As Christ followers, this direction can't be clearer. We are to pick up Jesus' earthly work and continue doing it. It's a personal message, and it applies to all of us.

Until the late eighteenth century, most Protestant Christians believed Jesus' commissions applied only to those disciples who actually heard his words. Church leaders proclaimed, "That was for the apostles. It doesn't refer to us." They failed to understand the implications of such a view. Obviously, Scripture addresses specific people in specific places; Jesus was in the company of his contemporaries when he spoke these words. But if we consider Bible study part of our Christian walk, then we understand the Bible to be a living document with relevance to God's people through the ages. So Jesus' words apply to the people he was addressing as well as to us and all believers. Like those people two thousand years ago, we are called and sent by God to go wherever and for whatever purpose God chooses.

2. "Make disciples of all nations..."

Two weeks following his commission in John 20, Jesus spoke the Great Commission, which was the second of the sending commands (Matt. 28:18–20). The Great Commission in Matthew is Jesus' best-known word of sending, and it clearly explains that the task of world evangelization is given to his disciples—then and now.

Because of his term "all nations," Jesus clearly intended for the gospel to reach lost people among what today missiologists call *every* people group and population segment. To understand this, church planters need to think less about political boundaries and more about the populations who live there. For example, in the nation of Canada live First Nations people (in the United States we use the term Native Americans, or sometimes Indians), large populations of descendants of French and English settlers, and a new, mostly first-generation Asian population growing in the West. This is an oversimplified list, of course, but let's use it to illustrate how even a relatively short one can be sliced and diced many ways to look not only at people groups but also at population segments.

Of the First Nations people are those who live on government land (south of the Canadian border Native Americans call this the Rez, or Reservation) and those who have assimilated into towns and cities, perhaps barely recognizable from other people groups in their neighborhoods. Of the descendants of French settlers are those who speak only French and those who are bilingual. Of the Asians settling in areas like Vancouver are those who came from different nations—Korea and India—but those who are first-generation immigrants and then the subsequent generations who may never have lived in Asia. And just to make things interesting, let's look at the people of English descent and agree to think of them in terms of lifestyles and interests—people who are just starting families, people who have retired from their occupations, people who farm, people who live in metropolitan areas, people who love music, people who love biking, people who have taken a liberal position on social issues. In this simple exercise, we have come up with *many* "nations" who we've been commissioned by Jesus to reach—and, yes, he told us to reach them "all."

How to do this? It's a process called *contextualization*. We recognize that different people groups and population segments have different values. The gospel is designed by God so the unchanging message can be put into changing "cultural containers" to reach people where they are and to take them where they need to go. All methods and worship should be centered on God and focused on the Bible. Contextualization is a skill that North American missionaries, like international missionaries, must learn and use.

Now let's look closer at Jesus' instructions to disciple, baptize, and teach. The Great Commission *is* church planting because Jesus called us to several activities. The Great Commission *is* church planting first because it calls us to disciple. Discipleship is the task of the New Testament church. Discipleship is not working when Christians must find their opportunities for spiritual growth outside the church. When a Christian says, "I can't get discipleship at church; I must get it at home, online, at conferences, Promise Keepers, Women of Faith, etc." it's likely the believer belongs to an unhealthy church (or the believer has an unhealthy view of discipleship and church). God expects the church to provide discipleship, which is not just a course or a series of studies. Discipleship centers on the salvation event. Discipleship begins with conversion and continues as an ongoing process. "Make disciples" means that the church is to win people to Christ and grow these new converts in the faith. That process is meant to take place in the local church.

Second, the Great Commission is church planting because it calls the church to baptize. Baptism is an ordinance of the local church. Baptism takes place in or among the local church. I say among because it does not have to take place within a church building. Many planters have baptized in bathtubs, lakes, and swimming pools. Baptism takes place wherever we can gather the church and wherever there's enough water to perform the ordinance. The Greek word *baptizo* means "ongoing baptizing," immersing each new believer. Baptism is a local church ordinance with local church responsibilities. The Great Commission is given to the local church.

Third, the Great Commission is church planting because it instructs the church to teach. We observe the fulfillment of this command to teach in Acts 2:42: "They devoted themselves to the apostles' teaching" which was the basis for their growth and fellowship. The Great Commission is fulfilled in churches by planting new churches and by teaching biblical precepts.

Some people note that the Great Commission does not use the term *church planting*. Thus, they argue that the Great Commission is fulfilled only through existing congregations (particularly in highly churched areas). But the early church was filled with the Holy Spirit, according to the book of Acts (2:4; 4:8,31; 9:17; 13:9). These Spirit-filled disciples planted churches. It's obvious by their actions that the first hearers of the Great Commission assumed its fulfillment required multiplying disciples and forming new congregations. The first believers heard the Commission, left their homes, and went out to plant. When we hear the Great Commission, we should also be motivated to go out and plant new congregations. The best indication of what Jesus meant can be found in how these first hearers responded. We should follow their example.

3. "Preach repentance and forgiveness"

Just before his ascension, Jesus again reminded the disciples of their task. The third command describes the content and location of their proclamation: "repentance and forgiveness of sins . . . to all nations" (Luke 24:47). Lost persons can be found only by preaching repentance and forgiveness, the message of every genuine messenger of the gospel. But this command contained Jesus' instruction to wait until they had received the power of the Holy Spirit in Jerusalem. Jesus' command to preach repentance and forgiveness of sins rested upon his resurrection. This is the content of the commission.

Church planting and church growth are rightfully subject to criticism when the content of the message is not Christ and Christ crucified, when the preaching is more opinion than proclamation of God's Word. On the other hand, many criticize any innovation, so I caution people who "have heard" or who "think" that a certain church is not preaching the gospel to go and find out for themselves. It may turn out to be hearsay not heresy. It may even turn out to be a misunderstanding based on style.

I have planted contemporary, seeker-sensitive and emerging churches that reach unchurched people with the good news. We achieved success by using creative methods. Criticism followed. But we determined that one particular criticism would never be true of us—that we preached anything other than Christ.

The message of church planters should never be anything other than the Word of God. Jesus expressed this axiom when he said to "preach repentance and forgiveness based upon the resurrection." Regardless of how seeker-sensitive we wish to be, we can never justifiably remove what for some is the stumbling block of the cross. The most biblical church is the one in which the cross is the only stumbling block for the unchurched. That's because lost people should face no church-culture stumbling blocks that keep them from Christ. Lost people need no additional reasons to stay away from church. The unchurched need to hear the good news of Jesus Christ, and that includes the stumbling block of the cross. Planters must not present any message other than Christ, and they should present it in a style that's culturally appropriate to the hearers.

4. "Jerusalem...to the ends of the earth"

The final sending passage from Jesus provides the geography. "You will receive power when the Holy Spirit comes on you; and you will be my witnesses in Jerusalem, and in all Judea and Samaria, and to the ends of the earth" (Acts 1:8).

Today we think of these geographic locations as concentric circles spreading from "our Jerusalem" or community. Judea may be seen as our state or province and Samaria as our continent (or more accurately, a different culture living in and near our Judea). This is helpful if we want to teach our congregations that missionary work is not all overseas but right here at home too. For many, that's a radical concept. Yet it's true, and it's biblical, based on Acts 1:8.

Another lesson from this passage is that the power appears here that Jesus promised in the sending account in Luke. When the Holy Spirit is present, the disciples—then and now—find themselves able to spread the gospel with confidence locally, regionally, and globally.

Early believers were sent (as we are) for the same purpose for which Jesus was sent: to disciple all people groups and to seek and save the lost—both locally and around the world. New Testament Christians acted out these commands as any spiritually healthy, obedient believers would: they planted more New Testament churches. The Great Commission instructs us to evangelize and congregationalize people. Furthermore, Jesus even supplied the content of the message as Paul described it, only Christ and Christ crucified (1 Cor. 1:23).

The sending God sent the Son. We join him in his mission of seeking and saving the lost. Then we become God's sent people to proclaim the message of repentance and forgiveness in the power of the Holy Spirit both locally and worldwide to all people groups.

New Testament Patterns

While differences exist in the way churches were planted in the New Testament, this section will demonstrate patterns of church planting used throughout the New Testament. Church planting convictions and endeavors should begin with the heart of God. Luke 19:10 states that Jesus "came to seek and to save what was lost." In focusing on unchurched persons, we align our lives with Jesus, who modeled and claimed, "It is not the healthy who need a doctor, but the sick. I have not come to call the righteous, but sinners" (Mark 2:17).

Many churches in North America have "called the righteous" with better teaching and more programs. Advertising claims of "programs for the whole family," "quality Bible teaching," and "full-featured choirs" seem designed to attract members from other churches. But Jesus claimed that he had come to call outcasts rather than the righteous. Like Jesus, the planter must seek the unchurched. In fact, through Luke's trilogy of parables (chapter 15) about the lost sheep, the lost coin, and the lost son, Jesus underscored the importance of seeking those who are lost in order to share God's good news with them.

Now the tax collectors and "sinners" were all gathering around to hear him. But the Pharisees and the teachers of the law muttered, "This man welcomes sinners and eats with them."

> Then Jesus told them this parable: "Suppose one of you has a hundred sheep and loses one of them. Does he not leave the ninety-nine in the open country and go after the lost sheep until he finds it? And when he finds it, he joyfully puts it on his shoulders and goes home. Then he calls his friends and neighbors together and says, 'Rejoice with me; I have found my lost sheep.' I tell you that in the same way there will be more rejoicing in

> heaven over one sinner who repents than over ninety-nine righteous persons who do not need to repent.
>
> Or suppose a woman has ten silver coins and loses one. Does she not light a lamp, sweep the house and search carefully until she finds it? And when she finds it, she calls her friends and neighbors together and says, 'Rejoice with me; I have found my lost coin.' In the same way, I tell you, there is rejoicing in the presence of the angels of God over one sinner who repents" (Luke 15:1–10).

The angel's response indicates the importance of conversion. Jesus promises in Luke 15:7, "I tell you that in the same way, there will be more joy in heaven over one sinner who repents, than over ninety-nine righteous persons who need no repentance" (NASB). Following the parable of the coin, he continues, "In the same way, I tell you, there is joy in the presence of the angels of God over one sinner who repents" (Luke 15:10 NASB). Although Jesus' words ending the parable of the prodigal son are attributed to the father in the story, the father clearly is a symbol for God. In the story, the father pleads with his "righteous son" to "celebrate and rejoice, for this brother of yours was dead and has begun to live, and was lost and has been found" (15:32 NASB).

Luke's Gospel certainly emphasizes heaven's joy at the conversion of lost ones. Luke continues this theme in Acts 15:3 with his reference to the early church's joy over the conversion of lost sinners when Paul reported his success among the Gentiles.

The New Testament Planter

Through the ministry of the apostle Paul, the New Testament provides a great example of the way we can minister to unchurched persons. Paul invited the recipients of his letters to "be imitators of me, just as I also am of Christ" (1 Cor. 11:1 NASB). What did Paul do that was worthy of imitation? What did he want his readers, including us, to imitate? Identifying the values and actions of Paul can enrich the ministry of every modern-day church planter.

Paul the Planter

1. Paul was personally prepared for his church planting ministry.

   - His world-class formal training gave him a broad understanding of divine history.
   - He was vitally connected with God (2 Cor. 12:7–9).
   - He became prepared by stepping out in ministry from the start (Acts 9:20–22).
   - He was teachable. He apprenticed under Barnabas. He was willing to be under authority before God put him over others (Acts 11:25–26).
   - He lived an exemplary life (1 Thess. 2).

2. Paul was an evangelist.

   - He began preaching the gospel right after conversion (Acts 9:19–22).
   - He was a net fisherman in two ways: he led whole families to Christ (Acts 16:25–33), and he conducted large-group evangelistic meetings (Acts 13:44; 14:1; 19:9–10).
   - He looked for those who were most receptive (Acts 18:6).

3. Paul was an entrepreneurial leader.

   - He had a vision and call from God (Acts 9:15; Rom. 15:20–23).
   - His vision was to be the apostle to the Gentiles by leading missionary teams into new territories to plant churches. He combined quick-strike evangelism with church planting. The wedding of these two powerful methodologies sparked movements that made an impact for generations.
   - He selected the workers and apprentices he wanted on his team. He was not afraid to ask others to make sacrifices for the cause of Christ (Acts 16:2–3). Sometimes he would not let people on his team (Acts 15:38). Paul also appointed long-term leaders for the churches he started (Acts 14:23). He even gave direction to his teammates as to where they should minister (Acts 18:19; 19:22).
   - He received direction from God as to where his team should plant, and his teammates had confidence in his decisions (Acts

16:6–10).

- He was a proactive strategist (Acts 13:14, 44–49). He established a reproducible pattern for his church planting (Acts 14:1; 17:2).
- He deliberately did advanced planning (Acts 19:21).

4. Paul was a team player.

- He was willing to be on a team (Acts 13:1–5).
- He always planted with a team (Acts 15:40; 16:6; 20:4).
- He had a sending base church to which he reported back (Acts 14:26–28).

5. Paul was a flexible, risk-taking pioneer (1 Cor. 9:19–21).

- He constantly penetrated new territory (Rom. 15:20).
- He targeted a new group (Rom. 11:1).
- He pioneered new methods of ministry (Acts 13).

6. Paul cared for people (shepherd role).

- He invested personally in the lives of people (Acts 20:31).
- He was like a nursing mother and an encouraging father (1 Thess. 2:7–11).
- He was vitally concerned with the growth and development of converts (Acts 14:22).
- He drew close to coworkers (2 Tim. 1:2).

7. Paul empowered others (equipper role).

- In order to lead this rapidly growing movement, he risked delegation to young Christians (Acts 16:1–3).
- His team planted churches on their first missionary journey and then a few months later came back to these new churches and appointed elders (Acts 13:13, 21; 14:21–23).
- He recognized his own strengths and weaknesses and delegated to others according to their strengths (Titus 1:5).

8. Paul stayed committed to fulfilling God's calling and vision even at the cost of extreme personal sacrifice (Acts 14:19–20; 2 Cor. 11:23–28).

- He never backed down, and he never gave up.
- He maintained a thankful attitude in the face of cruel and unfair treatment (Acts 16:25).

9. Paul was willing to let go of his church plants and move on to plant more (Acts 16:40).

   - It seems that Paul needed special encouragement to stay in a city for very long (Acts 18:9–11).
   - The longest he ever stayed in any one place was three years (Acts 20:31).
   - Ephesus was possibly his strongest plant and our best model (Acts 19:10).
   - He had faith in God's ability to keep the churches he started strong (Acts 20:32).
   - He was willing to let his best teammates leave his team in order to benefit best the kingdom of God (Acts 17:14).
   - He followed the example of Barnabas, who was willing to let go of the top position on the church planting team (Acts 13:6–12).
   - He modeled the church at Antioch that was willing to let go of its top leaders (Acts 13:1–4).[3]

A couple of points bear repeating. One component of Paul's example worthy of our imitation was his entrepreneurial personality. An entrepreneur starts new ventures from scratch. The fact that Paul was entrepreneurial is central to understanding his church-planting ministry. Effective church planters always demonstrate entrepreneurial leadership skills. As an entrepreneur, Paul was always thinking of new ways to evangelize and new areas to enter. We'll delve deeper into entrepreneurial leadership later in this book.

A second trait worthy of imitation was Paul's desire to remain a team player. Maintaining the balance between being an entrepreneur and being a team player challenges many contemporary planters. These two traits fit together poorly unless the Holy Spirit is allowed to guide an entrepreneurial planter to be a team player. Church planting, though profoundly entrepreneurial, is not a solitary effort; church planting must be a partnership.

Finally, Paul instructed others to follow the model he presented. For us to follow, we need to understand his strategy and his passion. Paul always asked, "How can I best reach unbelievers?" To reach them, he was willing to pay any price and change any methodology short of compromising the gospel. This willingness included the risk-taking of entrepreneurship and the accountability of partnership. Such traits are worthy of our imitation.

New Testament Church Planting

Church planting appears not only in the life of Paul but also throughout the New Testament, particularly in the book of Acts. Indeed, Acts becomes a remarkable document when read with an eye toward church planting. Take a look at the outline below through the lens of a church planter.[4]

Church Planting in the Book of Acts

I. Church Planting in Jerusalem (Acts 1–7)
- A. Its Origin
  1. Born in prayer (1:12–14)
  2. Bathed in the Spirit (2:1–4)
  3. Begun with proclamation (2:14–39)
  4. Baptized in the name of Jesus (2:41)
- B. Its Functions
  1. Doctrinal teaching (2:42)
  2. Fellowship (2:42)
  3. Worship (2:42, 46)
  4. Prayer (2:42; 4:29–31)
  5. Benevolence (2:44–45; 4:34–35)
  6. Identification with the community (2:47)
  7. Witness (4:33; 5:42)
- C. Its Growth
  1. Three thousand baptized at Pentecost (2:41)
  2. People saved daily (2:47)
  3. Two thousand saved on Solomon's Portico (4:4)
  4. Multitudes added (5:14)
  5. Priests believe (6:7)
- D. Its Organization
  1. Apostles (6:2)
  2. Deacons (6:3)

        3. Congregation (6:5)
        4. Elders (15:6, 22)

II. Church Planting in Judea and Samaria (Acts 8–12)
- A. Church planting done by laity (8:1, 4)
- B. Mass evangelism (8:5–6, 12)
- C. Village evangelism (8:25)
- D. Churches multiplied (9:31)
- E. Growth enhanced by miracles (9:35–42)
- F. Salvation extended to Gentiles (10:44–48)

III. Church Planting in the World (Acts 13–28)
- A. Scattered laity started Jewish churches (11:19)
- B. Christians from Jerusalem plant Gentile-Jewish church in Antioch (11:20-21)
- C. Antioch became the great missionary church
    1. Sensitive to the Holy Spirit (13:2)
    2. Submissive to the Spirit (13:3)
    3. Sending church (13:3)
- D. Paul's First Missionary Journey (13–14)
    1. Preached first in synagogues (13:5; 14:1)
    2. Shifted to the Gentiles (13:46)
    3. Moved from city to city (13:13–14)
    4. Appointed elders to lead the churches (14:23)
    5. Returned to check on the new churches (14:21)
- E. Paul's Second Missionary Journey (15:40–18:22)
    1. Employed a team ministry (15:40)
    2. Returned to visit new churches (15:41)
    3. Guided by the Holy Spirit (16:9–10)
    4. Evangelized households (16:15, 33)
    5. Taught in the marketplace (17:17)
    6. Contextualized the message (17:22–23)
    7. Emphasized responsive peoples (18:6)
- F. Paul's Third Missionary Journey (18:23–21:17)
    1. Returned to visit the churches (18:23)
    2. Established mother churches in urban areas (19:10; 1 Thess. 1:8)

3. Started house churches (20:20)
4. Encouraged stewardship in new churches (1 Cor. 16:1–3)

Church planting began in Jerusalem. Acts 1–7 describes the founding, growth, and early challenges of the Jerusalem church. The church was born in prayer (1:12–14), immersed in the Spirit (2:1–4), and bathed in the miraculous (2:5–13). God brought about a powerful ministry in Jerusalem, the center of the earliest church. It did not take long for the "found" of the church to preach the Word to the lost.

A study of Acts reveals that laypersons affected early church planting (8:1, 4). They performed mass evangelism (8:5–6, 12) as well as village evangelism (8:25). Through this lay movement churches multiplied (9:31). Miracles enhanced the growth of the church (9:35–42), and salvation reached increasing numbers of Gentiles (10:44–48). Later, lay Christians from Jerusalem witnessed about Christ and planted a Gentile-Jewish church in Antioch (Acts 11:20–21).

The founding of the Antioch church may be the most important moment in church planting history. Antioch would send missionaries throughout the world. Under the leadership of the Holy Spirit, the Antioch church became the first great missionary-sending church (Acts 13:3). On the other hand, the Jerusalem church turned increasingly inward and lost much of its vision, finally disappearing like the Judaizers of the early Christian movement. In contrast, the Antioch congregation reached the world by becoming the first church-planting church!

Few church planters have been blessed by the sponsorship of an Antioch congregation, a church that willingly sponsors new churches. Few churches volunteer, as Antioch did, to send the best of their leaders and to contribute significant amounts of money for the establishment of new congregations. The Antioch church did just these things.

Redeemer Presbyterian Church in New York City is a modern Antioch church. Redeemer knows that "no single church, no matter how large and active, can all by itself change an entire city. [Therefore] saturating greater New York with gospel-centered new churches is the only way to truly insure the transformation of our city that we so much desire."[5] As a result of their commitment, the Redeemer Church helps plant churches in New York and around the world. For the enduring success of church starting, planters need more Antioch churches to provide support.

Acts records that the church at Antioch sent Paul on his first missionary journey (chs. 13–14). He began by preaching the good news of Jesus Christ in Jewish synagogues (13:5; 14:1) to receptive and responsive people. Synagogues existed in almost every major community in the Roman Empire. Smaller communities hosted places of prayer where no synagogue had yet been established. Paul approached these people whom he hoped to be receptive and responsive, telling them the Good News of Jesus Christ.

Eventually, as Jews became more resistant to this approach, Paul began to emphasize reaching Gentiles (Acts 13:44–47). He began with God-fearers. These were Gentiles who demonstrated a hunger for true spirituality and authentic religion, and they worshipped with the Jews in their community synagogues. Although these seeker Gentiles could not become full members of a synagogue without undergoing the initiation rite of circumcision, they desired to worship the one true God of the Jews. Paul's move toward the more receptive Gentiles began with the God-fearers. To the Gentiles, the gospel (without circumcision) was good news indeed.[6]

During Paul's second missionary journey (15:40–18:22), he began to focus on contextualization. Much like North Americans today, the Athenians were people in search of spiritual truth. At Mars Hill in Athens, Paul took the revolutionary step of starting where the people were: "I see that in every way you are very religious" (Acts 17:22). Beginning at the point of their search, Paul provided them with a reasoned witness about the truth of Christ.

In the last few decades, a new movement—postmodernism—has been born in the West. One of its attributes is "spirituality," although it is expressed in ways foreign to most evangelical Christians. Postmodern generations are turning away from institutional Christianity in a way not seen in several generations.[7] Church planters who immerse themselves in the new culture without a commitment to traditional patterns will be the best change agents.[8] New churches are contextualizing as Paul did. This enables them to reach this new cultural expression—understanding that postmodern "spirituality" lacks the truth of the Holy Spirit.

On his third missionary journey (18:23–21:17), the apostle returned to the churches he had founded earlier (18:23). He also established strategic mother churches in major cities (Acts 19:10; 1 Thess. 1:8). These congregations would later become sending churches in their own right. The Philippian emissary, Epaphroditus, serves as a perfect example of a situation in which a major city church sent its own to serve, and probably to become an evangelist, in this case, alongside Paul (see Phil. 2:25–30; 4:18). Paul even encouraged stewardship in these new churches (1 Cor. 16:1–3; 2 Cor. 8:1–6; 9:1–5) so they could become self-supporting and reproducing, learning to serve others. Paul was concerned that these churches avoid developing external dependency.

Conclusion

The accounts and details we've considered in Acts demonstrate that Paul and other early Christians believed in and practiced church planting as a normal part of their lives—and specifically in response to the commands of Jesus. Planting new churches was not a novel or unique concept for zealous believers. Rather, church starting was the normal expression of New Testament *missiology*. Intentional church planting, under the guidance of the Holy Spirit, was the method of the early churches. Church planting explains how the early church exploded across the Roman Empire during the decades following the resurrection of Jesus.

The life of Paul and the action of the early church demonstrate that church planting was a primary activity. Any church wishing to rediscover the dynamic nature of the early church should consider planting new churches. Furthermore, the means that Paul and the early church used provide principles for us to apply in our current methodology. Though many of their strategies were specific to their context, we should find their principles universally applicable.

Resources for Further Reading

Allen, Roland. *Missionary Methods: St. Paul's or Ours?* Grand Rapids: Eerdmans, 1962.

Brock, Charles. *Indigenous Church Planting.* Neosho, Mo.: Church Growth International, 1981.

Shenk, David W., and Ervin R. Stutzman. *Creating Communities of the Kingdom: New Testament Models of Church Planting.* Scottsdale, Pa.: Herald Press, 1988.

Chapter 4

Models of Church Plants and Church Planters

Many different biblical methods are effective in planting a church, and God does not bless one way more than the others. The most common patterns or models explained in this chapter are based on research, observation, and conversation with church planters. As each model is described, a biblical example is provided (if available) followed by a modern example along with a discussion of strengths and weaknesses.

Model 1: The Apostolic Harvest Church Planter

Paradigm	Starts churches, raises up leaders from the harvest, moves to new church
Biblical Model	Paul
Historic/Modern Example	Methodist circuit riders; house church movement; networks of house churches

Principles

- Planter starts church and moves on.

- Pastor comes out of the church and then goes back into it.
- Pastor may or may not be classically educated.
- New churches provide core for additional congregations.

The apostolic harvest church planter is the most familiar model in the New Testament. Paul would go to an established urban center, teach and preach at the marketplace and/or synagogue, engage the intellectuals and elite, start worship, appoint elders-pastors, and then supervise the new elder/pastor via letter and occasional visits. In the graphic, the apostolic harvest church planter goes to an area, plants a church, calls out and trains a new planter (the arrows come from and back to the new church), and then leaves to plant another church (possibly with some core members from the previous church plant).

The apostolic model is what most laypeople picture when imagining church planters. This planter is seen as an itinerant journeyman starting

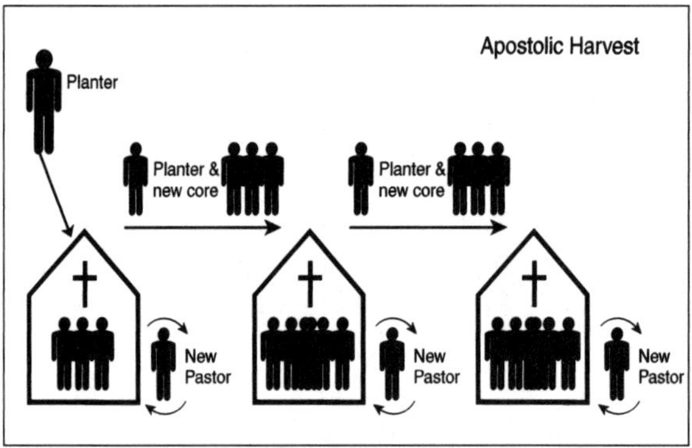

churches from town to town. The model has been widely used throughout history—from Gregory the Great's strategy in the sixth century to Methodist circuit riders of the U.S. Midwest in the eighteenth century.

Paul started an undetermined number of churches, primarily in Galatia, Asia, Achaia, and Macedonia. Many people think of this as the only model of church planting. It's not the only model, but it's certainly an important one.

Biblical Examples

An example of this paradigm can be seen in Acts 13–14.[1] Paul and his companions arrived at Pisidian Antioch (13:14) where they preached and "as many as had been appointed to eternal life believed" (13:48 NASB). Same pattern in Iconium (14:1, NASB). After preaching the gospel in Lystra (14:7) and Derbe (14:21), "they returned to Lystra and to Iconium and to Antioch, strengthening the souls of the disciples, encouraging them to continue in the faith. . . . When they had appointed elders for them in every church, having prayed with fasting, they commended them to the Lord in whom they had believed" (14:21–23, NASB). Notes John B. Polhill:

> The two apostles [Paul and Barnabas] returned the way they had come, revisiting the newly established churches along the route—first Lystra, then Iconium, and finally Pisidian Antioch. In each congregation they performed three essential ministries. First, they strengthened the disciples (v. 22a). This probably refers to their further instructing the Christians in their new faith. Second, they encouraged them "to remain true to the faith" and pointed out the "many hardships" they might encounter for bearing the name of Jesus (v. 22b). . . . The final ministry of the apostles was to establish leadership in the new congregations. For these early churches there was no professional clergy to assume their leadership. Consequently, the pattern of the Jewish synagogues seems to have been followed by appointing a group of lay elders to shepherd the flock.[2]

Historic Example

This paradigm can be seen in the rapid growth of the Methodist and Baptist denominations in nineteenth-century America. According to Justo L. Gonzalez, the use of itinerant ministers without formal education was a major factor in the growth of these churches:

> While other denominations lacked personnel because they had no educational facilities on the frontier, Methodists and Baptists were willing to use whoever felt called by the Lord. The Methodist vanguard were lay preachers, many of them serving an entire "circuit," always under the supervision of the "Connection" and its bishops. The Baptists made use of farmers or others who made a living from their trade, and who also served as pastors of the local church. When a new area was opened for settlement,

> there usually was among the settlers a devout Baptist willing to take up the ministry of preaching. Thus, both Methodists and Baptists became strong in the new territories, and by the middle of the century they were the largest Protestant denominations of the country.[3]

According to John Mark Terry:

> Circuit riders encouraged and appointed lay preachers to carry on the local ministry while they were busy along the circuit. These lay preachers played a great part spreading Methodism on the frontier. Normally, a young man who gave evidence of faith and speaking ability was encouraged to preach some trial sermons. If these efforts pleased the people, then the circuit rider gave the young man an "exhorter's license." Some of the exhorters became circuit riders, but many remained exhorters their whole lives.[4]

By the late 1800s, Methodist churches were multiplying so rapidly they were averaging one new church per day with plans for two. When a speaker at a Free Thinker's Society meeting in Chicago stated that the churches were dying across the land, it resulted in the composition of a song to serve as a rallying cry for churches to plant churches:

> The infidels a motley band in council met and said,
> The churches are dying across the land and soon will all be dead.
> When suddenly the message came and struck them in dismay,
> All hail the power of Jesus name, we're building two a day.
> We're building two a day, dear Bob, we're building two a day,
> All hail the power of Jesus name, we're building two a day.[5]

Also during the nineteenth century, one home missionary of the African Methodist Episcopal Church reported to the general conference in 1844 "that during four years he had covered 300 miles in his itinerant preaching, establishing 47 churches with a total membership of 2,000. He had seven other itinerant preachers working with him, and 27 local preachers had organized 50 Sunday schools with 200 teachers and 2,000 students."[6] As these itinerant preachers worked together, they appointed local preachers who pastored the churches they had started.

Contemporary Examples

Bob Gomez of Texas is an example of an apostolic harvest church planter. He planted his first church in Corpus Christi in 2002, followed by a second one the next year in Kingsville. Since then, God has given Bob a vision to plant churches across the southwestern United States. Between June and November 2005, he planted churches in five Texas communities—again in Corpus Christi and Kingsville plus Alice, Sinton and Portland. Gomez explained his strategy:

> We knew we needed to build teams made up of lay leaders. This idea came from growing up in a small church with revolving pastors. Every time a pastor left, a lay leader would always rise up and fill the gap until the next preacher came along. The preachers came and went, but the leaders inevitably arose to shepherd the people, and the people always followed. However, if you asked those men to preach, most of them would not accept. So, if we could develop leaders who would take care of the shepherding and caring, I would take care of the leading and feeding [through video].
>
> These same leaders also needed to be indigenous. Someone who grows up in a community often has strong ties. If the leader is new, he needs to find a local person of peace as soon as possible. We realized that in order for this vision to be fulfilled we would have to meet in homes. One of our values is to keep things simple, uncluttered, and easily reproducible. Our immediate goal is to saturate the Coastal Bend region with multiplying churches. In addition to that we are already praying about planting in either Laredo or San Antonio. Long term, we want to establish churches in the largest cities with Hispanic populations throughout Texas, and particularly the southwest United States.[7]

The house church movement is another example of the apostolic harvest model today.[8] John Dee has spent some time in China and offers a description of a typical underground house church.

> I thought you might be interested to learn a little about the house church system in China. This one church I will share about is typical. Its membership is approaching 100,000. Its radius is 300 miles.
>
> The leader is 30 years old, and he has a wife and a young son. I have been to this church and witnessed the brilliant young people in it. When a young person receives the Lord Jesus as Savior their immediate goal is to become a co-worker to be sent out for the Lord. They are not given an office with a computer, phone and fax machine. No retirement plans offered here or head Bishop post to shoot for. Without a doubt, they all know that sooner or later, they will be arrested, tortured and put into prison for the Lord.
>
> So the leadership is committed to teaching and raising up these young people to become full-time gifted anointed evangelists for Christ. As the revival continues to multiply in the area, this church sends out 30 full time workers into the countryside. Their meetings start at 5 a.m. and often last until dark. They gather in the dark and leave in the dark singing and praising the Lord in the Spirit as they go.[9]

Charles Brock, who founded Church Growth International, has served as a church planter both in North America and abroad. According to Brock, a normal process in the apostolic harvest church-planting experience (when working among receptive people) would take about eighty-two weeks. During this time, the group is led to Christ, congregationalized, given leadership training, then a study of Galatians, John, and Romans.[10]

After proper leadership is in place, the planter moves on to begin another church. Brock's objectives: (1) salvation of individuals; (2) birth of New Testament-principled churches; and (3) birth of an indigenous association of New Testament-principled churches.[11]

Can It Work Today?

Until recently, this model was primarily a theoretical idea outside of some ethnic communities. However, in the past two to three years, there's been a renewal of interest and raising up of leaders who are focusing on starting churches that are small enough to be called "relationally based."

Campus church plants are an example. They are often called "authentic faith communities" on college campuses such as the University of Texas at Austin. With a goal to start an authentic faith community in each of the more than five hundred student groups at UT, a group called Campus Renewal Ministries has united campus religious organizations to train leaders and start sixty new faith communities. Another group, Campus Church Networks (CCN), trains students to start campus churches that reach out to those around them in the U.S. and other parts of the world. A campus church planter who works with CCN and Youth With A Mission (YWAM) in Colorado Springs is seeing God ignite spontaneous prayer groups across the campuses that have a focus on praying for repentance and revival.

While there are fewer apostolic harvest church planters today than the traditional "vocational" church planter, there's a movement afoot of church planters who are bivocational or who work full-time in the marketplace *intentionally* (this is a paradigm shift from working in the marketplace for the salary to finance what they consider their real occupation: pastoring a church).

Scott Scrivner is starting a church in Oklahoma City while working as a graphic artist. Todd Hamilton is launching Pathway Church in Omaha, Nebraska, while working as a computer consultant. Matt Derfelt is starting a new congregation in Joplin, Missouri, while working as a nurse. These church planters see their secular work as their connection to the world, their opportunity to be salt and light plus a way to model the principle that *everyone* is a potential church planter. The apostolic harvest model is still found in North America today, though to a much lesser degree for several reasons:

Paul was single. Paul was able to move rapidly without considering family issues (which raises the question: how did it work for the people who traveled with him?).

Synagogues are less open to itinerant evangelists. Paul had an instant crowd—both at the synagogue and in the marketplace. The Hellenistic culture encouraged and participated in open public discourse and debate. This is no longer the case. Politics and religion, once staples of debate, are now on the forbidden list for most people. Thus, the apostolic harvest starter must generate a crowd because he will not have a ready-made crowd as Paul did.

Paul had apostolic authority. Paul could come to a town, plant a church, appoint pastors, and expect the laity to follow. (Of course, the reality is that even with Paul's God-given authority, the believers did not always follow well!) Most "apostles" in nonauthoritarian denominations don't have the same level of authority, so the process isn't as effective.

Paul established the church with miraculous signs. Most readers agree that either signs and wonders have ceased, or signs and wonders have decreased. Cessationist readers believe the gifts have passed away. Readers from a perspective open to or practicing sign gifts still probably haven't seen gifts at the apostolic level: people rising from the dead, regular healing, etc. With few exceptions, a new church is generally difficult to start based on miraculous signs.

Although the apostolic planter cannot operate in the same manner as Paul, there are similarities to today's world and advantages to Paul's model as applied today:

Cities are larger. An apostolic planter does not need to move from Philippi to Ephesus to Rome to start multiple churches. For example, Steve Childers at Reformed Seminary and Global Church Advancement outside Orlando can help to start churches throughout Central Florida, the United States, and even in Japan, without moving his family from Altamonte Springs.[12]

People can be reached en masse. Although no receptive synagogues are waiting for us to engage them, there are people who are receptive and responsive. Today we can reach thousands of people at the same time through e-mail, direct mail, phone campaigns, etc. Gathering a crowd has almost become commonplace: this many mailings produce this result; this many calls produce this result, etc. Today's apostle can effectively gather a crowd, evangelize and equip laypeople, raise up a pastor, and move on.

Pastors are readily available (for most areas). Ask one: "How would you like to pastor a one-year-old church filled with new believers ready for a long-term pastor?" Most will jump at the prospect. So if a leader doesn't emerge immediately from the group (best case), others are often available nearby.

The apostolic planter can be most effective when not pastoring a local church (although the planter might be on staff at a local church). Instead, the apostolic harvest planter's main focus is on reproducing congregations. This is seen today when church planters work as denominational church-starter strategists or catalytic church planters, bivocational or lay church starters, or itinerant apostolic church planters.

Laypeople also can be involved in apostolic church planting. God has gifted many laypersons with full-time work in a secular field and given them a passion to reach people. Such planters can gather a relation-based church through a Bible study in a home, workplace, or social circles, raising up leaders within the new church.

Model # 2: The Founding Pastor

Paradigm	Starts a church, acts as a "church planter" for a short time, and remains long term to pastor the new church
Biblical Model	Peter and the Jerusalem church
Historic/Modern Examples	Charles Spurgeon, Rick Warren
Principles	

- Planter starts and pastors the church long term.
- Pastor often moves from another location.
- Pastor often classically educated.
- Ideally, new church sponsors new congregations.

(c) Edward J. Stetzer, 2002

This is the most common model in North America. The pastor may come from outside the community to plant and stay. Or the planter might be a local layperson who plants a church, grows it, and becomes its pastor. (The lower right of the graphic (p. 62) emphasizes that even a founding planter needs to help plant other churches—keeping focused on kingdom growth.)

The founding pastor wants to plant, grow, and stay long term. The pastor may be a planted pastor or an entrepreneurial planter (discussed later in this chapter), but either way the founding pastor has a desire to stay at one church longer than an apostolic harvest planter stays. The founding pastor has a pastor's heart, so he doesn't become restless to move on like the apostolic harvest planter. Ideally, the pastor will lead the new church to start others but will remain as pastor of the original church because he's a pastor with a missionary's heart rather than a missionary with a pastor's heart. The founding pastor often learns church planting because it's necessary to start the church. Then the planter moves on to the issues of pastoring, eventually raising up others to plant another church.

Biblical Example

Peter may be a biblical example. Over time he emerged as the leader of the Jerusalem church after preaching its "founding" sermon in Acts 1. Peter was the spokesperson for the apostles and the church in Jerusalem, and he is singled out many times from the apostles:

- His speech is recorded in Acts 1:15–22.
- Peter is said to have taken a stand with the eleven (Acts 2:14).
- Peter spoke in the portico of Solomon (3:11–12).
- Peter spoke to the rulers, elders, and scribes (4:8).
- Peter spoke to Ananias and Sapphira (5:1–11).
- People desired Peter's shadow to fall on sick (5:15).
- Peter and the other apostles answer (5:29).
- Apostles heard that the Samaritans had believed and sent Peter and John to check it out (8:14).
- Peter took the gospel to the Gentiles (10:48).

Under Peter's leadership, the Jerusalem church helped start churches in Antioch and throughout Asia Minor. Peter was involved in church planting and ministry (which got him in trouble later). We know he visited Antioch, Corinth, and perhaps other places to establish or encourage new churches. Yet his focal point of ministry was Jerusalem. From that church he impacted the others.

Historic Example

Among the thousands, let's take a look at John Taylor. In 1783 Taylor and his family made a three-month journey by flatboat and horseback to Kentucky. After settling in Woodward County and establishing a farm, Taylor and several other Baptists formed Clear Creek Baptist Church. Taylor served as the pastor for nine years. He also had a part in founding seven other churches in Kentucky, Western Virginia, North Carolina, and Tennessee.[13]

Contemporary Example

Peter Wagner cites Rick Warren: "As Rick was finishing his work at Southwestern Baptist Theological Seminary, he prayed, 'I'll go anywhere you send me, Lord, but please allow me to spend my whole life wherever that may be.'"[14] Rick founded Saddleback Church, which held its first public service on Easter of 1980, and he's remained there ever since. Another reason Rick is a good example is because Saddleback has been such a prolific church-planting congregation. In the February 16, 2004 issue of *Forbes* magazine, publisher Rich Karlgaard wrote: "Saddleback has spawned [so many] daughter churches throughout the country...were it a business, Saddleback would be compared with Dell, Google or Starbucks."

Another good example of a founding pastor who is making a lifelong commitment to the church he started is Darrin Patrick of The Journey in Saint Louis, Missouri. He always had a heart for starting new ministries, going back to his high school and college years. He was disturbed to find that friends ranging from athletes to artists weren't connecting with a local church.

He made a decision to attend Midwestern Baptist Theological Seminary to be part of a church-planting team where he served for six years as youth minister. A few years ago he planted The Journey. His desire and vision is to stay there for the rest of his life, investing himself not only in this congregation but in a church-planting center that would be an outgrowth of The Journey, which is fast becoming a major resource for other planters. In its second year The Journey started mentoring new church planters. After celebrating only its third anniversary and passing 850 in attendance, The Journey under Darrin Patrick's leadership was helping five local planters by providing funds, coaching, and people to establish a core group. Now he's involved on a larger geographic scale, helping church plants throughout the Midwest and globally using Acts 29 (see www.a29.org.) through which they've assisted at least forty church planters around the world.

Other Types of Founding Pastors

Two other types of founding pastors I'll discuss are the planted pastor and the entrepreneurial pastor.

Planted Pastor (Founding)

Principles

- Organization and vision for new church usually external—from an apostolic church planter, mother church, or denominational leadership.
- Planted pastor usually has a shepherding heart with administrative ability but not a church planter's gift mix.
- Planted pastor by definition does not quickly leave but stays long term.
- Planted pastor is usually classically educated and comes from outside the congregation.
- Frequently, the pastor reaches and disciples the core. The crowd is attracted or created by someone other than the pastor.
- Ideally, planted pastor helps sponsor new works.

The planted pastor often asks: "Me, a church planter?" The answer is yes and no. Yes, the planted pastor is the first/founding/starting pastor. No, the planted pastor is not necessarily the type of person who starts things from scratch. The planted pastor is generally a pastor with strengths typically thought of as ministerial: preaching, teaching, counseling, and related abilities.

The planted pastor will lead the church as it's planted. The planted pastor may find and pastor the core while someone else (a larger mother church, an apostolic planter, or a denominational leader) provides the crowd. The diagram (p. 65) illustrates the point. The planter comes from the outside and, preferably, has developed some leadership in the core. Then the crowd is generated, leading to a successful new church plant.

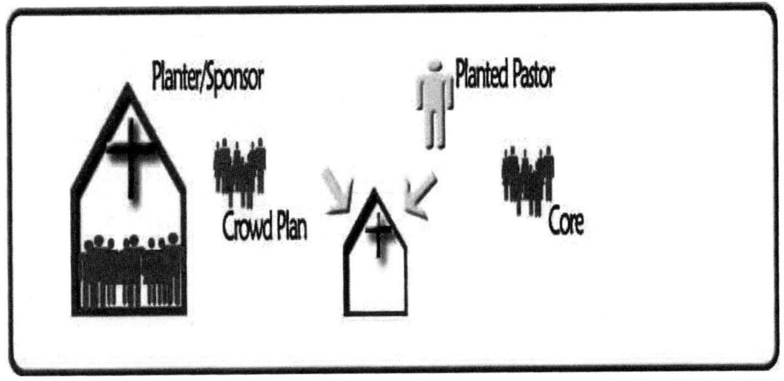

(c) Edward J. Stetzer, 2002

Wooddale Church[15] in Eden Prairie, Minneapolis, does an impressive job planting new churches. Tom Correll explains:

> We bring the church planting pastor on staff at Wooddale Church with the intent that he will start a church in six to nine months normally at a predetermined location. We launch either at Easter or Labor Day. While on Wooddale's staff and developing his ministry team the church planter has a "hunting license" to recruit anyone from the Wooddale body. We support this by having him give a faith story or preach and by sending letters from Leith [Anderson, Wooddale's pastor] to those living in the area where the church will be started encouraging them to be part of the new church plant. Oftentimes when introducing the planter in a service, Leith verbally encourages folks to leave Wooddale and be part of a new church.[16]

Their church plants are a testimony of their commitment to church planting:

When Wooddale plants a church like Westwood Community Church, the pastor does not need to have the same gifts as the church planter who is "parachuted" into a community. (Joel Johnson, the founding pastor, has incredible gifts including a passion for church planting. He helped develop the church planting strategy while at Wooddale and then was asked to be the lead pastor of Westwood.) Their commitment is well illustrated by this table:

Church	Year Founded	Approx. Number from Wooddale	Typical Worship Attendance Today
Woodridge Church www.woodridgechurch.org	1991	75	800
Woodcrest Church www.woodcrestchurch.org	1993	35	950
Westwood Community Church www.westwood-church.org	1994	250	3000
Bridgewood Church www.bridgewood.org	1998	50	600
Oakwood Community Church www.oakwoodonline.org	2000	35	150
Northwood Community Church www.northwoodcc.org	2000	25	250
Timberwood Church (150 miles distant) www.timberwoodchurch.org	2004	25-40 summer residents	200
City Church www.wooddalecitychurch.org	2005	75	225

The planted pastor has many gifts but not necessarily planter gifts. These gifts must include people skills, preaching skills, and pastoring skills. The planted pastor must be able to create a core congregation (with someone else gathering the additional people) and then pastor the crowd. The planted pastor can come at different times in the church development process. If there's a strong sponsor church, laypeople already may be planning the new church and can participate in the selection of the pastor. In other cases, the planted pastor is a staff member at an established church. The Anglican Mission in America actually has a resource for lay-initiated church planting that involves bringing in pastoral leadership later.[17]

Biblical Example

The closest biblical parallel to the planted pastor model is Timothy's ministry in Ephesus.[18] Although Acts does not record the origins of the church at Ephesus, because of the ministry of Priscilla and Aquila (Acts 18:18–19), Apollos (Acts 18:24–26), and Paul, the disciples grew in the faith (Acts 19:1–21). Some time later Paul sent a letter of instruction to Timothy, who was providing leadership to the Ephesian body of believers: "To Timothy, my true child in the faith. . . . As I urged you upon my departure for Macedonia, remain on at Ephesus in order that you may instruct certain men not to teach strange doctrines nor to pay attention to myths and endless genealogies" (1 Tim. 1:2–4 NASB). We can conclude that others planted the Ephesian church, and then God (and Paul) planted Timothy there as the pastor.

Historic Example

Although Charles H. Spurgeon is known mostly for his pulpit skills, he had a passion for new churches. When Spurgeon arrived at London's New Park Street Chapel, he found a dwindling congregation. Over time it grew to megachurch size, and Spurgeon established a ministerial school. Michael Nicholls has noted the impact of Spurgeon's involvement in church planting:

> Twenty-seven churches were founded by students from the Pastor's College between 1853 and 1867. In the second half of the nineteenth century, the number of Baptist churches in London doubled and nearly all of these were founded, in one way or another, under Spurgeon's influence. Students were sent out to new areas or existing churches, normally at the command of "the guv'nor," as students called Spurgeon.[19]
>
> Spurgeon joined with two other London ministers, Landels of Regent's Park and Brock of Bloomsbury, to found the London Baptist Association, with the goal of building one new chapel each year. Both Brock and Landels had planted their churches and started local missions, but Spurgeon's vision was London-wide.[20]

Spurgeon impacted London the most through church planting during the 1860s and 1870s. New Baptist churches averaged more than eight per year between 1856 and 1860. Forty-eight churches had been planted under

Spurgeon's guidance by 1878.[21] Spurgeon would send people out and set up places to plant new churches. Then he would plant one of his students there as the pastor of the new church. Spurgeon's students were planted pastors.

Contemporary Examples

The growth of church planting technology has enabled many people who don't have typical planting start-up gifts to plant successful churches. As mentioned, Wooddale Church in Eden Prairie, Minnesota, puts a high emphasis on church planting. They explain on their Web site: "Wooddale Church is committed to starting new churches. In the past ten years, churches started through the ministry of Wooddale Church have reached and blessed many, most of whom would never have become a part of Wooddale Church. These dynamic, contemporary churches share the common vision of helping people experience God's goodness in their lives."

This, too, may be a place to consider the multi-site movement. Although I do not include the multi-site church in church planting, it does resemble the model. And, in more and more cases, denominations are seeing multi-site churches as church plants. (For example, I recently spoke at the national Assembly of God chruch planting summit—co-led by their multi-site guru.) For more information on multi-site churches, see Geoff Surratt, Greg Ligon, and Warren Bird, *The Multi-site Church Revolution,* Zondervan Books, 2006.

The lesson here is that, as we look for church planters, not all of them have to be the ground-up types we might associate with the job. Instead, by planting pastors as well as churches, we open up the ministry for many who never would have considered church planting.

Entrepreneurial Planter (Founding)

Principles:

- Entrepreneurial planters love the challenge of starting churches but are often bored by pastoring the same church long term. However, entrepreneurial planters generally aren't attracted to the apostolic method because they love pastoring.
- The entrepreneurial planter often leaves before the congregationalizing is formalized (typically, three years).
- The entrepreneurial planter is often classically educated and comes from outside the congregation. In some cases the

entrepreneurial planter has avoided education due to boredom.
- The entrepreneurial planter may sponsor new churches.

Also a founding pastor, the entrepreneurial planter is usually an innovative and enthusiastic person who continually seeks a new challenge. That sometimes involves moving to a new church plant every few years, but that's usually not the plan at the beginning!

The entrepreneurial planter is more than a restless pastor who loves to start, grow, and move forward. Sometimes the entrepreneur is not interested, willing, and/or able to lead the church through its postplant phases. The entrepreneurial planter wants to build a core (year 1), launch and assimilate (year 2), reach out to the unchurched (year 3), and experience sustainable growth (years 4 and 5). Sometimes the entrepreneurial planter does stay but is always starting new ministries, outreaches, and programs to keep the challenge alive.

Some entrepreneurial planters don't want to lead the church through the solidification phase (three to seven years), so they leave before this phase begins causing a real problem: job security. Since all ideas do not work and all fields are not ready for harvest, there are times when the entrepreneurial planter will struggle financially. The same pastor can have different results in different communities even using the same methods. This person can often be viewed as unable to stay long term. Rather than recognizing the potential for church planting, many of these individuals will move from one established church to another.

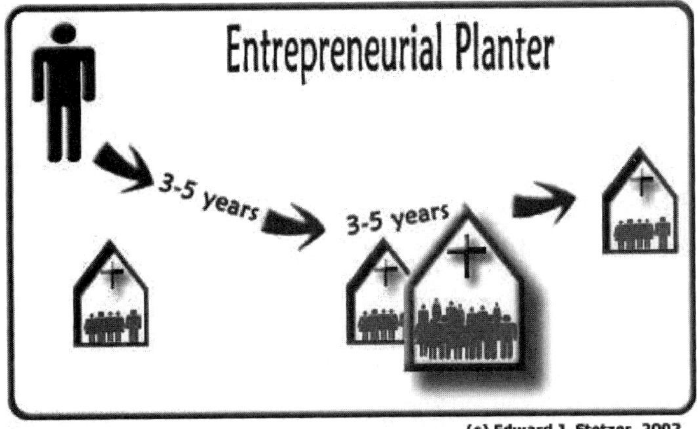

Ron Hale, who coordinates church planting in Illinois, provided a model to empower the entrepreneurial planter. Most denominations simply do not have an appropriate mechanism for funding entrepreneurial planters. Ron proposed a church planting evangelistic association modeled after the organizations of itinerant evangelists. In such a system a church planter would work with a group of supporters to provide ongoing funding for each additional church plant.

Hal Haller is an entrepreneurial church planter in South and Central Florida. After six years Hal felt led to start another church in 2003, so he moved to Lakeland to plant Church of the Highlands. Church of the Highlands publicly launched in April 2004. Hal now is in the midst of starting a new church near Disney World called Four Corners which is slated to start in April 2006. Haller has a vision to plant churches all along the I-4 corridor in central Florida. As an entrepreneurial church planter, Haller believes the biggest challenge for this type of planter is to receive validation for always wanting to plant new churches or start new ministries.

Although many entrepreneurial planters tend to move every three to five years, some do not. They're still entrepreneurs and must constantly be challenged by starting new projects such as ministries or churches that the entrepreneur doesn't lead.

Founding pastors, whether planted or entrepreneurial, are essential for kingdom growth. Statistics show that longer tenured pastors tend to grow stronger churches. When founding pastors plant strong churches that plant other churches, church growth becomes exponential, and the kingdom benefits.

Model 3: Team Planting

Paradigm	A group of planters relocates into an area to start a church. Often the team has a senior pastor.
Biblical Model	Paul (at times)
Historic/Modern Example	Missionaries at Iona, team church plants

Principles

- A team relocates to plant a new church. (Sometimes geographical relocation isn't necessary.)

- Church planting vision often comes from one key member of the team.
- Good teams have a gift mix.
- Team may amicably split up the mother church into multiple daughter churches or become traditional staff members of the founded church.

The team concept is attracting a lot of attention today. The method provides camaraderie, a division of gifts, and a strong leadership base. But it's the most infrequently used of all the models. The reason is simple: money. The cost of funding several full-time staff members is prohibitive in most church-start situations. Unfortunately, most church plant team members ren't willing to work bivocationally, which is a shame, because that factor alone may be preventing many successful church plants. For example, a successful team could include a full-time senior pastor and a team of bivocational staff, or even gifted, committed laypeople.

My friend Andy Williams, who helped with some of the revisions for this book, was blessed with an amazing team when he planted Heartland Community Church in Omaha, Nebraska, several years ago. Four families—eight adults and their kids who had long-standing friendships with Andy and his wife—moved to Omaha from other cities, and Andy was the only paid staff member in the bunch. Three of the men were techies and found computer programming jobs, and the other guy was an investment banker who started over with new clientele in the new city. All of them moved with no intention of ever being paid by the church for their services, even though all of them held key leadership positions in the church plant. Andy still says they were the most committed, sacrificial group of people he's ever been privileged to work with. Those ten began relating to their neighbors, coworkers, and within their social circles until the group was connected relationally to at least sixty non-Christians. That laid the groundwork for a launch of more than three hundred people who showed up for the church's first service.

This is the model we are using at Lake Ridge with one difference. At Heartland, Andy was the lead pastor. At Lake Ridge Church, we do not have a lead pastor; we function as a team of pastor/elders with different areas of leadership based on our giftedness. The preaching is a shared responsibility among the copastors. It's not always easy, and I don't recommend it for most young planters, but it works for me.

Biblical Support

The team method has strong biblical support. A large portion of Paul's ministry could also be described with this paradigm, first seen in Acts 13:2–3 with the church at Antioch sending out Paul and Barnabas to preach the gospel. In Acts 13:5, John Mark is seen as a helper. Eventually, Barnabas and John Mark traveled to Cyprus, and Paul departed with Silas to Syria and Cilicia (Acts 15:36–41). In Acts 16:1–5, Timothy joined Paul's team. In Acts 18:18–19, Paul traveled with Priscilla and Aquila to Ephesus. According to the scriptural account, Paul also had other traveling companions (Acts 19:29). We know that all of these people were involved in some form of ministry with Paul.

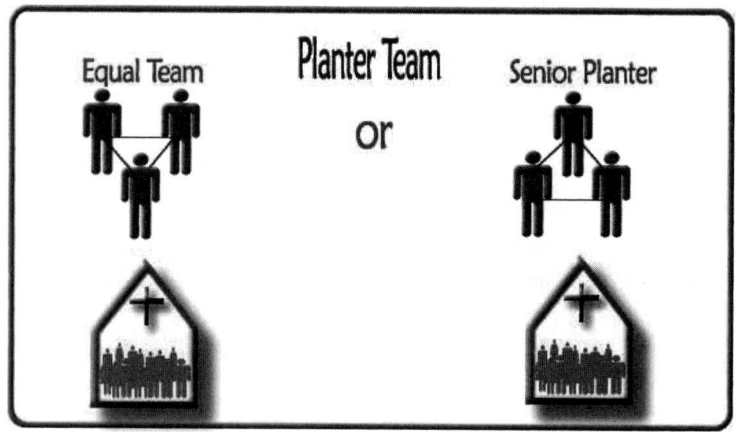

Historic Example

Columba's (521–597) ministry at Iona is a historic example of team planting. According to John Mark Terry:

> [Columba] founded several monasteries. . . . In 563 Columba took twelve fellow monks and founded a new monastery on the island of Iona near the coast of Scotland. The monastery at Iona was a base from which to evangelize the Picts, a tribe in northern Scotland. Even after Columba's death, the monastery at Iona continued to send out evangelists. One monk won a prince named Oswald to faith in Christ. When Oswald returned home

> to Northumbria, he asked the monastery to send a missionary to evangelize his people. The abbot sent Aidan, who not only evangelized the people of Northumbria but also founded a new monastery modeled after the one at Iona.[22]

In the Middle Ages, monasteries became centers of team planting. Teams would go out and plant a monastery (for example, Augustine of Canterbury) and then work together to plant churches in the surrounding villages. After churches sprang up around monasteries, the monks would move to a different location.

Contemporary Example

Many contemporary examples exist to support the team model's success with much of the current literature directed toward urban church planting.[23] James E. Westgate has divided the urban team approach into two categories: eastern model and western model.

The eastern model demonstrates the awareness of the need to develop a mini community in the midst of an urban pressurized society. Instead of sending one lone couple to face the difficulties and adjustments of complex urban culture, this model provides a network of supportive and complementary relationships to deal with the diversity and complexity of an urban setting. The focus of this team is not only to plant a church but to reproduce themselves by training others to plant reproductive churches.[24]

The eastern model "calls for a team of trainers equipping teams of church planters. The primary role of the team is to train others."[25]

Regarding the western model, Westgate writes:

> The team is committed to a bivocational approach to church planting. The primary goal of the team is to plant a church in a strategic place in the city. The primary focus of the team is evangelism, with each team member committed to disciple five to ten people during the first year, a potential of fifty people for the beginning of the church. The second year, the church is organized and the couples concentrate on training the new converts to share their faith while achieving their goal of leading ten more people to Christ. . . . During the second year the couples also

> choose someone to be trained in their own particular areas of skill, such as Bible study, or Christian education.
>
> The third year is a transitional stage for the church. Team members turn their responsibilities over to those whom they have trained. . . . Each team member then becomes the church planter for a new sister church and calls for four to six new couples to join them from a seminary or denominational sister church.[26]

More and more church plants are using a team planting model—and not just in urban settings. In 2004, Gary Lamb was in the planning stages of planting a church in Canton, Georgia. After planting a church as a solo planter in Iowa, Gary desired to start Ridge Stone Church as a multi-staffed team plant. Yet, like most church plants, they had no money. So Gary approached ten friends who had always talked and dreamed about starting a church together. He asked them to quit their full-time ministry jobs, raise their own support, and help plant a new church. Out of ten, three of them said yes. August 15, 2004, Ridge Stone Church launched with 287 in attendance.

From the first day they have had a full-time children's pastor, lead pastor, worship pastor, and administrative pastor. A year later they are all still together and all full-time with the church with the exception of their administrative pastor who moved on to enter into a church planting internship with the dream of planting his own church one day. Team plants can be tremendously effective.

My Ph.D. dissertation[27] focused on factors that cause a new church to have a larger attendance. I conducted an exploratory survey, providing room for comments. More than six hundred church planters responded, and many added their thoughts. One recurring theme was the desire for church planting teams. The survey revealed that attendance was higher (almost double) in plants with more than one church planting pastor on staff. (This doesn't take into account other factors that might be elevated by having multiple staff such as a large base, sponsor church, and ample funding. However, the mean attendance difference is clear.)

I also learned that it's not just the presence of *multiple* pastors that makes a difference. In fact, this increased mean attendance is most present when there are *two* staff members—not three or more. (With three or more I find that the new church struggles with making connections with the lost community. It's true that a larger number of pastors can build close team relationships; but, perhaps *because* they have close friends with one another, they don't make as many evangelistic contacts and relationships.) I concluded that having two staff members initially makes the most effective church planting team. (The survey didn't address whether both members of the team worked full-time, but in most cases I'd guess they did not.) From both the data and the comments I concluded that the combination of roles that make the most effective two-person planting teams are a full-time lead pastor plus a part-time second pastor with worship and evangelism skills.

Conclusions

God uses many types of people and methods to plant churches. The list above is not intended to be complete, but it might help you think through your role in church planting. Perhaps you have not fully explored what being a church planter involves. Maybe you fit into one of the categories, or maybe you see yourself as a combination of these models. The call of God and his provision of spiritual gifts will determine how each church planter accomplishes the work of starting new churches.

Resources for further reading

Nevius, John L. *Planting and Development of Missionary Churches.* Nutley, N.J.: Presbyterian and Reformed Publishing Company, 1958.

Sanchez, Daniel R., Ebbie C. Smith, and Curtis E. Watke. *Reproducing Congregations: A Guidebook for Contextual New Church Development.* Cumming, Ga.: Church Starting Network, 2001.

Steffen, Tom. *Passing the Baton: Church Planting That Empowers.* La Habra, Calif.: Center for Organizational and Ministry Development, 1997.

Wagner, C. Peter. *Church Planting for a Greater Harvest.* Ventura, Calif.: Regal Books, 1990.

Chapter 5

What Makes a Church Planter?

First, *who* can plant a church?

Do only churches plant churches? What about denominations? What about individuals? For that matter, must individuals be ordained, formally trained, and sent out by an agency or denomination?

In this chapter we explore the impact of sponsorship on church-planting success plus the qualifications of people called to be planters.

We'll start by exploring interesting patterns in the New Testament regarding the *who* of church planting.

Teams Plant Churches

We read that God raised up apostolic teams, especially in Acts and the Gospels. This was the practice of the apostle Paul, who consistently used team ministry in his church planting. In his intimate circle were Barnabas, Silvanus, and Timothy. Working with him as independent coworkers were Priscilla, Aquila, and Titus. Paul also worked with local church representatives, including Epaphroditus, Epaphras, Aristarchus, Gaius, and Jason.

"The churches, Ollrog argues, put these persons at Paul's disposal for limited periods. Through them the churches themselves are represented in the Pauline mission and become coresponsible for the work. As a matter of fact, not being represented in this venture constitutes a shortcoming in a local church; such a church has excluded itself from participating in the Pauline missionary enterprise."[1]

Individuals Plant Churches

When Philip went to Samaria (Acts 8:1–40), there is no indication that he was sent by anyone other than the Holy Spirit. As he won converts, the apostles sent Peter and John there, but Philip had already been baptizing converts and planting the new church.

Although an individual planting a church is the most common method today, it's the least common in the New Testament. This does not imply that it did not happen. Early church history reflects that several of the apostles set out in different directions to plant churches. This must have been a lonely endeavor and reminds us of the importance of bringing a team to plant—or developing one soon upon arrival.

Laypeople Plant Churches

Aquila and Priscilla are two names that appear frequently in the New Testament. They were laypeople, probably a married couple in business, and they probably started the church in Ephesus. They show up in several cities (Rome, Corinth, and Ephesus; see Acts 18:2–3, 18–19, 26; 2 Tim. 4:19).

They hosted a church in their home at both Ephesus and Rome (1 Cor. 16:19; Rom. 16:3–5). Since there is no record of the church in Rome being "founded," it is logical to assume that Aquila and Priscilla helped start the church that met in their house. They had a heart for church planting and the ministry of Paul and may have financed his trip to Ephesus. Richard Longenecker explains that they were probably traveling business owners:

> [They] were either transferring their business from Corinth to Ephesus or leaving their Corinthian operation in charge of a manager (as possibly they did earlier at Rome) in order to open a new branch at Ephesus. Perhaps Aquila and Priscilla, who seem to have been fairly well-to-do, paid Paul's passage as they joined him on board the ship for Ephesus—and perhaps also paid his passage on to Jerusalem. Being themselves Jewish Christians,

> they would have appreciated Paul's desire to fulfill his vow at Jerusalem.[2]

The fact that laypeople can plant churches raises an interesting point. It reminds us that those not called specifically to pastoral ministry can be involved in the ministry of church planting. It's a ministry for laypeople as well as pastors. If we want to create communities with a missional mindset, we cannot allow our churches to be held back because of a lack of *professional* pastoral leadership. Every believer is called to missions, regardless of a more specific vocational calling. Equipping more laypeople to lead ministries and churches is exactly what Ephesians 4:11–13 describes.

The Bible goes into too much detail about pastor/elders not to assume they were a normal part of the local church. But the qualifications are those of a godly person with one exception. The godly person must be "able to teach." Beyond the standards of godliness, that is the biblical qualification for a layperson functioning as a pastoral leader in a church plant. Laypeople can plant churches, assuming the pastoral leadership (or choose to bring someone else in), and plant Christ-centered churches.

Agencies and Denominations Plant Churches

Many people feel strongly that agencies and denominations should not plant churches because they're concerned about control and support. In my faith tradition, we believe in the autonomy of the local church, and we're skeptical of outside ecclesiastical control. In most cases, however, I find that agency/denominational church starting is not about control; it's about start-up. One of my former students put it best:

> [The Bible does not speak against] the idea of people collectively gathering and sending out people to do the work of the gospel. Paul was not supported solely by the Jerusalem church, from which he went out of on his missionary journeys. Paul traveled and was supported by many different people and churches (ex., Phil. 4:16) that he might do the work God had for him, and even had to support himself at times (Acts 18:3). Christians gathering resources and sending out workers into the harvest is what God has called his people to do, and while local church government seems to be restrictive, the work of the gospel is not. God has worked in many different ways throughout history, and

to place restrictions on God concerning this matter could cause many to miss out on the blessing of planting a new church.[3]

Churches Plant Churches

Although there is no requirement for "churches planting churches" in the New Testament, this method remains the preferred one today. In the New Testament, churches did commission people to plant churches, and some of their people did move from community to community in the process. "The real agent in the planting of the [church in] Antioch was the Holy Spirit. We see no evidence that the Jerusalem church as the 'mother church' or 'sponsoring church' took official action to send church planters to start a 'mission' or 'daughter congregation' at Antioch."[4]

But churches can, do, and should plant churches. The most effective church planting occurs when a sponsor/mother church is actively involved, a model historically called "church extension" where a mother church "extends" itself into another location. Today we call this church multiplication.

Mother churches tend to be involved at different levels, such as sending out a core group of members who work as a team or providing other resources: (1) mentoring or accountability relationships for encouragement, (2) financial support, (3) facilities, and (4) leadership. Another model I see emerging more in the twenty-first century is the mother or sponsor church creating satellite campuses that often look and sound like the originating church, the main difference being not only location but also a more contextualized ministry for the population in the different area.

Still others are cross-cultural church-starting models. In the first edition of this book, I dedicated a chapter to cross-cultural church planting models. That chapter is now available at www.newchurches.com.

However the partner church structures the relationship, church planting needs to be a priority of established churches. Phil Stevenson explains: "We cannot be a biblical church and abstain from planting churches. God never intended that the church should be just for us. His aim has always been to multiply the church.... This ancient method must be applied in new ways for a new time.... We need to rekindle the spirit of the Antioch church."[5]

This is a benefit for the daughter church when a mother church is involved. As the graph shows, attendance is higher in church starts with an involved mother church, especially in the early years. Each year the attendance of a new church with an involved mother church is higher than those without the participation of a sponsoring/mother church.[6]

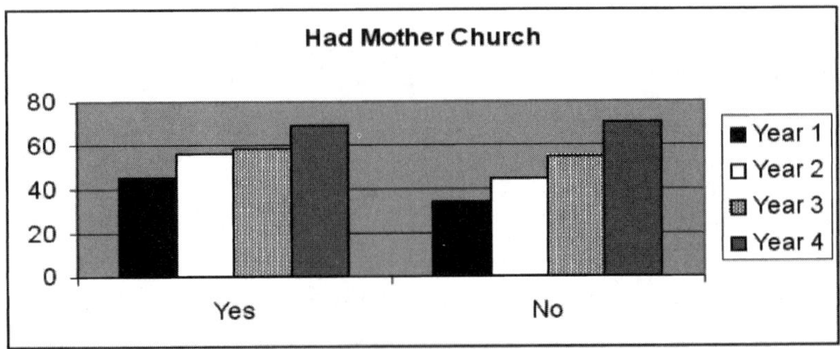

Church researcher Jeffrey Farmer is currently writing his doctoral dissertation on the effects of sponsoring a church plant on the mother church. After conducting a pilot study, he published a paper, "The Effect of Sponsoring a Church Plant on the Sponsor Church," and found that churches which sponsor church plants are positively affected in Sunday morning worship attendance, baptisms, and Sunday School attendance. Furthermore, churches which sponsor a new church plant every three to five years have the potential to sustain growth for an extended period. The study can be found at www.newchurches.com under "research."

Beyond the attendance numbers, a mother church can encourage and nurture the planters, a key ingredient to success. Many times I've sat with church planters who were discouraged because they did not have the support and encouragement of a sponsor or mother church. (To Whom It May Concern: to be fair, I've also spoken to church planters who were hindered in their work by a sponsor church that tried to be too controlling.) But church planters who had the healthy support of a mother church often flourished because, as they told me, they experienced the synergy of shared enthusiasm and excitement as well as outright help in practical ways. I conclude that having a supportive sponsor or mother church makes a big difference, and it's the best way to plant a daughter church.

So Who Can Plant?

A former student of mine wrote: "What was the criteria that Barnabas used in making his judgments on the church at Antioch? The Bible says he 'saw the evidence of the grace of God' (Acts 11:23). That is the only criteria that the Bible mentions. Thus, what Barnabas did was he recognized God at work in that church plant."[7]

Ultimately, God calls church planters and blesses new churches. God can use teams, individuals, agencies, and other churches. But without the Holy Spirit's work, we are not planting churches; we are starting religious clubs.

God can use different or multiple persons to plant churches. Over the last twenty years, people began to categorize and note certain characteristics of church planters. These common characteristics have been tracked and measured over the last couple decades, and groups began to develop assessments to evaluate church-planting potential.

What Does a Church Planter Look Like?

"Assessments" as a concept cropped up among church-planting leaders in the late 1980s. Today I see many levels of assessments. For some potential church planters, an assessment lasts one week and involves intensive psychological testing, one-on-one interviews, group interactions, and follow-up meetings. Other assessments are short and simple, intended to help the potential church planter clarify a sense of calling and giftedness. Still others are in-between, where the span of time is shorter, the face-to-face activity is limited; but some evaluation tools are used for informing the person making the decision with additional informers.

The task of church planting requires people who are uniquely gifted. Since you are reading these words, you may be asking, "Am I a church planter?" A quick assessment might clarify this question.

> Go to www.newchurches.com and click on assessment or go to www.churchplantingvillage.net and click on *discovery tools*.

A planter's SHAPE includes:

- *Spiritual gifts:* Gifts of ministry bestowed by the Holy Spirit
- *Heart or passion:* A burden to establish an outreach toward a

specific people group, in a particular location, or through a specific type of ministry
- *Abilities:* Entrepreneurial talents useful in planting (or perhaps in generating income in a bivocational church plant)
- *Personality type:* Analysis of personality types often appearing in church planters
- *Experiences*: Tools for describing experiences to help the planter understand when, where, and how to plant a church

Ridley Assessments

From his study of church planters in several Protestant denominations, Charles Ridley developed a helpful process for determining the probability that a person will succeed in church planting. Denominations across North America use his work to assess their planter candidates. It is the Ridley assessment to which most people refer when they speak of a church-planter assessment. Church planters who have gone through a Ridley assessment interview lead churches that are larger in attendance than those who do not.

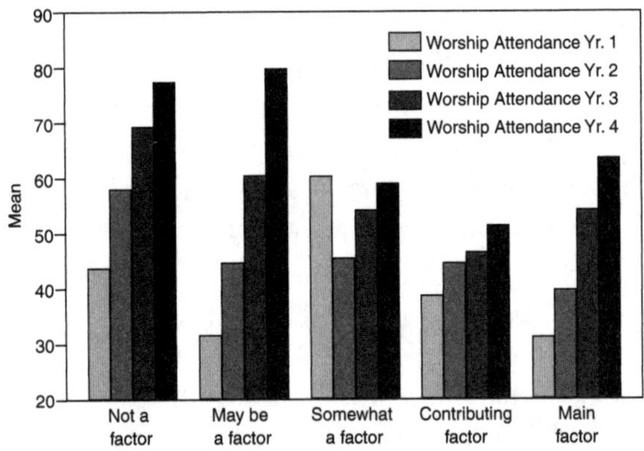

Attendance is a good indicator of church health (though not the only one). Although my graph refers only to attendance, most church planting leaders would acknowledge that a new church is more likely to fail when it's started by a planter who has not been assessed. Statistically, all other factors being equal, an assessment assures the selection of better church planters with a higher likelihood of success.

Ridley determined that most successful church planters share thirteen behavioral characteristics.[8]

1. *Visionizing capacity* is the ability to imagine the future, to persuade other persons to become involved in that dream, and to bring the vision into reality.
2. *Intrinsically motivated* means that one approaches ministry as a self-starter, and commits to excellence through hard work and determination.
3. *Creates ownership of ministry* suggests that one instills in others a sense of personal responsibility for the growth and success of the ministry and trains leaders to reproduce other leaders.
4. *One who relates to the unchurched* develops rapport and breaks through barriers with unchurched people, encouraging them to examine and to commit themselves to a personal walk with God. As an additional outcome, new believers become able to lead others to salvation in Jesus Christ.
5. *Spousal cooperation* describes a marital partnership in which church planting couples agree on ministry priorities, each partner's role and involvement, and the integration and balance of ministry with family life.
6. *Effectively builds relationships* is the skill to take initiative in meeting people and deepening relationships as a basis for more effective ministry.
7. *Starters committed to church growth* value congregational development as a means for increasing the number and quality of disciples. Through this commitment they increase numerical growth in the context of spiritual and relational growth.
8. *Responsiveness to the community* describes abilities to adapt one's ministry to the culture and needs of the target area residents.
9. *One who uses the giftedness of others* equips and releases other people to minister on the basis of their spiritual giftedness.
10. *A starter who is flexible and adaptable* can adjust to change and ambiguity, shift priorities when necessary, and handle multiple tasks at the same time. This leader can adapt to surprises and emergencies.
11. *Builds group cohesiveness* describes one who enables the group to work collaboratively toward common goals, and who skillfully manages divisiveness and disunifying elements.
12. *A starter who demonstrates resilience* shows the ability to sustain

himself or herself emotionally, spiritually, and physically through setbacks, losses, disappointments, and failures.

13. *One who exercises faith* translates personal convictions into personal and ministry decisions and resulting actions.

Others have been building on the Ridley assessment (and developing other tools) for over a decade. Some have addressed issues of relational skills, reason to plant, small group skills, etc.

For example, the Baptist General Conference offers assessment to help pastors determine their call: "An assessment for couples or singles seeking a confirmation to God's call to start a new church. The purpose of the assessment process is to increase the success rate of new church starts.... Currently the national average of church starts resulting in a successful plant is only 35%. Candidates who attend the Assessment Center and follow through with the conditions and recommendations are experiencing a success rate of over 85%."[9]

The need for assessment is obvious. Without properly assessing candidates, our effectiveness for the kingdom wanes. Our assessment must be more than a "they look sharp" or "my gut tells me" system. Assessments need to reflect accurately the giftedness of the candidate and match them with the appropriate spot in ministry. Tom Jones' group, The Church Planting Assessment Center, gives a brief description of their assessment by saying: "A Church Planting Assessment Center is an intensive multi-day experience which combines interviews, interactive exercises, individual and group presentations, and written evaluations by peers, assessors, and the candidates themselves."[10]

The North American Mission Board (where I serve) system started out based on the Charles Ridley approach where the behavioral interview was used as the assessment tool. Recently we have begun to change several categories in addition to yes/no decisions.

The mid-categories included:

- Not as lead planter but part of the team in another role,
- Not now but later after an apprenticeship experience.

The "assessment report" was also used for a point of reference to use in the development aspects for the planter and was to be used by the mentor in the mentor/planter covenant with the objectives for growth.

Joe Hernandez, team director at NAMB who oversees the assessment process, explained:

> We don't just use one tool now. Instead, we use the church planter selection process which includes additional tools to the decision-making process. A customizable process included inventories such as spiritual gifts, personality/leadership styles, passions, and additional inventories that the partner entity wants to include. The process encouraged a limited face-to-face engagement (thus keeping it to a one- or two-day activity) that not only included the behavioral interview but also any other activity from group dynamic to simulated activity to gain additional information for the decision-making process.[11]

Some assessments are more relational. "The Acts 29 Assessment process has essentially two aspects. The first is based on a series of exams, and the second is simply building relationship."[12] Even though some assessments are more simplistic in their formation, their intrinsic value is incomparable. Most assessments help the candidates discover much more than a simple self-examination. Most candidates believe they are already well equipped and often overlook their shortcomings and weaknesses. However, when planting a church these weaknesses will be revealed sooner or later. It is obvious that it is much better for everyone to find these qualities early on, as opposed to later.

Others include specific activities and interactions. The Mission to North America (MNA), a branch of the Presbyterian Church of America, involves "simulated church planting exercises, small group experiences, teaching modules, evaluation instruments and personal interviews."[13] Offering exercises to simulate real-life scenarios can be extremely helpful in discovering giftedness. Often tests can prove only as accurate as the truthfulness of the candidate; and especially in cases in which the denomination funds or assists in the plant itself, they desire to ensure much more than a written examination.

Every group has a different set of rules when deciding when to assess the potential planter, but Redeemer Church Planting Center in New York has a good grip on the subject of 'when' to assess vocational church planters (we will deal with lay planters later).

> Normally the assessment process occurs after a candidate has concluded his theological training and has had experience as an apprentice in a church planting situation or other church ministry. In order to better prepare the candidate for the task of church planting some seminaries are introducing a weeklong assessment process during theological training. This allows the candidate an opportunity to view his strengths and limitations and design his ministry focus accordingly. Although self-evaluation is important in understanding one's call, much can be learned by the objective evaluation of experienced church planters. This is what church planters call Assessment.[14]

You can expect a variety of answers from an assessment center. After assessment it is possible that the organization may receive all of the information they need to make their decision, but most of all you are bringing in an objective point-of-view to assist in the decision process. Regardless of their response, you need to be prepared for accepting a scenario that may be less than ideal. The Evangelical Covenant Church based in Chicago, Illinois, states their responses in this manner:

> Overall, participants desiring to plant a Covenant church were given three scenarios: (1) they were accepted wholeheartedly as church planters; (2) they were "conditionally recommended"—potentially a successful candidate for church planting—after following certain conditions before beginning a church plant; or (3) they were told that they should not become a church planter at this time. In all cases, evaluators pointed out the ministry gifts they saw in the church planter candidates and the reasons they were being given the evaluation they were given.[15]

Depending on the type of involvement your church will have in its denomination, and assuming that denomination requires assessment before you can receive funding; this process may not be an option for the church-planting candidate. However, if you are considering starting a church outside of a denomination or association that requires such, it is always a good idea to get a second opinion. Find a Church Planting Assessment Center and get more information. They can at times be costly, but the result is worth the investment.

Other Qualifications

Besides the qualities addressed by the SHAPE inventory and described by the Ridley categories, we find other qualifications in the New Testament. For example, although the requirements in 1 Timothy 3 target pastor-elders, they also apply to church planters. But, because church planters encounter issues typically not faced by pastors of established congregations, we need to consider several qualifications uniquely essential to church planters.

- **Certainty of call.** The first is a certainty of call to church planting. In Ephesians 3:8, Paul wrote, "To me, the very least of all saints, this grace was given, to preach to the Gentiles the unfathomable riches of Christ" (NASB). In times of doubt, pain, and struggle, Paul could look back to a specific time of his calling. This certainty of being called to preach to the Gentiles reassured him in difficult times. In 1 Timothy 2:7 he wrote, "For this I was appointed a preacher and an apostle (I am telling the truth, I am not lying) as a teacher of the Gentiles in faith and truth" (NASB).
- **Call to a community, culture, or people group.** Just as a call to the Gentiles compelled the apostle Paul, part of the planter's call is to a certain people. That call may be to the people of a specific community or a specific culture or demographic group.
- **Extraordinary faith.** Ridley mentions faith as a qualification equal with a dozen others, but it deserves much greater emphasis. The author of Hebrews wrote, "Faith is the assurance of things hoped for, the conviction of things not seen" (Heb. 11:1, NASB). Though every pastor needs faith, the church planter needs extraordinary faith. Although the church does not exist and cannot be seen before it is started, the planter must possess the conviction that the new church is a reality; it will come into existence. The planter who does not have faith that God is planting a church through his efforts should not be a planter.

Wrong Reasons

Many people plant churches for wrong reasons. Here are some inappropriate reasons:

- A strong desire to preach but no one will give you an opportunity
- Frustrated where you are because you can't do what you want to do
- Can't get an invitation to pastor an established church
- Out to prove something
- Need to get some experience—and church planting seems like a good opportunity to practice ministerial skills
- Dreaming of a large ministry to boost your own reputation or ego

None of these are adequate reasons even if your personality sounds similar to the characteristics described in this chapter. But if a person has the right reasons and the right wiring, the combination can lead to great church-planting potential.

Conclusions

After reading this chapter, you might be encouraged or discouraged depending on how you feel you "line up." If you're encouraged, consider connecting with church-planting leaders in your church, fellowship, or agency. Share your interest in church planting with them. The remainder of this book will contain practical steps that can be used to plant the church God has called you to plant.

If you read the categories and were discouraged, don't give up yet. First, ask those who know you if you have some of these characteristics. If they, and you, agree that they don't describe you, then reconsider being a lead church planter.

However, you could still serve on a church planting team, and you can certainly encourage and support others in church planting.

Resources for Further Reading

Mannoia, Kevin. *Church Planting: The Next Generation.* Indianapolis, Ind.: Light and Life Communication, 1994.

Ridley, Charles R. *How to Select Church Planters.* Pasadena: Fuller Evangelistic Association, 1988.

Chapter 6

Church Structure

Typical church planters can see in their mind's eye every minute of the church's first service envisioning a large, enthusiastic crowd; rehearsing the message; and imagining how every detail will unfold. On the other hand, the same church planters might have given zero thought to the new church's structure or form of government.

Elmer Towns, authority on church life and dean of Liberty University, says that changing ecclesiology causes many new churches to fail. My own church planting experience is probably a good example. I started my first church, Calvary Christian Church, with a public launch service of twenty-one people, followed by a weekly attendance of nine. Our plan was for the congregation to be cell-based and governed by a plurality of elders.

After a challenging first year, my own immaturity at being a twenty-one-year-old church planter, and pressure from "all nine" church members, I attended a conference on the effectiveness of Sunday school. Soon our church reorganized itself around Sunday school structures and did away with cell groups. We continued following a strong pastoral leadership model but de-emphasized elder plurality.

In less than a year we reorganized again, and this time emphasized deacon leadership. Obviously, I was feeling my way around, unsure of what governance approach was best and ignorant of the Bible's counsel concerning church structure. I adapted to whatever I'd learned at the latest conference or read in an influential book. (About this time in my life, I decided to attend seminary!) The church quickly became discouraged after each change.

Just as switching worship styles can divide a church, changing structure and leadership styles can polarize a congregation and sap morale. Selecting a new plan for church structure also frustrates people. The bottom line is that the church planter must decide on structure before hanging out the welcome sign.

Planters are often young, idealistic, and recent college or seminary graduates. During their academic training, they learn about ecclesiological paradigms; their school may have advocated one model over others. The planters decide which model to adopt as their own, perhaps even viewing the new church start as a way to demonstrate their chosen structure as the best. But planting a church to demonstrate an ecclesiological principle is a sure path to failure.

No Structure or Too Much Structure?

Some planters downplay the importance of biblical church structures. They believe that structures are theological afterthoughts or traps to be avoided for the sake of encouraging a streamlined organization. But when these are ignored at the beginning, they often become problems later.

On the other hand, some churches discuss their ecclesiology so frequently that they tie up meetings with endless internal business. Visitors wonder whether these churches can decide any matter without the approval of some board or body. I must admit that's how I started. After the first service at my first church, we had a thirty-two-page constitution for nine regular attenders—three pages for each attendee! Our committees outnumbered our people. We held monthly business meetings because I thought that was God's design. When a church *focuses* on structure, the planter spends more time servicing the structure and less time serving God.

The Bible provides us with a solid middle ground for church structure. Churches do need biblical ecclesiology that enables them to function with efficiency and integrity. Here are several popular options.

- **Elders.** The pure elder paradigm provides a true plurality for governance with no chief leader. It's practiced among Brethren denominations and in some Bible churches. Some biblical evidence supports this view.

- **Pastors and Elders.** This approach uses a plurality of leaders, including the pastor, who serves as an elder and is the "first among equals." Other elders may be laypersons or paid vocational (full-time) staff. Malphurs advocates full-time staff members.[1] This model best fits the biblical teaching on governance; and, in my opinion, elders may be either paid staff members or unpaid volunteers.
- **Pastor and Board.** The pastor is seen as the leader but looks to the church board to share in the tasks of leadership and major decision-making. The board may be comprised of either deacons or elders. This pattern describes the most commonly practiced form of church governance although I find little biblical support for it.
- **Board and Pastor.** This form acknowledges the pastor as an employee of the board, performing ministry at their direction. Although this model appears in many church settings, I find no biblical evidence to commend its use.
- **Pastor.** Churches that follow this ecclesiological system clearly follow only the pastor. This style frequently appears among independent Baptists and in charismatic and Pentecostal congregations. The pastor is the decision-maker for the church, sharing authority with no one except, perhaps, with the entire church under a congregational form of government. Some proof texts may be interpreted to support the approach, but I see dangers inherent to this structure. The most obvious one is the fact that other leaders haven't been developed, so if the pastor leaves the church (either for another ministry field or by death), the church may not be equipped to make decisions.

Scripture References

Passages to help us understand biblical teachings about ecclesiology include John 17:23; Acts 14:23; 20:17, 28–32; 21:18; 1 Corinthians 11:17–18; Galatians 6:10; Ephesians 4:3; 1 Timothy 3; 4:14; 5:1–2, 17–19; Titus 1:5–9; James 5:14–15; 1 Peter 5:1–5.

My best understanding of the biblical teaching is that the church should be led by a group of pastor-elders who serve in covenant relationships with one another. Generally, there will be a lead pastor-elder, but that leader will be drawn from the preaching team and the congregation as a whole. They might include pastors, bivocational pastor-elders, and lay pastor-elders. This is my best understanding of Scripture when I read the passages, but good believers differ on some of these issues. But it's important to find the basis for your style in Scripture and not just personal preference.

Congregational Purpose Shapes Ecclesiology

Churches should structure themselves for growth because the New Testament teaches that the church is here to evangelize the world, grow the body of Christ, and extend his kingdom.[2] Church governance should function like a human skeleton, as a necessity for structure and well-being but invisible to the naked eye. The structure should be biblical yet remain out of sight in its functional routine. Ecclesiological structure helps the church to be orderly. Scripture emphasizes that churches must be orderly because of the very nature of God: "God is not a God of disorder but of peace" (1 Cor. 14:33).

Jesus most frequently described his followers as a "flock." He called Christians his "sheep" and the church his "flock." This emphasis is also revealed in the term for a church leader known as "pastor." The Greek word *poimen* may be translated as either "shepherd" or "pastor." Pastors are to serve as shepherds—to feed, to protect, and to lead God's flock. The task of the pastor is to serve as assistant shepherd or undershepherd to the Good Shepherd (John 10:11, 14), whom Peter (1 Pet. 5:4) termed the Chief Shepherd. So pastors embrace the call to "shepherd" the flock that God has placed under their care (Acts 20:28; 1 Pet. 5:2).

All of these biblical principles of leadership point to the biblical concept of eldership (also interchangeably called "pastors" in Scripture). Pastor-elders were said to choose deacons (Acts 15:22), to "rule" (1 Tim. 5:17), and to intercede on behalf of the sick (James 5:14). These leaders were said to have received appointment—in at least one instance from a church planter (Titus 1:5).

Pastor-Elders

Several Scriptures explain the role. One of the clearest verses is 1 Timothy 5:17: "The elders who direct the affairs of the church well are worthy of double honor, especially those whose work is preaching and teaching." Another helpful text is 1 Peter 5:1–4: "To the elders among you, I appeal as a fellow elder, a witness of Christ's sufferings and one who also will share in the glory to be revealed: Be shepherds of God's flock that is under your care, serving as overseers—not because you must, but because you are willing, as God wants you to be; not greedy for money, but eager to serve; not lording it over those entrusted to you, but being examples to the flock. And when the Chief Shepherd appears, you will receive the crown of glory that will never fade away."

These two passages suggest that some pastor-elders teach and some do not (or else why the double honor?). The traditional pastor is not the only elder in the church. Some elders preach and teach; some do not. Furthermore, the elder is also called an "overseer" (Greek: *episkopos*, often mistranslated as "bishop") and the shepherd-pastor (Greek: *poimen*, translated as either "pastor" or "shepherd").

Therefore, a church is led by pastor-elders—some of whom function as teaching pastors. Pastors lead and feed the flock, help people find their place in ministry, and lead with the attitude of love found in healthy families. A proper understanding of the nature of the church and relevant biblical passages helps us understand the leadership qualities called for in church planters.

I find it interesting that in 1 Peter 5, the one whom Christ said "upon you I will build my church"—Peter—refers to himself as a "fellow elder." This is contrary to how some of our structures operate. Regardless of whether Peter was considered a lead elder (and I think he was), he still considered himself to share the same shepherding responsibilities as the ones he was addressing in this passage. Peter also reminds these elders that they are shepherding God's flock and not their own. How often do planters lose sight of the vision that the congregation they are building is not their own? It's easy to think that way because of all a church planter has invested in the ministry. Also, some planters build their ministry around their own personalities rather than creating a God-centered community. When a body of believers becomes God-centric, they'll recognize the spiritual leading of the pastoral team and/or elders when it's in line with his direction.

Deacons

According to the New Testament, deacons are servants who assist the church in accomplishing its ministry. In fact, the term deacon can also be translated "servant." Their role is a ministry role. In Acts 6, deacons took responsibility to oversee the church's social ministry to widows who needed the daily distribution of food. Deacons are to conform to certain lifestyle and behavioral requirements (1 Tim. 3:8–13). Paul greeted them as church leaders (Phil. 1:1). Deacons are ministry leaders who serve under the leadership of the church's pastor-elders.

Neutral Terms

At several of my church plants, we used neutral terms for the positions of elder and deacon. We called our pastor-elders the "administrative team" and our deacons "ministry leaders."

This approach has positive and negative aspects. Among the negatives, if these functions are biblical offices, wouldn't it be better to use biblical terminology? Neutral terms may overemphasize a businesslike model of the church; biblical terminology tends to emphasize the scriptural nature of the church.

On the other hand, neutral names can be understood by everyone. Because new evangelistic churches attract people without a church background plus people from other churches and denominations, this approach helps everyone make a fresh start in the new church. Otherwise, when a member with a Church of God background sees elders as leaders and deacons as servants of the church, he or she may be out of sync with the former American Baptist who sees deacons as the leadership "board" of the church. Newcomers can learn what title performs what function without having to unlearn old meanings. Furthermore, the case can be made that churches of the New Testament era understood elders as leader-servants and deacons as ministry-servants; clarity in terminology is just as important today. Some authorities in church planting recommend using terminology that's understood by most people in the new church without conjuring memories of old baggage—in other words, allowing cultural context to determine terminology.

The practicality of neutral names is a persuasive argument, but over the years I've become convinced that using biblical terminology is best. This allows the church to look to biblical texts for explanation and descriptions of leadership roles. The practice takes more work, but it enables the church family to personalize the Scripture text. When they read about elders, they have specific people in mind. When they read about deacons, they have a face to go along with the name.

Applications

How does this understanding influence the structure of a new church?

1. New churches should call out a few pastor-elders. Pastor-elders serve in such an important role that they should be high in spiritual caliber and few in number. A smaller group promotes greater intimacy and higher mutual accountability within the leadership.

These leaders should be called out slowly. New churches don't need many committees to function appropriately. Perhaps one administrative committee to oversee the plans of the new church will be a helpful accountability structure. Many new churches appoint a steering committee or a leadership advisory team in the early days of the church's life. This steering committee is not yet a leadership body; it's an advisory team that helps provide direction. Some, if not all, of those on the early steering committee can become pastor-elders when the new church constitutes.

2. The church should understand that pastors are elders. Thus, if the congregation follows a team of three pastor-elders, one could serve as the vocational pastor while the other two may be lay pastors. Depending on the congregation's growth, the church may want at a point in the future to call all of these pastor-elders as church staff or add other pastor-elders.

3. The congregation should allow its pastor-elders to "direct the affairs of the church." When congregations entrust most decisions to pastor-elders, those churches generally eliminate the need for constant church business meetings.

From the beginning of the new church, the planter-pastor should tell the people that the pastor will lead the church and that a group of other pastor-elders will lead the church alongside the pastor. This biblical structure will allow the pastor to lead under predictable accountability to maximize the effectiveness of the church. With proper accountability and leadership, the church will become fully empowered for its purposes of growth and ministry.

Conclusion

Nothing can take the place of effective leadership. In the established church, this is important, but in the new church it's basically all that exists. Everything rises and falls based on leadership. God-led leaders will serve their church plants through equipping and empowering others.

Resources for Further Reading

Baxter, Richard. *The Reformed Pastor.* http://www.ccel.org/b/baxter/pastor.

Dever, Mark. *A Display of God's Glory,* available for download at www.9marks.org.

Norman, R. Stanton, *Perspectives on Church Government: Five Views of Church Polity.* Nashville: Broadman & Holman, 2004.

Sanders, Oswald. *Spiritual Leadership.* Chicago: Moody Press, 1994.

Strauch, Alexander. *Biblical Eldership.* Littleton, Colo.: Lewis and Roth Publications, 1995.

Towns, Elmer L. *Getting a Church Started: A Student Manual for the Theological Foundation and Practical Techniques of Planting a Church.* Lynchburg, Va.: Church Growth Institute, 1985.

Warren, Richard. *The Purpose-Driven Church.* Grand Rapids: Zondervan Publishing House, 1995.

Chapter 7

Planter-Pastor Leadership Issues

Leadership is a big topic. Hundreds of books are available on the subject from both secular and Christian viewpoints. I won't attempt to duplicate their work here. But if you are untrained in leadership, it would be well worth your time to learn more about it. So instead of repeating what's already well covered, I'll address four subjects unique to church planting leadership: prayer life, daily routine, the challenge of cultural adjustment, and the importance of coaching/mentoring.

Putting Prayer First

Before we talk about a work week and cultural adjustment, it is essential to speak of a prayer life. You cannot lead people to godliness when you are not regularly encountering God. Church planters are not particularly prayerful people.

Prayer is not part of the typical vocational work; it is part of your personal spiritual jounrey that enables you to do the work of the minsitry. In a sense, it *is* the *work*, but it is something that you and every believer should take seriously. Unforunately, too few church planters put prayer first. David

Slagle, planter of Veritas Church (www.veritaschurch.net) and one of the church planters I mentor, has been working on a doctoral project to examine the prayer life of church planting. (When it is finished, we will post the dissertation at www.newchurches.com.)

David's study examined the role of prayer in church planting. Church planters were questioned about their beliefs and practices both before and during the planting phase. The vast majority of planting pastors experienced church planting as a crucible that revealed their deep lack of prayer and drove them more deeply to Christ.

Only a small number of pastors entered the planting experience with what they would describe as a healthy prayer life—more gold than dross. The majority, however, admitted to a preplanting prayer life that was sporadic and need oriented rather than relational.

The most striking feature of the study was that almost every pastor used the specific word *desperation* to describe how they felt as they fully entered the process of church planting. That desperation moved these pastors in one of two directions: to their knees or to the office. David wrote me:

> I'm happy to report that most pastors were driven to make prayer a practice rather than an aspirational value. A significant number, though, responded to the desperation by working longer hours. Planting pastors are driven, high-energy individuals. The great temptation to be busy rather than pray is compounded when this personality meets the multiple and varied demands of church planting. Those who did not cave in to the temptation to "do" rather than "pray" uniformly described a progressive climb out of the desperation and into peace, confidence, wisdom, and community. I would be remiss if I did not mention the incredible stories of God's provision in the lives of these praying planters. I listened to pastor after pastor describe healings from cancer, a voice restored just prior to preaching on launch day, multimillion-dollar donations, explosions of peace in the midst of unspeakable pain and disappointment, checks that arrive just in time, donated land and facilities, and hard-hearted individuals coming to Christ and ultimately leadership within the local body. Many times the provision was simply the courage and strength to keep one's hand to the plow when the church planting dream became a nightmare.[1]

Daily Responsibilities and Schedule

The planter's schedule is an expression of priorities in ministry. Many planters complain about the pastor's forty-hour workweek. Church planters need to know that many pastors don't ask key church volunteers to work just forty hours. They work forty to fifty hours at their job, and we ask them to volunteer another five to ten hours of work per week for the church. If pastors are to model leadership, a fifty-hour pastoral workweek is not unreasonable. Bivocational ministers may work many more than fifty hours per week.

Mapping out a productive work schedule is always a challenge. What follows is broken down for both full-time and bivocational starters.

Evangelistic Outreach: *fifteen hours per week (full-time); three hours per week (bivocational).* You cannot plant a church without spending time with lost people. If the planter does not set evangelistic outreach as a priority, the church cannot grow. If there are no core group members in the beginning, the planter has nothing else to do but knock on doors, make phone calls, or meet people. A prospect file helps the planter focus on a group of people who are receptive to follow-up visits.

Sermon and Study Preparation: *ten hours per week (full-time); three hours per week (bivocational).* Many seminary students have heard they need to spend thirty or more hours each week in sermon preparation. Realistically, a church planter, particularly a bivocational one, does not have that much time to devote to message preparation. Still, you must take the requirement for study seriously until you can reorder your schedule to spend more time in preparation. God mandates through Paul that we *preach the Word* (2 Tim. 4:2), not a series of opinions, or even opinions proof texted with Scripture. Church planters should make strong biblical preaching a priority, but that is not always easy to do when starting a new church.

One helpful way to balance good preparation with launch busy-ness, suggested by McNamara and Davis, is to prepare six months of messages before the launch service. They explain that it is critical that you "spend the majority of your time out in the community rather than cooped up in your study preparing messages."[2]

At the same time, the tools for sermon preparations have increased drastically. Bible programs can help exegete the text so that preaching is biblically sound. Other Internet resources can help you find cross-references and illustrations. Also, reading how several other communicators have worked through a passage can help to generate ideas. In fact, many ministries offer their sermons in text and audio files, sometimes even including their digital art and videos. These can be purchased (in some cases they're free), and they can make the process of planning sermon series much easier.

Administration: *ten hours per week (full-time); two hours per week (bivocational).* Like all pastoral functions, administration is essential but must be balanced with other tasks. For those with the gift of administration, meetings and planning can quickly fill up a schedule. For church planters, this time may include development of outreach materials and strategies plus related planning tasks.

Ministry: *fifteen hours per week (full-time); three hours per week (bivocational).* Many church planters become bogged down in this task area. New churches attract all kinds of troubled people who want the care of an idealistic, energetic, people-loving, people-seeking church planter. As a result, the planter can become overwhelmed ministering to these troubled people. Andy Stanley, pastor of North Point Community Church in Alpharetta, Georgia, says that "Sunday morning is for communicating, not counseling. In fact—and to some this may sound unspiritual—I don't think you can actually build a church on people who need counseling. When your church has grown and you have more resources, then those people can come back and be helped by the ministry you've built."

***

As a church planter, it's critical to pay attention to how you're using your time, where you're becoming too comfortable, and whether you're forming bad habits. Because so many tasks with a new church start require a tremendous amount of energy, it's easy for planters to procrastinate in areas that are outside your strengths.

For the creative, energetic church planter, administration is often an area of weakness, and it can be easy to ignore day-to-day details that go unnoticed until a crisis occurs. Use the weakness as a motivator to find people who can join your team and assist you in areas that challenge and frustrate you. The church planter who loves studying Scripture and finds lengthy sermon preparation comforting can successfully avoid the tumultuous experience of constantly meeting new people and sharing the faith and the vision of the new church.

Be self-aware or "awake" to how you're really using your time and be a faithful steward of that precious resource. Recognize that daunting areas exist for anyone who sets out to start a new church, then excel in your areas of strength, and do what you can in your areas of weakness while looking for others who can joyfully help you in the work.

Focus on people who seem likely to become reproducing leaders and on those who are able to minister to others. Planters too often spend time with a small group of available people without considering or realistically assessing whether these people will become reproducing leaders. It makes more sense for the pastor to invest time with potential reproducers, people who can help develop a church in which more and more people become equipped and trained for ministry. Then the church will be able to care for those who are needy, and the pastor also will have more time to minister to people with greater needs as necessary. This is not a matter of ministry but a matter of priorities and timing.

Culture Shock and Fatigue

Every planter needs to prepare for culture shock, a feeling of disorientation (think: fish out of water) while relating to so many unchurched people during the start-up phase of a new church. These people think, talk, behave, and react to life in a way that may seem foreign to the church planter, especially one who is fresh out of seminary or another setting that could be described as the comfortable cocoon of Christianity.

And it can get worse. Culture fatigue is a nagging weariness from culture shock. The constant feeling of working as a "stranger in a strange land" wears down the optimism of the planter, who at worst finally feels worn out, maybe even overcome with emotional exhaustion, thinking, *I keep telling them the right message, and they just don't get it.*

Be prepared for this inevitable challenge. Even if you're planting in your hometown, you'll find it surprisingly stressful to focus on the unchurched people there, even if the surroundings are familiar and so are the people. You may be from that town, but as a Christian who's making the enormous effort to plant a church there, you're coming at this once-familiar place with new eyes and from a different culture. In a way you're an alien there. And the longer you deny that to yourself, the more stress you'll experience.

Here are some ways to prevent the burnout that culture shock and fatigue can cause.

First, take the following warning seriously: every planter will experience some form of this cross-cultural struggle.

Second, identify an Ebenezer (1 Sam. 7:12). This marker is a memorial of God's help. It reminds the planter of God's call and God's promise that planting a new church, and planting in this place is the divine call. The planter must be able, in the midst of doubt and weariness, to look back to that "Ebenezer" moment when God's direction had been clear and unmistakable. I think of Jim Dumont, a church planter in Erie, Pennsylvania, who moved there in 1981 to start Erie Christian Fellowship. He had nowhere to live and didn't know anyone—he came solely in obedience to the call of God. He and his family lived in a campground for six weeks. Now, many years later, he says that every time he goes by the campground, "it reminds me of God's faithfulness." For Pastor Jim, this campground is his Ebenezer.

Third, develop a network of other planters and intercessors, a mentor, and a supervisor who can provide support during the high and low tides of weariness and hopelessness. You will need a community to support you on this journey. This leads to the issue of mentors and coaches.

Church Planting Mentors or Coaches

Church planters tend to be self-starters and often think of themselves as self-sufficient. That personality type is often resistant to the advice of others—thinking, *if I'd listened to other people, I would not be planting the church in the first place.* But planters who miss out on the benefit of coaching miss out on a tremendous help throughout the minstry journey. My analysis of more than six hundred church planters shows there's even a significant numerical value to having a mentor or supervisor.[3]

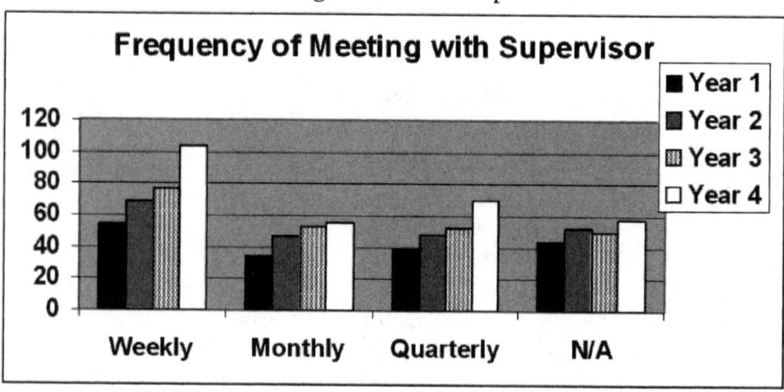

For example, the accountability to a supervisor correlates to a surprisingly high impact on attendance at the new church. Frequent meetings may indicate a heavy involvement by the sponsoring entity, and the planter would probably have a close and satisfying relationship with the supervisor. Most church planters I know would chafe at the idea of a weekly meeting with a supervisor, but, according to my research, it clearly makes a positive difference. Accountability leads to productivity.

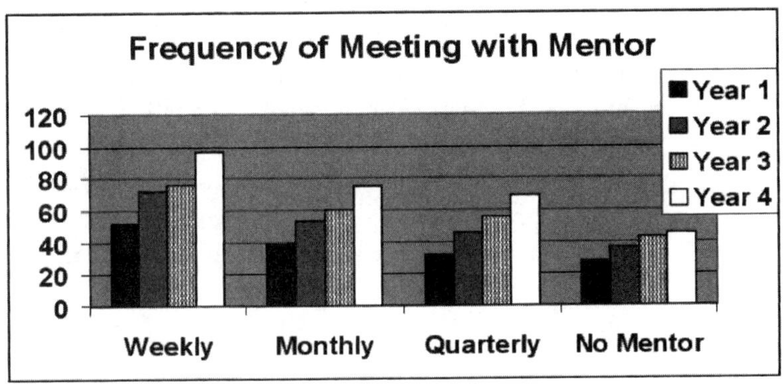

Meeting with a mentor has a similar positive impact on attendance. Planters who met weekly with a mentor, perhaps because they took seriously the process of learning from others, led churches that were almost twice the size of those that had no mentor. I believe a supervisor should focus on work issues, and a mentor should focus on personhood issues, providing encouragement and nurture to the church planter. Choose wisely in forming these relationships in the beginning, and give these individuals permission to ask you the hard questions—whatever they may be.

Steve Ogne is probably the best resource for insights regarding church-planting coaching. With Tim Roehl he recently coauthored a doctoral dissertation (soon to be a book) entitled *Coaching: a New Paradigm for Empowering Missional Leaders for Ministry in a Changing World.* In their dissertation they cited a church planting study from the Foursquare Church. (I served as consultant and advisor on the project.)

> That study, done in 2004, showed that two-thirds of church planters had the benefit of a coach as part of their church planting experience.... Of those who were coached, 77 percent reported that coaching had "some" to "very significant" impact

> on their personal effectiveness and productivity, with 54 percent reporting coaching had "significant" or "very significant" influence.... Of the 425 churches planted between 2001 and 2003, 90 percent of Four Square churches were successful. Of those that failed, 60 percent of the failed plants did not have planters who received coaching in their efforts.[4]

Relationships make leaders; wise leaders will also create learning relationships. This is not easy for most church planters, who tend to be free spirits and perhaps mavericks. But the best church planters combine innovation with learning and become leaders under accountability.

Finally, the planter must learn and remember, in spite of everything, that the God of eternity is faithful and that he is the God of the fiery furnace. He always accompanies his obedient servants into the midst of life's hottest fires (Dan. 3:19–30). Having a wise voice to remind you of this will be a tremendous help on the journey.

Conclusion

Leadership is essential. You may have plenty of funding, a full-time team, and a great location; but if your leadership skills are not developed and you are reluctant to invest in developing them, you will not succeed. On the other hand, you may have no funding, no team, and no place to live, but you will still be successful if God is at work through you as a leader. Elmer Towns wrote a church-planting book with a formidable but apt title: *Getting a Church Started in the Face of Insurmountable Odds with Limited Resources in Unlikely Circumstances*. The only way to overcome such obstacles is with Spirit-filled and Spirit-led leadership.

> Bob Rowley wrote an excellent doctoral dissertation, "Successfully Coaching Church Planters," that can be found at www.newchurches.com

Resources for Further Reading

Hiebert, Paul G. *Anthropological Insights for Missionaries*. Grand Rapids: Baker Book House, 1985.

Jones, Marge, and E. Grant Jones. *Psychology of Missionary Adjustment*. Springfield, Mo.: Gospel Publishing House, 1995.

Lewis, Larry L. *Church Planter's Handbook*. Nashville: Broadman & Holman Publishers, 1992.

MacDonald, Gordon. *Ordering Your Private World*. Nashville: Thomas Nelson, 1985. See pages 64–88.

O'Donnell, Kelly, ed. *Missionary Care: Counting the Cost for World Evangelization*. Pasadena, Calif.: William Carey Library, 1992.

Sjogren, Steve, and Rob Lewin. *Community of Kindness*. Ventura, Calif.: Regal Gospel Light, 2003.

Chapter 8

Involving Lay Leaders

Most church-planting teams have one lead pastor and several volunteer laypersons. The church planter needs to train and equip those lay leaders before the church opens for public worship.[1]

Stephen J. Ro, church planter, Living Faith Community Church of Flushing, New York, shares with readers of his article "How I Gathered the First 100 People to My Church": "Lay members used their gifts to collectively work toward the established vision and goals. They became outward focused and in turn, helped others to understand the gospel. Gift-use of laypeople is vital to keeping people at a small church."[2]

Trained, committed laypeople must become engaged in ministry before the church launch. This prelaunch stage resembles the period of human prenatal maturation during which a fetus develops systems to enable it to function after birth. A baby born without these systems developed and functional will not thrive. Similarly, certain operational systems must be fully functional by the time the church has its first public worship service. Otherwise, the church will be born prematurely and won't have the necessary parts to achieve success for the kingdom of God.

One warning: Take care not just to put a warm body in a spot you need to fill, a common mistake I see church planters making. Don't rush the process of finding the right person for the right job, or you could end up in the awkward position of having to remove someone. This, in addition to the time and energy lost, creates trust and confidence issues with the staff and congregation.

Five Indispensable Leaders

The team can come into the community with the church planter; however, most planters will raise up a local team, who can give helpful input regarding the community in which the church is being planted.

Bob Logan[3] identifies five key systems or processes (with volunteer leaders) that must be in place before the first public worship service: new member assimilation, network evangelism, spiritual gifts mobilization, a children's ministry team, and a worship team. Logan's systems could be "personalized" with the following team members: pastor (may also need an administrator), worship leader, preschool/children's minister, assimilation coordinator, evangelism networker, spiritual gifts mobilizer. At the end of this chapter, I will add two more I consider essential.

The *pastor* is a charismatic leader and vision-caster for the new congregation. This person does not need to be ordained. And, although administrative giftedness is helpful, if the pastor doesn't possess such skills, the team should complement the pastor and help supply those abilities.

The *worship leader* must be a talented music director with the ability to lead the congregation toward a culturally appropriate encounter with God. If this person does not direct the church's music, he or she should have the ability to assess and empower other leaders for music ministry. The worship leader's job is to put together a worship team. The worship leader makes sure attendees find the worship time appropriately structured, compelling, and meaningful—always pointing people toward God. Depending on the type of new church, the worship system may be so sophisticated that it includes a twelve-piece praise band backing up the worship leader with multimedia presentations and programs. Or the music may be so simple that it requires only one guitar and transparencies to show on an overhead projector.

Whatever the level of complexity, make sure the worship system is ready before launch day. In today's culture, people expect superior presentation quality, even from volunteer organizations such as churches. Poor quality may mean that first-time guests will not return. Don't misunderstand these thoughts. The goal isn't high quality presentation for the sake of entertainment; you're striving for a level of creative excellence that will facilitate an authentic encounter with the Creater of everything. And be realistic about the prayer and time required to reach this goal. Good musicians are in demand, and it may take awhile to piece together an effective worship team whose presentation is appealing without being distracting.

The *preschool children's minister* is a child-care worker (probably a volunteer) who sacrifices personal fellowship with the adult group to serve the children who attend. This person should mature in the ability to delegate tasks as the church grows.

It may be unfortunate, but an old adage worth paying attention to claims that the top three qualities people look for in a church (whether consciously or subconsciously) are good parking, nice women's restrooms, and excellent child care. The reality is that, as planters, usually we can only control one of these: child care. But, as with building up a worship team, to do it right the church planter must exercise the discipline to do it slowly.

I typically advise that church planters start with a preschool ministry during the church's earliest days. Because there are usually not enough volunteers, it is usually necessary to resist pressure to develop a program for children of all ages until the right players are identified and in place. This will be a challenge because most parents at a new church immediately want a full children's ministry. The best way to resist this pressure is to encourage parents to adopt the high quality of worship as their priority in the beginning, with the understanding that the goal you share with them is to grow the children's ministry in the near future. To buy yourself a bit of time on this, through worship you can give parents simple tools to use during the week to nurture their children spiritually.

Also, the right lay team gives parents a taste of the high-quality children's ministry you'll be developing by delivering the most important feature parents value for their infants and toddlers: security. Parents need to feel comfortable when they drop off their children at the nursery. Here are three standards you can adopt from the beginning:

1. Establish the rule that the parent who signs in a child should be the same person who claims the child after the service.
2. Agree on a clean, neat "uniform" (perhaps khaki slacks and white polo shirts, for example) that nursery workers always wear so that parents can easily identify who will be responsible for

infants and toddlers and to demonstrate a system of standards for parents who, sad to say, have every reason in today's society to be security conscious.

3. Consider investing in pagers for parents to take with them to services or, at minimum, a numbering system for each child so that parents can be "paged" via a discreet message on the worship screen. All of these assure parents that the more complete children's ministry of the future will operate with the same thoughtful standards of excellence.

The *assimilation coordinator* develops and oversees ways for involving church members and guests more deeply in the life of the congregation. Although we'll consider the area of assimilation in greater depth later, I'll define this layperson now as the organizer of small groups.

The assimilation system will involve guests and members in meaningful relationships, ministries, and services within and beyond the congregation. This is where they'll really bond with the church, making lasting connections that will provide a rich foundation for their spiritual growth. It's also the setting where their loyalty to the new church will be clinched, assuming it's a good experience.

Not having an assimilation system in place was one of my first mistakes while planting Millcreek Community Church. A total of 234 people attended our launch service. On the following Sunday, 167 people returned. Of the original 234 persons, we preserved 135. Although Millcreek outperformed the typical church plant (which averages 50 percent of the launch attendance one month later), it struggled without a well-developed, intentional assimilation system. A fully functional assimilation system of small groups can help new churches outperform the usual 50 percent rate of loss following launch day.

The *evangelism networker* promotes activities to reach the unchurched and also assists other leaders in evangelizing the unchurched through their existing networks. Riverside Church[4] in Cincinnati identifies this position as the "pastor of purpose." His job is to keep the church focused on the evangelistic purpose of the church.

Although evangelism should be the center of a new church's mission, too often it's overlooked in favor of tasks such as getting the music ready, recruiting nursery workers, and raising the finances. The evangelism networker helps the church stay focused by providing evangelistic projects and reminding the core members of their own evangelistic responsibility. For many evangelism may be a new skill; Christians who weren't evangelistic before launch day won't suddenly become experienced witnesses after the launch. So the evangelism networker has the responsibility to equip the new congregation to share Christ in their daily lives. Otherwise, evangelism can become just another program and not a way of life. We need to equip for the latter.

The church's *spiritual gifts mobilizer* is a coach who assists persons in identifying their spiritual gifts and their place in ministry within and beyond the congregation. Developing volunteers takes time, particularly if volunteers are recruited from among new believers. Taking the time to develop church systems during the prenatal stage will make postlaunch discipleship much stronger. To do this new churches need a systematic process for spiritual gifts discovery and ministry placement. The new church should develop a strategy to match spiritual gifts with ministries that are needed in the community. Be careful in the early days of the church plant to define broadly spiritual gifts and their practical applications. Focus on service, and develop the willingness to serve wherever needed—rather than in specific giftings. In a church-plant setting, you are going to need people to pitch in wherever needed and not refuse to take on some task because "it's not my gift."

Resources are available to the church-planting team for little or no cost to help people discover and use their spiritual gifts. A helpful program for the small church to develop a ministry placement system is Team Ministry (Church Growth Institute: 800-553-GROW). Saddleback Church also provides excellent small church resources through its Discovering My Ministry class (www.purposedriven.com). Network is an effective resource for larger churches (www.networkministries.com).

Recently some tools have started to become available on the Internet. PLACE ministries (www.placeministries.org) allows people to go through the process online. Churches can buy the process in bulk and provide codes to church members. Then the results can be sorted based on giftedness in a database, etc.

A tool that combines workbooks and electronic resources is BodyLife Journey (see www.lifeway.com). The heart of the resource is the Key Ministry Files (KMF). The KMF is a tabbed notebook representing spiritual gifts. Once people determine gifts, they can then find suggested places to serve in the file. The church can also use the provided templates to list their ministry need areas in line with the spiritual gifts.

All of these:

- teach about spiritual gifts, passions, and personality types,
- provide a measurement instrument of spiritual gifts (a gifts "inventory"),
- display a list of ministries that might match each gift, and
- recommend a way for one-on-one meetings so leaders can help new people find their place for ministry.

Two Other Important Leaders

In addition to the five leaders recommended in Logan's systems, I add two more:

A *welcome coordinator* organizes greeters, ushers, and other volunteers who make gathering with the church a warm and friendly experience for guests. Greeters help attendees feel welcomed and wanted. Volunteers must be able to tell arriving guests where to go and what to do.

These volunteers should be friendly, helpful people who smile. They should be trained to meet virtually every conceivable need. They should know the location of a first-aid kit, the site of the nearest water fountain, and the location of all departments, meeting rooms, and restrooms in the church. Other tasks for them:

- Greeting guests in the parking lot
- Clearly marking entrances
- Providing name tags for all attenders
- Assigning "seat shepherds" to sit in a specific area each week to connect guests with nearby members to make them feel welcome
- Promoting the "three-minute rule"—members must talk to someone they don't know for the three minutes following the end of worship
- A church must intentionally develop its volunteer-staffed greeter and usher system. A welcome coordinator will help fulfill this vital ministry.

The *financial organizer* oversees the new church's finances. This is especially important if a sponsoring church doesn't coordinate these matters for the new church. Either way, the prelaunch church needs this organizer to plan for specific on-site management of offerings, counting, transferring of funds, and reporting to the sponsoring church.

Good financial organization protects the congregation and planter more than it achieves any other purpose. Congregational offerings must be safeguarded and handled appropriately to protect the integrity of leaders and the reputation of the congregation. I have several recommendations:

- Tell attenders specifically how financial gifts are being used. This will reassure givers and even noncontributing guests.
- The planter and core group should agree well ahead of launch day on a strategy for safeguarding and accounting for finances. Put into place a system for two people to count the offering plus a second system of checks and balances when depositing the offering into the church's bank account.
- My strong advice is for the lead pastor/church planter to develop a system that prevents the planter from even seeing the money that comes in the offering. Yes, the church planter needs to know the status of finances and be well-informed. But I've known church planters who took the offering home, counted it, and made the deposit. That's a dangerous practice—with way too much temptation built in—and it creates more suspicion in unchurched people who may harbor a stigma about how pastors and churches handle finances.
- Many pastors opt out of even knowing what each individual member gives to the church so as not to show favor to one over another.

An Important Caution

Take whatever time is necessary to develop leaders. It's not enough to assign tasks; new churches must truly develop leaders. Pick leaders wisely—or suffer the consequences later.

Steve Sjogren warns churches to go slow in this process.

> It is common to trust leaders in the early phase of a plant, only to discover in short order these were "LWAs"—leaders with an agenda. As church planters we are in a conundrum for several years in a new plant—we need leaders desperately, but most of

> those available to lead aren't qualified. Why is it common for these faux leaders to find their way to new church plants? Those who have been rejected in the past from other churches find it attractive to start over at a new church where no one knows them. The challenge with leaders is this—to allow those who have failed in the past to get a fresh start, but at the same time make leadership decisions that will allow the church to grow in the years to come. This is my conclusion on this issue: I must more seriously take into consideration the larger work of God over individual leadership choices. It's a goose and golden egg question. The golden eggs (individual leaders) are wonderful, but I must protect the health of the goose (the local church) above all other considerations.[5]

Conclusion

The team outlined here does not have to move to the area with the church planter. Until we planted Lake Ridge Church, I never came with a team. Most church planters still will not come with a team; they will make one when they arrive. In my earlier plants, we formed the team on the field from the people we reached. They became the launch team, ready when we went public with our grand opening. However the team gets together, by moving to a community together or by emerging from the community, a team is needed before a church can be planted.

These team members and systems need to be identified and prepared before the launch service. In rare instances the team may be paid. Most of the time the team is made up of laypeople who often develop from a pool of new believers.

The church planter should limit prelaunch ministry positions to those essential for the new start based on its dreams, vision, giftedness, and systems for evangelism and ministry in the surrounding community. Save plans for men's and women's ministries until after the launch. All the new team members need to be focused on the launch until that is accomplished.

When these systems are well-grounded, the congregation is probably ready to begin public worship. With a good launch the church should find itself able to progress and grow rapidly. The indispensable role of laypersons in the development of these systems cannot be overstated.

Where do you find these laypersons? The next chapters will help explain where to find these people.

Resources for Further Reading

Cladis, George. *Leading the Team-Based Church: How Pastors and Church Staffs Can Grow Together into a Powerful Fellowship of Leaders.* San Francisco, Calif.: Jossey-Bass, 1999.

Cordeiro, Wayne. *Doing Church as a Team.* Ventura, Calif.: Regal Publishing, 2001.

Gangel, Kenneth O. *Team Leadership in Christian Ministry.* Rev. ed. Chicago: Moody Press, 1997.

Malphurs, Aubrey. *The Dynamics of Church Leadership.* Grand Rapids: Baker Books, 1999.

Ott, E. Stanley. *Transform Your Church with Ministry Teams.* Grand Rapids: Wm. B. Eerdmans Publishing Company, 2005.

Chapter 9

Understanding Cultures and Models

Effective church planting is missionary work. Insightful church planters must begin by determining their mission—exploring questions of personal call and conviction—and by learning missions principles. Then they seek to understand the culture they've been called to reach. How do the people who live here think? What are their values? What events shaped their collective history, affected their group psyche? What are their needs and desires?

It's not enough just to note the color of their skin or the value of their property or the amount of gray (or blond streaks) in their hair. The missional church planter is seeking information that's far more nuanced. The missional church planter is performing an "exegesis" of the target culture. Pronounced "ex-uh-GEE-sus," this term from Greek means "to show the way" or "to guide." So to exegete the culture is to study the setting in such a way that one receives guidance for understanding the meanings of cultural patterns, systems, and behaviors.

This is what it means to be missional; and this is why, in today's new world of establishing churches, every plant is different. It's because every culture is unique. And yet every culture has similarities to others. The result of the missional church planter's exegesis will be a cross-cultural understanding because in reality that's what we all are—products of many cultures with defining distinctives. As we study the cultures, finding their differences and similarities, we realize that we're really slicing and dicing the distinctives into finer and finer characteristics, until eventually we find ourselves looking at and understanding an individual a person, rather than simply *a postmodern or an African-American or a professional or a baby boomer.* Thus, an upwardly mobile suburbanite might be a product of divorce who in adulthood ran as far away as possible from a works-based theology that filled his youth with fear and guilt. Or an inner-city woman who because of her neighborhood appears down-and-out may, in fact, be well educated and holding a responsible position in a corporate office but unwilling to move away from her aging mother and aunt for whom she cares.

The two people I've described are more than composites. They have distinctives that belong to several cultures or population segments. And, in reality, these are the people who may one day populate your new church.

My point is that individuals are complex. This chapter is meant to serve several purposes in your understanding of church planting:

- To impress on you the importance of (1) identifying the members of your focus group, *Who is God calling you to reach for Christ?* and (2) understanding their culture. Not knowing them or understanding them will surely result in failure or diminished effectiveness.
- To remind you that demographic segmentations are helpful as guidelines, but the impassioned church planter must dig deeper. We can start with general information about large segments of the population—and I will point you to some on my Web site—but on launch day you must be prepared to meet not just Mr. Hispanic or Ms. Urban Dweller or Mr. and Mrs. Parents of 2.3 Children but rather *people to whom God is sending you to introduce to Christ.*
- To state what needs to be said before we look at the cold, hard facts of statistics. Although cultures and people are different, the gospel is the same for all of them. We cannot confuse appealing to certain kinds of people with the process of salesmanship. We're not "putting spin" on a message so it will sell to the masses. We're discovering how communication is received,

filtered, and understood by the people God is sending to us, so we can clearly and effectively tell the greatest story ever told.

In the first edition of *Planting New Churches,* I included chapters on different focus groups and provided some detail for each. You can still see all of that information at my Web site, www.newchurches.com. I've posted those chapters and additional information there. For now, let's look at a summary of frequently targeted focus groups.

Generations and Their Distinctives

> For more information on focus groups, go to my Web site www.newchurches.com.

In general, I'm not a big fan of demographic segmentations because they oversimplify people into artificial categories. But there's value in looking at the builder and boomer generations because they are at least definable by age. However, when we get to emerging postmodern generations, modeling by ages loses its usefulness because postmodernism is tied to mind-set or worldview(s) rather than generation. In other words, the generations in the second group listed below were born in the postmodern era, so they were exposed almost exclusively to postmodern thinking, yet not everyone in these generations embraces postmodernism. Likewise, the generations in the first group listed below were less likely to be exposed to postmodernism during their formative years, but some of them have embraced it. (We will only touch on postmodernism here. The next chapter will be devoted to people with an emerging postmodern mind-set.)

Most demographers divide North America into groups. The first is composed of two distinct generations:

- **Builders** were born before 1946. At the turn of the millennium, there were more than fifty million of them in the U.S. and eight million in Canada.
- **Boomers** were born between 1946 and 1964, the baby boom years following World War II. As of 2000, this was the largest single segment of the population, with more than seventy million in the U.S. and eight million in Canada.

The second group includes the emerging postmodern generations:

- **Busters** were born from 1965 to 1976 and total about thirty million in the U.S. and seven million in Canada as of 2000.
- **Millennials** were born in the years 1977 to 1994. At the turn of the millennium, there were seventy million of this generation in the U.S. and six million in Canada.
- Rounding out this generational tally are the **Babies**, born since 1994. At the time this book was written, this generation totaled about ten million in the U.S. and three million in Canada.[1]

Builders

Builders predominate in most churches, holding power in the majority of established congregations. Conflicts sometimes arise, even though they attempt to integrate younger groups with different cultural values into church life and leadership.

Builders are individualistic, shaped by heroes such as John Wayne and Roy Rogers, champions of the cinema who single-handedly defeated their enemies. Builders value personal responsibility and individualism. The theme song for this generation could be Frank Sinatra's "My Way."

Builders are thrifty and ambitious. The Great Depression was one of their defining events. They have a high work ethic and are dependable.

The other major defining event of this generation was World War II, a time of heroism and self-sacrifice. This toughened them and gave them the determination to return victorious, build a strong industrial-based economy, and face down any enemies that threatened America again.

Boomers

Boomers are so named because they entered the culture during the post-World War II baby boom of 1946 to 1964. Most new churches in the last two decades were focused on reaching this population. The style and governance of these churches look very different from the patterns of churches founded by builders.[2]

- Boomers are the first generation raised with absentee fathers because of the corporate and industrial marketplace that replaced the agrarian economy of previous generations. Boomers' grandparents had little influence on their life preparation and job skills.

- Boomers are the most educated generation in history. Racial integration of schools occurred during their school years, providing higher standards shared more equally. This generation took the issue of racial equality to higher levels and then applied many of the same principles to equality for women—educationally, professionally, and personally.
- Boomers were raised with affluence and opportunities, but because of inflation they can't afford to live at their parents' high standard of living. They also accumulated credit-card debt trying to "keep up with the Joneses" and worked hard to earn more and more.
- Boomers are the Cold War generation. From the dropping of the atomic bomb that ended World War II and through Korea, Vietnam, and the nuclear-arms race, this is the first generation that's lived in fear of being destroyed by a nuclear bomb or war. It's also the first generation to question en masse the value of war as a process for settling conflict.
- Boomers were the first generation to be reared with television as a significant communication and parenting tool. Television brought with it advertisements, fads, and up-to-the-minute news and video coverage—something that radio was never able to do with just words. It has contributed to a unique North American culture.
- Boomers were the first to have varied choices in birth control and family planning, allowing parents to determine their family size. This also enabled boomers to be the first generation to be promiscuous without consequence of pregnancy.
- Boomers grew up with a team-oriented approach to organizations. The stereotypical heroes of the boomer era appeared in the 1966 television serial *Star Trek*. The crew, though a team, did not always follow the captain's orders. This motif of individualism within teamwork both shaped and described boomer culture, including the major musical shift brought about by boomers, the "rock generation." For example, North Americans remember John, Paul, George, and Ringo more

as the Beatles than as individuals. This phenomenon describes the cultural shift from the strong individualism of builders that moved toward a team or a combination approach for boomers.

- Boomers lived through assassinations of their President and other cultural leaders. Boomers experienced the moral decline of a President who left office in disgrace. And a boomer serving as President startled even his own generation by claiming that his adulterous behavior was not really sex.

Boomer Churches

Boomers are the largest single segment of the population, and they've shown they're open to God.[3] Other traits:

- Their Bible teaching emphasizes practical living.
- They place a healthy emphasis on relationships.
- They prefer fewer titles and less formality.
- They understand the new family in America.
- They share their faith by what they say and do.
- They recognize the abilities of women.
- They place an emphasis on worship.
- They have a high tolerance for diversity.
- They are action-oriented.
- Every year into the twenty-first century the boomer generation becomes more of a senior adult generation. Any boomer-targeted church plant or ministry must consider that, as boomers age and retire, they tend to become more interested in matters of the afterlife.

The 1980s and 1990s saw the growth of baby boomer churches across North America. Some were church plants, but others were established churches reinventing themselves to reach out.

African-American Church Planting

One out of every six churches in North America is African-American, yet the number of unchurched African-Americans is constantly rising. The need for planting new churches in African-American communities intensifies every year, especially in light of the gradual erosion of interest in traditional worship styles among African-American young adults.

Three helpful resources have been produced by African-Americans to assist planters in starting new churches in their communities. The first is the 1989 book *Church Planting in the Black Community,* edited by Sid Smith. The second is the 1993 collaboration by Joe Ratliff and Michael Cox, *Church Planting in the African-American Community.* The most recent work, published in 2000, is *Church Planting in the African-American Context* by Hozell C. Francis. The author focuses on sociological factors not covered as thoroughly in the other works. A careful reading of all three will sensitize the planter to crucial cultural and methodological issues in planting churches in African-American communities.

Ratliff and Cox speculate that pastoral leadership in an African-American church plant is even more important than in an Anglo church plant.[4] There are differences in leadership expectations and style from Anglo to African-American churches. According to Francis, an African-American pastor must carefully balance the demands of "social, political, and spiritual" needs to be effective.[5]

Other than what's here plus what I've posted on my Web site, www.newchurches.com, I hesitate to write more about African-American church planting since I'm not African-American and haven't served in that context. The best resources are listed above. Consult them if you plan to start an African-American church. This book shares principles, but the listed books offer context and cultural discernment, which is the essence of missional church planting. I would welcome more scholarship on this vital subject from church planting experts and authors who have personal experience to share.

Ethnic Church Planting

Although most growth in church planting in recent years has occurred among ethnic groups, comparatively little has been written on the subject. Noteworthy exceptions are Oscar Romo's *American Mosaic* and a series of church-starting guides focusing on various ethnic groups, published by the Home Mission Board of the Southern Baptist Convention in the early 1990s.

The Internet is the best source for up-to-date information about ethnic church planting. The Ethnic Harvest Web site (www.ethnicharvest.com)

is a must for those planting ethnic churches. The Church Planting Village (www.churchplantingvillage.net) contains some excellent resources by ethnicity (use the search function to search by ethnicity). Also, the Research Team where I serve maintains a North American networking resource for cross-cultural church planting engagement at www.peoplegroups.info.

From its beginning, America has not been the mythical melting pot but instead has been marked by its diversity.[6] Today more than 10 percent of the population of the United States was born outside the country. Canada has always valued diversity and has always been a multicultural nation as well.

As with the material in this chapter on generations and African-Americans, the information presented here is supplemented on my Web site, www.newchurches.com. But I'll whet your appetite to learn more about the ethnic diversity of North America with just these four factoids:

- French Canadians are the largest unreached group on the continent.
- Seventy-eight percent of Los Angeles residents are ethnics.
- More Jews live in New York City than in Israel.
- Chicago is the second largest Polish city anywhere in the world.[7]

Reaching people living within a culture requires a missional approach to church planting. In fact, reaching ethnics may be the ultimate missional task. Bible translators tell us that people never will be reached effectively for the gospel until the gospel is in the language of their souls. Planting churches in the heart language of the people groups of North America is an essential strategy if we are to reach North America.

A major component of this continued growth is the emergence of cultural (indigenous) leaders among ethnic groups. When an ethnic church sponsors a new ethnic church, 98 percent of the pastors come from that ethnic group. When leaders encourage indigenous leaders to arise within ethnic population groups, the growth of churches of that ethnic segment often doubles.[8]

Conclusions

Missional church planters should learn distinctives about generations, races, and ethnicities as guidelines for understanding the people God is sending them to reach. It's interesting that the need for this understanding will only grow as we take a look at one intersection of generation and ethnicity statistics. The 1990s was the decade of immigration with the foreign-born population of the United States increasing at least 27 percent to more than twenty-five million.[9]

This means emerging generations have greater racial diversity than previous generations, a diversity that will continue to increase as we move through the twenty-first century. A key to ministry in the new era will be the creation of multiethnic faith communities that reflect the demographic makeup of their population.[10]

Following is the projected change of the ethnic mix over twenty years:

Ethnicity	2000	2020
American Indians/Native Alaskans	1%	1%
Asian/Pacific Islanders	4%	6%
Hispanic	16%	22%
Black, non-Hispanic	15%	16%
White, non-Hispanic	64%	55%

Resources for Further Study

Francis, Hozell C. *Church Planting in the African American Context.* Grand Rapids: Zondervan Publishing House, 2000.

Hesselgrave, David J. *Planting Churches Cross-Culturally: A Guide for Home and Foreign Missions.* Grand Rapids: Baker Book House, 1980.

Jones, Landon. *Great Expectations: America and the Baby Boom Generation.* New York: Ballantine Books, 1986.

Light, Paul. C. *The Baby Boomers.* New York: W. W. Norton & Co., 1988.

McIntosh, Gary. *Three Generations.* Grand Rapids: Revell, 1995.

Murren, Doug. *The Baby Boomerang.* Ventura, Calif.: Regal Books, 1990.

Pillai, Rajendra K. *Reaching the World in Our Own Backyard.* Colorado Springs: WaterBrook Press, 2003.

Ratliff, Joe S., and Michael J. Cox. *Church Planting in the African-American Community.* Nashville: Broadman Press, 1993.

Romo, Oscar I. *American Mosaic: Church Planting in Ethnic America.* Nashville: Broadman Press, 1993.

http://www.ethnicharvest.org.

http://www.churchplantingvillage.net.

Chapter 10

Church Planting in Emerging Culture

When we talk about planting churches in emerging culture, two problems arise. First, some who are connected with the "emerging church" have moved away from historic biblical doctrines and practices. Some would expect a book on church planting in emerging culture to revise the gospel in the context. That is not what I am advocating. For those who want to revise the gospel and abandon Christ's church, this is the wrong book. When I talk about planting a biblical church in emerging culture, it is both *biblical* and *church*.

The second problem is that many others promote the idea that *all* of the trappings of the modern church are biblical and, thus, unquestionable. The reality is that many of the forms of minstry in our churches today were once helpful but are no longer so because they were based on temporal traditions rather than eternal truths. When we talk about planting biblically faithful churches in emerging culture, our focus is on the "biblically faithful" part first and then how that expresses itself in "emerging culture."

When entering any culture as a missionary, there is a discerning way to approach the worldview and culture of a people. Cross-cultural missionaries have used tools to approach new cultures. One way to understand cultural engagement is to understand that there are parts to every culture we adopt, parts we adapt and parts we reject. That is how we approach emerging culture for the purpose of missionary engagement.

At the outset, I indicated that the focus here is on planting missional churches. There are many contexts in which that might occur, as the last chapter indicated. However, for most of the readers of this book, our focus will be on and in a culture impacted by postmodernism.

It's hard to try to keep current with trendy terminology. A few years ago, it was *Gen X* (more about that below). Recently, it was *postmodernism*. Now there seems to be a backlash against that word. *Emerging* is now the new term. However, my interest is not in being trendy but in being helpful to people wanting to plant churches. To reach people of a culture, you need to understand the culture. Outside the emerging church community, now in a fuss not wanting to be labeled as anything, the worldview of most North Americans is what we call "postmodern." Rather than focusing on postmodernism, I will instead focus on the people called "postmoderns," who they are and why it matters. In this case, postmoderns are simply a short-hand version for understandng the majority of people in our culture today.

Emerging generations have no universal worldview. They recognize a series of worldviews. It's an error to think that Gen Xers can be neatly described like every subsequent generation or that millennials all think one particular thing. This is actually a good time to set aside the idea that postmoderns can be neatly categorized. The concept of baby boomer was easily recognized if you were white and middle class. But just because one generation had some similarities does not mean that subsequent generations can be easily described.

Why Not Gen Xers?

The transition between the modern era and our world today has been taking place in and among what commonly has been called "Generation X." The stereotypes were primarily demographic flags placed on this age group by Madison Avenue. The stereotypes about Gen Xers changed so quickly it was hard to keep pace with the shifts. In the early 1990s a rash of new books described Generation X, claiming that young adults who were unable to find meaningful work were often cynical and unconnected, and they experienced prolonged adolescence. Books described how to reach such societal dropouts.

Then came the dot.com boom. Suddenly, Xers were affluent. Church growth books in the late 1990s told how to reach the newly affluent, up-and-out Generation X with cutting-edge strategies. The boom was followed by the dot.com bust, which changed the cultural landscape again. It was enough to illustrate the danger of generational-focused ministry based on rapidly changing trends.

It's good that the Gen X, buster, and millennial terminologies have fallen into disfavor. Those who used the terms recognized that the groups they sought to describe were bound together more by attitude than by age.

While the church needs to be careful not to focus too much attention on the oracles of the marketplace, we must admit that specialized ministries to Gen X opened the door to a better understanding of ministry in emerging culture. But there's no longer real value in using such labels, and we need to dispose of them. With the switch from modernism to our current situation, it's no longer good strategy to identify an age group, analyze its current situation, and then make pronouncements of how to reach them. Economies are too unstable, and fads are too short-lived. Good missionaries uncover the deeper issues—underlying values, thought processes, and ideas of a culture or people group. Using this information, they develop a plan to reach them based on these deeper issues.

Reaching Emerging Generations from a Modern Evangelicalism

The church wants to reach and should reach out to emerging generations. The church struggles because it is so deeply rooted in modernity. It needs to reach people in emerging postmodern culture, but it must not adopt postmodernism. Postmodernism comes up short; in many ways its basic presuppositions are actually antithetical to the gospel. We cannot "move with the times" and embrace postmodernity without strong discernment. So the modern church is not being successful with postmoderns in its current state, and the church cannot become postmodern. A middle course needs to be found.

Most churches have focused on how we can reach emerging generations by getting them to come to us, missing the fact that the Christian church is no longer the first choice of those who seek a spiritual reality.

We can no longer think of ourselves as the preferred source of truth to the unchurched.

Evangelicals need to adopt new approaches—not just use the old ones over and over. What we're doing isn't working; people don't get the picture anymore. It's time to discover new clues so we can connect with them. But we must not love our clues more than their needs.

Contrary to what some have written, the death of modernism is not a cause for panic. We've been here before! The church has been in the midst of a pluralistic milieu, and it reached millions. The first century was much more pluralistic than North America is today, but the church remained faithful to its witness and saw great results.[1]

Though not a cause for panic, this is surely a cause to think differently. The church has waited hundreds of years for the world to come to it in repentance. Today we must go to them. We're in a missionary location because North America is a mission field in the same way we once considered the undeveloped world the mission field.[2]

We need to think like missionaries to a new-world situation.

"We Must Go to Them"

A few years ago, I was discussing mission strategy with church leaders in Kumasi, Ghana, West Africa. The mission was seeking to reach the primarily Muslim Walla people from Wa, in northwest Ghana. We had a few minutes of discussion about how best to go about the strategy. During this time an insightful missionary and former Muslim asserted, "We must go to them." Everyone quickly agreed and started speaking of going to Wa. In the midst of the discussion, he interrupted and explained, "Yes, we must go to Wa and plant churches there, but they are here in Kumasi as well. Almost every man who carries lumber on his head to the market is Walla." The result was a mission strategy for reaching Wa and another for the Walla. Missionaries went north to the town of Wa, and missionaries went into the lumber markets of Kumasi. Both were focused on the Walla people.

The same can be said for North America today and its unreached emerging postmodern contexts. Churches need to be planted in Buckhead (metro Atlanta), Marin County (San Francisco), and at the University of Wisconsin. These are just a few of the hometowns for the cultural creatives on the edge of the postmodern cultural context. But the Walla are not just in Wa! People who are transitioning out of modernity also live in upstate New York, rural Alabama, and New Mexico. We must go to them everywhere.

Emerging Generations Are People in Need of Christ

Starting a new Korean church is an obvious response to an influx of Koreans. The church would reach people who swim in the water of Korean culture. The same must be done for emerging postmodern generations, who are swimming in the new North American culture.

Evangelicals have struggled with responding to these new realities, finding reasons not to respond. It's important to note that the shift to postmodernism has not happened everywhere. The shifts have not yet impacted many in the church culture, because the church culture acts as a protective shield, unmolested by a secular culture's music, literature, and values.

Large pockets still exist in North America where people live out their lives in much the same manner as their parents before them. These people have more toys, but they still go to church (or at least feel guilty if they don't go), still have relatively stable family lives, and still espouse the "old values" of America. Most evangelicals live in these pockets and have been somewhat insulated from the societal changes. Still, television can't be avoided. In our fallen world, something seems to be wrong. These people see the shifts coming. While the societal shifts may not have impacted them yet, they see the changes reflected in their children's eyes. The chart here illustrates this point.

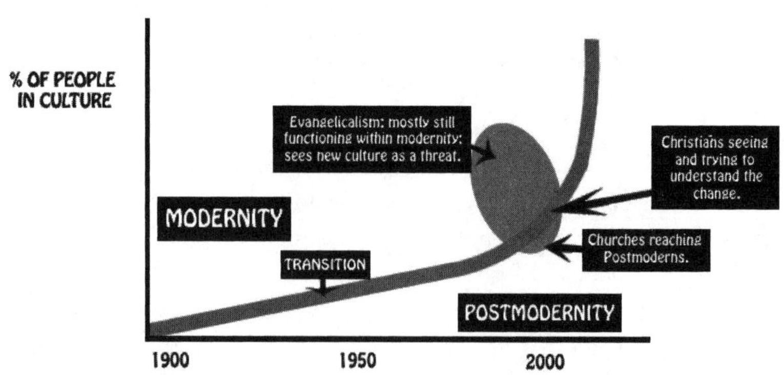

The chart also helps to explain that being a postmodern is not an age or generational issue alone but a "cultural postmodernity" cutting across generational lines. I place the transition after World War II, which coincides with the influx of the generation known as boomers. True, it may be more prevalent in today's younger generations simply because these people were exposed almost exclusively to postmodern thinking. But it's not limited to them. A sixty-year-old artist from San Francisco might be thoroughly entrenched in postmodernity while a twenty-four-year-old banker from Memphis might hold more modernist values.

Many evangelicals haven't engaged postmoderns because they don't want contact with the value systems of the postmodern world. It's much easier to deny its power than to acknowledge its influence.

As a result, many evangelicals will choose to sit out the changing culture and remain isolated. Many nonevangelical churches have decided to be edgy and adopt what they see as postmodern values and try to hitch their fading star to the newest value system. (Yes, that will be as embarrassing as it was when they tried to adopt the values of the 1960s, 1970s, etc.) Thankfully, some churches will choose to engage the culture in radically biblical ways—becoming missionaries to a culture they have not traveled to but which has instead traveled to them.

Churches must think differently to reach this different kind of people. This will obviously be hard to do in established churches. Some churches are just now adopting the music of the 1970s (and consider this to be a radical change). To postmoderns, the debate about traditional versus contemporary music in churches is about as important as listening to dad and granddad fight over the television remote. The churches most likely to become missional will be new churches founded for and primarily led by indigenous postmodern leaders. Their methods and media will be radically different from the present church, but their message will be deeply biblical.

Some historians identify 1968 as the transition point from modernity to postmodernity, calling that year the 1960s decade in microcosm.[3] This would be the year the first boomers finished college. During that year the North Vietnam Tet offensive foreshadowed the inability of a superpower nation to overcome a small revolution, Moscow crushed the "Prague Spring" by invading Czechoslovakia, Martin Luther King Jr. and Robert Kennedy were assassinated, and a young man in Paris gave up hope for

Enlightenment ideas. Eleven years later in 1979, Jean-François Lyotard wrote *The Postmodern Condition,* which helped define the values of the emerging shift from modernity.

Understanding Postmodernity

Postmodernism means "that which comes after modernism." Much of what defines postmodernism is a reaction against modernism. Erickson provides some helpful categories. Postmodernism is based on the following values (my version of their cultural expression is in parentheses):

- *The denial of personal objectivity* (I do believe in God, but that's really the influence of my parents. Nobody can know for sure.)
- *The uncertainty of knowledge* (The government says the Atkins diet doesn't work, but who really knows if it's true.)
- *The death of any all-inclusive explanation* (You know, things just don't fit into a nice, neat explanation.)
- *The denial of the inherent goodness of knowledge* (The more knowledge out there, the more dangerous the world is becoming.)
- *The rejection of progress* (I have all this technology, but I'm still not happy.)
- *The supremacy of community-based knowledge* (It's arrogant to think that I, alone, have figured out spiritual truth.)
- *The disbelief in objective inquiry.* (Here's what I think that verse means, but I could be wrong. What's your interpretation?)[4]

While modernity and postmodernity hold some things in common, as a whole postmodernity tends to be more cynical. Maybe that's the point—modernism and its hopeful notions of progress seem quaint in a post-rational era.

I've tried to simplify with three overarching themes. In this book I'll explain one of these, called "From Meta-Narratives to Mini-Narratives." Go to my Web site www.newchurches.com for explanations called "From Text to Interpretations" and "From External to Internal Truth." They may help illustrate the shift toward postmodernism. Each section starts with a

For more information, go to www.newchurches.com.

vignette from the church and then from the broader culture—illustrating how these philosophical shifts have impacted our thinking.

From Meta-Narratives to Mini-Narratives

In the Church

"Don't tell them all about the whole biblical story of Jesus. Tell them the story of what Jesus has done for you" (from an evangelism training manual).

Though it's not a bad thing to tell of one's personal experience, the focus has moved from the big story of redemption to a personal story of redemption. This is both a good and a bad thing. However, the culture has shifted from the big stories (meta-narratives) to the small ones (mini-narratives).

In the Culture

"I don't buy into your comfortable suburban American dream," explained the man sitting at the airport lunch counter. "You tell me about God, but what it really seems is that you want me to fit into your standard of what I should be. My partner and I have found our own happiness. I don't buy your values."

The description is not uncommon. People don't want what they're "supposed" to want. People are "supposed" to want a nice white picket fence in the suburbs. That's the American dream—work hard, play by the rules, live in the suburbs, retire in Florida. One problem: fewer people are committed to that "story." Instead, they set their own view of what an idyllic existence would include. They create their own story (mini-narrative) rather than buy into the grand story of the culture (meta-narrative).

The one thing everyone agrees on about postmodernism is that it represents the death of a single, universal worldview.[5] Jean-François Lyotard defined postmodernism as disbelief toward universal worldviews. "Simplifying to the extreme, I define *postmodern* as incredulity toward meta-narratives."[6] He believed the point of this new movement was to help liberate men and women from the idea there was a universal point or reason for existence. These universal values, whether they are the American dream, Christianity, or capitalism, are called meta-narratives.

A meta-narrative is a unifying cultural value that explains and gives purpose to life, meaning, and existence. It's the reason people go to work and live their lives. Thus, in a sense, Christianity is a meta-narrative. It includes truth, meaning for life, and the purpose of our existence. However, capitalism is also a meta-narrative. It provides truth (profit is good), meaning (providing more for you, your family, and children), and existence (getting ahead is a key value).

It's important to note that individuals often hold to more than one meta-narrative, perhaps a mix of different values. For example, the meta-narrative of most North American Christians would be a mix of Christianity, capitalism, and the American dream.

Philosophical postmodernism, often represented by the views of philosopher Michel Foucalt, explains that meta-narratives and all constructs of truth are used by those in power to control the disenfranchised. The mental pictures of how things are (or should be) are not "value-neutral."[7]

It's true that meta-narratives have been used to oppress throughout the ages. The meta-narrative of medieval Catholicism suppressed and persecuted heretic Protestants, the meta-narrative of Victorian Christianity kept women in their "right place," and the meta-narrative of the American dream tried to keep African-Americans in quiet submission. Good postmodernists not only resist such "categories" for themselves; they also must deconstruct them for others, believing this is just the right thing to do.

Instead of finding grand, universal, and timeless truths, postmoderns find truth to be that which is expressed by a community of people. Truth is that which is agreed upon by the community to be beneficial to that community. Only those within our group have the ability or right to comment upon or criticize "our" truth.

Finding the Truth

If all the "big truths" aren't true and are really there to control the people, where do we find the truth? People are still looking for truth, meaning, and existence. However, now they're finding it in little stories that don't claim to be universal. For example, rather than proclaiming the universal value of the American dream, a postmodern might say, "I can instead find truth, meaning, and existence in the writings of Deepak Chopra, and I wouldn't dare claim that this truth is something for you. It's my mini-narrative—my personal story that gives me peace."

Consider this: "Native American spirituality can bring me peace, while my neighbor can find peace in Kabbalah (Jewish mysticism)." There's no "big story," so we each hold tightly to our own "little stories" that bring us peace and serenity.

The implications for ministry are important to grasp and may provide a window on our culture. It's unlikely that the average person on the street would say, "I think this meta-narrative you're promoting is intended to oppress me." Nevertheless, this is exactly what many people think when we try to evangelize them. They see us attempting to "impose" a truth that we consider universal. This truth has been used to oppress women and slaves, and now we want to oppress them. Since they already have their own mini-narrative, we must be seeking to destroy it. In the minds of some people, evangelism is not just wrong; it's a hate crime.

Richard Rorty, a radical postmodern philosopher, believes that all truth is *made* and not found. Thus, any value or moral belief is "made up" by the person or the group to which he or she belongs.

Deconstructionism, a term in academic postmodernism, plays a large part in the process. In the postmodern world there are no valid truth claims; all must be deconstructed by the new postmodernist. This means that "wise" people make a point to "take apart" (deconstruct) false truth claims. Since all truth claims are false, that's a full-time job!

Culturally Relevant Ministry in a Postmodern World

Being a missionary is never easy, but when the culture change has taken place in one's own home, it's even more difficult. We are much like Anglos living near Eighth Street (Calle Ocho) in 1959, during the era when locals were overwhelmed by new immigrants. Anglo churches in south Miami had two choices—think like Cubans and understand how to function in their world or move. Most chose to move rather than engage the new cultural shift.

The church does not have such an option. Our job is to reach the lost world and bring greater glory to God. Yet, rather than engaging the new cultural change, the most prevalent Christian response is to pretend that there's been no shift.[8] The church continues to function as it always has—protecting its youth in summer camp, keeping its members listening to Christian music, and, as a whole, staying away from change.

This is the easiest approach, but it's not the way of Christ. Those trying to preserve the existing church unchanged have little time to think about what the future of the church should look like.[9] Most churches don't even have the vitality to be a healthy modern church, let alone to make the transition from a modern to an emerging world. Some predict that the new millennium will see the death of thousands of local churches, which won't be surprising, considering trends.

Even the casual observer sees that Christianity has been disestablished as the primary belief of North Americans. Being part of the clergy was once considered a position of prominence, leading to service on boards and commissions. Now being clergy is more a detriment to such involvement.[10] The idea of being "spiritual but not religious" is becoming the highest value.

On the other hand, many Americans are still churchgoers. The United States is second only to Ireland as the highest church-attending Western nation.[11] Unfortunately, though these statistics are still high, they're declining. More important, it's the social influence of Christianity that's declined. Attending church doesn't necessarily indicate true belief and may no longer determine lifestyle.

Keep in mind that churchgoers are usually people in the older generations, not the ones who have been exposed almost exclusively to postmodernism. For the most part, emerging generations don't have a biblical heritage or a Christian cultural identity. They don't necessarily accept the Bible as an authority for their lives until they've seen how it applies to them.

"Won't They Grow Out of It?"

Church leaders may ask, "Haven't we seen youth cultures claiming a new way of thinking eventually merge back into the greater culture? Won't they grow out of it?" The 1960s are a good example. Many people thought hippies would grow out of their values. People rightly assumed that slogans such as "never trust anyone over thirty" wouldn't last beyond their thirtieth birthday. And most did assimilate into the broader culture, cutting their hair and putting on ties. But they also brought some of their values with them. (Consider the sexual revolution and antics of Bill Clinton.)

Perhaps this emerging mind-set is a fad that will pass. But if the 1960s are a barometer, note that many of today's church leaders were touched by the Jesus Movement while they were still wearing beards and bell-bottoms. At that time they could not have been touched otherwise. The argument for moving aggressively into the emerging culture and not avoiding it is strong. Emerging culture has only a few of the characteristics of an enduring value system (in that it's often described and defined more by what it's not than what it is), but mainstream popular culture has already embraced its values or nonvalues. This compounds the problem.

Oprah Winfrey's show is a good example of postmodernism expressed through popular media. Her influence is hard to overstate. A recent book, *The Gospel According to Oprah,* reveals that she once considered becoming a missionary or teacher. Oprah 101 has become the cultural classroom of America. A guest will talk about his or her alternative understanding of morality or spirituality—sex before marriage, etc. Oprah then asks the audience for questions, and an individual might say, "Well, the Bible says..." (We immediately throw up a quick prayer that Christians won't be embarrassed!) But the person continues, "The Bible says that God's best is found in a committed marriage."

Oprah will nod and smile but say something like, "That may be true for you, but who are we to judge, as long as people are happy and not hurting anyone else." ("Judge not" is often misinterpreted to justify the notion that intolerance is the major sin in today's culture.) That's postmodernism, that's media influence, and that's now the majority view of our culture.

Oprah might not know she's influenced by a cultural system called postmodernity, but postmodern values permeate her show. She's not alone. Talk shows, "reality" programs, and even the news illustrate the values of postmodernism. Postmodernism is the reigning cultural paradigm in popular media. Postmodern values touch all those who are exposed to popular media, everyone who watches television! And that's virtually everyone.

Emerging Planting Models in a Postmodern World

How we plant churches is in many ways determined by the location and focus group (where and among whom we plant churches, which is the subject of the next chapter). Emerging generations will most likely be reached by new and yet to be developed models. This section focuses on models for reaching emerging postmodern generations.

Based on my observations, the ten most frequent traits of impactful, emerging postmodern churches are expressed in these key values:

- Being unashamedly spiritual
- Promoting incarnational ministry
- Engaging in service

- Valuing experiential praise
- Preaching narrative expository messages
- Appreciating and participating in ancient patterns
- Visualizing worship
- Connecting with technology
- Living community
- Leading by transparency and team

Being Unashamedly Spiritual

People tired of the modern belief that everything can be answered by science and reason are open to answers that are "mystical and spiritual." This hunger runs rampant in postmodern pop culture.

Proud of their spiritual quests, people hold beliefs in many things, including astrology, New Age, tarot cards, psychics, ESP, channeling spirits, reincarnation, witchcraft, palm reading, UFOs and aliens, mother earth, crystal power, and Eastern or African spirituality. From Hollywood to politics, spirituality is at a popular high. Go to your video store and notice the popularity of titles like *The Passion of the Christ* and *The Chronicles of Narnia*. Celebrities who embrace religions based on "spirituality" (but not necessarily Christianity) talk about it openly and enthusiastically (which makes you wonder why the Christian stars aren't getting that exposure). Music has been influenced by postmodernism, one example being the popularity of Gregorian chants.

It may be difficult for many Christians to see the current emphasis on non-Christian spirituality as a potential openness, but Paul emphasized that very thing, noting with enthusiasm that the Athenian philosophers were "already very religious," which he obviously considered a beginning point for presenting the gospel.

Postmoderns want a spirituality that's applicable to all areas of life, not one that only lasts for an hour on Sunday morning but one they can rely on all week. They eschew a spirituality that doesn't "work"—bring peace, improve relationships and quality of life. (Memo to church planters: Christians without joy are an anti-evangelism strategy!) Postmoderns want a spirituality that's authentic above all else; it doesn't have to be perfect, but it must be genuinely and humbly held.

The most surprising news of postmodernity is that postmoderns are on a "spiritual search and not an intellectual quest."[12] They're willing to take that quest with Christians, if we're genuine and live a holistic faith.

Promoting Incarnational Ministry

What's more, if Christian worship services and small groups embrace a participative spirituality, postmoderns see that their participation might lead to a genuine faith experience. Authenticity is essential, and authenticity only comes when we're real and present. That "presence" is what theologians call incarnational ministry.[13] Postmoderns are looking for people who are genuine and transparent. Their question isn't, Is it true? but, Is it real? They want to see Christ through people who've earned their respect and trust.

Many people feel they're entering an alien culture when encountering evangelical Christianity. But it's not the job of the unchurched to enter our culture; it's our job to invade theirs. We do that by recognizing this as mission work, which is the same everywhere; the missionary must radically engage the culture. Evangelism to emerging generations is a day-to-day effort. People no longer want to hear about Christianity; they want to see Christianity in action.

Evangelism must adopt "Jesus type" methods. We must go to people in culture in order to reach them—live in their neighborhoods, eat at their restaurants, drink coffee at their coffee shops, shop at their stores. Living in Christ must become a daily reality. Being a Christian is not a label or a banner flown only on Sundays; it's a way of life.

Engaging in Service

People are looking for opportunities to serve by being hands-on and active.[14] Volunteerism is huge as people want to make a difference in their community and world. Organizations such as Habitat for Humanity and the Peace Corps are opportunities for postmoderns to make their mark on society.

Churches can connect by offering an outlet for their passion to serve. Genuine faith always expresses itself in ministry. As people observe that faith produces service, the validity of the faith is proved. One way is to engage emerging generations in mission work and not just service in international locations and not limited to traditional ways of evangelizing those who don't know Christ. Downtown Community Fellowship in Athens, Georgia, takes advantage of its proximity to the college campus. The pastor explains, "We hand out icy-pops and hot chocolate downtown and at the University of Georgia campus in order to meet people, share God's love and invite them to worship with us."[15]

My friend Andy Williams of Omaha planted a seeker-driven church in a movie theater in the 1990s but now engages his community in more incarnational approaches. He's moved from quality music, drama, and video as attraction tickets to offering projects with a purpose to draw unbelievers to lock arms with Christians as they cooperate to do good in the community. When Hurricane Katrina hit the Gulf Coast in 2005, Andy pulled together a group of his friends, about half of them not yet believers, and they worked together to adopt displaced families. He says some of the most enthusiastic calls he got were from "friends who don't know Jesus who were calling *me* to see what we were going to do to serve and love these people."

Valuing Experiential Praise

A significant change over the last two decades was discovering what constituted a seeker-sensitive service. In many large boomer churches, seeker sensitivity involved a high degree of anonymity. This may be changing in the postmodern culture. Being sensitive to the postmodern seeker means involving him or her in the learning process.

A community that provides people with a dynamic and participative worship is providing a powerful apologetic to people open to the spiritual yet unaware of how to connect with the Spirit. Those without Christ cannot worship God. However, through such worship these "already religious" people can see true believers praising God in spirit and in truth, a worship that will attract them and be unintentionally evangelistic.

Emerging worship is not antiliturgical. It may find its manifestation in liturgical expressions as modern-generation Christians focus on becoming "like" Christ by "participating in the divine nature."[16]

At Lake Ridge Church, we draw our worship from more than just the contemporary music scene. We believe people experience the fullness of worship through singing contemporary music but also reciting a creed, kneeling in prayer, and learning a hymn from the fifth century.

Emerging churches often provide people with experiences of classic mystical practices or spiritual disciplines. For worship to promote evangelism, Sally Morganthaler says it must include four elements: "nearness—an awareness of the presence of God; knowledge—worship that is centered on who Christ is; vulnerability—worship that involves opening up to God; and interaction—participating in the worship of God."[17] She's correct. Her book *Worship Evangelism* should be required reading for every church planter seeking to reach postmodern generations.

Preaching Narrative Expository Messages

The power of story has engaged people in culture today. More churches are recognizing the power of the biblical story in preaching. Emerging churches value the power of story, often spending more time on the Gospels where the modern church spent more time on the Epistles. Since Jesus, life is presented not as an essay, doctrine, or sermon but rather as a story, the truths of Jesus are often told in story form. People have grown accustomed to stacked narratives that move in and out of varying stories, like television shows with several interwoven plot lines per episode.

Eugene Peterson observes:

> We live in an age when story has been pushed from its biblical front-line prominence to a bench on the sidelines, condescended to as "illustration" or "testimony" or "inspiration." Both inside and outside the church, we prefer information over story. We typically gather impersonal (pretentiously called "scientific" or "theological") information, whether doctrinal or philosophical or historical, in order to take things into our own hands and take charge of how we will live our lives. And we commonly consult outside experts to interpret the information for us.[18]

Early church preaching was often story focused. A return to narrative preaching is a good thing as long as the focal narrative is the narrative of Scripture. Jesus frequently used narratives in his preaching. Often the story was the point. But we're told to preach the Word and not just tell meaningful stories. Preaching must be both narrative and biblical. To some, narrative preaching is telling a contemporary story with biblical texts sprinkled in. This is not enough. New Testament churches need to be biblical and to present Scripture as their text and focus.

Appreciating and Participating in Ancient Patterns

In the post-seeker age, churches are again beginning to appreciate the wisdom of a community of faith that stretches back two thousand years. Responding to the transition to contemporary worship and seeker-sensitive services, there's a backlash among emerging generations to reach toward the stability of the past. This explains why so many with a postmodern mentality, including boomers and those born later, are attracted to liturgical worship rooted in biblical text.

The church of the modern era failed to answer many of the questions postmoderns were asking, but the ancient traditions still hold the mystery of the transcendent and the experience of spirituality. "The philosophical shift from reason to mystery provides an opening to the discussion of a supernatural view of the church connected with the work of Christ."[19] Liturgy and ancient patterns often provide that link to the transcendent mystery of the gospel.

Visualizing Worship

Many people look to the prevalence of MTV as the reason churches should use multimedia if they want to reach emerging generations. That's not a compelling reason to me. Instead, we recognize that truth is often expressed in images. Visual images and art can illustrate the written truths of Scripture in a powerful way, and worship has become more visual. For us at Lake Ridge Church, we don't just project the words of the music on the screen. We use images that describe that theme. When we sing of blood, we show blood. When we sing of Christ, we use art from the ages to show Christ.

Emerging generations don't want to be entertained; they seek to be engaged. So a worship service in a sterile auditorium led by worship leaders so professional that they come across as slick won't appeal the way it did in the modern era. People want reality, and they want visuality. Many emerging churches are discovering the value of banners and liturgies that connect postmoderns with biblical truth.

Connecting with Technology

Technology is so much a part of our cultural experience that it's not optional for a church reaching emerging generations. In fact, some credit technology itself with the rapid spread of emerging culture.

A good example of a church using technology in worship services is Cornerstone Church in San Francisco (www.cornerstone-sf.org). They use light gels to transform their worship into a liturgical church, projecting stained glass where there is none.

Cyberspace has had a leveling effect on people, presenting a myriad of religious options at their fingertips, including opportunities for evangelism. Most postmoderns do research before trying something new, and most research will be online. Ginghamsburg Church in Tipp City, Ohio (www.ginghamsburg.org) is a good example of a church that's using the Internet for evangelism. They actually have a staff person for cyberministry.

When we planted Lake Ridge Church, we used Church Plant Media (www.churchplantmedia.com) to provide us a Web site that would connect with our target community. They focused on the Web site and updated as requested, and we focused on reaching our community.

Some churches are exploring the use of technology to foster community. At Lake Ridge, we use Church Community Builder (www.churchcommunitybuilder.com) to create online communities for our church family. Like ours, most churches using the Web for community aren't doing so in place of personal interaction; they're doing it *to enhance interpersonal interaction*. (Internet churches without meaningful community beyond chat rooms are just occasional anomalies. Steer clear of them.)

Living Community

Community will be a central value in all organizations of the future, whether secular or sacred. This is good news for the church because community is central to its mission. Also, spiritual growth best takes place in community.

People are searching for the security provided by relationships with like-minded people, forming a family bonded by friendship rather than kinship. The rise of reality television, with it hyper-accelerated relationship building and breaking, points to the longing of people in culture for community.

In spiritual things people long to belong and are hungry for a *we*-centered approach to growing spiritually rather than a *me*-centered approach.

Groups seeking to build relationship will not be short-term study groups but rather longer term commitments of two or more years before becoming true communities with trust and intimacy. The key to evangelizing emerging generations is the presence of Christian community, a biblical concept since relationship with God and others is the foundation of the faith. There's no church without community. We're rediscovering that truth today.

Emerging churches are reaching out by inviting people into their community. They're allowing the spiritual journey to begin before conversion. Spiritual seekers are invited to participate in the faith community before they share the faith. Allowing someone to belong doesn't mean that he or she is incorporated into the body of Christ.[20] It means they're seeking in a safe place.

You can't buy community, program community, or fake community. It's the reality of the relationships that makes Christ believable to an unbelieving society. The devout atheist and the homosexual will not come to Christ until the love of Christ annihilates the worldview upon which they depend. Community is the love of God manifesting itself in and through the people of God. That's the advantage the church has in this society.

Leading by Transparency and Team

In the modern context the leader was penalized for transparency. Leaders who shared their struggles frequently regretted it later as it became an example in future arguments. Today struggle has more value, giving the "wounded healer" validity. We can look to Paul as an example. He admitted that he often found himself doing the things he shouldn't be doing, and he admitted that a "thorn" was placed in his side to keep him from being exalted above others. As a leader, he favored a level playing field.

Leaders in emerging contexts prefer a team-oriented approach to leadership. When we decided to plant Lake Ridge Church, we began with a team of pastor / elders, functioning as a plurality of elders. Our desire is to model team at our leadership level for a church that will be made up of people teaming together for the sake of the gospel.

The community-style of leadership means that governance assumes a participatory culture rather than a representative culture. *Participatory* assumes that people want to make their own decisions and have multiple choices; leadership emboldens and empowers others to lead; individuals will make sacrifices for the good of the whole; human systems are self-organizing, and people can be trusted to invest wisely of their resources and time. *Representative* assumes that people want and need to be controlled and have decisions made for them; the task of leadership is to administer guidance and regulations; people do only the things they're rewarded for doing; and people can't be trusted to use their personal freedom in service to the society or organization.

Teams are messy, painful, difficult, and rewarding all at the same time. We're fallen creatures with fallen motives. But, ultimately, the work is worth the reward. The covenanted leadership team models Christian community to the whole church. The church, in turn, models community to the world.

Resources for Further Study

Dockery, David S., ed. *The Challenge of Postmodernism: An Evangelical Engagement*. Grand Rapids: Baker, 1995.

Gibbs, Eddie. *ChurchNext: Quantum Changes in How We Do Ministry*. Downers Grove, Ill.: InterVarsity Press, 2000.

Grenz, Stanley J. *A Primer on Postmodernism*. Grand Rapids: Eerdmans, 1996.

Guder, Darrel L. *Missional Church*. Grand Rapids: Eerdmans, 1998.

Hunsberger, George R. "The Newbigin Gauntlet." In *The Church Between Gospel and Culture*. Ed. George R. Hunsberger and Craig Van Gelder. Grand Rapids: Eerdmans, 1996.

McLaren, Brian D. *Church on the Other Side*. Grand Rapids: Zondervan, 2000.

Shenk, David W., and Ervin R. Stutzman. *Creating Communities of the Kingdom: New Testament Models of Church Planting*. Scottsdale, Pa.: Herald Press, 1988.

Sweet, Leonard I. *Soul Tsunami: Sink or Swim in New Millennium Culture*. Grand Rapids: Zondervan Publishing House, 1999.

Sweet, Leonard. *Aqua Church: Essential Leadership Arts for Piloting Your Church in Today's Fluid Culture*. Loveland, Colo.: Group, 1999.

Van Gelder, Craig, ed. *Confident Witness—Changing World*. Grand Rapids: Eerdmans, 1999.

Chapter 11

Choosing a Focus Group

One of the church planter's earliest decisions is how to select the group that the church will reach—called "focusing," an essential process in international missions. International missionaries talk of focusing on taxi drivers in Calcutta or farmers in Mexico. To consider how people group segmentation (focusing) works, let's begin with the objection some people have to the idea of selecting a particular people group for a church plant. Their concern is that planters need to focus on everyone, and they believe that focusing is perceived as an exclusionary process. My answer is that a better description is that planters are open to everyone, but the new church is focused on a certain people group.

If you object to the terminology, let me challenge you. If you choose contemporary music, aren't you focusing on people who prefer it? Wouldn't you be excluding some people who won't like that music? Or, if you're a Hmong church using the White Hmong language, are you likely to reach Kurdish immigrants?

Focusing acknowledges that people generally prefer to come to Christ without crossing social, racial, or economic boundaries.[1] Every international missionary is aware of this and focuses on a selected receptive group of people. When I was in Malaysia training church planters, my class had

Indians, Malaysian-born Chinese, other Chinese, Iban aboriginal people, Westerners, and a few others. I didn't have to explain that Iban are more likely to reach Iban. They used traditional Iban music and expressions of worship, even though they might speak the same language as others in the class. There was not an attitude of division or segmentation, just a mature recognition that Iban people would be more likely to come to Christ in an Iban church.

This can be explained not just in a cross-continental experience but even within our own neighborhood contexts. Dimas Salaberrios, pastor of Infiniti Church in New York, describes the difficulty of their location this way: "Finding the meeting place is always difficult in a large city. Currently, they are meeting at Fort Independence Community Center. The space is large and will hold a couple hundred people. But the Center is right in the middle of Crip territory—a place to where any Blood member might think twice about going."[2] When looking at their community, Dimas understands a key aspect, that focusing on his target audience will affect even the simple questions of location.

Focus group is about evangelism—who will you reach first. *But, their evangelism was not their fellowship.* The evangelism was focused on reaching the Iban or people in an urban context. But the church fellowship was representative of every tongue, tribe, and nation, as expressed in Revelation 7:9. So, although the music was Iban, the church also included those from other ethnic groups who enjoyed the Iban expression of worship.

Developing a Focus Group

Here are some guidelines:

Who lives here? Different types of people live and earn their income in every geographical area. Ask: What are the people here like?

Example. Saddleback Church in California is probably the church best known for focusing in the North American context. It has developed a profile of "Saddleback Sam," a composite image describing the typical Saddleback person's values, income, education, and lifestyle preferences. Saddleback Sam is well educated, enjoys his work, likes where he lives, listens to contemporary music, prioritizes fitness, and is skeptical of organized religious expression.[3] Saddleback's process for profiling (not their profile, *per se*) provides a model for planters in North America.

The Central Question. How do we proclaim the gospel to focus the audience in a manner that's effective and life changing and fits within the context of the culture? The answer materializes when church planters understand the people group God has called them to reach. According to the New Testament, Paul spoke differently to Jews than he did to Greek philosophers. He considered their different lifestyles and backgrounds (1 Cor. 9:19–23). Church planters need to follow his model.

Begin with Data. Research using census data, economic profiles, and other databases to learn demographic, socioeconomic, cultural, ecclesiographic, and spiritual information on the focus group. Effective missions and church-planting methodologies are contextual and indigenous, meaning the planter is "from the area" and dresses, talks, etc. like those in the area.

> Much more information can be found in *Breaking the Missional Code.*

The Fallacy of the Average. Information such as age, household size, educational level, median income, housing type, and ethnicity can help to refine your strategy. But beware of the "fallacy of the average" which may skew the application. For example, a community of two age groups, one in their late sixties and the other in their early twenties, may present its median[4] age as early forties, but few middle-aged adults may actually live in that community. It is better to graph the information and look for groups in need of a new church.

Census Tracts, Not Zip or Postal Codes. Researchers may be able to avoid this problem by focusing on census tract studies (available at public libraries) instead of larger, potentially more diverse zip code-focused studies. Even so, there's no guarantee. Data must be tested by other research. "Soft data" surveys with community leaders, local people-helping agencies, etc. will help provide verification.

Christ for the World

The church planter's ultimate objective is nothing less than winning the whole world for Christ. But such a huge focus can frustrate and overwhelm the planter. The journey of a thousand miles begins with a single step—immediate focus on the people group whom God has placed on the planter's heart, then expand to other groups.

Multiplied Efforts. This strategy involves first reaching a particular subgroup of the unchurched and then teaching those initial converts to focus on and reach other unchurched groups. This reinforces the first converts' journey toward faith and allows the church to reach others who may be different from that first generation of converts. Planters must focus on and reach lost people. But their task is not finished until they have influenced their converts to reach others as well.

Cross-Cultural Planting. For example, an African-American church planter believes God has called him to reach Hispanics in Des Moines, Iowa, a calling to church planting and also to cross-cultural missions. The African-American church planter then starts to teach new Hispanic Christians to become the primary evangelists in the Hispanic community. The cross-cultural church planter becomes a discipler, teacher, and mentor for the next generation of leaders.

Missionizing the Unchurched

Church planters can missionaize the unchurched, even cross-culturally, if they're able to reach receptive persons, to understand lost persons, to understand felt needs, and to overcome resistance to church relationships.

Identifying Receptive People. In your area, who are they? Often, they're people experiencing the pressures of a major life transition, such as relocation, forced employment change, divorce, marriage, childbirth, or the illness or death of a loved one. These circumstances cause people to respond more positively to the good news. An example would be an area where new subdivisions are being built. As people move into new homes, they're likely to consider a new church. At the churches I have started, we purchase the names of people in transition so we can contact them. At Lake Ridge Church, we have used reachingamerica.com. They use timely new mover lists, generate a set of three personalized mailers, and send them out for us each week. Our best responses come from new movers and this helps us communicate with them.

North Cross Baptist Church in Cumming, Georgia, is attempting to take a new look at identifying receptive new people in their community. Rather than just sending an invite to new movers, they're unifying community leaders to give new movers to the area a crash course in community involvement. The new mover will discover more than a church that cares about them; they will also plug in with their elected officials and local business leaders. Identifying these new people and coming up with creative ways to reach them is part of this task.

Informal Discussions. Many unchurched people resist connecting with a church for several reasons—both real and imagined. One way to break through is to find out what they think about church. The planter should probe the focus group for perceptions of church and denominations, perhaps through in-home discussion groups or coffee-shop conversations.

Simply going to the local restaurant or coffee shop is the perfect place for this kind of simple line of questions. Gary Lamb, founding pastor of Ridgestone Church in Canton, Georgia, would hang out at the local restaurant. Sitting in the waiting area near the bar, he would pay the hostess one dollar for every group she sat next to him while they were waiting for their table. He would then ask them their thoughts on church and Christ. You would be surprised what you will find if you go into the community. Many of us try to find out the answers to these questions within our church communities, but that will give us a churched view, not an unchurched one.

When All Else Fails, Ask, Then Listen. One way—the best and most affirming way—to find out what unchurched people think about church or what they need is to ask them. Word of warning: Lock your lips and really listen, resisting the temptation to fashion arguments for what they're saying. Most of our evangelism methods have been geared toward talking, when what's often needed most is the fine art of asking good, deep, compelling questions and then truly listening to the answers.

Felt Needs Are Exposed for What They Are. While building relationships, the church planter may discover opportunities to offer support for meeting group members' felt needs, such as a class focused on parenting, addictions, or weight loss. Parents may discover that resolving marital struggles and overcoming selfishness between mates is the greatest need in the family. People in "recovery" ministries need to know that there is a true "higher power" in Christ. The dieter may find that low self-esteem prompts overeating and inappropriate self-nurture with food. In addition, high-trust relationships will afford the planter opportunities to introduce group members to the answer for their deepest need—a lasting relationship with Christ.

What Is That Music They Hear? Worship style is a barrier for many unchurched people. The planter may ask focus group members about their musical taste. Some church planters identify Arbitron's five highest-rated music radio stations in the area. In all likelihood, focus group members are tuned in—stylistically, as well as literally—to those stations. Then ask what style of music would best connect with these people.

Consider Styles and Values. Patterns of time management and type of recreation can shape church planting. The planter's awareness of patterns of recreational, political, and other social activities can help to develop a strategy.

From Felt Needs to Real Needs

Many unchurched persons feel no need for a savior. They conclude that they need something, but they don't know what that something is. Moving an unbeliever from felt needs to real needs happens by applying a relevant strategy to help unbelievers identify the true nature of their needs. It's a process. Twice a year, during fall and spring, we present topics related to felt needs because most of our focus group initially attended during those seasons. During winter and summer we focused on moving people to deeper spiritual needs.

Church planters can't afford to remain at a felt-needs level. We may begin with felt needs in order to gain a hearing for deeper needs, but life change occurs with a systematic process of moving from felt needs to real spiritual needs. Felt needs preaching leads to spiritually immature people and churches, but there are times when felt needs can be addressed in a strategic matter.

Strategizing by Discovery. The wise church planter strategizes to meet real needs by discovering the longings of the focus group. The Bible determines our message, and our focus group's needs determine when, where, and how we communicate that unchanging message.

Strategizing by Repeated Analysis. As planters strategize, they determine the focus group's needs and what methods may work most effectively. Beyond an immediate plan, however, effective strategizing must also include maintaining a network of resource people able to provide information updates, so the planter can address the ever-changing needs of the focus group.

Crucial Questions. In *Reconnecting God's Story to Ministry*, Tom Steffen encourages readers to ask crucial questions when engaging a new culture.[5] First, what's the worldview of the focus audience, no matter if they're a tribe in Pakistan or postmoderns in Seattle? Second, what are their decision-making patterns? This helps isolate the redemptive analogies that best describe the culture. This process also demands that the planter seek to identify what this culture group believes about the basic components of the gospel. Other questions: Is this focus group a "shame" or a "guilt" culture? How will they understand Christian rituals? What's the best delivery system for exposing them to the gospel?

Materials Relevant to the Focus. The church planter develops relevant materials to connect effectively with the focus audience. One planter discovered that many in his focus group believed sermons were boring. The church was careful to affirm, in an early informational letter, that many sermons *are* boring, promising no boring sermons at the new church.

Different Context, Different Concerns. When I planted Millcreek Community Church and its daugheter churches, we were in the northeastern United States. Our focus group had different concerns than many other places. We were planting among nominal Catholics who wondered whether we were a cult because we didn't own a church building. They worried that we would hold long worship services in which people would act in bizarre ways. Many came from a background they called "the great Catholic guilt machine." They expected us to beat them down verbally with guilt-laden preaching or to emphasize legalism. Our focus group had other worries than boring sermons.

In order to address their concerns, we provided direct-mail pieces describing us as "rooted in historic Christianity." I reassured prospects that our service would begin at 9:35 and end by 10:45 and that no one would pressure them or attempt to make them feel guilty.

Those are not the same concerns where we are planting now, and our outreach is now appropriately different. By designing materials that addressed the concerns of our focus group, we alleviated some of their fears and were also able to present the gospel in a nonthreatening environment.

Objections to Focusing

We should hear and respond to people who object to focusing as a strategy.

Exclusivism. Donald McGavran's Homogenous Unit Principle[6] identifies the reality that people generally prefer to come to Christ without crossing social, racial, or economic boundaries. Some planters fear this tool will be used as an excuse for racism or to exclude others from new church starts, perhaps people whom members find "undesirable."

It is probably true in many cases. I find it odd that most church planters I know seem called to the same upscale communities that other church planters do. Too often, they choose their focus group based on their financial preferences rather than the call of God.

But the data shows that new churches more readily attract those from the lower socioeconomic strata in their community than from the higher. Upper-income people are generally less religious and less interested in spiritual concerns. So the planter who targets Rich Roger might consider targeting Average Al instead. The greatest mission fields in North America are those abandoned by others, including the inner cities.[7]

Focusing and Moving Outward. Focusing is essential because it enables the congregation to concentrate its light, enabling accomplishments and successes in a way that diffusion of light cannot. Focusing should not be exclusivism. Rather, it should enable the congregation to concentrate on reaching increasing numbers of unchurched people with the good news of Jesus Christ by beginning with one group—the focus group—in order to expand its influence to many other groups. Reaching the unchurched with the gospel can be summed up in one word: evangelism.

Resources for Further Reading

Apeh, John E. *Social Structure and Church Planting.* Shippensburg, Pa.: Companion Press, 1989.

Brock, Charles. *The Principles and Practice of Indigenous Church Planting.* Neosho, Mo.: Church Growth International, 1981.

McGavran, Donald A. *Effective Evangelism: A Theological Mandate.* Phillipsburg, N.J.: Presbyterian and Reformed, 1988.

———. *How Churches Grow.* New York: Friendship Press, 1959.

Wagner, C. Peter. *Church Planting for a Greater Harvest.* Ventura, Calif.: Regal Books, 1990.

Chapter 12

A Church-Planting Fault Line

My friends who live in earthquake country tell me it's no big deal for them anymore when the rumbling starts. That is, unless it's one of those rare quakes that make it to the major level. In some parts of the world, earthquakes are recorded daily on local seismographs but generally not felt—a level 1 to 3. Level 3s to 4s are often felt but cause no damage and magnitude 5 quakes that are widely felt and cause slight damage near the epicenter. Anything higher than that and you start to move into the type of earth-shaking that can cause sizable damage and even loss of life of the famous "great earthquakes" of San Francisco in 1906, the Alaska in 1964, and one recorded in Oregon in 1700.

Why this geology lesson? Well, I have become convinced that some rumblings beneath the surface are now starting to move to the "major" magnitudes. Fault lines are starting to break on the church-planting landscape in North America. North American church planters are faced with compelling new issues. Now it might barely register with most people. As we go about the business of church planting and church growth the same way we have for the past thirty years, most church leaders barely notice. But it's rumbling just the same.

For some, this is an extension of what is already taking place internationally. Mission researcher David Barrett (cited by Alan Hirsch) believes there are 394 million Christians around the world in roughly twenty thousand networks. "According to Barrett, these Christians reject historical denominationalism and all restrictive central authority, and attempt to lead a life of following Jesus, seeking a more effective missionary lifestyle. They are the fastest-growing Christian movements in the world. Barrett estimates that by the year 2025, these movements will have around 581 million members, 120 million more than all Protestant movements together.[1]

If George Barna's most recent research and conclusions are to be believed, earth-shaking transitions are emerging here in North America as well. In his newest book, *Revolution*, Barna chronicles research that is uncovering a "growing sub-nation of people, already well over twenty million strong." He is calling this group of people "Revolutionaries." And as such, Barna says these modern-day disciples of Christ are doing what revolutionaries do—seeking to "overthrow or repudiate" and "thoroughly replace" established systems. He describes this emerging group:

> Revolutionaries eschew ministries that compromise or soft sell our sinful nature to expand organizational turf. They refuse to follow people in ministry in leadership positions who cast a personal vision rather than God's, or who seek popularity rather than the proclamation of truth in their public statements, or who are more concerned about their own legacy than that of Jesus Christ. They refuse to donate one more dollar to man-made monuments that mark their own achievements and guarantee their place in history. They are unimpressed by accredited degrees and endowed chairs in Christian colleges and seminaries that produce young people incapable of defending the Bible or unwilling to devote their life to serving others.[2]

You could probably measure those tremors at about Level 3 in the church in North America. They are beginning to be felt, but not doing considerable damage to existing structures. Barna predicts, however, that these for-now-under-the-radar Revolutionaries will have level 5 and higher impact on the face of the American church. In the next twenty years, Barna predicts the complete reshaping of the way people experience "church" in America:

> The U.S. will see a reduction in the number of churches, as presently configured (i.e. congregational-formatted ministries). Church service attendance will drop. Donations to churches will drop. Churches' already limited political and cultural influence will diminish even further at the same time that Christians will exert greater influence through more disparate mechanisms. Fewer church programs will be sustained in favor of more communal experiences among Christians.... To some, this will sound like the Great Fall of the Church. To Revolutionaries, it will be the Great Reawakening of the Church. New scenarios do not mean mayhem and dissipation. In this case, they represent a new day in which the Church can truly be the Church—different than what we know today, but more responsive to and reflective of God.[3]

In one chart, he describes the transition to churchless Christianity, much like that we have already seen in some international fields. Barna reports and predicts:

Primary Means of Spiritual Experience and Expression

	Local Church	Alternative Faith-Based Community	Family	Media/ Arts Culture
2000	70%	5%	5%	20%
2025	30–35%	5%	40–35%	30–35%

These future projections are based on current research and observation of recent trends. But even if they turn out to be half true, the American church and its church-planting engine are in for a dramatic shift. These American Revolutionaries will drastically rethink and retool the way church planting has been done for the past thirty years. Forms of church planting that have exploded worldwide but have historically struggled to gain a foothold in the U.S.—particularly house churches—could appear on the scene and multiply at a rate never seen in this country

Even megachurches are seeing this trend. When Hurricane Katrina blasted the Louisiana and Mississippi Gulf coast region in late August 2005, Saddleback Church—Rick Warren's megachurch in California—asked permission to use the house church resource *Getting Started Course* (from Tony and Felicity Dale) to train Katrina survivors in the basics of starting house churches. With thousands of church buildings destroyed and months or years from being rebuilt, the crisis called for a different kind of church. Perhaps the crisis that is the North American church might also call for such a bold reaction.

Several new books have been written on the relation-based church. And unlike years past these books have begun to sell. Another recent release, *The Way of Jesus*, is the recounting of Jonathan and Jennifer Campbell's journey out of organized, established church structures and into what we will call a "missional/incarnational" approach. Jonathan describes what that might look like when he states: "We've been amazed at the number of people we have met around the world who are on their own journey of deconstruction and discovery, breaking out of the complexities of religion to get back to the powerful simplicity of life in Jesus. They likewise have seen the widening gap between *talking about Jesus* and *walking with Jesus*. It's not that they are against church; they are just making more room in their lives to experience the living reality of Jesus in community with their family and friends."[4]

I brought Jonathan into the seminary where I taught for a dialogue. Jonathan came and advocated a missional/incarnational model without paid clergy, buildings, or programs. The other presenter promoted a crowd-to-core model of a large launch church plant. The dialogue was interesting, but the reaction of the students was even more so. The students, who were preparing for vocational ministry, lined up to talk to Jonathan and to learn what church might look like when not driven by budget, buildings, and programs. One of the students soon after resigned from a local megachurch to plant a house church in Louisville.

In the next chapter we will explore these three forms of church that seem to be positioning themselves somewhere along this church-planting fault line: house or relation-based churches, missional/incarnational churches, and emerging churches. One thing is clear: The rumblings have definitely begun. This is both good news and bad.

The good news is that everybody should know by now that things are not thriving in North America. The church is not advancing, and the gospel is not graining ground. For us to cling to the current model (what some call the Constantinian model) of pastor + program + building = church, when it is not working, is silly at best and negligent at worst. For us to eschew models that are "relational" and "small," when that is exactly what the New Testament described, is absurd.

Many church planters are now considering this more simple approach to church planting. They are seeking to live out their Christian lives while engaging their neighbors with the truths of the gospel. Less program, budget, and building; more life, community, and gospel. If Barna is right, significant numbers of American believers are already engaged in the movement and many more will be in the coming decades.

However, there are some challenges as well. Simply put, many of those I have seen involved in such alternative faith communities are not there for missional reasons. They are there for emotional ones. They have been hurt, disappointed, or marginalized by the institutional church. And the faith communities they create are more reactionary than biblical. So, when I describe missional/incarnational models and house church models, I will try to describe what a biblical version of each looks like. Of course, that means I risk the wrath of some revolutionaries who want no restrictions, but the boundaries I describe are not my boundaries; they are the scriptural ones.

The Bible is not simply the journey of Jesus. It is also the story of the church he founded. Some wish to separate Jesus and his church. Liberal scholars have simply declared Jesus' reference to the church to be later additions to the text. As evangelicals, we cannot allow such a separation to exist.

For a church to be biblical, whether missional/incarnational, house, or institutional, it must hold to the biblical values of church. The church is not simply a group of people who choose to get together and talk about spiritual things. Talking about spiritual things is good, but it is not church. In Scripture, Jesus spoke of the church as a body; and regardless of size and location, that body of Christ has certain characteristics.

Part of the challenge is confusion about the fact that two and three can gather in his name, and Jesus is there (Matt. 18:20). The presence of Christ does not necessarily mean that a local church exists in that context. A church, as described in Scripture, has certain elements that make it a *church*.

The increased interest in new expressions of church is a sign that evangelicals are open to new missional approaches. This is good news. However, as with any new emphasis (or in this case a reemphasis of New Testament practice), evangelicals do not merely need to search the Scriptures for permission to function in the manner described. We also need guidance in how to implement the practice—taking into account the full biblical teaching on the matter.

Yet we also must guard against the false requirements of cultural Christianity. Keller and Thompson explain, "We must distinguish between those Biblical absolutes for church structure and form which God has laid down for the church at all time[s] and those vast areas of church function and practice where we are free to shape ourselves in order to reach our communities for Christ."[5]

Their popular book *The Shaping of Things to Come* explains that our Christology (understanding of Jesus) shapes our missiology (our understanding of mission) and creates our ecclesiology (how we function as church). They advocate that planters not start with the mission, vision, and values of your church—which is exactly where most church planters start, the authors contend. To get an authentic expression of church in each culture and among each unique people grouping, we must first live out the answers to the first two questions, and "church" will form on the back end—not be the driver and shaper of things on the front end. Their explanations leave the realm of church planting open to new, alternative forms of church expressions that can't even be imagined until we are in the midst of them.

Although that sounds persuasive and there is much that is helpful in the book, it is not complete; it underemphasizes the role of Scripture in our understanding of all Christology/Missiology/Ecclesiology. I believe a better way to represent the intersection of Christology, ecclesiology, and missiology is as follows. First, we have to recognize that all of these flow and must be based on Scripture, and Scripture has much to say on each topic. For us to think we can make up new paradigms without consulting the Scripture would be odd indeed.

There are some obvious teachings about who Christ is and about the mission that he gives us. Both of these are most clearly birthed from the Scriptures. However, ecclesiology and ministry are not simply a result of missional thinking. The Bible has much to say (and mandate) about church and ministry. Missiology impacts how these things are done, but the Bible requires that certain things should be done.

What things does the Bible require for church? What scriptural evidences are necessary for a church genuinely to be church? There are many, but a few of those should include:

A Covenant Community. For a church to be a church, it has to consider itself a church body; and that includes the understanding that some are a part and some are not. This does not mean that people cannot be in community with the church, but the community of church is one that holds one another accountable for godliness and growth, and sometimes people are "removed" (see Matt. 18 and 1 Cor. 5:9ff). The church has a covenant and expectations in the community, whether it meets in a house or in a cathedral.

Meeting. As odd as it seems to have to say this, churches *meet.* Churches are not just gatherings on the Internet or occasional meetings at a coffee shop. Though a church can meet in a coffee shop, it needs to meet; and the New Testament church did that weekly, normally on the Lord's Day. Christians can and do gather at other places and other times, but they do not always gather as a church.

Biblical Leadership. The Bible spends too much time describing leaders called "pastor/elders" and "deacons" not to have them as a normal part of the life of a New Testament church. Paul spent too much time appointing such leaders to consider them unnecessary. A church can still exist where there are no delegated leaders, but New Testament churches work toward the normal offices of church leadership, whether they have employed staff or volunteer leaders living in a missional/incarnational setting. They are not required to be paid, schooled, or titled, but the Bible records their appointment and functions, and we will be remiss to ignore that delegated leaders are a part of New Testament churches.

The Ordinances. Again, the Scripture teaches and history shows that the early church placed great import in the participation in the ordinances of Lord's Supper and baptism. These are not quaint relics of a forgone era; they are commanded celebrations ("do this in remembrance; make disciples… baptizing them…") given by Christ to remind us of his death and resurrection. And, the Bible gives information about when and how to partake in such celebrations.

Preaching. Preaching is not a thing of the modern era to be thrown out as irrelevant to today's world. Certainly the idea of a suit-wearing, leather-Bible-carrying, wood-pulpit-pounding preacher is not what happened in the New Testament days. But there was an expectation in the New Testament church that the word would be preached—and two thousand years later that word needs to be preached, even when that means a soft-spoken man sharing in his living room to a house church. The form is not commanded, but the function of preaching is.

So, clearly ecclesiology is not a blank slate to draw out of the cultural situation. The Bible tells us that certain things need to exist for a biblical church to exist. Certainly, *how* we do some of those things is determined by the context, but *that* we do them is determined by the Scriptures.

The following diagram that I call "The Missional Matrix" may help explain the interaction of Christology, missiology, and ecclesiology.

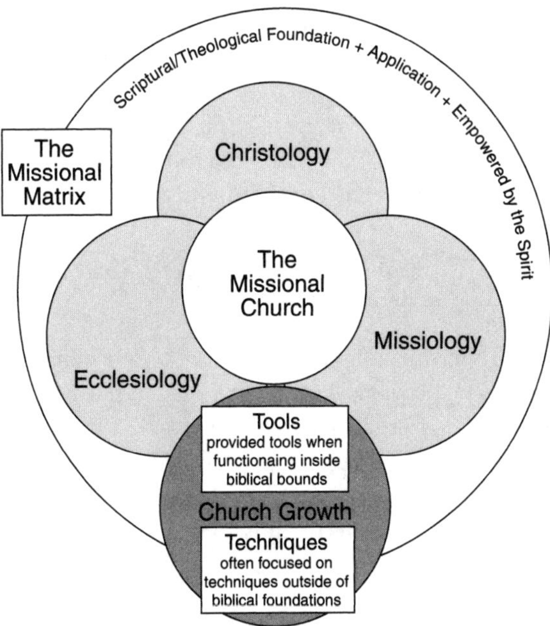

Bob Roberts, pastor of Northwood Church and founder of GlocalNet, was recently looking for a staff member to lead his church-planting efforts. He told me something that stuck in my mind. He wanted someone who "loved it all"—house, mega, emerging, purpose-driven, and whatever other biblical expression was out there. When we "love it all" then the issue is not a slavish adherence to a model but a biblical application of the life and teaching of Christ (Christology), lived out in a certain cultural context (missiology), with a New Testament church (ecclesiology).

A better approach is to wrestle through who God has called you to reach. Instead of coming with a model-specific vision, such as, "I want to plant a megachurch" or "I want to plant a house church," we need to come with a scriptural understanding of Christ/mission/church. Planters need to abandon a model-specific vision and bring the gospel into a context asking the question, "What cultural containers—church, worship style, small group ministry—will be most effective in this context?" That is a missional-appropriate strategy.

Montreal urban missiologist Glenn Smith proposes three fundamental questions to be asked when developing a praxis for urban mission. He says to address three issues, and they are appropriate in every context:

- Strategic—Where is the church in the midst of all this diversity and complexity?
- Missiological—What relevant church-planting strategies need to take place? How do we listen to the Word of God while at the same time we are confronted with missiological concerns?
- Theological—What will the church look like in all this diversity/complexity? How does the church pursue the reign of God with incarnation as its strategy?[6]

When taking such an approach, more and more planters and churches will move to less institutional forms of church. Why? Because these less institutional forms of church are becoming more effective as the institutional church is losing its appeal. It is not the church that is losing its grasp; it is the culture-specific model of the modern church. In the next two chapters, we will examine the missional/incarnational and the relation-based (house) church.

Resources for Further Reading

Barna, George. *Revolution*. Tyndale House, 2005.

Lewis, Robert, and Wayne Cordeiro, with Warren Bird. *Culture Shift: Transforming Your Church from the Inside Out*. J-B Leadership Network Series. Jossey Bass, 2005.

McNeal, Reggie. *The Present Future: Six Tough Questions for the Church*. Jossey-Bass, 2003.

Miller, Donald. *Blue Like Jazz*. Thomas Nelson, 2003.

Chapter 13

Missional/Incarnational Churches

As I speak to church planters, I hear more and more of them embracing church planting as a way of life rather than a strategy. They are asking, "Who is Jesus? What has he called us to do—our mission on earth—and how do we follow him and his example?" Then, through relationship and minstry, church is emerging. Rather than starting with a prescribed vision of what the church will look like (most good church planters spell this out in a vision prospectus or fund-raising proposal), proponents of this new way of planting churches let their incarnation of Christ drive the mission in their community and beyond; and the church emerges out of that journey.

Church planters who are adopting this way of life may see themselves as church planters and pastors, or they may view themselves as something totally different and refer to themselves as such. They may be business owners or work part-time or full-time in the marketplace—on purpose, not just as a way to get the church started so they can enter full-time vocational minstry. They pray and move intentionally as God moves to see people come to Christ in their various contexts—work, neighborhood, social circles, etc. They aim for new faith communities to spring up naturally, birthed out of relationship. The Gospel of Mark explains: "Again Jesus said: God's kingdom is like what happens when a farmer scatters seed in a field. The farmer sleeps at night and is up and around during the day. Yet the seeds keep sprouting and growing, and he doesn't understand how. It is the ground that makes the seeds sprout and grow into plants that produce grain. Then when harvest season comes and the grain is ripe, the farmer cuts it with a sickle" (Mark 4:26–29 CEV).

They take Jesus' commands to go into the world and make disciples, and his admonitions for his followers who are "in the world," as marching orders to "plant seeds" of prayer, love, kindness, good deeds, and witness in all of the circles where God allows them to roam free: home, work, neighborhood, social circles, kid's school, and sports teams, etc. Rather than moving into those contexts with a goal of "attracting" nonbelievers to a church service, these spiritual entrepreneurs see their job as living out the first question in those contexts: Who is Jesus? (incarnational). "The missional church is *incarnational,* not attractional, in its ecclesiology. By incarnational we mean it does not create sanctified spaces into which unbelievers must come to encounter the gospel. Rather, the missional church disassembles itself and seeps into the cracks and crevices of a society in order to be Christ to those who don't yet know him."[1]

They desire to show the love and care of Jesus Christ in those contexts and *be* Jesus there—"come see Jesus" ministry rather than "come to a church service" attraction (missional). As they live out the mission they have been given in those circles—Jesus' mandate to love God, love your neighbor, love one another, love the least, etc.—they look for the opportunity to harvest and gather communities as God moves.

For church planters who fall into this camp—with proponents such as Frost and Hirsch, and hinted at by Steve Sjogren with his servant evangelism approach—life and ministry seem to be much more spiritual than strategic, more about prayer than planning, and more spontaneous than organized. If you ask them for their long-term goals and strategies, they may have some, or they may not have a crystal clear idea where God will take things; they are trying to follow that closely. But they are firmly planted in their cities, striving to live how Jesus has told them to live there, sowing seeds faithfully in the places God puts them and praying and waiting for the harvest.

The term that some have used is "missional/incarnational." My intent is not to say that other models are not missional or incarnational, but this is the primary focus of this approach. Thus, the movement defines itself by the mission and incarnation of Christ.

The 411 NYC is such a faith community. Planted in the heart of Manhattan, The 411 has not been a typical church plant from its first day. With a deep desire to become influencers of the entertainment, information, financial, and cultural centers of the world, pastor Scott Rourk led his team to do something extremely rare in the church-planting world: pray and serve—with no strings attached. Scott's church has even made the *New York Times* because of its radical approach to service. For eighteen months they did nothing but pray and serve in the community and did it very strategically.

Rourk and his team mapped out a three-hundred-block section of Manhattan; broke it down into three, one hundred-block zones, twenty-five-block areas, and five-block sections. They then invited volunteer teams from churches and other church plants all around the country to come to the city and talk to people they met to find out real needs there and to pray. I remember talking to Scott about his grid and wondering if he could fill them all, but he continues to do so.

As the volunteer teams interviewed residents of the city, and prayer-walked three to five hours a day while equipped with digital cameras, volunteers were able to map the areas and pass on to The 411 team:

1. How do we pray for these people?
2. Where are the spiritual strongholds?
3. Where are the points of light where God is already moving?
4. What relevant, real service is needed?

Scott explained, "This was a tool for us to analyze the area, join God in where He was already working and lay the foundation with prayer. That is where we wanted to start. Some people who were supporting us pushed us to start something a lot sooner and wondered when they were going to get some results. But I just kept telling them, 'We're not going to battle in a place like this without praying.' And that's what we did."

To that intentional prayer base The 411 team added intentional service in the community. It started simply, with water and granola bars or hot Krispy Kreme doughnuts and Starbucks in sub-zero weather as busy New Yorkers were hustling to work early in the morning. The group's service expanded from handing out bubbles to kids in the park to weeding the now-famous Daffodil Hill where the Red Cross brought bodies after the 9/11 terrorist attacks.

The 411 team even scrubbed rubber mats where kids played in a neglected park and cleaned bathrooms that were too nasty to open before. The group's black T-shirts, which have the appearance of "stage crew" apparel among the area's artist community, got to be so well-known that New Yorkers started asking where The 411 group was serving that day, what they were giving away, or if someone would pray for them. "We wanted to redefine what church is for people in New York City," Rourk said. "We wanted to establish ourselves as a faith community that gives back instead of taking away." So for eighteen months, The 411 NYC prayed and served intentionally before even thinking about launching an official Sunday morning worship service.

Logos in Atlanta is another such missional/incarnational community. Church planter Danny Presten, on staff at the six-thousand-member First Baptist Church of Atlanta for six years, sensed God was leading him to plant a church in downtown Atlanta among its various subcultures.

Presten's initial idea was to rent a storefront property, put together in his words a "cool worship band and cool speaker" (himself), and "people would come. They just weren't going to church because it wasn't cool enough—I thought," Presten said. Presten found out by talking to people in the area that downtown residents weren't interested in going to any church and weren't really all that interested in Christianity, either. They had heard it all before and might have even given the cool versions of church a try. "We figured out that all the attractional stuff might draw transfer Christians and eventually their Christian friends because it was a little cooler than their church. But that's not why we came here. We're here to reach lost people."

So Presten shifted his strategy to renting a storefront and staging different events every night that would attract the different subcultures—skateboarding competitions for the skaters, poetry readings and concerts for the artists, etc. Presten's place would be where the various subcultures of people wanted to hang out and a church would eventually result. That, too, ended up to be flawed thinking, according to Presten. "We started looking for storefront property and realized all those things were already going on around us," he said. "There was already a skating place where they had competitions all the time. There already were three concert venues on one block. Did we really need a fourth that was owned by a Christian? It finally hit us that we needed to get involved in those cultures that were already going. Instead of owning our own place and trying to get people to come there, we needed to go to those venues already in place and be Christ there." Incarnational and missional—even though Presten really hadn't heard those words and wouldn't have called it that at the time. "We just saw it as the church going out and living like missionaries," he said.

Living and doing church planting that way also would require that team members become legitimate "insiders" in those subcultures and love people in Jesus' name there. So Presten took his Suzuki 650 and got a job at a motorcycle shop. In two weeks of working at the shop, Presten built deeper relationships with people than six or seven months of "outsider" ministry had produced. He now is becoming an expert and the go-to guy at the largest weekly gathering of motorcyclists in the country. Another team member, a musician, is penetrating the musical performance community and works in a music store. Another team member has gone to law school at nearby Macon, Georgia, and is building relationships and praying for a faith community to emerge there. The goal is for each faith community that starts in an "insider" context to spawn one church every year. "We may be a church of one thousand some day, but they won't all be in the same place," Presten said. "We see them being one hundred churches of ten each led by a lay leader and everyone in the group seeing themselves as missionaries who are coming together to encourage one another, worship God, and go back to the fields."

The 411 and Logos are illustrations of this emerging missional/incarnational approach to church planting. They don't define themselves simply as gatherings on Sunday morning. They do gather for worship, an important function for biblical churches as discussed in the last chapter, but these churches define themselves much more by how many people they serve and how "members" live out their faith in their particular circles all week long. It is not a "come and see" approach, but rather is a "go and tell."

Missional/Incarnational are two sides of the same coin, reflecting Christian community that moves both outward (missional) and deeper (incarnational) into culture. Those within an M/I church movement view themselves as "sent ones" (apostolic). The central focus of the community is the shared, common mission. Evangelism and mission are synonymous in that both occur regularly across cultural barriers even within the same city. (For example, my current hometown area, Atlanta, is such a multicultural melting pot.) Success is measured in multiplication of churches and quality of disciples.

In contrast, for the past several centuries (over a millennium), the Western church has been operating primarily in an Evangelistic/Attractional mode reflective in the "church growth" movement and the Constantinian model ("Constantinian" referring to the church becoming the state religion of the Roman Empire under Emperor Constantine). This worked for the most part, but in this post-everything culture, it is not nearly as effective. In the county I live in, 70 percent of the population is completely unchurched, meaning they have little to no connection or interest in Christianity. We have already reached most of the people who are open to the "come and see" approach. Therefore, the E/A church (the majority of all churches) is effectively reaching only 30 percent of my local neighborhood, and I live in Georgia!

The Evangelistic/Attractional church is "extractional" by nature, meaning converts are brought out of their cultures and assimilated into a new culture (Christian/church). Evangelism occurs within the same/similar cultural context; hence, homogeneous church demographics. Whereas, mission occurs outside the culture. Therefore, the E/A church does not regularly reach across cultural barriers unless they are engaged in "mission" (often "mission" is programmed as sending missionaries, going on short-term mission trips, etc.). Success in the E/A church is measured in numbers of church members, baptisms, program attendance, etc.

But as Barna's statistics bear out and Frost and Hirsch state so powerfully for the local church and church planting as we look to the future: "It is absolutely vital for the gospel to be incarnated into thousands of subcultures that now exist in our complex, postmodern, tribalized, Western contexts. It is vital that these multiform people and subcultures encounter Jesus within their own cultures and from within their own communities, for only there can they completely comprehend him."[2]

As stated earlier, these stirrings are relatively new, and the water is just beginning to simmer. But even groups such as Church Resource Ministries—the Colorado-based ministry famous for spawning Bob Logan and the standard-setting "Church Planter's Tool Kit"—have scrapped attractional church-plant training and have shifted to a missional/incarnational approach (www.missio.us). With training modules that include ZerOrientation (a one-day missional reorientation), Zer0 Church plant training (3–4 day seminar), and MCI (a consulting process for implementing change strategies), Zer0 emphasizes "developing spiritual leaders who faithfully pursue Christ in their community and their culture with unwavering grace. We teach habits of living out faith and inviting in sojourners. This process involves transformation for the entire community, leaders and sojourners alike," according to the group's Web site.

CRM chose the name Zer0 for its new focus when team members considered "the great need for equipping teams and leaders to reach the vast number of people completely disconnected from North American church subcultures. We needed a term that described looking at the harvest with fresh eyes. Zer0 implies starting at the beginning, as if on the threshold of a door that has just swung open." The group's site continues, "A Missional Approach is specifically designed for contexts where people think they've heard the gospel, but have yet to experience the Life. When paradigms of life and reality change, so must the forms of church and most importantly the type of leaders required to move this new church forward. Missio seeks to help move churches from 'a place where adherents go,' to a 'community of apprentices where every member participates.'"

Hugh Halter, a former Seattle church planter who heads up CRM's Zer0 focus and is leading a missional community in Denver, said the new direction in thinking and practice began with smashing the assumptions that have driven modern-day attractional church planting. Halter said research into churches that had been started during the "Toolkit" days showed that many churches were planted, and many of them grew substantially, but 98 percent of the growth was still transfer growth. "The biggest assumption we had to get rid of is: If we build it, they will come to us, if we just do it well enough," Halter said. "We had to start assuming they are not going to come. The only ones that are going to be drawn to our programs are Christians, for the most part, and conversion is not based on just trying to figure Jesus out."

As Halter and his teammates have "engaged culture" in Denver—step 1 of the missional process—those cultures have begun to form communities where "saints and sojourners come together." Non-Christians are "joining in the journey" in a natural, relational, life-on-life way. "As we started engaging the culture, we had an entire Starbucks in our home on a Saturday night," Halter said. The third stage, according to Zer0 principles, is to multiply and structure those communities into a missional congregation—something the Denver group is beginning to experience as eighty gather in smaller communities and are beginning to gather in a larger group setting.

Halter said another distinctive of the missional/incarnational community is just that—the emphasis on community. It's no longer enough to be a strong personal evangelist, a lone crusader who continually brings new sheep into the fold. "We start with an inspirational person, but very quickly it must be about an inspirational community," Halter said. "I'm not enough anymore, and the community we're all part of is becoming the primary apologetic. The baseline for us is we're trying to learn how to become a community where the saints go deeper with God and one another, and we want sojourners along on the journey."

Changes Are Here but Still Coming

A church-planting changing of the guard is no doubt taking place. The seeds are too numerous in various pockets of the country, and the rumblings—from George Barna to CRM to new communities forming in cities around the U.S.—are loud enough that it can no longer be ignored. It's too early to predict the scope of this shift and determine its measurement on the church-planting Richter scale. As one church planter said, "We're not sure how much fruit we will see from what God is leading us to do right now. But we see ourselves laying the foundation for future generations. It may not even be my daughter's generation but maybe her daughter's that will witness a widespread church-planting movement where all Christians see themselves as a missionary and starts churches in the places God puts them."

There are still more shifts that need to come. Right now, much of the missional/incarnational emphasis is practiced internationally. There is little in the preceding paragraphs that would be surprising to the missionary resident among the Dinka of Sudan. However, the support system for such missionaries in North America does not now exist (nor will it likely exist anytime soon).

For church planters who desire to engage in this kind of ministry, common sense and mission strategy dictate that these models be intentionally nonpaid from the beginning. It is unwise and counterproductive to begin as a full-time church planter when your model, by definition, will be slow and organic in its growth. Missional/incarnational church planters do not need a prospectus, strategy plan, and time line; they need a job in the marketplace.

When I coordinated the North American seminary church-planting program for my denomination, we sent out church planters—many of them funded. In the last year I ran the program (2003), we sent out 122 church planters. Most of those who planted using standard models with funding support did well. Most of those who planted relation-based churches without funding did well. However, those who wanted to plant relation-based churches while receiving funding did not; their funding ran out too soon, and people in the context wondered who was paying the salary in the first place.

Missional/incarnational models are gaining in prominence because many planters have grown weary of the long lists of processes, systems, and programs and want something simpler and more biblical. That is a good thing. However, the weariness of systems is not reason enough to plant a church. As the church grows, that anti-establishment approach breaks down. Soon, the Hellenistic widows start complaining about being overlooked, and systems need to be born (Acts 6); the people start grumbling that they are not having their needs met (Exod. 18); and some who are in the community refuse to live godly lives, and lines need to be drawn (1 Cor. 5:9ff).

Len Sweet and I recently discussed models, and he shared his impression that "as soon as it becomes successful, it is then illegitimate" because it requires organization and systems. If this approach to church planting leads to missiology and Christology but not a solid ecclesiology, it will be incomplete and not the full expression of biblical church.

Yet, if this approach leads to thousands of committed believers not entering vocational ministry, but instead entering the marketplace to plant churches in homes, businesses, community centers, etc., that is good news.

Resources for Further Reading

Campbell, Jonathan, Jennifer Campbell, and Brian D. McLaren. *The Way of Jesus: A Journey of Freedom for Pilgrims and Wanderers*. John Wiley and Sons, 2005.

Frost, Michael, and Alan Hirsch. *The Shaping of Things to Come: Innovation and Mission for the 21st-Century Church*. Hendrickson Publishers, 2003.

Gibbs, Eddie, and Ryan Bloger. *Emerging Churches: Creating Christian Community in Postmodern Cultures*. Baker Academic, 2005.

Minatrea, Milfred. *Shaped by God's Heart: The Passion and Practices of Missional Churches*. Jossey Bass, 2003.

Chapter 14

Koinos Churches

The term "Koinos Church" is birthed out of a frustration. There is a need to describe this phenomenon often called "house church," but people in this movement do not like being identified by a "house." They point out that these churches do not just meet in a house, they also meet in a restaurant, business, or other settings. What defines these churches is not location, but emphasis. (The dislike of the "house church" term is not the case in the whole movement, as house2house.com is a good example.)

Still other Koinos churches have coined terms that describe their particular movements. It is not my desire to desribe a certain kind of house church, so I am intentionally not using those terms. However I do want to accurately describe what this movement does. Thus, I am using the term "Koinos Church."

Koinos churches are churches that function completely by face-to-face relationship. If everyone can not be "in common," the church is no longer a Koinos Church. Frank Viola explains,

> First, everyone in the church knows one another. And quite well. We spend time together outside of religious meetings. There is a fraternity of sorts among us. We are like family in many ways… [E]veryone is free to lead a song or request a

> song… [T]he ministry comes from anyone who wishes to share… [A]nyone can ask a question or add an insight when someone else is sharing. This happens quite frequently and it is spontaneous and very edifying… [W]e realize that all of us are responsible to care for one another (we are the church). We make decisions together as a Body. We plan our meetings, our activities, and we decide how to handle our problems. We decide how to use the money we give… [W]e exhort one another in our meetings… My spiritual growth is dependent on an entire Body of believers who minister the Lord to me every week… We fellowship throughout the week, and we mutually encourage each other.[1]

The term "koinos" is used infrequently in Scripture, but we see it in Acts 2:44 where the believers had "all things in common." Koinos churches are churches that, at their core, have committed to have face-to-face relationships in such a way that they truly live life together. This requires a commitment to community beyond larger churches in that they will always intenionally stay small so that people cannot be a part of the church without being truly connected in biblical community. Thus, I will use the term "koinos" but will also use the term "house church" when appropriate.

Up until recently, the concept of Koinos church in North America was relegated to the back burner in the church world. This continues to be the method God uses in most parts of the world to rapidly expand his kingdom (China is a great example, with estimates of more than fifty million "underground" Christians meeting in house churches). But house-church proponents in the U.S. have often been painted as "disgruntled" Christians who are pulling out of established churches, or as groups that quickly become in-grown. Koinos churches have been an intriguing, though limited, experiment among Christians in the West—with little succes in the past for sustaining a movement of this simple strategy. But the phenomenon seems to be picking up some steam, and even caught the attention of the *New York Times* several years ago: "A growing number of Christians across the country are choosing a do-it-yourself worship experience in what they call a "house church." Although numbers for such an intentionally decentralized religious phenomenon are hard to pin down, as many as 1,600 groups in all 50 states are listed on house church Web sites."[2]

That number is growing, with rapid multiplication beginning to occur in such pockets as the Authentic Faith Communities popping up at the

University of Texas and other college campuses and increasing interest in a koinos church as a viable alternative for committed Christians—on purpose, not by default or because people are angry with the institutional church.

Each Labor Day weekend, at the annual House Church Conference in Colorado, house church leaders gather for planning and strategy. A meeting that started in Tony Dale's home several years ago with 120 house church leaders from around the country, the 2005 Labor Day conference drew more than four hundred people—with over one hundred network leaders at a preconference briefing—and has featured such speakers as author John Eldredge (*Wild at Heart; The Sacred Romance*) and leaders from the Barna Group.

Koinos church planting is being noticed and considerd by an increasing number of evangelicals. Global house church trends-watcher Wolfgang Simpson of Germany estimates there are five thousand house churches in North America. Barna researcher Thom Black stated at the Labor Day gathering that their best estimate is that one million people are invovled in house churches in North America.

Koinos Churches by Choice

Throughout history, Christians have tended to meet in larger and larger groups under more highly trained leaders when they have the freedom and ability to do so. When government restricts the use of large buildings, the church thrives in homes, as it has in China. When church buildings are out of the question because of economic factors, the church can thrive by meeting under trees in a village. But when it has been possible to gather in larger groups, Christians have historically done so.

For many years, some Christians have promoted the Koinos church as a viable alternative for the Christian church. One book written in 1972 explained, "It was after this first year as a congregation that some of us discovered, to our surprise, that groups elsewhere called themselves House Churches. Through our reading we were discovering, too, that the House Church had appeared in the early life of the church. The importance of its historical roots and its contemporary emergence slowly dawned upon us."[3]

Some are calling for the "third reformation" that will restore the New Testament church structure:

> In rediscovering the gospel of salvation by faith and grace alone, Luther started to reform the Church through a reformation of theology. In the 18th century through movements like the Moravians there was a recovery of a new intimacy with God, which led to a reformation of spirituality, the Second Reformation. Now God is touching the wineskins themselves, initiating a Third Reformation, a reformation of structure.[4]

There is a genuine feeling that this expression of church will lead to a great move of the Holy Spirit: "A new wind is stirring in the land! A mere zephyr, but we expect it to become a hurricane which will alter the landscape of Christendom. The wind is the Spirit, who in our time is again doing new things. He is bringing renewal and transformation to the individual and corporate lives of His people, His church."[5]

Many people have advocated that the church abandon its buildings and embrace the relational nature of the Koinos church, but before now this has not caught on in the North American church world. Koinos church adherents may consider it a failure of the church, but Christians and the unchurched generally have not chosen to worship in small house churches. Although, there are signs that may be changing.

Barna's comments in the previous chapter may back up the claim many have expressed for years that this expression of church structure will be prominent in the future. Observers of church growth have heard this claim during the Jesus Movement of the 1960s, the charismatic movement of the 1980s, and the Koinos church networks of the 1990s. None provided a long-term viable model of church structure. When their visionary leaders passed, they dissolved or reverted to more common models.

However, the culture shift into postmodernity may have the escape velocity that the other movements lacked. This remains to be seen. There have been a few models but no great successes. Yet we cannot deny that the potential for Koinos churches is great in a culture that values intimate relationships, shared leadership, transparency, and teamwork. And there are new signs—along with Barna's assertions—that house churches could be a significant part in the wave of the kingdom future in North America.

I personally long for this model to become the norm, but I have not made the step into the movement. Why? As a missiologist, part of my role is to ask if certain models are being effective in culture. Right now, Koinos models have not been able to break through into the cutlure of lostness as a few more common models have. I pray that Christians might gather in missional Koinos communities, practicing solid New Testament church structure, and reaching out to their neighbors. I have seen a few such examples. This encourages me that more are possible.

What Is a Koinos Church?

A significant amount of literature on Koinos churches has emerged. Since the newest emphasis on the house church started in the late 1990s, much of the literature is available on the Internet. I have assembled some of this information at www.newchurches.com/house. I will not attempt to duplicate these materials here; you can find them at the Web site. Instead, I will focus on what Koinos churches may look like in our emerging cultural context.

A basic understanding of the difference between Koinos church and home cells might be helpful. A home cell is a part of a larger church and supports the ministry of that church. Most churches planted in the last few years have had a large celebration service for worship accompanied by meeting in homes for small group care.

The Koinos church is different in that it doesn't see itself as part of a larger body—it is a church. The Koinos church performs all of the functions of the church—baptism, Lord's Supper, study, giving, etc. It is a church.

Koinos churches do not start in a home with the hopes of moving to a larger rented or permanent facility "when it grows up." The home is their permanent facility. The church is a church in a home.

I recently trained church planters in Romania. Their church-planting strategy involved building a "mission house" or a "house church" where the missionary church planter would live. The missionary would reach out to the people of the village and invite members to meet with him in his home—which included an extended living room with benches. As the church grew, it would then build its own building.

The same pattern is very common in North American church planting today. The vast majority of new churches start as churches meeting in a home. But they do not stay there. Eventually they move to a larger facility.

The Koinos church is different. Fundamental to its design is the idea that it will remain a Koinos church. As it grows, it will multiply into other homes, businesses, coffee shops, etc.—not enlarge.

Understanding Chuches that Meet in Houses

Most readers have had some contact with house churches—either by personal experience or by reputation. It is difficult to define the house church because it has so many expressions. Frank Viola wrote an article that described the streams of the house church movement.

> Stream 1. Those influenced by Gene Edwards. This stream is often referred to as the "radical wing" of the House Church movement. These groups tend to be anti-formalist to the extent that they claim no leadership, no order, no structure, no organization, and other traditional elements.
>
> Stream 2. Those influenced by Watchman Nee and/or Stephen Kaung. These groups are typically centered around Christ, his eternal purpose, and the Scriptures. Most follow the teaching (some loosely, others strictly) outlined in Watchman Nee's *The Normal Christian Church Life*. Deeper life themes are often stressed in these groups.
>
> Stream 3. Those influenced by T. Austin-Sparks. These groups tend to be virtually identical to the above but are inclined to stress the heavenly and spiritual nature of the church more than the practical and earthly side.
>
> Stream 4. Those influenced by Witness Lee (Living Stream Ministry). This camp is ardent in its belief that Lee now has the "Divine baton" and is the vessel that God is presently using to recover his purpose and the truth about "the local church." These groups were more militant in the 1970s (often "taking over" other weaker home fellowships) than they are now; yet many still regard them as exclusive and divisive.
>
> Stream 5. Those who are fundamentalist in their orientation. This strand of House Church tends to rigidly stress a specific pattern for meeting, regarding it as the pattern to follow. Most hold to Reformation theology right down the line and/or party-line fundamentalist themes.
>
> Stream 6. Those who are neo-evangelical (or post-evangelical) in their orientation. These House Churches tend to color their interpretation of Scripture with modern biblical scholarship and

often contribute fresh insights to old questions. They are highly relational.

Stream 7. Those associated with Word-faith teaching. Although few in number, these House Churches (as well as a network directed by C. Alan Martin) are built around the prosperity-faith teachings of Kenneth Hagin, Kenneth Copeland, Fred Price, Charles Capps, and similar personalities.

Stream 8. Those influenced by the Sonship teachings of the Latter Rain. Sam Fife and/or George Warnock are often regarded as the fathers of this camp. Many of these groups meet in intentional communities, are self-sufficient, and often act as refuges for people who need extreme help and can't make it in the streets. They are Pentecostal in nature, adventist in outlook, and place a heavy emphasis on the preparation of God's end-time remnant for the time when the "sons of God are manifested."

Stream 9. Those who circle their lives around the 3 H's (home church, home school, and home birth). Many are influenced by the teachings of Bill Gothard and believe that God wants virtually all Christians to raise large families that are home schooled. According to some, these groups have often become their own subculture, wholly disconnecting themselves from the larger culture (including Christian) and from anything that is conventional. Some House Churches of this ilk have a penchant for keeping the Jewish customs.

Stream 10. A few groups are characterized by a sovereign leading of God's Spirit to meet according to New Testament principles. This stream has little or no human influence (consequently, folks who swim here have probably never heard of any of the above streams.)

Stream 11. The eclectic types. These folks swim in two or more of the above streams.[6]

There are committed believers meeting across North America (and the world), worshipping in biblically balanced and theologically faithful Koinos churches. Unfortunately, many people lump all Koinos churches in the same category. This is an unfair stereotype. This is why I am attempting to avoid this stereotype by using the term "koinos" instead of "house" church.

At the same time, if a Koinos church is genuinely a *church*, then it should function as one. As mentioned earlier, the Bible teaches that churches have pastor/elders and other leaders. Biblical churches covenant with one another. These churches participate in the Lord's Supper and baptism. All the characteristics of a New Testament church need to be present in a Koinos church for it to be a biblical church. (For more information, see "Church" in *Perimeters of Light: Biblical Boundaries for the Emerging Church* by Ed Stetzer and Elmer Towns.) One of the weaknesses of the Koinos church movement is the lack of some of the scriptural foundations of church.

In the New Testament, "the word 'church' was applied to a group of believers at any level, ranging from a very small group meeting in a private home all the way to the group of all true believers in the universal church."[7] Many biblical passages refer to local house churches and they clearly are churches (1 Thess. 1:1, the church of the Thessalonians; Rev 2:1, church at Ephesus, etc.).

However, part of the challenge is that many enthusiastic Koinos church proponents have neglected some of the ecclesiology described in Scripture by de-emphasizing New Testament patterns of leadership, misunderstanding the role of covenant and related church discipline, and failure to practice the biblically prescribed ordinances. The North American Mission Board partnered with Stan Norman to develop (and then formally adopt) a guiding ecclesiology to help assure that *churches* are being planted, whether they meet in a home or a brick building.

(See http://www.churchplantingvillage.net/v3_pages/7Steps_Partners/EcclesiologicalGuidelines.pdf for this document.)

The biggest challenge to Koinos church planting may not be the few well-meaning groups that have minimalized ecclesiological principles. In most cases, these are errors of enthusiasm rather than doctrine. Instead, the greater problem for the biblical house church is the millions of believers who consider their brick, institutionalized, non-multiplying church to be a more biblical model than the fifteen people meeting in a home with a passion to reproduce and multiply.

Luther expressed it five centuries ago (in his preface to the German Mass and Order of Service): "Those who want to be Christians in earnest and who profess the gospel with hand and mouth should sign their names and meet alone in a house somewhere to pray, to read, to baptize, to receive the sacrament, and to do other Christian work."[8] Something so biblical should be an encouragement to us all.

How Does It Work?

How does the Koinos church work? There is no one answer. Some people say the house church should "keep it simple—no corporation, no name, no statement of faith, no property, no titles, no salaries, etc.—just believers gathering simply, in His Name."[9] Others say such churches need some of these things. But they all agree on one thing—Koinos churches do not need a building. It is fundamental to the new Koinos church that it meets in a nonfacility. As it grows in size, it multiplies into other houses—but not to a church building.

The house is a perfect place for such a Koinos church to meet. The culture has begun to build houses as sacred places. Ceilings are named for cathedrals. Stained glass is common in many houses. While people seek for their houses to look and feel like churches, what better use is there than to actually place a Koinos church inside such a house.

A relational church stays relational by staying small. Koinos churches usually multiply into smaller groups before reaching thirty people. It makes sense that emerging generations, with strong interest in authentic relationships, would be attracted to churches that are built upon relationships and not highly organized systems.

Charles Brock, well-known church planter and trainer, explained: "Many years have passed since I wrote *The Principles and Practice of Indigenous Church Planting*. In that book I said there are four absolute essentials in church planting: the Seed, Spirit, Sower, and Soil. Today I am more convinced than ever that these are the four essentials which are indispensable. Caution must be observed when adding anything beyond these four essentials. Anything additional may be detrimental to healthy church planting."[10]

Brock goes on to explain, "We must answer clearly what a church is before we can think of objectives and strategies. . . . I believe a perverted and tarnished view of what a church is constitutes one of the greatest hurdles faced by church planters."[11]

These things became confused over time. Soon people began to "go to" church instead of being the church. Church began to be recognized as a place instead of a way of life. This struggle was most pronounced on mission fields of the nineteenth century. Missionaries struggled to determine what made a church a church. Roland Allen sought to teach that what was needed was only what the Bible required: "[believers] were members one of another in virtue of their baptism. Each was united to every other Christian everywhere, by the closest of spiritual ties, communion in the one Spirit. Each was united to all by common rites, participation in the same sacraments. Each was united to all by common dangers and common hopes."[12] It was simple, it was biblical, and it did not require a building or a budget.

Floyd Tidsworth lists several items that a church should possess before it constitutes as an autonomous church. In *Life Cycle of a New Congregation*, he asks, "Does the mission have enough members to do basic work without help from the outside? Do the members have enough money to carry the financial responsibility of the congregation? Is the mission mature and stable in its biblical beliefs?"[13] All of these can be answered yes in many Koinos churches, but they would not possess the typical outward signs of church structure.

Koinos churches often exist in networks. They are not solitary groups of Christians, but they are related to other churches in a given region. These churches may meet together for fellowship with other Koinos churches, but this is usually not done weekly and it is not seen as "real church." Real church takes place every time the church meets.

What Next?

My attraction to the house church springs from its simplicity and faith. I have been a part of larger and larger church starts. Each involved more and more money. In my heart, I often feel that church planting should be simpler. I like this definition of a church: "A New Testament church of the Lord Jesus Christ is . . . an autonomous local congregation of baptized believers, associated by covenant in the faith and fellowship of the gospel; observing the two ordinances of Christ, governed by His laws, exercising the gifts, rights, and privileges invested in them by His Word, and seeking to extend the gospel to the ends of the earth."[14]

Others may prefer this older definition of the church: "Unto this catholic visible Church, Christ hath given the ministry, oracles, and ordinances of God, for the gathering and perfecting of the saints, in this life, to the end of the world: and doth, by His own presence and Spirit, according to His promise, make them effectual thereunto."[15]

A New Testament church exists when its people function as a church and see themselves as a church. A Koinos church of ten is a church if it functions as a church and sees itself as a church.

If you want to plant a house church, you can use some of the principles in this book. Many of the patterns in this book would be applicable in the Koinos church setting. Some would not be as appropriate, particularly issues related to the "large launch" and facilities.

Several excellent resources are available at www.newchurches.com/house. These include *Houses that Change the World* by Wolfgang Simpson and *Planting House Churches in Networks* by Dick Scoggins.

Resources for Further Reading

Allen, Donald R. *Barefoot in the Church.* Richmond: John Knox, 1972.

Banks, Robert. *Paul's Idea of Community: The Early House Churches in Their Historical Setting.* Grand Rapids: Eerdmans, 1980.

Banks, Robert J., and Julia Banks. *The Church Comes Home.* Peabody, Mass.: Hendrickson Publishers, Inc., 1998.

Barrett, Lois. *Building the House Church.* Scottsdale, Pa.: Herald Press. 1986.

Birkey, Del. *The House Church—A Model for Renewing the Church.* Scottsdale, Pa.: Herald Press, 1988.

Bunch, David T., Harvey J. Kneisel, and Barbara L. Oden. *Multihousing Congregations: How to Start and Grow Christian Congregations in Multihousing Communities.* Atlanta: Smith Publishing, 1991.

Felicity, Dale. *Getting Started: A Practical Guide to House Church Planting.* Austin, Tx.: House2House Ministries, 2002.

Hadaway, C. Kirk, Francis M. DuBose, and Stuart A. Wright. *Home Cell Groups and House Churches.* Nashville: Broadman Press, 1987.

Kreider, Larry, and C. Peter Wagner. *House Church Networks: A Church for a New Generation.* Austin, Tx: House to House Press, 2002.

Simpson, Wolfgang. *Houses That Change the World.* Authentic Media, 2001.

Scoggins, Dick. *Planting House Churches in Networks: A Manual from the Perspective of a Church Planting Team.* A downloadable manual produced in 2001 and accessed via http:www.dickscoggins.com/pdfs/church_plantin_manual.pdf

Towns, Elmer L., and Ed Stetzer, *Perimeters of Light: Biblical Boundaries for the Emerging Churches.* Chicago: Moody Press, 2004.

Viola, Frank. *Rethinking the Wineskin: The Practice of the New Testament Church*, 3rd ed. Gainesville, Fla.: Present Testimony Ministry, 2001.

http://www.homechurch.com.

http://www.housechurch.ca.

http://www.home-church.org.

http://www.fcpt.org.

http://www.house2house.tv.

Chapter 15

Evangelism in Church Planting

Does it seem odd to include a chapter about evangelism in a book on church planting? It's ironic that recent technological developments in church planting—direct mail, Web pages, etc.—have undercut evangelism as the foundation for birthing new churches. At the same time, many Christians think that evangelism is passé and out-of-date in today's world. (Ironically, "Starbucks evangelists" are all over the Web using the word *evangelist* and proclaiming the good news of their "salvation.") Yet in the church, evangelism has such a bad reputation that my friend John Avant writes a column, "Making Evangelism Good News Again." Church plants need to take evangelism seriously because there is good news to tell.

Developing a plan is a crucial issue. It may surprise you that starting a church without evangelistic effort is actually possible. In fact, it's easier to start a church by drawing Christians from other churches than to win new disciples from the community. Developing a strategy to reach people takes effort and creativity. Remember, the gospel remains the same, but methods change from culture to culture. This chapter addresses the need for a culturally appropriate evangelistic strategy and how new churches can reach people in culture.

Intentionality

Authentic church planting—planting a church that reaches unbelievers—requires what we might call "the soil of lostness."

First, the church planter must be intentional about developing an evangelism strategy, figuring out how to reach the lost instead of just rearranging church members in a given community. Without intentionality, evangelism remains undone. Intentionality causes the planter to plan for personal evangelism and leads to the creation of a strategy characterized by a high level of commitment to reach the unchurched. Staff members at many new churches hold one another accountable for building relationships with the unchurched.

Second, intentionality means having a system of organizing evangelistic contacts. Many computer programs provide tracking software for prospects that can be useful. We use a Web-based system from Church Community Builder so our team can have common access from any computer. Or a simple index card system may suffice. The idea of keeping a prospect list may seem contrived to many today, but it's essential if you are going to be intentional and reach beyond immediate relational connections. (See chapter 13 for those who would prefer only a relational approach.) When using an organized system, people are never just names on a card. You must show concern for those you're seeking to reach and that you care enough to remember them and stay in contact.

Third, intentionality means developing a plan. The planter's first goal should be to design an evangelistic plan that might include training lay ministers to share their testimonies, sharing the simple plan of salvation as the worship hour begins, or including it in the order of worship. Every service should include instructions on how to turn to Christ, but the plan does not require a weekly ten-minute evangelistic sermon.

Rock Springs Church of Smyrna, Tennessee (www.rockspringschurch.com) explains that their strategy, borrowed from North Point Community Church in Alpharetta, Georgia (www.northpoint.org) is to "invest and invite." They encourage the church family to invest in the lives of their unbelieving friends by spending time together, serving and encouraging them. After laying this foundation of genuine involvement, caring and love, the church members are encouraged to invite their unbelieving friends to church. Pastor Chris Brewer explains, "We partner with our people. If they'll invest their lives in the unchurched and then bring them to church, we'll have activities to help lead them to Christ."[1]

Evangelism as a Process and Event

Authentic evangelism is progressive, not just a one-time event. As Andy Stanley, North Point Community Church, puts it: "Nobody goes from atheism to faith during a sermon. . . . Salvation is not a process, but coming to faith is."[2] Each step to faith in Christ is part of a journey and not a destination. There's a point where each person must have his or her name written in "the Lamb's book of life" (Rev. 21:27). Conversion is an event, but evangelism is helping people on a journey to conversion and then on to maturity.

Imagine a missionary who's traveled the globe to a tribe that's never heard the gospel, never seen a Bible, or never heard the name of Jesus. Imagine that the missionary preaches immediately upon arrival, "All you need to do is repent of your sins, believe the Bible, and ask Jesus into your heart." Only blank stares would follow. The church planter can't assume that people understand who Jesus is or what sin has done to their lives, even in North America. This is especially true in the emerging culture with the proliferation of material on spirituality and with all the different beliefs in circulation. The end result is that many people are often confused. They may have borrowed ideas and beliefs from several worldviews and philosophies in a smorgasbord approach. It's naïve to think that people who are that spiritually open but fragmented will hear the gospel once and fall on their knees to confess Christ.

The Engel Scale

One tool for measuring spiritual awareness is the Engel Scale. This linear scale[3] resembles a number line depicting a series of steps from complete unawareness and ignorance of the gospel to a maturing commitment to Christ.

The Engel Scale classifies awareness in a range of steps from -8 to +3, as follows:

-8: Awareness of a supreme being but no effective knowledge of the gospel
-7: Initial awareness of the gospel
-6: Awareness of the fundamentals of the gospel
-5: Grasp of implications of the gospel

-4: Positive attitude toward the gospel
-3: Counting the cost
-2: Decision to act
-1: Repentance and faith in Christ

REGENERATION

+1: Postdecision evaluation
+2: Incorporation into the body
+3: A lifetime of growth in Christ—discipleship and service

Negative 1, repentance and faith in Christ, is the crucial step, but not necessarily an isolated event. Reaching this point demands a process. God can make repentance and faith in Christ an instantaneous event, but it's usually a process that leads to this event. In fact, Engel erroneously places repentance before regeneration. Theologians have historically held that regeneration precedes (and enables) repentance.

Following conversion or regeneration, the new believer begins to evaluate the decision, is incorporated into a fellowship of believers, and becomes a person who actively shares the gospel. The church planter's task is to partner with God in order to move people toward understanding the gospel, toward the point of repentance and faith in Christ. The effective evangelist-planter will learn to recognize that people are at different stages on this scale when they attend worship services or when friendship develops.

In this partnership process the planter may meet a person who seems to stand at minus 6. The wise Christian will not rush into the reasons the Bible says we need Christ. Such an approach assumes that person believes in the authority of Scripture and its personal application to his or her life. A better approach might be to share biblical passages that can help the non-Christian understand more about Christianity and to show the person what faith looks like by living it out in front of them over time. Before a person can make an intelligent choice for the gospel, he or she must know what the gospel means. Jesus encouraged men and women to "count the cost."

Again, we must recognize that people are at different stages in their spiritual development. For instance, one young woman in a former pastorate came to my church and was crying by the end of worship. Speaking with me later, she said, "I know I need to receive Christ into my heart because I'm separated from him." She stood at the point of conversion. All

I had to do was offer her assistance in taking the step of faith. On the other hand, when I served in a Chinese church, I encountered many people who had no awareness of Christianity. I began evangelizing them by teaching the existence of God as displayed in the Scriptures and displaying Christ in my life and our relationships.

Culture has changed in North America. In the twenty-first century, we live in a post-Christian culture in which many people are farther back on the Engel Scale than their parents were.

The Gray Matrix

The Engel Scale has two problems. It tends to be linear when most people are not. It also doesn't take into account that people can misunderstand or reject parts of the truth. The Gray Matrix[4] is a modification of the Engel Scale that may help people better understand the evangelism process:

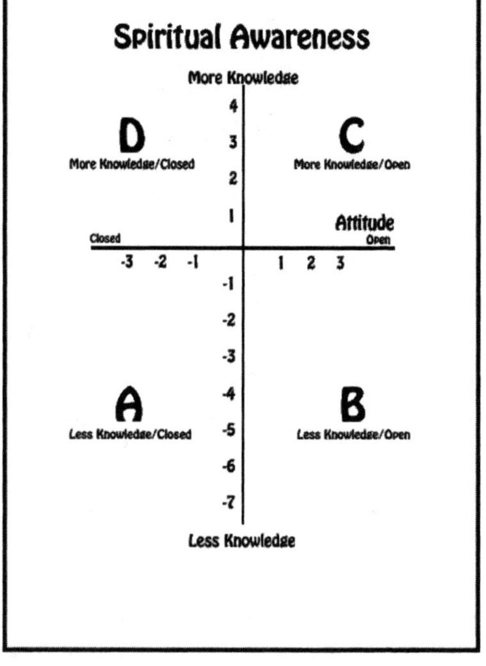

- Anything which moves people from left to right across the scale is "evangelistic." This might include acts of service and friendship, mom and baby clubs, medical and development work—many things which are not apparently "preaching." Yet, in fact, the word Jesus used when he told us to "preach the gospel" has a much wider meaning than speech. It refers to communication.
- If we can understand roughly where a single person or target group of people is situated on the scale, we can choose an appropriate approach to reach them.

- If people are near the bottom of the scale, we must not use Christian language and ideas which will mean nothing to them. We must assess our message through their eyes, not ours. It may also be inappropriate to give a heavy preach-for-a-decision message at this point.

- Pressures of society and culture, and the strategies of Satan, will tend to pull people down toward the bottom left hand of the scale. God's purpose is to draw people to the top right hand side by his Spirit, through the witness of his people.[5]

An Alternative Evangelism Process in an Emerging Culture

Evangelism is more than a scale, and it's not complete with the matrix. I believe that evangelism is a journey involving stages or steps. Thus, Engel is right. But Gray is also right because evangelism is more than a neat linear process. I suggest a new idea—the Stetzer Evangelism Journey, a combination and revision of the ideas of Engel and Gray with some additional clarification of the journey taken from Darrell Guder's *The Missional Church.*[6]

There are two conversions—one temporal and one eternal. The first conversion is the conversion to community. With few exceptions people come to Christ after they've journeyed with other Christians, examining them and considering their claims. They can come into community at any point. Thus, the funnel-shaped lines (representing community) stretch all the way to the top of the diagram. At any point a person can decide to begin a spiritual journey toward Christ.

Pastor Mark Driscoll expresses this move toward community-based evangelism this way: "As long as Christians fail to repent of self-righteousness, we will continue to speak of evangelism in terms such as outreach, which implies we will not embrace lost people but will keep them at least an arm's length away."[7] Instead, it should be understood that "the transformed lives of people in the church are both the greatest argument for, and the greatest explanation of, the gospel. Therefore, it welcomes non-Christians into the church, not so much through evangelistic programs as through informal relationships like Jesus developed with his first disciples... (this evangelism) considers it vital that lost people be brought close enough to witness the natural and practical outworking of the gospel in peoples' lives." [8] That is why a conversion to community matters.

In the diagram, the circle represents the church. Church and Christian community must not be the same thing. Unbelievers can and should be invited into the community, but they cannot be part of the church. A church is a body of believers (more on that later). A person becomes part of the church with the second and eternal conversion, the conversion to Christ.

Each curved arrow is representative of evangelism. For example, a person who has rejected God and is living in rebellion can be challenged to live a different kind of life by a committed believer. In this context lost people can decide to consider the validity of a just God in conversation with Christian friends. They may begin to believe that God is real and may then consider the claims of Christ. At some point they begin to consider these things in community with believers.

The journey is not intended to be the same for each people group, worldview, or culture. The central line remains the same; it's the universal journey of evangelistic discovery. For each culture the misperceptions and reasons for rejection are different. The only thing that's constant is the center column. The sides depend on the people involved. For example, among Muslims the chart might look like this:

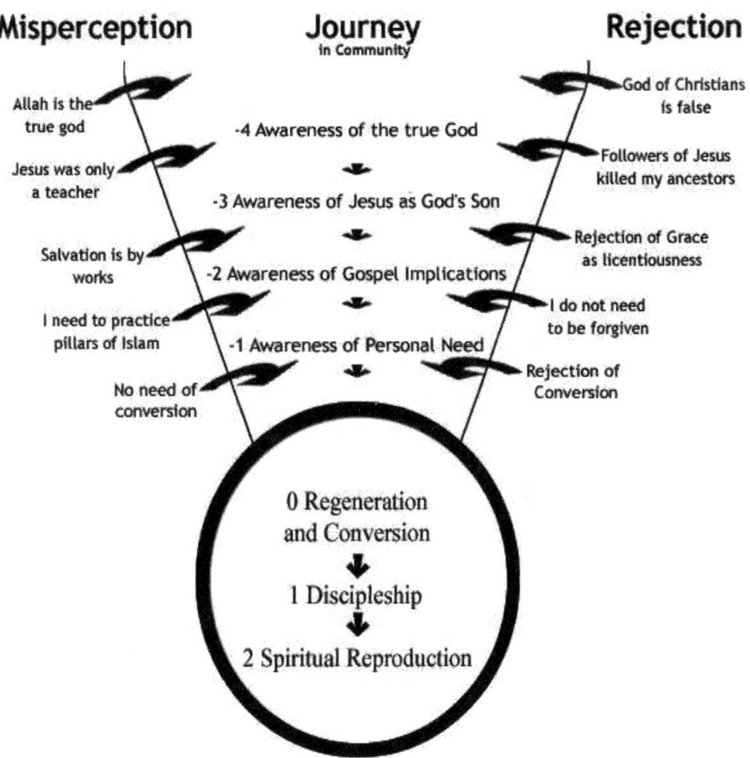

The same process can be seen in the postmodern world. Of course, in a postmodern community in the predominately ex-Catholic Northeast, the journey will look different from the eco-pagan Northwest or multicultural Canada. Here's an example of a postmodern evangelism journey in New York City's lower East Side.

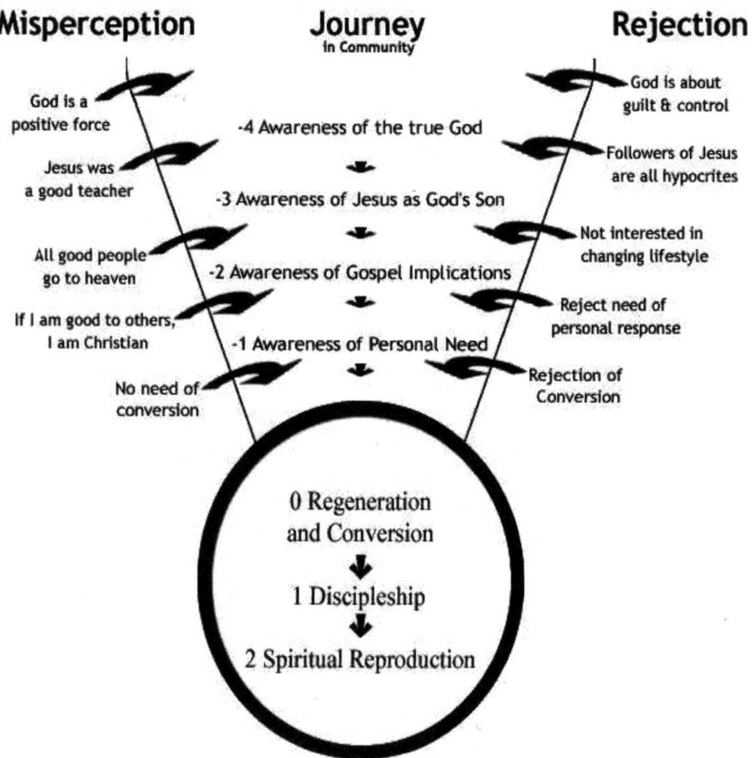

Every planter should consider making a diagram of their people group's worldview. In this way, when sharing about faith, the church planter will know the needs of those being reached. When sharing Christ with

Muslims, we need to explain that grace isn't an excuse to indulge the flesh even though they watch television from "Christian America" and see that very thing. Postmodern people in New York may see no need for grace. Their concern is not licentiousness but need; in their mind they're already good enough.

As mentioned earlier in the book, culturally appropriate evangelism answers the actual questions that are being asked by the culture rather than those that the church believes the target culture should ask. "But in your hearts set apart Christ as Lord. Always be prepared to give an answer to everyone who asks you to give the reason for the hope that you have. But do this with gentleness and respect" (1 Pet. 3:15). The process is:

- Understand the issues in the worldview.
- Address those issues (misperceptions or rejections) with redemptive witnessing opportunities based on where the listener is.
- Encourage the listener to consider the truth claims of Christ.
- Invite the listener to journey with the faith community as they live out the truth claims (invite "conversion to community").
- Invite the listener to make a faith commitment (invite "conversion to Christ").

Losing Evangelistic Focus

I've asserted that it's possible to plant a church without evangelistic emphasis; but even when churches begin with a heart for evangelism, they may later lose that focus. This tragedy occurs because two typical problems arise—large-group panic and vision hijacking.

Large-Group Panic

This challenge arises when significant numbers of unchurched people come to Christ quickly. The new church can feel overwhelmed, and some people may think that even the church needs a break from evangelism.

When I planted and pastored Millcreek Community Church, one committed believer approached me about slowing down our outreach in order to disciple the large number of new believers. I responded with a request that he take on the discipling ministry as his primary concern while others continued with the outreach emphasis. The plan worked. I saw him at the church's ten-year anniversary last month, and he is helping new believers grow toward maturity.

If the church planter is not intentional in evangelism, the planter—and very soon, the new church—will lose its evangelistic zeal. A reduced evangelistic focus foreshadows the long-term loss of evangelistic zeal. Missional churches need to model Christian community and to invite others to join the journey of faith while practicing intentional evangelism.

Vision Hijacking

The second problem that often kills new church evangelism and zeal is "vision hijacking." In nearly every new church, a portion of the core group makes the attempt to redirect—to hijack—the original vision shared by the church planter and the core group (more about this later).

The stress and difficulty involved in reaching the unchurched often prompt attempts to hijack. These attempts often involve the loss of evangelistic passion. Reaching other believers is much easier than doing evangelism. The offerings of believers are greater, their children behave a bit more calmly in worship, and they have skills for leading church programs. The fact is that tension exists whenever a church planter or planting team reaches lost people. The planter must be prepared to deal with this tension.

Use Sound Evangelistic Methods

Following are sound evangelistic methods that can be used in all church planting efforts.

Meeting and Engaging Unchurched People. It's essential to build relationships with the unchurched, not just so they can be "prospects" but because we genuinely care about the people. Not only is this the right thing to do; it's also practical: unbelievers usually have good antennae for insincerity. This can be a difficult task for many of us; as we are so far removed from the culture of the unchurched, there is a fear to get close. Be careful not to accept every unchurched action to be one you must engage in, but we do need intentionally to visit places and involve ourselves within communities outside of our church communities. We can only gain a grip on how to engage their culture by invading it.

Relationship Building. Intentional relationship building often begins with community leaders. Planters often meet leaders by becoming team or club chaplains, by becoming involved in a community organization, or by personally contacting the mayor and other government leaders.

When church planters intentionally build relationships, people begin to know who they are and why they're there. Some may even come to the new church. Intentional relationship building with community leaders adds credibility to your church.

Howard McNamara, church planter in Princeton, New Jersey, serves as a good example. He signed up for a ten-week course entitled "Start Your Own Business" at the local rotary club. Each week three prominent business leaders made presentations. Each week they all concluded their presentation with, "If there is anything we can do, give us a call." Howard was able to meet thirty business owners, a few of whom became prospects for his church.

Marketplace Farming. This is the process of consistently making contacts with friends or neighbors, building relationships leading to an opportunity to share Christ. Church planters should know their neighbors. Planters can't afford to spend all their time with church people and must become acquainted with unchurched people who live nearby. Marketplace farming is also an intentional process.

When moving to a new area, move your bank account into that community, purchase your gasoline and meals and groceries from local businesses, and become acquainted with the clerks and servers by name. Our culture continues to move toward nonpersonal service; whether it be self-checkout lines at the grocery store or pay-at-the-pump gas stations. Becoming intentional, however, means oftentimes not taking advantage of all of the convenient services in an attempt to build relationships.

Marketplace farming guides the planter into an intentional routine. I bought my gas at the same establishment for three years, no matter what the prices at their pumps. That's the price I paid to build marketplace relationships. Our culture relentlessly leads us toward isolation. We can order goods and all our books over the Internet. We no longer have to meet real people to purchase the items we want. Such options are not open to church planters. We must be intentional about meeting people.

My copastor, Travis Vaughn, has a tremendous ability to build relationships in the marketplace. In less than nine months, because of his networking, our church has a weekly coffeehouse at a local coffee shop (with an owner he led to Christ), a marriage café meeting weekly with his neighbors, and an early Friday morning Bible study at the local office of an international business firm.

Prospect Cards. Bob Logan developed "marketplace farming" as an intentional process for meeting people on a regular basis. According to Logan, the planter must meet people six times before a relationship can be established.[9] Prospect cards are one way to keep up with these contacts. Following each visit or telephone conversation, the planter should record the time and nature of the visit.

Your first prospects could be people in transition or under tension, maybe families who relocated into your area. As a planter, you can order the names and addresses of newcomers to your city from many different companies.[10] We used a full-service company, Reaching America (www.reachingamerica.com), a service that allows you to choose which area to focus on. You prepick the style card you prefer and your message, and the service will address and mail them for multiple contacts, then bill you for a reasonable fee. Other options include contacting newly married couples and new parents. A simple card of congratulations on a marriage or on the birth of a child is an excellent way to contact prospects. The planter can provide an even more direct and positive witness by adding a reminder on the importance of spiritual things.

Existing Relationships. Ministering through relationships is paramount. Your church people already have a circle of friends. In one pastorate, I challenged the church family to reach their own "seeker seven," seven people they were praying would come to Christ. (The Billy Graham Evangelistic Association's Operation Andrew, now called Friend to Friend, provides a simple format to teach intentional friendship evangelism.)

Every person knew seven people who would be particularly open to a gospel witness. After the believers wrote their prayer lists, we helped those members work toward inviting the important family members and acquaintances on their lists to a Friend Day event.

Three-Minute Rule. Preparing the congregation for guests is essential, including the "three-minute rule." The concept is simple: Members talk only to guests during the first three minutes following a worship service.

Our human inclination is to fellowship with people we know, communicating an unfriendliness we don't intend. Evangelistically speaking, attention spent on one another would be better spent on guests for the first three minutes after the service.

Every-Sunday Registration. The use of a churchwide registration every Sunday is an excellent way to track guests without causing them to feel uncomfortable. This process, usually completed at the end of the worship hour, often uses a registration clipboard that attendees complete and pass toward the end of the aisle.

Welcome Cards. For anonymity and more candid communication of personal needs, cards may be a better option. Everyone in attendance (not just visitors) completes a card at the end of worship. Regular attendees need to complete only their name and any prayer requests. They should wait until the very end of the service to complete the card, along with guests and visitors, so guests won't feel self-conscious or "spotlighted." I have put several examples at www.newchurches.com.

Guest Follow-up. The next step is obvious: follow up quickly by making a personal contact with guests. Although anonymity is clearly a value for many guests, they give you permission to contact them if they've communicated their name, address, and phone number. Even the unchurched know that submitting a card will prompt contacts from the church.

The first contact should be made immediately by a layperson over the phone. Initial contact could also be made by a personal visit if the person has given his or her address. This contact should be made first by a layperson. One study revealed that "clergy" follow-up reduced the effectiveness by one-half (compared to laypersons doing the same).

"No other single factor makes a greater difference . . . than an immediate visit to the home of first-time worshippers. . . . When lay persons make fifteen-minute visits to the homes of first-time worship visitors within thirty-six hours, 85 percent of them return the following week. Make this home visit within seventy-two hours, and 60 percent of them return. Make it seven days later, and 15 percent will return. The pastor making this call, rather than lay persons, cuts each result in half."[11]

Although I prefer a phone call to a house visit, the key is involvement of laypeople in guest follow-up.

Door-to-Door Contacts through Mission Teams. Most people don't like door-to-door surveys even though they're good and time-tested methods. In spite of people's misgivings and even my personal dislike (although I've planted several churches), I understand that door-to-door visitation is part of the overall prospect development process. One of the best ways to address this challenge is to get someone else to make door-to-door contacts with you or for you. Prepared and trained mission teams are excellent resources for this task, including those from other churches and areas. Here are some guidelines:

1. **Communicate goals.** When contacting the team, make sure each person understands the purpose of door-to-door survey: starting a relationship.

2. **Agree on tasks ahead of time.** Many mission teams want to perform activities irrelevant to church planting. For the sake of outreach needs and congregational protection, the planter should insist on a simple rule: no mission team may serve the field unless they agree to at least twelve hours of contact work during their visit (typically less than a week for out-of-town teams).

3. **Prepare for the team.** Prepare precise maps of the area to be surveyed, including drop-off locations. Plan to send the team into at least four distinct areas. Give them enough houses to contact so they don't waste time doing nothing. Most teams can survey twenty houses per hour. Drop off the teams, give them time to work, and return to pick them up at an appointed time.

4. **Train the team to do outreach.** A mission team can be an invaluable resource if they know what to do. Underused teams get frustrated.

The church planter must be prepared and organized for their arrival because they have the potential to lead to "the best of times" or "the worst of times." Using mission teams is productive and satisfying, if the planter prepares for and trains the team, and if the team has agreed to the church planter's goals and agenda for their visit. If there are no teams available, the church planter must do door-to-door alone.

Conclusion

The church planter must become intentionally evangelistic. This commitment includes developing a pool of unchurched people to reach. Evangelizing lost persons does not happen by accident. The mature church planter will not expect unchurched people to show up for services just because a new church has arrived.

The planter should use every available means to contact and invite unchurched and lost persons. Mission teams, door-to-door visitation, prospect listing, telemarketing, and follow-up are good tools for evangelism. But a church planter's most effective resources for evangelism and eventually for developing a core group are commitment, hard work, and Spirit-led prayer.

Resources for Further Reading

Burke, John. *No Perfect People Allowed: Creating a Come as You Are Culture in Your Church*. Grand Rapids: Zondervan, 2005.

Hunter, George. *Radical Outreach: Recovery of Apostolic Minisry and Evangelism*. Nashville: Abingdon, 2004.

Long, Jimmy. *Generating Hope: A Strategy for Reaching the Postmodern Generation*. Downers Grove, Ill.: InterVarsity Press, 1997.

McRaney, Will. *The Art of Personal Evangelism*. Nashville: Broadman & Holman, 2003.

Webber, Robert. *Ancient-Future Evangelism: Making Your Church a Faith-Forming Community*. Grand Rapids: Baker, 2003.

White, James Emery. *Rethinking the Church: A Challenge to Creative Redesign in an Age of Transition*. Grand Rapids: Baker Books, 1997.

http://www.namb.net/root/evangelism/thenet/default.asp.

Chapter 16

Developing a Launch Team

The most difficult phase comes early, when the church planter is attempting to attract a launch team. At this stage the planter can offer no relationships, no meeting place, no programs, and no music. People have difficulty committing themselves to a dream they can't see. Recruiting a launch team is challenging but essential. It's when the planter lays a foundation for the birth of the new church.

In the first edition of this book, this chapter was called "Developing a Core Group." The terminology has begun to change because most church planters do not have their launch team intact one year after they start having public worship. Thus, if it is a "core team" and then the "core" leaves, it can demoralize the church. Instead, if people are on a "launch team," they can leave afterward without it seeming to be a betrayal. They helped it launch and then moved on to other things—no negativity implied.

Developing a launch team is the first step—the prenatal stage if you will. The prenatal stage of new church development is similar to the prenatal stage of human development. An unborn child must develop different biological systems to enable it to function effectively after birth, and they must be in place when birth takes place for proper development to continue. Same for a new church. Key systems must operate, or the church may not succeed after it's born.

Earlier we looked at five indispensable systems with corresponding leaders which must function at the time of a congregational launch, according to Bob Logan.[1]

1. Assimilation process
2. Evangelism network
3. Program to mobilize spiritual gifts
4. Children's ministry team
5. Worship team and a plan for early worship services.

The heart of the church start is the launch team that ultimately helps birth the new church and provides the ministry muscle for these systems. These ministries will not exist without core member volunteers.

Launch Size

Today most planters wait longer to begin public worship. For launch teams, Malphurs explains that bigger is better.[2] The group's size should be determined, for the most part, by the kind of church being planted. Churches starting with large (launch) first services should have one person in the launch team for every ten people they hope to attract to the first service (core to crowd ratio of 1 to 10).

Finding Launch Members

The process of gathering a launch team is not an easy task. With the right training, almost anyone can plan the launch, mail appropriate advertising, and prepare for people to come on the launch day. But molding an effective launch team is another story. There are several ways to find such people committed to start a new church with you.

Members of the Mother Church. One possible source for launch team members is a sponsoring church which can appeal for volunteer families (sometimes called "extension members"). Bob Roberts, pastor of Northwood Church and founder of GlocalNet, has started ninety churches out of his church (and many more in partnership with GlocalNet). Their local church is directly mothering ten new churches each year. In several cases, he has sent out members to start these new churches. Bob explained: "When we sponsor a daughter church, each church is different. Generally for a new plant, sending out three to eight families from our church is the most. We sometimes send staff as well. We don't recruit this much because we have found that core groups from established churches can slow a plant down. A planter will start a small group and multiply it while an intern at Northwood. If they can't do that, they can't plant a church. I give them 100 percent fishing license with those people."[3]

This presents both positives and negatives. A strong positive is that the planter has a launch team almost overnight, and the length of start-up time decreases considerably. The church can begin services while developing one-on-one relationships. In addition, the planter usually finds that these volunteer families are solid believers who can assist immediately in the development process.

On the negative side, not all of these people come from churches like Northwood Church! These "experienced" believers may have strong feelings about the form of worship, leadership style, and other matters. Such convictions, if different from the vision of the church planter, can create significant conflicts in the early development of the congregation. These conflicts may quickly put at risk the continuation of financial support from the sponsoring church. I recommend using this recruiting method for launch team development only if the sponsoring congregation is highly similar in philosophy and style to the new church, and the planter and the context of the new start is similar to the context of the sponsoring church.

Developing a SWAT Team. In settings where extension members are unavailable or their use would be unwise, several other means for recruitment are possible. One alternative has been termed a SWAT team, an acronym for Servants, Willing and Temporary. SWAT team members commit themselves to the new church for a short time, usually six months. These volunteers staff the nursery, teach small groups, serve on set-up teams, or fill other roles in the first months following the launch. John Worcester has planted TEAM Church as a SWAT team church. John explained:

> TEAM Church meets on Sunday PM so its members are free on Sunday AM's to go on "mini mission trips" to help the churches we are planting all around the metroplex. It is common for us to send multiple teams of 5–15 workers to help church plants on any given weekend. This involves manning their children's ministry, helping with music, setting up and taking down

> during preview services, grand opening, and several Sundays after their weekly startup. We also send teams out on Saturdays and other times to do listening surveys and conduct block parties. Basically, we seek to take up a "John the Baptist" servant's attitude to pave the way for our church planters success. This strategy has helped us plant four churches a year during our first three years of existence, with a combined "orchard" attendance on Sunday AM of about fourteen hundred. It has given our members a firsthand vision for church planting, ministry and teamwork experience, and a sense of accomplishment.[4]

TEAM Church is obviously unusual. However, many churches will send their people for a short while to help a daughter church. For example, Pentaluma Valley Baptist Church loaned about thirty of its members for a six-month to one-year period to help plant Living Faith Church. They did children's ministry, music, setup. Both are growing successful churches. Despite their initial short-term commitment, some SWAT volunteers often become permanent members of the church when their short-term commitment has ended.

Leadership on Loan. Christians from nearby churches who want to become part of a new church are a third source for core development. However, for the sake of trust and to preserve a reputation of integrity, the planter must ask permission of the pastors of these churches before approaching their members. These people must be genuinely committed to planting the kind of church the planter has envisioned.

Advertise. Another means for recruitment is purchasing Christian radio and television ads. Posting notices in Christian bookstores also may help locate volunteers.

Know the Risks. These common methodologies for recruitment present their own risks. Christians often envision helping birth a "perfect" church. They may anticipate that their involvement will help them realize their vision. Difficulties quickly arise when "borrowed" or volunteer core members' ideas conflict with the planter's vision for the new church.

The planter must ensure that these volunteers understand and agree with his vision. If not, the planter faces the unpleasant task of asking such workers to find another place for involvement. When you choose core members, choose carefully!

Even though it's best to have a launch team, the reality is that their presence doesn't make much of a difference as the church grows. It helps in the beginning, but their impact seems to become less important by the third and fourth years.

Core Development from the Unchurched

Although recruiting core members from outside sources may be helpful, it's better to find non-Christian evangelistic prospects and recruit them for the launch team. One of the best ways to recruit the unchurched is through intentional relationship building. This is done in three ways: strategic contacts, door-to-door surveying, and phone outreach.

Many church planters argue that they prefer to recruit by direct mail and/or personal relationship. But the fact remains that even those prospects may not come without personal contact of some kind. Kevin Sullivan at Highpointe Church[5] in Seattle knocked on fifteen thousand doors to build his launch team. Six months later he launched his new church with five hundred first-time attendees. By going door-to-door, he built a launch team and established goodwill within the community that helped attract people for the launch service. This approach complemented his use of direct mail.

Core Development through Relationships

One of my favorite new churches is Sojourn in Louisville, Kentucky. The church planter is one of my former students, Daniel Montgomery. He decided that he did not want to use any "artificial" forms of relationship building. Instead, he made a point of hanging out in coffee shops, music venues, and festivals in the Highlands area of Old Louisville.

As he built relationships in this artsy bohemian community, he decided he needed an intentional strategy to build prospects from the community. He rented, renovated, and transformed a building into an art gallery before the church ever held public worship. This became a place where he and the launch team built relationships (and gained credibility) with the art community.

Core Development through Outreach Events

There are many ways to build relationships by connecting through intentional outreach events. Church Planting Solutions (www.church-planter.org) is a Web-based coaching tool for church planters. (We use the resource at Lake Ridge Church to help us work through the details of church planting; it is a great help.) They provide a list of outreach ideas to build up the core, including:

- Neighborhood picnics/barbeques
- Sponsoring existing community events (e.g., home-owner association events)
- Backyard VBS
- Car wash
- Drink (water bottles, lemonade, coffee, etc.) giveaways (e.g., to commuters, along bike paths, at ball fields, etc.)
- Face painting or balloon sculpting at other community events
- Food/deserts for local public servants (e.g., police, firemen, EMT, nurses, etc.)
- Hand out smoke detector batteries (door to door)
- Hand out one-cent or two-cent stamps at the post office after postage increases

Core Development by Using the Phone

Although personal visits ultimately follow, several methods can help the church planter jump-start the core development process. When we planted Lake Ridge Church, we started by using TellStart (www.tellstart.com). In just a few days, their equipment made thirty thousand phone calls and we had two hundred people leave their name requesting more information. Of course, we had to screen out the problem people, but today several families are now part of our new church because of the TellStart outreach.

Others have also used a more direct phone-calling campaign to contact core members. Some planters will be bothered by the idea of using the phone. First, be aware that there is nothing illegal when you call people; churches are not covered under any rule that prohibits phone solicitation. You are not soliciting. Second, few people get upset at such calls. Church planting leaders Roger McNamara and Ken Davis explain, "We have found that one out of every thousand phone calls elicits a negative response. If you are honest, upfront, and friendly with people, they will respond positively to your phone call."[6]

Core Development by Using the Core Development Mailer

Another way to jump-start the process of core development is to use a mailer. This piece enables simultaneous contact with large numbers of people that the planter would not normally be able to contact. Keep in mind that mailers just make the initial contact. People are reached most effectively through relationships.

This core development mailer asks for a response different from the prelaunch advertisement. The grand opening mailer is designed to convince the recipient to attend a public gathering. As such, it answers objections, calms fears, and announces the event.

On the other hand, a core development mailer is designed to convince interested, receptive people to respond by completing a postage-paid return address card. Although overall response to business reply cards is low (our experience was less than .5 percent), people who do respond often demonstrate high motivation and interest.[7]

One recommendation for the core mailer is a trifold brochure or letter design. It should include basic information about the church, some biographical information of the planter, and a business reply card to return. The message of such a mailer is simple: it should communicate the start of a great new church and that the leaders of the new church invites the recipient to be part of the new church start. For examples of this, see www.newchurches.com.

The core development mailer doesn't need to be expensive. You can use Operation Epistle, a strategy that involves volunteers hand-addressing and applying first-class postage stamps to the mailers. These volunteers generally come from sponsoring churches around the country. In the end the new church pays only printing costs and the start-up fee to open the QBRM (Qualified Business Reply Mail) account. Established church members are often enthusiastic about participating in mission activities such as this.

Filtering the Prospects

Building a launch team may attract unbelievers, backslidden believers, new believers, and even mature believers. It may also attract people who are disenchanted, hurt, or power hungry—such people may be difficult to assimilate. Knowing this ahead of time will allow the planter to use caution and wisdom in building a launch team from these respondents.

Two weeks after I arrived in Erie, Pennsylvania, a family asked to become part of our new church. During our conversation I learned that their church had recently closed. They tithed regularly, longed to be a part of ministry, and wanted good Bible teaching. Though they sounded great, they were not an appropriate match for the new church. They demonstrated strong convictions about what a church should be, and they seemed unwilling to accept the direction that our new church would take.

Although reasons may vary with every new start, the planter will have to turn away some people who want to be included in the launch team. This becomes easier when the vision statement, mission statement, and core values are in place. These tools help to provide direction and protection for the new church. The launch team should be asked to "sign on" to these values as a prerequisite for becoming a core member.

Conclusion

Core development is hard, labor-intensive work. After telephone and mailing campaigns, the planter faces the difficult task of filtering out persons who will not mesh with the new launch team. But if these efforts net a few dozen appropriate, interested people, then the work should be well under way.

Developing a launch team is indispensable to the long-term life and vitality of the new congregation. Great effort, time, and money should be invested in developing strategies that will help form a solid launch team who will ultimately determine the future of the congregation. Use whatever methods are necessary—visitation, mailings, telemarketing—to achieve this task. Time and money at this stage of the development of a new church will be well spent.

Resources for Further Reading

Long, Jimmy, et al. *Small Group Leaders' Handbook: The Next Generation*. Downers Grove, Ill.: InterVarsity Press, 1995.

McIntosh, Gary, and Glen Martin. *Finding Them, Keeping Them: Effective Strategies for Evangelism and Assimilation in the Local Church*. Nashville: Broadman & Holman Publishers, 1992.

McNamara, Roger N., and Ken Davis, *The Y.B.H. Handbook of Church Planting: A Practical Guide to Church Planting*. Longwood, Fla.: Xulon Press, 2005.

Neighbour, Ralph. *Where Do We Go from Here? A Guide for the Cell Group Church*. Houston, Tex.: Touch Publications, 1990.

Chapter 17

Small Groups

Small-group ministry is essential to the health of any church. Small-group organizations include cell groups, home groups, Sunday school classes, and other gatherings that promote relationships in the family of faith.

Each healthy church with more than fifty in attendance must develop a multiplying network of small groups which may take different forms but accomplish the objective of binding a church together.

George Gallup found that 70 percent of Americans say that the church is not meeting their needs. When asked what these needs were, there were six common responses:

1. To believe life is meaningful and has purpose.
2. To have a sense of community and deeper relationships.
3. To be appreciated and respected.
4. To be listened to and heard.
5. To grow in faith.
6. To receive practical help in developing a mature faith.[1]

These needs can be met in a variety of settings but most effectively in a nurturing small group. This may help explain the rise of small groups in both secular and church settings in modern society.

Cultivative Bible study

The cultivative home group is a Bible study of a different kind. The planter uses this home group to cultivate the unchurched person's relationship with Christ and to develop the new leader's maturity in Christ.

In agriculture, *cultivating* is the continued attention to a planted seed by nurturing, refining, and preparing it to become a well-established, healthy, reproducing crop. In church planting, we cultivate people, beginning when they are seedlings through the time when they accept Christ and grow to become full-grown, healthy believers and individual members of a church family. We would call the farmer foolish who ignored his crop during the four to five months before harvest and yet wonders why he has no crop. Yet, as church planters, we often scramble to attend the latest conferences and study the latest trends, hoping to grow our churches quickly while ignoring opportunities to incorporate people into ongoing cultivative relationships with others.

Acts 2:42–47 describes the activities of the early church:

> They devoted themselves to the apostles' teaching and to the fellowship, to the breaking of bread and to prayer. Everyone was filled with awe, and many wonders and miraculous signs were done by the apostles. All the believers were together and had everything in common. Selling their possessions and goods, they gave to anyone as he had need. Every day they continued to meet together in the temple courts. They broke bread in their homes and ate together with glad and sincere hearts, praising God and enjoying the favor of all the people. And the Lord added to their number daily those who were being saved.

Notice the frequency with which the disciples met in homes. The text says they met in the temple, but Luke was careful to describe the home meetings that took place on a regular basis.

Verse 42 tells us that the disciples "devoted themselves to the apostles' teaching." That teaching-learning process became a central part of their growth in discipleship. The text also points out that fellowship took place. The disciples broke bread, indicating that they took the Lord's Supper together in homes.

These Jerusalem believers also prayed, devoting themselves to prayer. Signs and wonders took place, presumably on a regular basis. God was performing miraculous deeds. These people, who loved God, also loved others and cared for their needs.

Verse 46 indicates that they worshipped together at the temple and met in homes for the Lord's Supper and other matters. Then as now, small-group ministry involved people in worship. Praise and significant numerical growth followed the early church's ministry through home groups ministering in a variety of ways. We should use small groups to achieve all these purposes: worship, prayer, study, and fellowship while meeting for a doable amount of time for busy schedules (about an hour and a half including snacks).

Worship

The small group typically begins with worship. In the past it was difficult for nonmusicians to lead worship. But modern compact discs (CDs), computer midi files, and other tools have largely solved this problem. These resources enable a gathering of five to sound like a chorus.

You can coach your small group leaders by encouraging them to use music they may already know from your church's weekend worship gatherings. Especially during the first few meetings, keep it simple and allow people to join in at their own level of comfort. Leading a small group can be nerveracking for someone the first few times they do it. You can be supportive by walking your leaders and hosts through basic logistics of music selection, having it ready, and setting the tone for this part of the group. And always keep it simple.

I recommend intentionally incorporating upbeat, positive songs into this time. From a practical standpoint the weaker vocalists won't feel as exposed in these songs simply because the notes aren't held out as long. This can also help the facilitator. It's easier to begin speaking to a group of any size when the mood is up, high, and positive rather than somber and reflective. But there's definitely a place for many styles of music in small-group gatherings.

I encourage worship through music in every kind of small group except one: gatherings of fewer than four people. Groups of this size seem uncomfortable with singing, particularly if they aren't used to singing in the presence of others.

Prayer

Prayer generally follows and grows out of worship through music. This time can bind group members and empower their growth. The planter should recognize that small group prayer often becomes a time of high anxiety for people who aren't used to praying. Encourage people to pray at their level of comfort and with the type of words they use every day.

Excellent resources are available on how to pray. Maybe you could start modeling prayer by praying through Scripture. Help people take small steps and give them moments of experience to begin understanding this somewhat intimidating aspect of "talking to God" and what it's all about. Be prepared so that each group will have at least one person who is embarrassed to pray aloud. Make sure not to single anyone out, but do your best to equip them to pray. Even times of individual silent prayer can be extremely powerful because such times allow everyone to share in the prayer time regardless of their fears. Teach them that prayer is an important element of small groups because it is our means of communication with God.

Bible Study

Worship motivates prayer, and prayer prepares the group for Bible study. Cultivative studies are student-focused and Bible-centered, not teacher-dominated. Make sure the study doesn't turn into a lecture, even though a cultivative Bible study assumes little biblical knowledge on the part of the learners.

The best and most effective cultivative studies avoid church language such as "washed in the blood of the Lamb" and other phrases familiar to most long-term church members. A cultivative Bible study should lead learners to conclude that Christ is the answer by magnifying him so that they recognize the gospel in a personal way. Here are some fundamentals for leading a cultivative Bible study.

Make it a discussion, not a lecture. The leader guides the discussion and summarizes regularly. Start by asking easy, icebreaker questions to get the members talking out loud and feeling comfortable early on. Especially for quieter members, speaking up early in the discussion seems to increase their comfort level for opening up during more challenging parts of the study.

Prepare leading questions. These will cause the learner to think, to feel emotions, and to probe a passage for God's hope or expectations. Leading questions enable the learner to draw personal conclusions based on the study content. Avoid yes-no questions or those that are easily answered with one word.

Stay focused. Involve every participant, eliciting comments from each one, but stay focused. The study should not evolve into an opportunity for unknowledgeable group members to share their confusion about certain issues. For example, instead of teaching on the differing views of the end-times, a cultivative Bible study could focus on how to make Christ the center of one's home.

Avoid sidetracks. Some group members will attempt to sidetrack the discussion toward unrelated topics. Sometimes these arise because the student has real questions that need to be answered, but the cultivative study is not the time or place. Sometimes those who lead the group astray are attempting to steal the leadership role from the facilitator or to thwart the Christ-centered purpose of the study. Christians often unwittingly present great difficulties for the unbeliever or new believer by introducing complex subjects such as the fate of those who have never heard the gospel, different views regarding end-times, or charismatic gifts. These matters are important, but the cultivative study is not the time to discuss them.

Here's where your role as coach comes in. After a few weeks many new small-group leaders wish they had double majors in psychology and theology before jumping in with both feet. To combat their feeling overwhelmed, each week give them one or two practical tips on how to keep the discussion on track or how to redirect learners to discover answers to unrelated questions outside the meeting so that everyone present can concentrate on learning more about God and one another. If your small-group leaders feel that you're supporting them and believe in them, over and over again God will amaze you at how he uses them to cultivate a maturing body of believers in your church.

Use the same Bible text and translation. Most unchurched people have no idea where to find Matthew (to say nothing of Habakkuk). Providing students with the same Bible as your Bible allows you to list page numbers and other details in notes you can supply during the study. Another option, especially when finances are tight, is to print text passages for each study from www.crosswalk.com.

Supply a bulleted list of points or principles for each lesson. These should number about three to five truths from the passage which outline the meat of the study. These points may have individual headings (for example: (1) The Need of Humanity; (2) The Provision of God; (3) The Response of Faith). But pay more attention to the wording of questions or comments under each point, making sure they will spur reflection on and conclusions about Jesus Christ.

Formulate questions carefully. Penetrating questions help to ensure a good cultivative Bible study and distinguish it from other types of small-group studies. The best questions don't lead to yes/no answers. In addition, they should not ask "interpretation" questions. Coach your leaders not to make the common mistake of asking the learners: What's your interpretation of this passage? An effective Bible study won't ask unchurched persons to determine what a passage means. Instead, your questions should be worded to assume that the text has a meaning. The task of the study leader is to guide participants in a discussion to unearth the meaning.

Use the power of silence. Silence usually terrifies the new leader. Refuse to be afraid of participant silence. The best questions should provoke enough thought that most students won't be capable of answering—intelligently—at least not immediately. Also, the leader should avoid supplying the answers. If students know the leader will always provide the answers, they'll become dependent on the leader to do the thinking and feel no need to try to give answers themselves.

As students become accustomed to the process of the study, they will feel comfortable in answering questions. Reassure participants and be consistent in helping them believe that wrong answers are acceptable.

Draw conclusions. The closing segment of the cultivative Bible study should be application which is intended to ask "What should the learner do, be, and feel as a result of this study?" From the application, participants should conclude how to allow the Bible text to reshape their lives.

> Visit www.newchurches.com/examples for a template and dozens of cultivated Bible studies written by my students.

Foster leadership. From the earliest stages, encourage your small-group leaders to recruit other group members to lead elements of the Bible study. Even if a group member leads only for seven minutes and asks the first two questions of a study, that's two more than he or she has probably ever asked before. Nowhere is it written that to become a leader you have to take huge steps. As your small-group leaders guide the members to facilitate sections of the group time, each will grow a bit toward leadership because of the discipline of thinking more intentionally about their small but important responsibilities.

Fellowship

The final element of the cultivative Bible study is a time for fellowship. Although the other segments of the study develop spiritual understandings, the fellowship period develops congregational social relationships. Before your new church initiates Sunday worship, the cultivative Bible study may be the congregation's only opportunity to encourage many attendees toward spiritual maturity.

The cultivative Bible study often brings about another vital, though secondary, result. Intended primarily to win lost persons and weave believers into the body, effective groups also identify gifted leaders and train them to lead future groups. The most effective church planters usually delegate Bible study leadership to maturing lay leaders when the time is right. The cultivative study serves as a training ground for discovering and equipping leaders who eventually will direct other cultivative studies or church cell groups.

The Importance of Small Groups

Thirty years ago many church planters started new churches by using small group Bible studies. From that stage the progress followed uniformly and logically: Bible studies became chapels, then missions, and then finally constituted churches. In the new millennium, most new churches no longer emerge through such a neat progression.

Most modern planters develop people in a cultivative Bible study, out of which emerges a core group. During this time the planter trains leaders, and then the church goes public—an event usually called *the launch*. But the launch cannot replace congregational core development. Congregational leaders must be solidly in place at the time of the launch. Some planters have attempted to start churches with a large crowd and without a core group. These rarely succeed because the congregation has no hub at the center of the wheel to bear the weight and carry the load.

The cultivative Bible study serves as the best building block to prepare for congregational and organizational maturity prior to the launch. Despite the effectiveness of direct mail, Internet communication, advertising, and telemarketing, nothing can replace small groups, and specifically the cultivative small group.

Small-Group Ministries

In *Prepare Your Church for the Future*,[2] Carl George establishes a strategy for church growth by dividing a congregation into small groups. He describes this type of fellowship as a "metachurch."[3] He uses this term instead of *megachurch*. According to George, metachurches can be any size.

Though a metachurch uses cell groups, pure cell-based churches differ from metachurches in that a pure cell-based church is a congregation of small groups, not a church with small groups (metachurch). Thus, a cell-based church usually focuses on large-group weekly worship but gathers in homes (or other sites) during the week. Aside from Sunday worship all church life takes place in home cell groups.

A metachurch can take various forms. It may be a pure cell-based congregation, or it may be a Sunday school-based church that offers care and ministry through small groups. It may be an intentionally Bible study-centered gathering in which attendees break into small groups on Sundays or on Wednesday nights. In this case, the church does not typically meet in homes at all.

Exodus 18 provides one of the best examples of small-group ministry found in the Scriptures. In this passage the father-in-law of Moses, Jethro, recommended a means by which to avoid exhaustion because Moses was overworking himself and failing to delegate tasks to others.

> It came about the next day that Moses sat to judge the people, and the people stood about Moses from the morning until the evening. Now when Moses' father-in-law saw all that he was doing for the people, he said, "What is this thing that you are doing for the people? Why do you alone sit as judge and all the people stand about you from morning until evening?" Moses said

> to his father-in-law, "Because the people come to me to inquire of God. When they have a dispute, it comes to me, and I judge between a man and his neighbor and make known the statutes of God and His laws." Moses' father-in-law said to him, "The thing that you are doing is not good. You will surely wear out, both yourself and these people who are with you, for the task is too heavy for you; you cannot do it alone. Now listen to me: I will give you counsel, and God be with you. You be the people's representative before God, and you bring the disputes to God, then teach them the statutes and the laws, and make known to them the way in which they are to walk, and the work they are to do. Furthermore, you shall select out of all the people able men who fear God, men of truth, those who hate dishonest gain; and you shall place these over them, as leaders of thousands, of hundreds, of fifties and of tens. Let them judge the people at all times; and let it be that every major dispute they will bring to you, but every minor dispute they themselves will judge. So it will be easier for you, and they will bear the burden with you. If you do this thing and God so commands you, then you will be able to endure, and all these people also will go to their place in peace" (Exod. 18:13–23, NASB).

A planter-pastor who wants church members to feel satisfied and loved by their church should encourage a strategy in which members receive love from leaders other than the pastor. Planters will never find the time and energy to express sufficient love to meet the congregation's needs.A small group can meet such needs because they can build relationships that make a difference.

A brief study of the Exodus passage above helps us understand the effective contribution of small-group ministry. Jethro's suggestion to Moses outlined an administrative system for Moses to follow. For the church planter the principles are clear. The planter must begin dividing the people into small groups from the beginning of the new church. The people must learn from the outset that the planter is not the sole caregiver in the church.

Christ the King Anglican Church[4] in Monument, Colorado, applied the Jethro administrative system to its church organization. They began by designating a lay leader for every ten families. The lay leader leads the small group in "four components of historical/biblical Christianity: 'They devoted themselves to the apostles' teaching, and to fellowship, to the breaking of bread and to prayer (Acts 2:42).'"[5]

That leader's specific task was to nurture those ten small-group families. An advantage to this approach is that a leader is not asked to oversee a large group. Ten is not too many to feel overwhelmed. Also, the size allows more contact from the leader. Since they only have ten families, they could contact those ten on a weekly basis.

In Carl George's system every small-group leader with ten people also supported an apprentice leader who served as an understudy to the group leader for a period of time. Many expect each small group to multiply itself within a year. The original group would spin off a second small group that the apprentice would oversee. If the group failed to reproduce itself within a year, some churches close the group and fold members into small groups that demonstrate greater success in reproduction. Incorporating the less successful members into more productive groups enables those members to catch a vision for multiplication.

While planting and pastoring, we expected two noteworthy individuals to emerge within every group. Carl George calls the first individual the EGR (Extra Grace Required). It seems that every group attracts at least one particularly needy person who wants to be the center of attention and to have the group obsess on his or her problems at every gathering.

The second noteworthy individual for every small group was the seeker, one who was hungry for true relationship with God—a non-Christian seeking to know Christ. During our small group meetings, we insisted on leaving a vacant chair to represent a seeker. Every week we prayed for that additional person, that God would fill that chair with his chosen one to whom we should minister.

The church planter should decide whether small-group membership should be required of all church members. Regardless of whether participation is required, a recommended goal is having 60 percent of Sunday attendance involved in small groups.

If the congregation decides to use Sunday school units instead of cell groups, it's best not to attempt pastoral care through the Sunday school organization. The reasoning for this recommendation is simple: Sunday school classes often grow beyond a size in which pastoral care remains manageable.

If the church still wants to conduct pastoral care through the Sunday school structure, two recommendations are appropriate. First, classes should be limited to approximately ten people. This size facilitates a healthy mix of comfort with accountability. Second, classes should not spend their entire hour on Bible teaching. Groups must devote a significant period of time to people's needs. Time should be set aside for pastoral concerns, especially since pastoral care will be carried out in the Bible study organization.

No matter what form these small groups take, every healthy church needs a multiplying network of small groups that aid in binding the church together. A church without small groups will often struggle to connect the members of the church with one another.

One of the greatest gifts you can give to yourself, your small-group leaders, and the kingdom of God is good coaching and support as they take on these leadership roles. Remind them regularly that they don't have to know everything to please you or their group, nor do they have to do everything. Encourage them to give every job they can away to someone in the group. Snacks? Delegate. Hosting? Delegate. Phone calls to the group? Delegate. Leading worship and prayer time? Delegate. Will this make your small-group leaders lazy? No, it will make them disciple makers. They will reproduce themselves through others, and more groups will grow from people who have experience serving in different roles. Pour your life into them and encourage them to pour their life into their small group, and you will be amazed to see God at work.

As your church grows, there are several principles to consider. Small-group expert Rick Howerton at Serendipity House shared with me several principles for new churches to consider as they mature and multiply small groups:

- **Make sure the model group continues to be the model group.** Small-group leaders lead their groups to do what they have seen done. Be certain your first group/groups accomplish everything you expect all groups to do for generations to come. Then, during huddle meetings, remind group leaders of their responsibility to do what they saw modeled by the leader who modeled small-group leadership for them.
- **Make leaders, not just small-group members.** Every spiritually mature person in each of your groups must be seen as a future

small-group leader. Small-group leaders must not only lead their group toward Christian community but also must note and raise up every person who is a potential leader.

- **Make the telling of one another's stories a primary feature of group life.** Until people really know one another, they will not consider themselves a meaningful part of the body of Christ. One of the core needs in life is to know others and be known by them.
- **Multiply when necessary, not when recommended.** Integrating the masses into all aspects of church life is more important than a few people experiencing the highest levels of intimacy. Most small-group gurus will recommend that groups be together eighteen months to two years before multiplying. Church plants do not have that luxury.
- **Multiply masterfully.** Multiplication without meaning makes for miserable people, and miserable people will make you miserable. When multiplying groups divide the group by spiritual gifts rather than by which people seem to enjoy one another the most, by the wants and wishes of the apprentice and leader, or by the whims of the group.

In small groups you will see the wonders of God at work. Marriages find support and healing. People find hope in Christ. Parents find strength. Singles find significance and connection. No matter what numbers you see during your large weekend services, the numbers that will matter most are the ones in these small-group gatherings throughout the week. Those will be your church.

Conclusion

No matter what form these small groups take, every healthy church needs a multiplying network of small groups that aid in binding the church together. Churches that plan to grow must focus on both the large-group worship gathering and the small group. The church planter that focuses solely on the Sunday worship service will not plant a healthy church. A church without small groups will often struggle to connect the members of the church with one another.

Resources for Further Reading

Arnold, Jeffrey. *The Big Book on Small Groups,* rev. ed. Downers Grove, Ill: InterVarsity Press, 2004.

Corrigan, Thom, and the Pilgrimage Training Team. *How to Build Community Through Small Groups.* Littleton, Colo.: Pilgrimage NavPress, 1998.

Donahue, Bill. *Leading Life-Changing Small Groups.* Grand Rapids: Zondervan, 1996.

Frazee, Randy. *The Connecting Church.* Grand Rapids: Zondervan, 2001.

McBride, Neal F. *How to Lead Small Groups.* Colorado Springs, Colo.: NavPress, 1990.

Stanley, Andy, and Bill Willits. *Creating Community: Five Keys to Building a Small Group Culture.* Portand, Ore.: Multnomah, 2005.

Chapter 18

Finding and Handling Finances

Planters frequently ask me, "How do I get the money to start a new church?" We'll examine the funding of church plants led by paid staff and funding that involves partnerships with denominational systems. This chapter addresses sources of funding, start-up costs, the handling of funds, and missions giving.

Bob Logan and Steve Ogne do an excellent job in *Churches Planting Churches* spelling out what a church-planting proposal needs to be effective.[1]

> Visit www.newchurches.com for examples of church-planting proposals.

Church-Planting Proposal Contents

Why start a new church?

- Demonstrate a clear calling.
- Communicate an exciting vision.
- Identify reasons for good church planting.
- Demonstrate an understanding of the need for new churches.

Who is the ministry focus group?

- Describe the ministry focus group.
- Show understanding of the community's needs.
- Include appropriate demographics.
- Identify the proposed location.

What kind of church are we trying to plant?

- Clearly state your core values.
- State and expand your mission statement.
- Describe the church's ministry style.
- Define a ministry model.
- Include a ministry flowchart.

With whom will this church be planted?

- Describe the proposed launch team.
- Include a profile of any confirmed ministry partners.
- Define the specific roles to fill.
- Clearly identify team members needed.

How and when will this church be planted?

- Outline a comprehensive strategic plan.
- Include a detailed time line for the first eighteen to thirty-six months.
- Provide a detailed explanation of how the core group will be gathered.

Sources of Funds

A new church requires a regular flow of money. It's possible to start a new church successfully with a completely unsupported bivocational planter, but usually the congregation needs additional support for a meeting place, program, or other costs. Also, there are times in the life of many church plants that require a special infusion of funds—launch activities, outreach projects, sound and video equipment, gathering events, and the like.

Denominational entities, congregations, and individuals have joined efforts and provided resources to underwrite new church starts across North America. However, it seems that church planters and their denominations often struggle with how to define the relationship.

Ralph Moore, founder of the Hope Chapel movement, has an excellent section on "How Can a Denomination Help?" in his book *Starting a New Church*. He explained: "You will soon find that your denominational support comes with strings attached. If you receive this support, you will be required to participate in denominational functions. This can be frustrating. Officials will busy themselves with programs that focus on the forest while you try to nurture a single small tree."[2]

Many new church plants are dissimilar in worship style to the majority of churches in their denomination. However, if God has called you to be a part of a denomination, then it's your job to reach across that divide (and others). When denominations help fund church planters, it's an integrity issue. Church planters who receive denominational funding should have the integrity not to be ashamed of those who made their ministry possible. This does not necessarily mean the name of the denomination needs to be reflected in the name of the church, but they should have the denomination in their values.

I have several anecdotes but one in particular illustrates this principle. A woman heard from a friend that the church she'd been attending for many months was started with funding from my denomination. Before that she had no clue. She asked the pastor if the information was true. For fear of someone having a problem with the issue, he was afraid to explain the church's involvement. While it's a possibility that someone will be turned off by learning of the connection between a certain denomination and your church plant, don't deny who you are. That creates an air of secrecy, and when people learn about it, they can feel betrayed. If people will have a problem with your denominational connection up front, they'll probably have a problem with it later. You don't need to broadcast it, but don't be ashamed of it either. If you are ashamed of it, either get a different denomination or go nondenominational.

Generally denominations have policies regarding fund-raising that planters should get from their denominational leaders. If there are no restrictions, some of the ideas below may help.

Build networks. During my final year with Millcreek Community Church, we succeeded in gathering $200,000 for church planting and growth—money we couldn't have generated by ourselves. By building various relationships and partnerships, we found resources to start two daughter churches on the same day with over two hundred at the first service for each new church. Our denomination helped; we were given an empty church building (which we sold), and we raised funds. Some church planters find themselves underfunded because they function as Lone Rangers. They refuse to take the time to build relationships and maintain strategic partnerships.

As we are planting Lake Ridge Church, we are working again with our denomination but also with other partnerships from people, to churches, to networks like Acts 29. Both of my co-pastors raised their own full support for one year and most for the second year.

Get others involved. Other persons and churches may become involved as contributors. Many church planters find Christian businesspeople open to supporting a new church. If you approach businesspeople for funding, be sure to have your strategic and fund-raising ducks in a row. Financially successful people like to see specifics in at least three categories: (1) achievable goals; (2) how you're stretching to meet those goals; and (3) how their money will be spent. They also expect to be kept up-to-date on progress and results.

Talk their budget language. Donors have different "pockets" or line items from which they resource others. While established churches or other denominational entities are often willing to give, if the planter asks for church-planting money (which they don't have) instead of ministry or evangelism money (which they do have), the planter may be disappointed. Doing some research ahead of time to determine how a congregation or donor has given in the past may help a church planter find valuable resources when approaching others to establish relationships and request funding.

Talk their heart language. Before you request help, learn about a potential donor's or congregation's passion. Some respond to need, but most respond to vision.

"Soft needs" or brick and mortar? My colleague donates gifts to his college alma mater in the form of student scholarships. Other people prefer to purchase "brick and mortar" gifts for new buildings or renovations. Some donors contribute to people projects or needs while others want to help with tangible projects. Knowing a donor's preferences can be helpful in your church's presentation of needs. Many big givers prefer to write a one-time gift check for a tangible item rather than make out monthly checks for church-planter support or items such as building rent.

A hand up, not a hand out. Other supporters contribute hands-on involvement more than monetary support. The "$39 Launch Day Operation Epistle Project," in which churches commit to hand-address envelopes and pay for one hundred stamps[3] is a popular proposal with partner churches. The supporter's primary contribution is the time to address one hundred envelopes, not the payment for stamps. A sister congregation recruited two hundred people to participate in this project with us. In the end this church spent more than $6,000 for a special project, but they probably would not have given us the same amount in cash.

Multiple churches may be involved as sponsors. Steve Allen, church planter strategist in New York City, explained their plan to involve multiple sponsors with a new church:

> In an area where the cost of living and operational expenses are among the highest in the nation, New Hope New York has sought to enlist a plethora of partners for each new plant. Multiple partners of a single Metro NY / NJ church plant/planter often provide for various needs, including:
>
> - Money
> - Mentoring
> - Manpower
>   —whether S.W.A.T. teams
>   —those permanently hived off or provided through a Fishing License (Fishing License: A pastor gives permission to another pastor to gather people [fish] from the church for a new church plant.)
> - Material support (furnishings, nursery shower items, etc.)
> - Mediation—prayer support
> - Moral Support—help for the planter's family such as child care or transportation needs.
> - Mobilization—cultivation of the church planting field.[4]

Individual Donors

Individuals also contribute financial resources for new churches. The church planter may begin tapping such resources by developing a fund-raising brochure, a fund-raising letter, and a fund-raising conversation. In this approach, the planter should prepare the promotional letter and brochure, including a cover letter of commendation for the new church from a respected, well-known leader in the denomination. This brochure should be mailed to potential donors, especially to persons who have demonstrated interest in new work. Before approaching individuals who are involved in local churches, it's a good idea and a move of integrity to get permission from that potential donor's pastor.

After a few days the planter should follow up with a telephone call to answer questions using the information outlined in the fund-raising conversation. As needed, the planter may volunteer to pay a personal visit to the prospective donor. A concise, well-designed PowerPoint presentation given during the visit may help the donor catch the vision for the future of the new church.

Fund-Raising Principles

Psalm 50:10 describes God as owning "the cattle on a thousand hills." The real problem in fund-raising is not divine resources or believers' unwillingness to give resources. Church planters have not because they ask not or because they ask wrongly (see James 4:2–3). This is the first principle in fund-raising.

Another principle is that people give to vision, not to need. Begging donors probably will not generate a great response. But communicating one's story in a convincing, spiritual way can touch donors deeply. When God's people understand that the planter's life investment is worthy of their support and financial investment, they'll become involved.

The Local Congregation

If the new congregation begins to think they can rely on outside sources for pastoral support, they will never develop maturity in giving. In *Church Planting Landmines*, Tom Nebel explained that "fear of money" was one of the ten land mines for church planters in their first years. Tom speaks boldly, "In general, I trace the fear or neglect of money issues to church planters' personal rejection issues, coupled with a skeptical society rampant with stories of financial abuse."[5] Instead, we need to find ways to teach biblical stewardship in an appropriate way for a new church.

Church planters can and should mention giving and tithing in Sunday messages, but new churches should not do a tithing series. Instead, the planter should address stewardship whenever it comes up naturally in preaching and should leave the in-depth stewardship study for a more committed group.

A setting even better than an individual message for discussing new church finances is a class on spiritual maturity or a message series with small-group support. If a stand-alone class, it should be aimed at a more select group of believers at various levels of maturity and offered several times during the year.

At Lake Ridge Church, my copastor Philip Nation developed our class. All of our spiritual formation classes are called "practices." In the case of stewardship, we call the class "Practices of Simplicity." We are convinced that teaching tithing as the first lesson of stewardship makes no sense in our context; people are already living at 120 percent of their income and making it 130 percent only frustrates them. We need to teach people to reorder their lives, put God first in their finances, and then live below their income level. By guiding people in this manner, we accomplish a great deal more than a simple focus on their checking account. Instead, they are able to see that finances are an indicator of greater issues of spiritual formation. You can download our class at www.newchurches.com.

Get a Job

A secular job can also supply funding for the church planter. Just because the denomination or a church can't fund the planter's church start doesn't mean the planter can't plant a church. If God has called a planter to begin a church, the planter must go forward in faith. Congregations and individuals must remember that denominations don't call church planters; God calls church planters. If God has called but finances don't follow as expected, the planter can't argue that God has closed the door. Finances are not the determining factor in God's will; God is the determining factor in God's will. If God expresses a call, the planter must help make a way where there is no other way—by working at bivocational employment, at least for a period of time until the church has grown to support the pastor.

In their excellent church-planting book *Community of Kindness*, Steve Sjogren and Rob Lewin advise church planters to work outside the church until their congregation reaches two hundred in attendance, even those who have the financial backing to dedicate their full time to the congregation. They point out five advantages you gain in bivocational work:

1. You will meet people to invite while on the job.
2. You will help "destroy the sacred-secular conflict. . . . By that we mean the natural inclination of most already-converted people who think working in the church is more valuable than working in the marketplace—that it's more valued by God."
3. You will continue to send the message that you aren't trying to live off of other people. Be sure to give substantially from the money you can earn outside the church to the church. Great leaders are always one of the top givers in their church.
4. You will be required "not to be available and allow for your congregation to work out their issues on their own on occasion. . . . Taking an outside job creates an understanding in the church that you aren't there as their free therapist."
5. You will be forced "to interact with the people in the marketplace," and they will see you "functioning in the role of a 'normal' person outside the rank of pastor."[6]

Many jobs are well suited for bivocational ministry. Dan Ramsey, author of *101 Best Weekend Businesses*, suggests the following as good jobs for bivocational church planters:[7]

Antique restoration service	Apartment preparation service	Auto detail service
Baking service	Bookkeeping service	Caregiver
Carpet-cleaning service	Catering service	Child care
Chimney sweep	Collection service	Companion to the elderly
Computer instructor	Computer maintenance	Construction cleanup service
Cooking instructor	Crafts business	Desktop publisher
Driveway repair service	Food-delivery service	Fund-raiser
Furniture refinishing	Handy-person service	Housecleaning service

House-painting service	Importer	Income tax preparation service
Information broker	Kitchen utensil-sharpening service	Mail-order sales
Masonry service	Newsletter publisher	Newspaper stringer
Personal consultant	Photography service	Picture-framing service
Plant-care service	Pool cleaning	Rental preparation
Research service	Resume writer	Reunion planner
Word processing	Security service	Small appliance repair
Teaching your skills	Telephone survey service	Translation services
Tree-trimming service	Tutoring service	Used car sales
Video-copying service	Wallpaper service	Wedding planner
Window-cleaning service	Woodworking	Writer

There are always cautions in bivocational ministry. For some people, being bivocational is a permanent ministry choice. For those planting missional/incarnational or house-church communities, this should be their funding strategy. For others, it will be a step into full-time ministry service. Both approaches are valid. For those who are working bivocationally with plans for full-time ministry, Steve Sjogren writes:

> If you are bi-vocational in the launching stage of your plant, don't forget why you are doing all of this—to launch a church. You did not move there to build a career in the secular workforce. If your job is robbing you of energy and enthusiasm beyond reason, find a new job. The ideal arrangement is a job [that] looks something like this:
>
> - pays an hourly rate
> - daytime hours so your evenings are freed up to build leaders and launch small groups
> - doesn't overly drain you emotionally or physically
> - puts you in touch with a good cross section of your city.
>
> I have found that jobs in sales or education tend to be ill-suited for planters.[8]

Many people already have a career. Others will find a job for the purpose of establishing the church. Bivocational and lay church plants are time-tested, biblical methods every church planter should consider.

When I was unable to find adequate funding at my first church plant, I took a job insulating houses. I could start early in the morning and supervise several crews from my car and mobile phone. At the same time I could do visits on my own time if I was in the area. My employer was flexible and gave me the freedom to clock in and out as needed. The job served as a good place for connections and ministry. It also helped pay the bills when the new church could not.

The Nuts and Bolts of Finances

Typical start-up costs for a church include outreach, facility rental, and purchasing sound and video equipment, the initial costs of doing kingdom business.

The first concern for the new congregation is to develop a start-up budget. Many new churches must start with nothing more than a guitar and an overhead projector. Some mission agencies no longer support pastoral income needs, but they will give one-time start-up grants for new churches to enable the best worship service from the very beginning. Pastoral support amounts or duration may be reduced if money goes to start-up, but a few denominations actually offer both pastoral support and start-up money.

Safeguarding funds is a fundamental issue of reputation and integrity. The number of church starts that become tainted by mishandling (or mere appearance of impropriety) is significant.

In order to avoid any appearance of wrongdoing, church planters should not set up an account tied to themselves. Even if the account is in the church's name, don't use your Social Security number. If you do, all money deposited to this account is taxable income. It's easy to get an Employer Identification Number (EIN) from the IRS by calling their toll-free number or go to www.irs.gov. Use the EIN to set up a checking account for the church.

The church should hold no account in its own name until significant safeguards have been put in place. Until a treasurer and a financial secretary have emerged and have been bonded, the account should not be opened. If the need for paying bills is great, then the treasurer of the mother church, a designated treasurer from among the sponsoring church missions team, or a qualified individual from the denomination may act as a temporary manager of the new church's funds.

The treasurer should not handle offerings *and* write checks. By having different persons functioning in these roles, the congregation holds accountable both the treasurer and the counter of money. Some local or regional governments even require separate persons to handle the separate functions. No matter how the state feels about it, allowing one person to handle all financial tasks for the church is risky. One individual should not be given so much responsibility. It's both a great temptation and a poor witness to the world.

A third group to appropriate the handling of finances consists of counters for offerings and other receipts. They should always count in teams of at least two persons. Counters are responsible for counting the money; the financial secretary should deposit the money; the treasurer should write checks for disbursing the money. Expenditures should always be made by using written checks to maintain a record of money management.

Two unrelated persons, neither of whom is the church planter, should sign all checks for the church. The planter must be protected by remaining at arm's length from monetary matters. Our culture already thinks that pastors have problems with finances. The planter must give no reason or excuse for anyone to point a finger of accusation.

A treasurer must be equally aboveboard with all the finances in how reports are given. Reports should be regular (monthly), readable and straightforward, and reputable in their accounting for all funds and accounts—the more detailed, the better. With the many software programs available, the church should have little trouble managing money and producing financial reports.

From the first day of its life, the new congregation should begin to give to missions from its undesignated receipts. By giving to support missions in North America and around the world, the new church is immediately giving back. Even the smallest new church can be a part of worldwide missions.

I recommend that each new church tithe to missions from its local undesignated giving. Although I'm not making a theological statement that the local church needs to tithe, the new church can model sacrificial giving from the start. Some new churches should and will give more; we have chosen to give 10 percent to our denominational mission program,

3 percent to our district association, and 7 percent to direct church planting from our first Sunday.

The pastor and overseers of the church (however church polity is organized) should ensure that the church does not give to the mission fund from mission funds. For example, if the new start receives $12,000 per year through partnership funding, the treasurer must not send 10 percent ($100) of that income each month to missions. In effect, that money is a "designated" receipt—mission funds intended specifically for starting a new mission.

The total amount of money may seem insignificant to the congregation at first (almost a "why bother?" issue), but learning to establish a percentage, to maintain it, and to increase that amount over time will mean that many other church plants and other missions endeavors may go forward because of the young church's gifts. At the very least this attitude of generosity teaches by example that congregation members should give their tithe and beyond.

I've even known of church planters who gave away every dollar of the offering taken during the first public worship service to another church plant. This sends the message: This money is not ours, and we're going to be generous and give to expand the kingdom. Church planters who decide to do this may have to swallow hard when they realize how generous that first offering was. But God always rewards generosity by pouring more in your lap. It's a promise he makes.

Conclusion

When you examine the financial picture, the real resources are already in the hands of God's people—whether great foundations, wealthy donors, wealthy churches, or simply typical, individual believers—who want to become involved in kingdom enterprises that are worthy of their gifts. The planter and the new congregation should be faithful and ethical in handling financial matters and also in how they approach donors and partners for money. May the planter be wise, and may God resource the church plant miraculously and marvelously that both the planter and the planted congregation exult and proclaim in praise, "We couldn't have done it on our own, but God brought in the resources; now we want to give back so that others might have a miraculous new church experience of their own."

Resources for Further Reading

Callahan, Kennon L. *Effective Church Finances: Fund-Raising and Budgeting for Church Leaders*. San Francisco: Harper and Row, 1992.

Mission Service Corps Support Development School, www.namb.net/beonmission/volunteers/msc/msc_orientation.asp.

Powers, Bruce P., ed. *Church Administration Handbook*. Rev. ed. Nashville: Broadman & Holman, 1997.

Chapter 19

Choosing a Name and Logo

Choosing a name and a logo are significant decisions when beginning a new church. These leave first impressions (and maybe, last impressions) with the community about the new church.

Names for new churches in the twenty-first century should be meaningful and contemporary. Exceptions always exist, of course, but logic urges that contemporary names are more likely to attract people. The only reason your church has a name is to identify it to outsiders, so you should plan accordingly and choose a name that appeals to the unchurched.

What's in a Name?

I discourage using some types of names or categorical descriptions which were contemporary yesterday but not today. The church should not be called a *mission*. The term can evoke pictures of a skid-row rescue ministry or perhaps a Roman Catholic ministry in the southwestern United States. Neither is *chapel* a good idea. Many denominations frequently used this term in naming new churches during the 1970s. By now the term has come to suggest a site used specifically for weddings, or worse, for funerals. Even the term *fellowship* may no longer serve the best interests of a new body of believers. I recommend that the planter and congregation call themselves what they are—a church.

It's also wise to avoid names that are street specific. Walnut Street Baptist Church would obviously identify the location of a church on Walnut Street. But there's no Walnut Street in Louisville—at least not any longer. The city changed the name to Mohammad Ali Boulevard to honor the hometown boxer. The church was not enthusiastic about changing its name to a convert to Islam. The name has no meaning to those who aren't familiar with the former street name.

The word *church* still has significance for our culture. Although most people may not understand the lofty theological implications of the term, they at least know that *church* is strongly related to the Christian faith and that it's a place where Christians go.

There's a trend today among emerging postmodern churches to use a single name: Sojourn, Journey, Veritas, etc. This isn't necessarily a bad practice since the names have meaning, but they aren't as easily identified as Christian churches.

Some church planters at the dawn of the twenty-first century choose generic names such as Community Church, Christian Church, or Bible Church. Planters have used generic names to attract people beyond their own denominational boundaries, to appeal to antidenominational baby boomers, or to identify with a specific area.

Peter Wagner cautioned the church planter to "think twice before using the name of your denomination. . . . Not that these names should never be used, but ask yourself what they mean to the *unchurched* public."[1] On the other hand, Elmer Towns believes that if your denomination (in his case Baptist) has a bad name in the community, the church planter should work to make it a good name since people will attend a church because "of what it is doing, not because of its name."[2] Most new churches being planted today don't identify their denomination in their names.

A denominational church planter who decides not to include the denominational label needs a well-thought-out explanation for the choice. Simply following a behavior commonplace among church planters is insufficient. A church planter needs to have a solid understanding of the issue and be prepared to explain the reason to the denomination if asked.

If the church planter should decide to develop a church name that's free of denominational labels, that name must make a good impression on the target community. The name should convey reliability, theological meaning, and the church's commitment to reach and serve the unchurched community. Therefore, ask. Ask denominational leaders, the core group, and your focus group what name they prefer. Most important, following efforts in asking leaders, the core group, and the target group, the church planter must pray through the name issue. Since the planter is likely to feel pressure from every direction during the process, listening with an open mind and then quietly seeking the Lord's counsel is a wise process for sound decision making.

In the debate about church names, a new church is different from an established church. I chose neutral names for every church I planted because I thought it was the best decision for each location. When I've pastored established churches (in two cases, revitalizing struggling or dying churches), I've recommended that the church not use a neutral name because they already have an identity in the community.

Views of Unchurched toward Major Denominations

George Barna has done some excellent research on the subject. Below is one graph from his presentation analyzing the views of the unchurched toward major denominations.[3] This graph deals with the attitudes of the unchurched. It describes their perceptions of major denominations. One interesting note: he found that pastors thought that the unchurched had a more negative opinion of the denomination than the unchurched people actually did. The average unchurched person is simply not aware of most denominations. A small percentage have negative views. The vast majority have positive views or have no awareness of most major denominations.

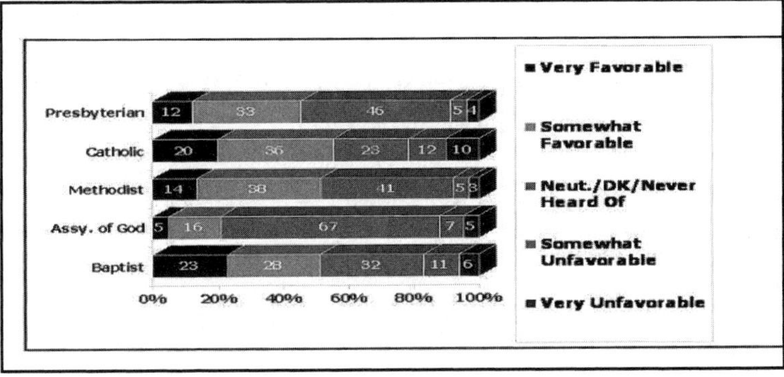

Some have said that the name of the church makes no difference to the unchurched. However, that conclusion cannot be applied when speaking of new churches. If the only thing people know about a new church is the name, the name certainly makes more of a difference.

Developing an Effective Logo

Pictures and logos are worth a thousand words. A church brands itself with its logo and/or a symbol. We identify many businesses or products with a symbol alone. Many people will begin to see your church the same way in the community.

Go to www.newchurches.com/research for further information on naming your church.

Also, the community will form its initial impression of the church from its logo. Since that impression can be either positive or negative, the planter and church should exercise great care in designing the church's logo. Every image, whether a rugged cross or a brilliant sunburst, summons powerful emotional and intellectual responses from the community. Images that appeal to believers may not only fail to appeal to unchurched people but may also repel them.

The meaning of a logo should be clear. A church using an image cannot assume that the unchurched people who see it will understand what the congregation thinks it says. For example, one cannot immediately discern whether an image of the sun on the horizon conveys daybreak or the day's end. Does it signal the dawn of hope or the end of hope? Birth or the end of life? Dawning light or impending darkness?

We must ask ourselves what our visual images—buildings and facilities, signs and logos—say to our community about the church's values, attitudes, and morale. The design of any visual image must communicate the messages that the congregation wants to communicate.

Technical Considerations

Manlove Church Marketing[4] provides excellent logo service, including technical recommendations that the church planter should keep in mind when designing a logo:

- A logo should quickly communicate the identity of a company or organization.

- The logo should reproduce well in various sizes.
- A logo should look great in gray scale. Oftentimes a logo looks great in four-color; but when it is rendered in gray scale, it is unrecognizable or loses all its impact. The best approach to logo design is to establish that the logo is great in gray scale and then to add the complementary colors.[5]

Thinking through a Logo

A congregation's name and logo should "give permission" to the unchurched to visit and become acquainted with the new congregation. Church people forget how timid and anxious unchurched people are in beginning a relationship with a church. The church's logo, signage, and other public displays should attract and comfort potential members. A trained artist can suggest colors that transmit warmth and welcome.

The message of the logo must be consistent across the spectrum of church communication. Stationery that welcomes and invites must be complemented by other visual images. Although church signage may proclaim, "Alive and warm toward visitors," those words painted in gray and black, sitting in a yard without grass and surrounded by an eight-foot chain-link fence topped with barbed wire hardly convey an inviting image. Passersby must be able to look at a building, signage, the lawn, and the logo and experience comfort, warmth, and welcome.

As Eric Ramsey and I described in *Strategic Outreach: A How-to Manual for Pastors and Church Leaders:*

> All communication, internal and external, should present a consistent identity. Ideally, no letterhead, signage, business cards, brochures, or other written materials would be developed or distributed until an official name, logo, and theme is ready to be utilized. Once a logo is developed, the following elements should be designed and produced:
>
> - Letterhead
> - Envelopes
> - Postcards
> - Mailing labels
> - Business cards

- Note cards
- Web site
- Signs
- Fliers
- Church transportation
- Door mats[6]

Chances are that nothing will help unbelievers say, "This church looks really good," but at the very least they should be thinking, *It doesn't look that bad*. The church must remember that unchurched people are already "scared to death" about coming to church. The name and logo make it easier for them to take the next step.

Resources for Further Reading

Stetzer, Ed, and Eric Ramsey. *Strategic Outreach: a How-to Marketing Manual for Pastors and Church Leaders*. San Diego: Outreach, 2005.

http://www.1800mylogo.com.
http://www.churchlogogallery.com.
http://www.outreachmarketing.com/.

Chapter 20

Finding a Meeting Place

Every new congregation must have a place for corporate worship. This is true, no matter the place or the size of the new, growing church—from the smallest house church to the largest megachurch. By their nature house churches do not need an external facility. All congregations, with the exception of house churches, require a facility—temporary or permanent. This chapter addresses the facility needs of both new and growing churches.[1]

Finding the Right Location at the Beginning

The new church's location is like a hospital; it's where the birth of the new church "happens." The location of your congregation will determine the available facilities. I attended a new church on the Upper West Side of Manhattan called Journey[2] that meets in the Triad, a trendy community theater. They began meeting in the theater because it was available, and it connected with their focus group.

Their "foyer," where they hand out coffee and church programs, is on the West 72nd Street sidewalk. Attendees have to walk to the second floor to be seated (above the bar). There's no room for child care, but there's little need. People who live in the Upper West Side have dogs, not children. Journey found a facility that met their needs. Every church needs to find a facility that connects with their people group. There are common trends and general guidelines for finding the right facility, but these must be applied in your individual context.

Save Money; Rent Facilities. The young congregation can save money—probably a great deal of money in the long run—by renting facilities in the beginning of its life. New churches with no credit history are often unable to get mortgages for the purchase of land or a building. Purchases demand closing costs and a host of other expenditures. Fast-growing new churches may be wise to save for a significant period of time before they buy or build permanent facilities. This allows the congregation to actualize its membership potential before building in order to concentrate on internal relational matters, to continue defining and refining its mission and purpose, and to save money for a later purchase. It is also usually wise to avoid long-term lease agreements until it is clear that the new church is viable and can fulfill such an obligation. Bottom line: keep your overhead low so you can spend money on supporting the ministry staff and on outreach and community events instead of on buildings.

Choosing a temporary facility means that the congregation must develop a "portable approach" to ministry. One excellent source for portable equipment is Portable Church Industries.[3] Knowing the new church's specific needs, this company can design and arrange portable church furnishings and supplies to allow the congregation to hold public events in temporary settings without looking temporary. This approach can be a little pricey, but PCI also has good deals on used equipment from churches that have outgrown it or new churches that didn't make it.

The most common place where new churches meet is inside other churches, a tried-and-true practice. Many ethnic churches meet within another part of a church's facilities, sharing the building with the mother church. Outside of other churches, the most common meeting place is in public schools.

Many complain that there's a need for a permanent location in order to grow; however, West Ridge Church (www.westridge.com) runs more than three thousand and is still meeting in a high school gymnasium. Another community, New Spring Church (www.newspring.cc) in Anderson, South Carolina, also runs more than four thousand in attendance and remains portable. Even Saddleback Church remained portable through its formative growth years. Remaining portable is not a hindrance, and it can be an advantage.

Court Decisions on School Rental. Any congregation which desires to rent school facilities in the United States needs to be aware of Lamb's Chapel. The U.S. Supreme Court ruled that school districts could not discriminate against churches seeking to rent facilities on the basis of speech or the message of the renting group. This ruling was clarified even further in 2001 with *Good News Club vs. Milford Central School*. In this case, the court ruled that evangelism and discipleship were allowed in a school building if other nonschool groups used the facilities for their purposes.

> There is much litigation about churches using schools today. Since this may change, you can find up-to-date articles about U.S. and Canadian laws at www.newchurches.com/legal. Also, you can find a sample letter that explains the law to school administrators.

Schools that rent to other nonschool groups must also rent to you whether you're showing Christian films, doing Bible clubs, or even having worship. But with this privilege come some limitations. If the school district believes that weekly worship would "excessively entangle" the state with the church, they can decline use of their facility. Schools may also set a time limit on the length of your stay or require that a new church show this is a temporary arrangement by the presentation of near-future building plans. Eventually, this specific case will need to be heard and settled by the Supreme Court.[4] Until then, have your facts and ask (or act) wisely. Do not force your way in; you might regret it later. The Christian Legal Society maintains some excellent information on the use of schools (see www.clsnet.org).

In Canada, the legal issues are not as problematic, but renting from schools is still a challenge. One Canadian church planter (and seminary professor) explained:

> Churches are on their own to negotiate as they can. Many school systems use a broker to negotiate for the entire system. We were refused, but there are at least four others who are in schools, usually because they have relationship with someone in the administrative system. Community Centres are happy to rent to churches, but there is no rental protection (at least not in

> Alberta) so the church is often victim of the whims of the community council. Again when the church demonstrates that it is involved in the community, doing things that matter to the community, things (including rental) go much better. There are also a few church plants who have found good deals in hotels: conference rooms, setup, and coffee all provided . . . one church pays only a dollar a head for their rental agreement.[5]

Other Rental Site Options. Another common location for new congregational rental is a day care center. Although centers which consist of small meeting rooms may not serve as good locations, many day care centers have large, open rooms that can be adapted as a worship area.

Movie Theaters. Many churches are meeting in theaters and finding them to be helpful locations. One of the owners of Regal Cinemas is a Christian and wanted to see his theaters used for church services. They started a program for churches (see http://www.cinemeetings.com/power_churches.html). Other movie theaters have followed their lead. One of the church planters I coach, David Bryan, is planting Christ Church, an Anglican Mission in America church. They meet at a theater in Murrell's Inlet in South Carolina and explained how it works for them: "We use one auditorium for our main worship service and a second one for our children's ministry (each with a fee). Regal allows us to use common areas for our nursery and fellowship areas. We take advantage of the big screen in these auditoriums by using Media Shout software, video clips and other multimedia presentations. Obviously and thankfully the chairs are in place in these auditoriums, so we simply bring in extra lighting, sound & projection, equipment, tables (including an altar table), signs and instruments."[6]

Restaurants and Meeting Halls. These provide another type of location for new church meeting places. One of my former congregations met for a time in an American Legion hall that contained a restaurant and a large dance hall.

Other Alternatives. Depending on the community, fire department meeting halls may offer a great choice for rental space. Many volunteer fire departments have a large room they use for fund-raising or other events. Some Roman Catholic churches rent their fellowship halls to other organizations and even other congregations. Seventh-day Adventist churches, which worship on Saturday, often provide space for congregations that worship on Sunday.

Make Your Geographical Selection Wisely. The planter and congregation must be careful in choosing not only their building but their meeting area as well. Familiarity with community needs, history, and feelings will help the church avoid poor choices. In some communities certain buildings have a bad reputation, are in an unsafe location, or have some other problem which may turn prospects away.

Facility Needs

A large launch is likely to demand a large auditorium (more about that later). Many more options exist for smaller new churches that are planning on being larger than a house church. The smaller new church may consider a recreation room in an apartment or condominium complex, a large living room, the back room of a restaurant, a school cafeteria or gymnasium, or vacant retail space in a mall. Sometimes older congregations are pleased to rent unused space in their building. Wherever the congregation meets, the space must be affordable, pleasant, logistically manageable (see the next section), and culturally suitable for the focus group. The needs of the focus group, not the cost, should serve as the determining factor. A low-cost facility that turns off the focus group is not a good choice.

Rental Fatigue

New churches normally rent facilities for a limited period of time. At first, they usually rent for Sunday morning worship only. These rented facilities are dramatically different from traditional church buildings whose furnishings remain in place from service to service. When renting space, "rental fatigue" develops. This describes the weariness experienced by the core group from having to set up and tear down week in and week out over a long period of time. This challenge may not sound ominous, but finding volunteers willing to get up at 5:00 or 6:00 every Sunday morning for two to three hours of setup wears people out quickly. Unless specific church members sense such activity as their calling and receive great satisfaction from doing it, fatigue can erode enthusiasm quickly.

Value of Portability. Overcoming rental fatigue is challenging but not impossible. The planter's first step might be to commend portability by various means of communication—from the pulpit, through newsletters, and if possible, by the testimony of laypersons who have experienced its value personally. The planter may want to underscore the importance of portability because the church is still in formation. Bill Easum and Pete Theodore's book, *The Nomadic Church*, provides helpful direction on how to cast a compelling vision for building-less churches. In the same way that Israel used a portable tabernacle during the forty wilderness years and well after, so the new congregation can be a portable church.

Good Stewardship. The planter can help church members understand portability as good stewardship. Many people benefit from pastoral reminders to invest money in church staff members and in efforts to reach the unchurched, rather than in building or buying a facility. Refocusing members on priorities for reaching the community through stewardship of resources will help members center on such priorities for many years to come. By the time the church does build, members will have matured to the point where they view the building as a tool for ministry.

Call Out Workers. Many people cannot teach or lead in worship, but they can set up chairs or the audio system—and will enjoy doing so. Involving them in set-up efforts is important not only to make everything ready for worship, but also to cultivate their participation and their faithfulness in service. Although the pastors or core group leaders could perform the task, involving others who have no other church job enables them to feel that they are making a valuable contribution. Leaders should praise these people publicly and privately for their faithfulness in this important ministry. Such persons are "body parts" in Christ who, though seemingly of lesser value, actually become more valuable through their service to the kingdom.

Seven-Day Facilities. Although it is almost certain to be more expensive, another way to avoid rental fatigue is to lease a seven-day facility. This around-the-clock rental arrangement provides building access every day for office space and weekday ministries. It also solves the portability problem because no one else uses the building or needs to have the church's furnishings removed each Sunday. Even if this arrangement is initially impossible (or unnecessary) for the new church, the congregation might consider the feasibility of such a facility within the first few months. Several factors—rental fatigue, developing church ministry needs, and financial ability, among other factors, signal the church's readiness for a seven-day facility.

Nomad Churches

Although the thought surprises our building-centered values, some congregations actually find a nomadic existence—moving to new meeting sites as needs change—a way of life. This approach to church planting has become increasingly popular, particularly in expensive urban settings. The reasons for such developments are understandable.

No Available Acreage. Land in some urban settings is prohibitively expensive. In other areas churches find that purchasing land on which to build is legally impossible because very old—occasionally even dilapidated—buildings have received civil protection as historic landmarks. This most frequently occurs in the northeastern United States where many communities guard their colonial heritage. Some open land in urban areas is off-limits to development for houses and churches as a matter of wildlife protection. In still other places, religious, political, or social pressures may prevent a new congregation from purchasing land or from putting up a building.

Available but Insufficient. Even if land is available, it may not be large enough to meet needs. Generally, since churches need one acre for every 150 persons, a projected congregation of fifteen hundred will need ten acres of land. Manhattan Island, in the heart of New York City, contains no available tracts that size. (Redeemer Presbyterian meets on the campus of Hunter College in Manhattan.) Northern Virginia offers virtually no land for purchase today. Even if available, land costs may soar to a price of millions of dollars for one acre.

The Singapore Solution. The island nation of Singapore, which lies just off the tip of the Malay Peninsula, faces overcrowding and shortage of space, just as in some North American urban areas. As a result, churches have met for many years in hotels, office buildings, and similar structures. "It is almost impossible to find any meeting place to rent in the city on Sundays as the Christians have already taken up everything available."[7]

New Paradigms for New Times. If evangelicals are to succeed in reaching North American urban centers in church planting, we must abandon the thinking that ten acres of land and a brick building are essential in order to be successful. A true New Testament church can meet on the sixteenth floor of a high-rise building just as surely as any First Presbyterian Church can meet on the county seat town square. With the birth of the twenty-first century and the changes it has ushered in, we must redefine good stewardship in the context of land purchase and buildings. We need new paradigms for new times. For those who are not called or convinced by a house church model, we still have to abandon a building-centered model if we are to reach this new reality.

Shared Facilities

Sharing facilities is another alternative to the exorbitant costs of building permanent church structures. Congregations across the United States and Canada have discovered the economic advantages of this approach in which two congregations—or even multiple groups—share the same meeting space. This practice sometimes includes churches of different denominations and, certainly, of different ethnic backgrounds.

A Permanent Building

At some point the congregation may desire a building to call their own. Although not every call for a permanent site signals the time to buy or build, there are times to consider the need. In some places churches don't really break through until they have a building.

Cultural Needs. For example, if a church cannot secure even marginally adequate facilities at a reasonable price, few realistic options remain except to buy or build. Another common situation is the community's perception of the church's permanence.

Buffalo, New York, is a heavily Roman Catholic area. As a whole, Roman Catholics (as well as others) seem to be "building centered." Despite the fact that our prospects were nonpracticing Catholics in many cases, they would hardly give our new church a second glance until we "had a church"—until we owned our own building. On a number of occasions, I heard prospects or contacts say, "When you get a church, I'll come to see you." In response to this cultural need, we eventually purchased a 150-year-old church building and remodeled it to suit our needs and the needs of the focus group. Cultural preferences sometimes dictate the need for a new church to occupy its own facility.

Just One Chance to Get It Right. The church should never let the shoe determine how big the foot will become. If it decides to build or buy, a congregation must be certain that the space it chooses does not limit the growth of the church. Churches that are determined to build must look as far as possible into the future to determine whether their planned building will be sufficient for next week as well as the future. Churches can overcome underplanned facilities but not without headaches and great costs. They have only one chance to get it right—the first time they build.

With a rented facility the church simply moves when it has outgrown its space. Over several years Seminole Community Church met at a funeral home, a gym, a movie theater, and an elementary school before building a more permanent facility.[8] They moved to a different site as their needs changed.

Location for Building

If a congregation decides that it must build, location is a highly important consideration. Many have observed that location does not always matter—particularly to strong, established churches. For example, North Point Church in Alpharetta, Georgia is one of the largest churches in America. I drive by the entrance to the church regularly and am continually surprised that people can find the church with its small sign, tiny frontage, and zero visibility. Because the church already had established its identity in the community and was growing rapidly, its location did not keep it from becoming a megachurch.

Location, Location, Location. When a new church decides to build, its choice of location is crucial because it's different from an established church. The new congregation does not have an established reputation in the community. Visitors will not easily find the church facility unless it sits in plain view and is easily accessible. A building located on a convenient, accessible site can enhance the fledgling congregation in developing its community identity.

Many Acres; How Much Use? The congregation must consider how much of the land will actually be usable. One of our daughter churches in Pennsylvania, Lakepointe Community Church, purchased twenty acres of land for construction. Approximately one-third of that land is wetland and not available for construction. Fortunately, the congregation knew well before the purchase that the land would not be useful for their construction purposes, and they planned for that reality. But not all churches are so fortunate or thorough. Skilled consulting engineers can help the church avert costly, discouraging problems.

Zoning Laws

Along with plans for purchasing land, the congregation should develop its awareness of local zoning issues. Failure to do so can prove costly to the new church. The "Religious Land Use and Institutionalized Persons Act of 2000" addressed the creeping problem of local zoning laws by giving more power to local churches. Under the new law the government must have a "compelling governmental interest" to exclude a church from a zoning category.

Laws to Restrict Churches. Churches should clearly understand that government entities sometimes use zoning laws to restrict the activities and development of churches. The Web site of well-known Christian activist/attorney Jay Sekulow explains that churches are "increasingly facing discrimination from local zoning authorities."

Search and Obey. If a new congregation plans to build, it must find real estate that meets three criteria: first, it must provide adequately for the present and future needs of the church, as described above. Second, it must be financially affordable. Third, its intended use must conform to zoning laws.

The consistent U.S. Supreme Court pattern over recent years has been to rule on the side of governments, not on the side of churches in matters regarding zoning. These decisions send a chilling message to congregations that hope to build facilities in the near future, particularly congregations that aren't recognized and respected by local government officials. The recently passed national Religious Land Use Act may make things better, but as of this writing, it has not been tested in court. (See www.newchurches.com/legal for updates.)

A Place to Begin. In order to avoid costly and frustrating battles over zoning issues, the congregation should begin its building plans in the zoning office of the local government. Informed representatives of the church should first determine the present zoning of the proposed site. Next, they should determine whether local government entities already have or are preparing to change zoning regulations in ways that would impact the church's plans. Although new legislation in the United States holds out renewed hope for churches, congregations must be careful in their dealings with local government agencies and agents.

Building Campaigns

If a congregation plans to build, it must have a plan not only for building but also for financing its purchases. As a rule of thumb, most consultants feel that a church can raise three times its annual budget income for a building campaign. LifeWay Christian Resources administers one such plan through their Together We Build program for fund-raising.[9] This program has proven its worth over a number of years and has been used by all kinds and sizes of churches.

However, I don't recommend new congregations engaging professional fund-raisers. Many of these agents, while superb in their skills, require costly fees that can discourage the financially challenged church, which usually pays 5 to 15 percent of the fund-raising proceeds to the agent.

Other Alternatives. An alternative program, "A Time to Build,"[10] was designed by and successfully used by Saddleback Church for their building campaign.

Another option is to request the services of your denominational consultant who can be skilled in effective, nonmanipulative fund-raising techniques. His or her skills should help raise the money. In addition, the consultant should leave the congregation matured in their stewardship and feeling respect for the agency that dispatched the agent to the congregation.

Church Loans

A new church has several options for securing a building loan.

Conventional Loans. Lending institutions such as banks, savings and loans, and credit unions may provide the resources a church needs. The church may find borrowing locally of some advantage in building a solid reputation in the community.

Local Denominational Entities. Some denominations loan money for church building purchase or enhancement. Even if all needed funds are not available through these groups, they may provide sufficient seed money to enable the church to pay for architectural plans and other start-up costs.

Foundations. Many states and localities have small agencies or wealthy laypersons with resources for grants and loans. You should ask local churches or denominational leaders what opportunities are available. For example, the Oldham Little Church Foundation[11] provides grants for church building repairs and upgrades. Although their grants are not large, their target is small churches. Many small, new churches may find this brick-and-mortar agency helpful.

Only One-third of Income for Debt Service. Regardless of the lender or means by which a new church purchases property, it should commit no more than one-third of its weekly receipts for debt service. Many church planters will confirm that churches which don't heed this warning place a strain on the spirit of the congregation and choke its life and ministry.

Conclusion

A meeting place is indispensable to the life of a church, but facilities should never control the direction of the church, whether by their cost, their size, their need for maintenance, or some other factor.

Whether you rent or buy, pay cash or secure a loan, build new or remodel another congregation's structure, the building in which you meet is God's gift for ministry, not a monument to be protected. Plan its use well.

Resources for Further Reading

Bowman, Ray, and Eddy Hall. *When Not to Build*. Grand Rapids: Baker Book House, 2000.

Easum, Bill, and Pete Theodore. *The Nomadic Church: Growing Your Congregation without Owning the Building*. Nashville: Abingdon, 2005.

Callahan, Kennon L. *Building for Effective Mission: A Complete Guide for Congregations on Bricks and Mortar Issues*. San Francisco: Jossey-Bass, 1997.

Warren, Rick. "Bigger Buildings?" at http://www.purposedriven.com/articles/practice/display.asp?id=41.

Chapter 21

The Launch—Birth of a New Church

Some planters put so much effort into the conception-prenatal period of planting that they fail to remember the importance of the actual birth *day*. This chapter outlines the final days immediately before birth and the day of the launch. We also will consider a few matters related to the first days of new church life after launch day.

Prebirth Announcements: Advertising the Launch

You can use several ways to tell the community that your new church is about to be launched. Some people have compared the prelaunch period to a pregnancy. The vision for the new church is the conception. The prelaunch growth of the new church is the prenatal period. The launch day is the birth.

Most church planters use advertising to announce the birth. They know that a birth is worth annoucning. And a new church is worth announcing as well—particuarly when we are announcing a church that glorifies the exalted Savior.

Advertising is a proven means for reaching large numbers of people in a limited amount of time. Effective advertising can generate a large attendance, but it can also break a budget. Church planters may choose from a number of options when advertising the birth of the new church. Following are some of the best-known advertising options.

Direct Mail

Aubrey Malphurs notes the two most effective ways to gather a crowd are direct mail and telemarketing.[1] While telemarketing is used much less frequently today, direct mail is common and the most cost-effective. In a focus group of seven church planters from across Canada and the United States,[2] I asked their thoughts on direct mail. Three ranked direct mail as their most effective outreach tool, two thought it was moderately effective, and two thought it was ineffective in their context. Direct mail is working—but not everywhere.

You need to consider how many other churches may be using this method in your target area; doing this can prevent overspending an advertising budget that will become less effective because many other churches are using it. When people receive multiple mail-outs, they are less likely to pay attention.

While many are giving up on direct mailing, LifePoint Christian Church (www.lifepoint.org.) in Alpharetta, Georgia, believes strongly in it. They send out multiple mail-outs many times a year and attribute much of their visitor attendance and presence in their community to their mail-outs. We used direct mail in the same area as LifePoint and estimated that it generated more than one hundred visitors for us over a two-month period. Many of those people are now a part of Lake Ridge Church.

I continue to be surprised at where direct mail is working. Many churches are using direct mail and having success. This surprised me because many discard the idea, yet many others are still using it as a tool to reach into all kinds of communities. The key question is: Will it work among my focus group? Consider some direct-mail strategies that church planters are using.

Single Mass Mailing. An invitation letter is the most widely used one-time mailing. It is most effective when the letter identifies and addresses the particular needs of the focus group. The letter should express enthusiasm and excitement for the future of the new church, the readers, and those who become involved.[3] The letter must anticipate and overcome the reader's concerns about church and spiritual matters. It should help the reader put aside fears that surface at the mention of "church." It should be understandable and completely free of theological and church terms as well as grammatical errors. As recipients finish reading the letter, they should feel energized and ready to attend the new church.

Double Mailing. Some churches have found it more effective to do two mailings—one ten days before the first service and one five days before. The impact of the mailer is multiplied, and the message is reinforced with two mailers.

Multiple Mailings. When it comes to advertising, more is usually better. Some churches have sent five or more mailers to the same area to reinforce the message of the new church, but more mailers cost more money. Those wishing to start with a big first service generally find that the single mailing does not produce the best results.

When we planted Lake Ridge Church, we used the multiple mailing approach and had good results (at least fifty new guests at each service). We used Outreach, Inc. (www.outreach.com) and developed a theme for a series of several mailers for our preview services and for our launch. We have posted these at www.newchurches.com.

Telemarketing

Even today the second most widely used method for initiating contacts is telemarketing. This methodology must not be thought of as merely making phone calls but as part of a combined phone-and-mail strategy. This usually involves people calling from a local mother church or a phone bank.

Another option is an automated call system like Tellstart. The ministry, a part of Southside Community Church, explains:

> TellStart is a program whereby we telephone up to fifty thousand homes per day on your behalf, seeking interested people for your church. . . . Essentially, we take about five seconds and ask if the person answering the phone would be interested in a new (or re-focusing) church in the area. . . .

> If they press #1 they are given an additional one-minute message containing details about your church. At the close of this section they are invited to leave their name and address for follow-up and more detailed information. Those who have left their names after the tone are prospects for your church.[4]

We used it to plant Lake Ridge and found more than two hundred families asking for more information. Several families from the project are now part of our church.

It is obvious that telemarketing is becoming less effective over time. Caller ID and unlisted numbers indicate that this strategy will become less and less helpful. Also, so many people are reacting negatively to unsolicited phone calls that now a national Do Not Call Registry (www.donotcall.gov/default.aspx) has been established.

But telemarketing still works. It can help jump-start the process to making relationships with the unchurched. If telemarketing was unproductive and fruitless, business marketers would stop using this methodology. Those called may not respond every time, but they are much more likely to respond if they perceive a personal need for the "product," in this case, a church, offered by the telemarketer. This method can reach a husband and wife who recently discussed returning to active church life. It can stir to life the individual whose interest in spiritual matters has grown because of watching a Billy Graham television event. Marketers cannot reach everyone every time, but they do reach someone every day.

Millcreek Community Church's fifty-five thousand dial-ups before the launch service helped develop a list of 2,151 persons who agreed to receive more information. From that list, more than two hundred people in addition to our core group attended the first service. At the time, we were the largest Southern Baptist launch service in history in the northeastern United States. Telemarketing served as a superb resource—a major reason Millcreek Community Church became a church-starting success.

The most obvious objection is to the telemarketing itself. But one church planter described the results as follows:

> When people comment on [telemarketing], they frequently say that it will not work in my area because people are adverse to telemarketing. . . . I held the same opinion. I hate telemarketers—though Jesus tells us to love our enemies. However, after

> a lot of prayer, I felt God calling us to use the phones for your strategy. We made more than 13,000 phone calls and ended up with 330 people at our launch.
>
> I found that while people were negative toward telemarketing, they were excited to have a phone call from a new church. We only had one truly negative response out of 13,000 dial-ups. Because all of our phone numbers were newly assigned, they either did not identify the caller on people's caller ID's or people were just curious. Frequently, we had people get our number off their caller ID and call us back to see what we wanted. Go figure![5]

The Phone's for You. The best-known procedure for telemarketing was designed by Norm Whan. He created The Phone's for You! Whan designed his excellent resource on a marketing formula assuming a 10 percent positive response. A caller making twenty thousand phone calls would identify about two thousand persons willing to receive more information about a new church. More than twelve hundred churches used the program in 2002.[6]

After Calling, Mail. After collecting the needed information, the church sends a series of five mailers to the two thousand respondents. Whan discovered that typically 10 percent of the original pool of positive respondents do so because of mailers, and they attend the first service of the church.[7] Since these figures vary somewhat from place to place, Whan developed a test instrument of one thousand calls in order to help telemarketers project the predictable response in any given market.

Telemarketers' Target. Church planters who use telemarketing are looking for people who are not involved in church. Their sample question in some way asks whether the person is "actively involved in church." In some areas of North America that are influenced heavily by cults or sects, the sample questions could be modified to: "Are you actively involved in a church that teaches the Bible?" The caller's question should be contextualized to the area.

Next Step. The telemarketer's second question, if the first generates interest, is: "May we send you information about a new church that will be starting in the area this fall?" The vast majority of people will decline.

Of those who say yes, about 10 percent will remain sufficiently open and actually attend the church's first service.

Telemarketing is not for everyone. In some communities, it may even cause the church's reputation to suffer. But it has worked in many locations and continues to be used widely.

Preview Services

The preview service came to prominence in the last ten years. It usually consists of a series of monthly meetings just before the first official service of the new church. It allows many people to be exposed to the new church while gradually increasing the size of the attendance that will show up at the first official service. Be cautious not to do such a large mailing for the first preview service that there are two hundred in attendance at a preview service and then only one hundred present at the first official service. This shift in size becomes anticlimactic, and the momentum will be lost.

Do not have more than three preview services before the launch. People soon begin to get impatient and want to start regular services. The preview services also give the group an opportunity to try out the worship leaders. Tell the people who are present, "We're glad you're here for this service. This is the first time we've been together, so everything might not be perfect." The worship team is allowed some slack to make a few mistakes that generally aren't permitted after the launch service. Many churches have found this a successful method of core building through existing relationships.

E-mail

E-mail is a controversial method. Just as people receive junk mail at home, junk e-mail can be sent to the inbox on a computer. Every day pornography and "get-rich-quick" schemes are sent out to random e-mail accounts. But the world is already using the Internet, and the Internet is ripe for the gospel of Jesus Christ to be proclaimed via e-mail methods. The key is to do it in a way that gets people's attention without offending them. Most people use an "opt-in" approach where friends submit their names to electronic invitation cards, and they can choose to be added to the mailing list if they are so inclined.

No matter what approach is used, complaints should be expected. When we used the telemarketing approach, we were amazed at the number of people who were using *69 and calling us back wanting to know who we were and why we called. If you use a postage-paid return address card, there will be responses that don't always glorify the Lord. Some people will believe you are interfering because to them their faith is a private matter.

Some church planters have decided to avoid all methods of mass outreach. They reason that a postmodern world is now relational and that all forms of outreach will be received negatively. This has not been my observation. The only postmoderns I have seen offended by mass outreach are Christians who have determined it worldly or lacking authenticity. Spiritually-seeking postmoderns are generally not offended by outreach.

Statistical evidence supports that new churches using a big-launch method are larger than those that do not. Although the difference is not as significant as I expected, those who use a "large first meeting" to start their church do evidence a larger attendance in the second through fourth years:

Approaches to Avoid

I usually don't encourage church planters to use the newspaper. In most cases it covers too broad an area for a local church, and newspaper ads are expensive. However, local and ethnic papers of small towns may be exceptions. If you do use the newspaper, make sure your ad is professional looking and eye-catching. But, to be honest, many younger generations are disregarding the local paper altogether and getting their news solely from the Internet.

I also usually discourage the use of radio which also touches an audience that's too broad, meaning you usually aren't able to reach your target. If you decide to use radio, make sure you do so through a station that uses the musical style to which your church is accustomed or the style your church will use when it launches. For example, do not advertise on a classical station unless there will be classical music in the worship services.

Billboards are another media source generally to be avoided. They are too expensive for the amount of return they yield. People who have used this method tend to put up an eye-catching billboard with a countdown to the first service. When Big Sky Church[8] used a billboard, they placed a big invitation with a note advertising their launch Sunday. A major problem with billboards is that they're so common along highways they often go unnoticed.

The only billboards people really look at are those that catch the eye. Television time is also extremely expensive. Cable access is one possible exception. Commercials on one of those thirty-minute cable access programs where someone sits in a chair with a Bible and preaches are not effective in missional church planting. Some cable access channels do sell local time on CNN, MSNBC, and FOX news. Local ads on national networks may work.

Gathering the Large Group

The point of using any of these methods is to gather a large group so you can move from one stage to the next. No matter the number of people you begin with, when you go public with the worship service, make it an important event. Encourage the core people to invite all their friends. Tell the core group: "We're starting a new church. Let's bring all our friends. Let's focus together and see what God can do in this new church." The launch might attract thirty people or three hundred. Either way, make sure you use your methodology wisely.

The Launch Event

Most new churches today start with a "large launch." The core group works to attract a large crowd for the first public worship service. Getting unchurched people to come is one task; helping them feel comfortable about being there is another.

Seven out of ten people in attendance at the launch service are typically unbelievers without church experience. Two out of ten may be churched, but they don't know anyone at this church. It's a challenge to create an atmosphere that will break down anxiety and stimulate the desire of the attendees to hear of and experience God's presence.

I encourage church planters not to launch with a crowd more than ten times the size of their core group. A core of twenty should not plan for a first service of more than two hundred. I call this the crowd-to-core ratio. If a core of ten launches with more than three hundred people, the core is frequently overwhelmed because there aren't enough workers for music, child care, assimilation, etc. New churches should plan their launch service to match an adequate core group.

Conclusion

Planting a church eventually involves a public worship experience. Church planters have learned that a public launch is often most effective. But such a launch requires efficient planning and quality execution. The kingdom of God is to be built up in a strategic and biblical manner.

The church's worship must not alienate unbelievers but lead them to Christ. We will explore this topic in the following chapter.

Resources for Further Reading

Chaney, Charles L. *Church Planting at the End of the Twentieth Century.* Wheaton: Tyndale House, 1991.

Logan, Robert. *Church Planter's Tool Kit.* St. Charles, Ill.: ChurchSmart Resources, 1991.

Rainer, Thom S. *Surprising Insights from the Unchurched.* Grand Rapids: Zondervan, 2001.

Chapter 22

Worship in the New Church

The purpose of church planting is to begin a church that gathers to praise God in corporate worship. John Piper reminds us that missions still exists because worship does not yet exist everywhere. We are planting a church. By definition, churches are "people of worship," but writing about worship is like talking about driving. Everybody does it and thinks they do it best.

Much has been written about worship in recent years. Worship authorities debate the "right" musical styles for worship. Seeker sensitivity has spawned controversy. Many committed believers question what forms are appropriate in the worship setting. Elmer Towns and I tried to tackle the subject in our book *Perimeters of Light: Biblical Boundaries for the Emerging Church.*

Some believe worship has been given only to Christians. They reason that the church should gather for worship and Bible teaching; then the people will be built up spiritually to go out and evangelize. This notion is incomplete. The church and its worship are not intended solely for believers. We are called to please God. This includes the edification of believers, but the true purpose of the church is as broad as the purposes of God. It is the *missio Dei*—the mission of God. It includes all that God includes because we are an extension of his work in the world. The *missio Dei* includes worship but also evangelism, ministry, encouragement, and pastoral care as well.

Some church attendees are being drawn to Christ and are "called" but have not yet committed to Christ. The Bible refers to the church as the *ekklesia*—the "called out ones" who have made a commitment to follow Christ. When the called are brought together, the planter must present God's message in such a way that it challenges believers and also encourages unbelievers toward commitment.

Hundreds of years after the birth of the church, Augustine still lamented the impossibility of separating the wheat (faithful) from the tares (unbelieving). His implication is plain: in this church age the unchurched and Christians will always coexist in the local congregation. If this were not true, why would Paul have to write the Corinthians about what unbelievers think when they enter the worship service? (See 1 Cor. 14.)

The purpose of the worship service is not just to arouse attendees' passions to hear preaching. The true objective is to enable believers to encounter God in worship and the Word. The purpose of worship is also to allow unbelievers to observe the divine-human encounter and to yearn for their own personal relationship with God.

Congregations such as Willow Creek believe that their seeker service prepares seekers for the presentation of the gospel message. This argument rests upon their strategy for reaching the unchurched population through large group meetings. Going to Willow Creek on Sunday morning is the equivalent of going to an evangelistic crusade. It is not intended for the worship and edification of believers. The worship and edification of believers occurs at the midweek "new community" service.

Much of the criticism directed at the seeker-driven church is a result of the misunderstanding of their strategy. In seeker-driven churches, Sunday morning is not supposed to look like church; it's designed to be an ongoing evangelistic service. A student who visited Willow Creek with me commented that the service looked like a Young Life meeting, a low-key evangelistic service with an opportunity for those who attend to go deeper at another time. The strategy has worked for Willow Creek, but it's not one I embrace for theological reasons.

Instead of focusing on a seeker-driven worship service, I believe it's better to ask why the church exists—and then to ask questions about the content of the worship service. Churches should exalt God, edify believers, and evangelize the world.[1] Worship services, first and foremost, should exalt God. This statement underscores the imperative of God-centered worship. Believers should also be built up in the faith. Finally, authentic worship can evangelize unbelievers.

Believers who assert that the church is intended only for Christians assume continued preaching to believers will mature them to the point where they will evangelize the unchurched. I have yet to see this happen. Churches that are not intentionally evangelistic do not become evangelistic through quality Bible teaching alone. If knowledge led to evangelism, we would have reached North America years ago.

When the church exists for feeding believers only, those believers become spiritual sponges who absorb more and more knowledge. If those sponges do nothing but soak in a pool of their own learning, they eventually sour. An unchurched person can hardly feel welcome in such a setting.

God-Centered Worship

The challenge is to create an atmosphere for worship that's appropriate for both believers and unbelievers. The worship service should be God centered or even God driven. Unchurched persons benefit from seeing believers enter the presence of God. Sally Morgenthaler's book, *Worship Evangelism*, is an excellent resource for this type of worship experience.[2] Churches should recognize that the unchurched need to experience the presence of Jesus—not because they are Christians but because they are around Christians. They need to see Christians worship God.

Seeker-Comprehensible Worship

I used to call this section "Seeker Sensitive Worship." Unfortunately, that word has come to mean different things to different people. You should be sensitive to seekers. Everyone is even when they say they are not. However, the real issue is to be understandable to seekers. The primary means for creating a welcoming atmosphere for unbelievers is designing worship that's sensitive to their needs, building bridges by beginning where they are.

Churches must center on the worship of God and the proclamation of his Word while also being aware of the needs of seekers. In other words, the desire to reach seekers must not take the place of Christ-centered, Bible-based, Spirit-led worship. In order to reach unbelievers, effective churches must be sensitive to the understandings of the unchurched. However, they cannot be driven by those concerns, or else the focus is on man and not God.

One of the most effective evangelistic methods a church can use is exposing the unchurched to the authentic worship of God. Unbelievers learn worship as they witness the worship of believers. Seeker-comprehensible worship gatherings create an experience of both "God-centrality" and openness toward the needs of seekers. Seeker-comprehensible worship is a gathering that offers God honor, through worship and the preaching of the Scriptures, while providing a relevant atmosphere in which unbelievers are challenged to come to saving faith in Christ.

Seeker-*comprehensible* and seeker-*driven* worship gatherings are not the same. Seeker-comprehensible worship asks, "How can we make the unbeliever understand and feel as comfortable as possible in this context?" We must remember that the unbeliever cannot be made completely comfortable because the cross is not seeker sensitive, but the message of the cross still contains good news. A biblically sound seeker-sensitive church asks, "How can we conduct worship and communicate convictions in ways that welcome outsiders yet simultaneously honor God, his Word, his directives, and Christian practices."

Every church is seeker-sensitive to some degree. If we are worshipping in the local language, wearing local clothing, and singing music written in the last one thousand years, we are using a worship style that's sensitive to those who attend. (The pre-Vatican II Roman Catholic Church was a good example of a truly nonseeker-sensitive church. They worshipped in Latin regardless of the location.)

The real question is: To what degree will we be seeker sensitive? Will the church explain what the song means? Will the church tell when everyone will stand? Will the church demonstrate how to take the Lord's Supper? Will the church avoid the use of confusing language? Every church has seeker-sensitive worship, but *how* sensitive is it? My main concern is that the actions of the church are understandable to the unchurched, sensitive to their needs, but not changing the message to be sensitive.

An Atmosphere of Acceptance

Part of a church's task of sensitivity toward unbelievers is simply making them feel wanted and welcomed. Many pastors preach "How to Be Friendly" messages to their congregations. Creating an atmosphere of acceptance is not as easy as one might think because unbelievers and the unchurched do not act or live like Christians.

Acceptance Is Not Approval. Accepting people without approving of their lifestyles can be challenging. While loving people, we must be careful not to appear to approve or condone their un-Christian behavior. Leading such people to life-changing discipleship is not likely to occur unless they hear the claims of Christ during a worship event. The church must allow unchurched persons who are living in sinful lifestyles to enter and hear. These persons will not disrupt the well-being of the congregation or taint the saints.

Here We Stand. The church's stand on holiness should emerge at the point of church membership. Allowing sin to go unchecked among members is fundamentally different from welcoming the unchurched to a worship service. New churches need to have a biblical view of membership from the start.

The church must make clear that anyone may come and find acceptance, no matter their lifestyle. But coming to Christ and becoming His disciple requires a life change. Christ expects change, and the church should expect change. Part of the congregation's commitment to new members must be to ensure that members' lives mature in Christ. Congregational integrity demands such accountability. The church should love unbelievers as Jesus loved them, but it should also call members to life-changing discipleship, just as Jesus did.

Meeting Spiritual Needs in Worship

Needs of believers and unbelievers are often similar; they both need the power of the gospel to transform their lives. Christians suffer from the same rate of divorce as non-Christians. Christians face the same rate of emotional breakdown as unbelievers. Christians and non-Christians alike need help with parenting, finances, and priorities. God's Word applies to all in need, and his power is available to those who call on him, through conversion or for Christian growth. God's Word relates to all kinds of life issues. The church must proclaim God's Word to unbelievers in such a way that they are encouraged to take new directions in life under the power of the Spirit. Making the scriptural and musical messages understandable aids this transformation process.

Make the Music Clear. We must never underestimate the power of music to transform lives. For many people, music can touch the heart in a way that preaching cannot. Since music has an intense power in the formation of the human spirit and in the transmission of truth, we must ensure that the worship songs are theologically sound and worship appropriate.

Music should relieve anxiety and create interest for unbelievers who have not attended church for years. When people enter, they have no idea what's about to take place. Spiritually empowered music can relieve their anxieties and stir their hearts to hear God's voice.

During our second service at Millcreek Community Church, we sang "The Lord Reigns." It's a great song, but the chorus can confuse the unchurched. The lyrics read, "A fire goes before him and burns up all his enemies. The hills melt like wax at the presence of the Lord."[3] We needed to explain those words to those in attendance in order to make the lyrics understandable to the unchurched.

Electronic Aids. Electronic communication through overheads, PowerPoint presentations, and video clips also enriches worship. At the very least, the church should print the morning's Scripture texts and provide a fill-in-the-blank outline to help listeners stay engaged as the preacher presents the information using an overhead projector.

More than six out of every ten Protestant churches (62%) use a large-screen projection system in their communications. That's up 59 percent since 2000 when just 39 percent used this technology.[4]

Build a Theme. When we planted Lake Ridge Church, we used banners from Group Imaging (www.groupimaging.com) that connected with our fall theme. We live in a part of Atlanta known for an especially long commute. So our theme was, "ReThinking Reality: Living for More than the Commute." The banner matched our other banners (at the road, at the front door, at the worship center, and at children's areas) but announced our theme every week.

Consider Preaching a Series of Messages. Besides the use of electronic and written resources, another way to help listeners stay engaged is to develop a thematic series for preaching. These plans will help unbelievers and young believers alike build a body of knowledge that will serve as a foundation for their faith development for the rest of their lives. Preaching is God's chosen method for communicating the Word of God. Effective preachers will use multiple approaches to give their preaching the greatest possible impact. (See chapter 23 for an in-depth treatment of preaching in the new church.)

Consider language and behaviors. The typical evangelical church often demonstrates confusing activities: everyone suddenly stands and shakes hands on cue, everyone contributes an offering, and people walk down the aisle after the sermon. The unchurched guest, given no explanation, may find these actions strange and uncomfortable.

Aubrey Malphurs says it well: "Rather than attracting new people to Christ, many worship services are distracting them from Christ."[5] Church planters should remain sensitive to the concerns of the unchurched. If we consider visitors as guests, then we should treat them as guests. We must be careful to explain everything that could cause confusion in their minds.

Music

If church planting is missionary work, then the church planter and the planting team should think like missionaries in planning worship music. Leaders should choose the music based on the context. Music should be missiological ("like a missionary") and serviceable in the context.

Early Hawaiian missionaries failed miserably in this regard.[6] When they arrived on the islands, they had the islanders dress in Western clothing, and they taught them European music and hymns. These insensitive activities limited missionary effectiveness for that time and, perhaps, for all time among the indigenous people of Hawaii.

Although members of liturgical churches in colonial North America enjoyed stately English hymns, persons of lower station neither liked nor understood them. One creative missionary along the frontier adapted a tavern tune to tell the gospel story in response to that reality. The church then learned the good news from the lyrics of "Amazing Grace, How Sweet the Sound."[7] Contextual music is always better, but we must remember that songs that were clear hundreds of years ago may not be understandable to many people today.

The sensitivities expected of international missionaries should compel North American church planters who also work in pluralistic cultures.

Planters and team members should select worship music that's culturally appropriate for their specific context.

One way to determine the music is to know your focus group. What is their favorite musical style? This can be determined by listening to popular radio stations or looking at a local music shop in a culturally creative neighborhood.

Once we've determined their preferred musical style, wisdom calls us to adapt our own tunes and style to the preferred style of our focus group. Just like the frontier evangelist who adapted the tune of "Amazing Grace," we must also write or adapt Christian lyrics suitable to that particular style. As the frontier evangelist might have said, "There's no such thing as Christian music, only Christian lyrics." Adapt the unchanging gospel to a changing musical style.

Statistical evidence supports the fact that worship style does impact church size. When comparing six styles and looking at new church worship attendance over four years, contemporary and seeker churches tend to be larger than the other worship styles:

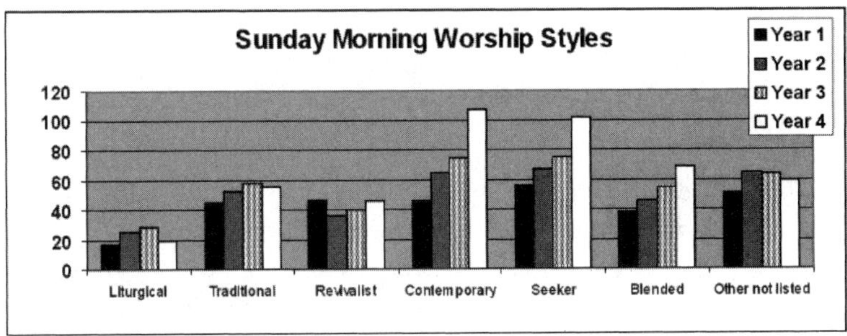

The Enduring Struggles

The church planter must decide whether to think like a missionary (missional) or be constrained by the values and vision of supporters who are already Christ followers. In my new book, *Breaking the Missional Code*, we have a section called "The Sin of Preferences." Too many pastors and core groups are planning their worship style based on what they like, their preferences, rather than what will help people they are reaching understand and participate in worship.

An effective church planter needs to demonstrate a great concern for gospel expressions that relate to unchurched people. Effective missionaries don't ask the focus group what their content of their preaching and music should be; they ask what vehicles—preaching style and music style of the focus group—will change their lives in the most effective way.

If the style of music or preaching overwhelms the message, the missional church planter is making a serious mistake. Worship requires words of truth. The vehicle—music, style of proclamation, and so forth—must edify Christians and encourage the unchurched to consider following Christ.

Conclusion

Worship should touch the heart and the mind. It should be cognitive, touching the brain like the kenotic hymn of Philippians 2; it should be affective, stirring the emotions like the Psalms. We need both experiences in new churches today.

Not every service has to include both elements. These elements should receive attention in order to touch and change the lives of your focus group. Every worship time, regardless of stylistic content, should emerge from the leadership of God and rest solely on his Word. True worship must be both God-centered and seeker-sensitive.

Resources for Further Reading

Baker, Jonny, and Doug Gay. *Alternative Worship: Resources from and for the Emerging Church.* Grand Rapids, Mich.: Baker Books, 2004.

Kimball, Dan. *Emerging Worship: Creating Worship Gatherings for New Generations.* Grand Rapids, Mich.: Zondervan, 2004.

Morgenthaler, Sally. *Worship Evangelism: Inviting Unbelievers into the Presence of God.* Grand Rapids: Zondervan Publishing House, 1995.

Sorge, Bob. *Exploring Worship: A Practical Guide to Praise and Worship.* Canandaigua, N.Y.: Oasis House, 1987.

Chapter 23

Preaching in the New Church

There is much confusion about preaching today. Some are advocating only one form of preaching; others seem to have abandoned preaching in the name of cultural relevance. Neither of these positions is helpful as you plant a new church. But the preaching of the Word is a mark of a true church whether that preaching is in a circle of ten in a house church or in front of thousands at a rented conference center.

Preaching in a new church offers unique challenges. In a gathering made up of believers and nonbelievers, preaching must both edify believers and encourage nonbelievers. We must grow in our preaching skills if we cannot do both. While Jesus preached a straightforward gospel, he demonstrated that preaching is not just opening the Bible, reading words, and providing commentary.

In a new church, preaching should be simple but not simplistic. The Scriptures are given not only for information but also for transformation. The preacher may impress listeners with arcane theological truths that offer no life and hope, or the preacher may help transform lives with the truths of Christ's life-changing presence. The latter result is God's intention for Christian preaching.

Yet for many, preaching is seen as almost an embarrassment. Some new churches want to abandon preaching in their attempt to be more relevant. I've walked that road myself. I've preached a lot of sermons that were more about my opinions than God's Word. Sure, they were based on biblical principles ("love your wife," "don't worry," "work hard") but not grounded in the biblical story of redemption. Then, Donna (my wife) told me that after all our years together she felt that she did not know the Bible well. As her pastor, I had taught her how to be a godly person but not how to understand our God revealed in the Bible.

The need for biblical preaching has never been more urgent. Biblical preaching is more than commonsense truth with biblical proofs taken out of context. Instead, it is letting the agenda and shape of Scripture determine the agenda and shape of the message. I've learned that I have not taken it seriously enough, and I think I am not alone. As we have planted Lake Ridge Church, we have made sure that the Bible and the story of redemption are more central in our preaching.

Good preaching usually does not focus on theological truths without application; both are present. When the Bible presents theological truth, it almost always weds that revelation to relational application. The high kenotic hymn in Philippians 2:6–11 says this about Christ: "Who, being in very nature God, did not consider equality with God something to be grasped." This is theological material, but it's important to remember how the hymn begins: "Have this attitude in yourselves which is also in Christ Jesus." Any presentation of the theological truths (about the preexistence of Christ, etc.), needs to include practical application (about how our attitude is to be changed by Christ's example).

The reverse is true as well. Almost all relational truth comes from passages of Scripture rooted in the story of redemption. You can't preach the last part of Ephesians (no unwholesome words, love your spouse, work hard) without preaching the first part (we were dead and God made us alive, his incomparable power working in us). If we preach "do good" and "try harder" without the truth of the power of God working in us, we have presented an applicable sermon without the power to apply it.

Listeners need a time for hearing technical theological truths because these serve as foundations for life changes. The challenge is a balance of theological content and life application. At the beginning of the new church, preaching may be more practical; but felt-needs preaching is not a long-term, viable strategy for preaching.

Expositional Preaching

All biblical preaching should be expositional preaching. Exposition means a presentation of the meaning or intent. All true preaching explains the meaning and intent of the Bible. This does not necessarily mean that preaching has to be a verse-by-verse study of the Bible. It does mean that it has to convey accurately the meaning and intent of the Bible.

The unmistakable admonition of 2 Timothy 4:2 is, "Preach the Word." These verses do not commend personal opinions, nor do they validate fads. Paul's directive to Timothy was, "Preach the Word."

Scripture-based preaching is not always popular. Unchurched people and believers who haven't defined their biblical values often take offense at the preaching of the cross. Such thinking may create friction between the pastor and unchurched people. The church planter, nevertheless, has been called to "preach the Word; be prepared in season and out of season; correct, rebuke and encourage—with great patience and careful instruction" (2 Tim. 4:2). The church planter must allow the text to set the agenda and to address the issues.

It's been interesting to be a part of (and now an observer of) the church growth movement of the 1980s and 1990s. Some people taught cultural truths with scriptural footnoting. They would describe some universal truth (you should be good to your spouse, for example), and then explain that the Bible agrees. In the last few years, such preaching seems to be less common. Increasingly new churches reaching emerging generations are saying, "This is what the Bible says, and this is how to apply it. We are trying our best to apply it in our lives, and you can too." I think that's good news.

On the other hand, there seems to be a significant minority who say that all preaching needs to be verse by verse. For some people, expository preaching has become synonymous with verse-by-verse preaching. This causes some to argue that verse-by-verse exposition is the only valid form of preaching. If that were true, then the early church heard no preaching at all for at least 350 years, until the time of John Chrysostom, who popularized this form.

For the purposes of this book, I'll define expository preaching as "proclamation that exposes people to the truths of God's Word." Albert Mohler says, "For a sermon to be genuinely biblical, the text must set the agenda as the foundation of the message, and not as a spiritual authority cited for spiritual footnoting. Scripture should be central."[1] Expository preaching does not make statements and look to the Bible for support; it begins by examining the Scriptures.

Contemporary churches have been criticized for their lack of expository preaching. Some of it is from misunderstandings. However, some of it is also because some new churches have abandoned biblically based, expositional preaching. The Bible is not their sermon text; it barely impacts their sermon text.

I've seen too many churches advocate subtly that winning people to Christ necessitates laying aside the Bible. One pastor in a Bible Belt state explained his strategy as having people attend a "little pep talk" each Sunday morning in order to offer them encouragement and then send them home. That church has shortened its service time to a maximum of forty-five minutes. The end results will be disastrous if the pastor-planter does not preach the Word. The pastor-planter *must* preach the Word.

We need innovative preaching, but we also must take people to the Word, not just give them commonsense wisdom they can get watching Wayne Dyer on PBS.

I recently interviewed Andy Stanley for a future project on key leaders and their characteristics. I believe Andy expressed the concern for biblical preaching well. Andy explained:

> [Preaching] is a journey… I am going to start by making sure… everybody knows where we are going… and they know why they need to go with me. Once I have built enough tension for someone to give a rip about what we are going to talk about, then I am going to take them to a passage of Scripture where somebody resolves or expresses that tension. And I am going to stay there long enough so hopefully they will go back that afternoon, and they will say, "I understand this part of the Bible." Then I am going to talk about what to do and what a wonderful world it would be like if we all just do this. It is really that simple.

That requires taking the time to prepare biblical sermons. Mark Driscoll of Mars Hill Church explains how he prepares: "In studying a passage to preach, I ask three questions: Who is God? How is He revealed in this text? What are the most natural inclinations that resist or deny that truth? Then, for the rest of the sermon, I seek out that resistance and break it."[2]

Most importantly, biblical preaching is gospel-centered preaching. By gospel-centered, I am not referring to continual evangelistic preaching—every week a sermon on how to get saved. Instead, the gospel is the means by which life change occurs. Tim Keller of Redeemer Presbyterian describes the process of being sure that the gospel always is presented as the means of transformation:

> At the heart of Redeemer's ministry and its philosophy of preaching to post-modern audiences is the conviction that "the gospel" is not just a way to be saved from the penalty of sin, but is the fundamental dynamic for living the whole Christian life—individually and corporately, privately and publicly.... It is more accurate to say that we are saved by believing the gospel, and then we are transformed in every part of our mind, heart, and life by believing the gospel more and more deeply as our life goes on.[3]

Four Kinds of Expositional Preaching

The four most common are: verse by verse, thematic, narrative, and topical.

Verse-by-Verse Preaching. This is the systematic reading and explanation of a biblical text, involving one book of Scripture and its piece-by-piece analysis. I quoted Mark Driscoll earlier because Mars Hill Church[4] in Seattle is a well-known church that's effectively reaching unchurched people in Seattle. The church Web site explains, "The beginning, the end, and everything in between. The Bible defines Mars Hill."[5] The site lists recent messages from Pastor Mark Driscoll and other teaching pastors including text and MP3 files of each message. Recent messages include studies of Song of Solomon, Romans, Jonah, and other Scripture texts.

Thematic Expository (or Doctrinal) Preaching. Thematic preaching is an excellent form for preaching Bible doctrine. The speaker can focus on everyday topics by expounding on a specific biblical text. The pastor can focus on Bible sayings on any relevant subject by a careful study and exposition of relevant biblical passages.

Thematic expository preaching generally appears in a sermon series over several weeks and introduces many Scriptures focused on the same theme. Thematic messages may include as many as ten or twelve Scripture passages in each sermon. Since the Bible tends to provide teachings on themes dispersed through different books, this form of preaching is a good way to preach the "whole counsel of God." This method also introduces new believers or unschooled unbelievers to general themes and patterns that appear throughout the Bible.

For example, Darrin Patrick at The Journey, a new church in St. Louis, has been preaching on themes of love and marriage, drawing from the Song of Solomon and other biblical texts. The focus is what the Bible teaches about those themes, and the source for that is the Scripture, not his opinions or preferences. His messages are available at www.journeyon.net.

Narrative Expository Preaching. Narrative preaching presents the biblical text in the form of story and follows that story to completion. A narrative sermon functions as a lengthy illustration that uses a biblical text as its beginning and end.

When using this form, the speaker shares a story from the gospel such as the account of Jesus and the Samaritan woman (John 4). In telling the story, the preacher asks the listener to join in the narrative. As a result, the listener sees the fullness of Jesus' words and teachings. This type of expository preaching can be highly effective in postmodern North American culture, which has rejected most of our traditional approaches.

Some time ago I discovered the value of narrative preaching during a church-starting crusade in West Africa. Although I believed I had preached a great message on the first night of a crusade, I found that the nationals had not connected with my verse-by-verse exposition of Luke 14.

On the second night I adapted my style to use narrative exposition of the Nicodemus story from John 3. Those in attendance responded to the unfolding story with enthusiastic applause at key points. Their excitement grew. When I told of Nicodemus's presence at the foot of Jesus' cross, the crowd exploded with joy. Many responded to the gospel invitation that night. More than one hundred attended the first service of the new church.

Narrative preaching will grow more popular in the coming years. This is good news as long as the narratives remain consistent with biblical texts. Jesus demonstrated the value of narrative preaching by his use of parables.

Topical Expository Preaching. Of the four forms of exposition, I recommend this form the least. Its weakness grows out of the limits of time and the speaker's inability to include enough biblical text about the topic in one sermon. Although I discourage this form, it's helpful at times.

Topical exposition generally revolves around one passage, centering on one theme. It is topical because it's usually a single message on a single subject. It's expository, because it uses the biblical text as its source.

Most preachers use this form on special occasions such as Mother's Day, Father's Day, and Easter, but topical preaching does not provide adequate time to address the whole counsel of God as other methods do. Topical preaching limits opportunities for presenting proper understandings of the context as opposed to verse-by-verse preaching. In addition, the topical approach does not offer the opportunity to use the graphic and powerful images of narrative preaching. The church planter will probably use topical exposition, but it should be used sparingly.

Application

Any good message starts with the primary question: What's the purpose of the sermon?[6] If people find the purpose interesting, they will listen. Pastors often don't answer the questions people are dying to ask or resolve because of what's going on in their personal lives. The pastor may be preaching on the benefits of the Old Testament law while a woman in the pew is wondering if her marriage will last. The pastor may be explaining the importance of the chiasma in Philippians while a husband is considering an adulterous relationship.

The pastor needs to answer the questions that people are asking and answer them in a way that influences people's lives. The sermon should be biblically sound first—and then mnemonically effective, visually stimulating, and encouraging.

Mnemonically Effective. The most effective sermons are those that are simple and easy to remember. Paul provides some examples. Pithy sayings can be effective. Each of the following Scripture passages can be readily quoted:

"Bad company corrupts good character" (1 Cor. 15:33).

"For the letter kills, but the Spirit gives life" (2 Cor. 3:6).

"If a man will not work, he shall not eat" (2 Thess. 3:10).

"Don't you know that a little yeast works through the whole batch of dough?" (1 Cor. 5:6).

Visually Stimulating. Paul used illustrations from many sources, including athletics and the military.[7] These were appropriate because they were from the world in which he lived. Illustrations are essential. Good messages have memorable illustrations.[8]

Encouraging. Paul had no difficulty in appealing to the emotions of his hearers.[9] Chris Seay, now pastor of Ekklesia[10] in Houston, explained how he shared his struggles with honesty and transparency. He wanted to show others that they could make it if he could: "Basically, my preaching style is to get up in front of them and say: 'This is where God "beat me up in the Word" this week, and this is an area where I have sinned.'"[11]

Instead of trying to amaze congregations with the use of primary sources and exegetical methods, a wiser course is to share personal shortcomings and struggles as you explain the text.[12] This is where genuineness comes into play.

Paul was not considered a great orator. Much has been written about this topic, and it seemed to be a great weakness of the apostle Paul.[13] Delivery hardly seemed to be of great importance to the spread of the gospel. It was said of him, "His letters are weighty and forceful, but in person he is unimpressive and his speaking amounts to nothing" (2 Cor. 10:10). But Paul's heart was always open. He derived his speaking authority from his genuineness and broken nature.

Shaped by the Listener

I remember sitting in a well-known church after a national tragedy. The pastor did not mention or address what was on everyone's mind—why do such things happen? Instead, he continued through his text as he had planned months before. He failed to take into account the needs of the listener.

The Scriptures model a different paradigm. For example, Paul varied his message depending on the needs and spiritual conditions of the listeners. The chart below illustrates his changing style:

Text	Place	Audience	Approach
Acts 13:15–41	Antioch of Pisidia	Interested Jews	Much history and Hebrew Scripture
Acts 14:15–17	Lystra	Idolaters	Nature is a bridge to the gospel
Acts 17:22–31	Athens	Educated philosphers	Quotes a Stoic poet and acknowledges their religious quest
Acts 22:3–21	Jerusalem	Mob of Jews	Gives a personal testimony

Conclusion

When a new church is launched, the messages won't tend to be as deep as they might be in the future. In the beginning stage of a new church, the sermons should be more like what Larry Moyer defines as an evangelistic sermon—a message with a sharper focus, an awareness of the biblical illiteracy of the audience, less work with the text, simple organizational structure, revealing of life, filled with illustrations, and humorous.[14] Good preaching in a new church will eventually evolve into a more thoroughly biblical yet practical preaching. Some have called this "life-situation preaching."[15]

We must not only stay immersed in the Word, but we also must study the culture in order to understand the people to whom we preach.[16] The most effective form of preaching in emerging churches is not trendy and culturally driven. Instead, it is holding up the Word of God as the source of truth and allowing the listener to be challenged and shaped by it. We don't have to talk them into anything or convince them that the Bible makes sense; instead, we can share the Bible as authoritative and allow them to decide whether to accept it.

Calvin Miller explained that the purpose of the sermon is not education; it's encounter with God.[17] I hope I can lead people into that encounter while remaining faithful to the Word of God. My desire is to be able to repeat the words of John Calvin: "I have not corrupted one single passage of Scripture, nor twisted it as far as I know. . . . I have always studied to be simple."[18] Preaching in our age, as in any age, needs to be biblical preaching. Styles of delivery should change, but we still must "preach the Word." It is good news that more and more congregations are rediscovering the value of biblical preaching.

A school of thought emerged in the 1990s—in order to reach the lost you had to water down the biblical content. Ralph Moore explains: "We at Hope Chapel sometimes take a little heat for our bibliocentric approach. One time a delegation from another congregation visited my church. As soon as I asked people to open their Bibles to the text for the evening, these people began rolling their eyes and punching each other in the ribs. Later I discovered they were young pastors in training. They had been taught that it is not sensitive to the unchurched to use the Bible in church."[19]

If you don't know where I stand on this issue by now, I'll be more direct: *The only message you have is Christ and the Bible.* Downplaying the prominence of that message for any reason is a dangerous compromise. You can reach out to the unchurched and still be honest about your message and the Book that contains that message.

My friend John Mark Clifton shared this with me, and I thought it an appropriate ending for this chapter:

> I give each of the church planters with whom I work a copy of Piper's book, *The Passion of Jesus*. It contains fifty messages on the power and meaning of the cross. Here is the deal: the cross is enough. It is enough to save, to heal, to give hope, to give peace, to give joy, to overcome discouragement. I tell my guys that you don't have to teach your people everything, but they do need to know, to believe, and to live as though the cross is enough. Get to the cross in every message. It is not only about salvation, it is about life, struggle, victory, and sacrifice; and it is missing in most church planter preaching.[20]

Resources for Further Reading

Anderson, Kenton C. *Preaching with Conviction: Connecting with Postmodern Listeners*. Grand Rapids: Kregel Publications, 2001.

Nelson, Alan. *Creating Messages that Connect: 10 Secrets of Effective Communicators*. Loveland, Colo.: Group Publishing, 2004.

Piper, John. *The Supremacy of God in Preaching.* Grand Rapids, Mich: Baker Books, 2004.

Stone, David. *Refining Your Style: Learning from Effective Communicators*. Loveland, Colo.: Group Publishing, 2004.

Stott, John R. W. *Between Two Worlds: The Challenge of Preaching Today*. Grand Rapids, Mich.: Wm. B. Eerdmans Publishing Company, 1994.

Willard, Dallas. *The Divine Conspiracy: Rediscovering Our Hidden Life in God*. San Francisco: Harper & Row, 1998.

York, Hershael, and Bert Decker. *Preaching with Bold Assurance: A Solid and Enduring Approach to Engaging Exposition* Bold Assurance Series, 2. Nashville: Broadman & Holman, 2003.

Sermon materials on the www.pastors.com Web site.

www.preachingplus.com.

www.sermoncentral.com.

Chapter 24

Spiritual Formation in the New Church

Church growth expert Win Arn lists eight characteristics of an "incorporated member." These characteristics describe a person successfully assimilated by a new church, and they help the congregation develop methods for assimilation.

1. New members should be able to list at least seven new friends they have made in the church.
2. New members should be able to identify their spiritual gifts.
3. New members should be involved in at least one (preferably several) roles/tasks/ministries in the church, appropriate to their spiritual gifts.
4. New members should be actively involved in a small fellowship (face-to-face) group.
5. New members should demonstrate a regular financial commitment to the church.
6. New members should personally understand and identify with church goals.
7. New members should attend worship services regularly.
8. New members should identify unchurched friends and relatives

and take specific steps to help them toward responsible church membership.[1]

Spiritual Formation / Discipleship

At some point the church planter must move beyond immediate follow-up to create an ongoing spiritual formation process. Disciple development occurs through opportunities in which individuals consistently grow toward spiritual maturity.

Discipleship does not happen by accident. Jesus told his followers, "If you hold to my teaching, you are really my disciples. Then you will know the truth, and the truth will set you free" (John 8:31–32). Church planters are called to create disciples, not just believers. By definition, a disciple is a follower of Christ. A disciple is a learner.

A disciple is also a believer who practices biblical habits that enable him or her to live the Christian life effectively. A mature believer displays many behaviors or habits such as prayer, sharing faith, Bible study, and fasting. The disciple must intentionally practice these habits in order to develop effectively as a disciple.

Many churchgoers and leaders assume that younger believers develop these habits because they hear about the need to practice them. This is not true in new or older churches. Habits leading to Christian maturity must be practiced in order for a disciple to become developed.

The important question is whether the church's approach produces maturing disciples. As long as the spiritual formation process is biblically based and God-focused and produces maturing believers, it's a serviceable disciple-making approach.

Part of the church planter's task is to create an atmosphere—a congregational culture—in which discipleship and disciple-making surface as core values. For most churches, there is a difference between what is said and what is done. New members hear about the spiritual formation process but observe that the vast majority of church attendees don't participate. They choose to listen to the culture rather than the leaders.

A better course is to get the entire church valuing and participating in a spiritual formation process. Then it is not just the leaders exhorting people to spiritual formation; it is the culture of the church that does so.

Sequential Discipleship Plans

The L.I.F.E. class curriculum[2] is probably the most common approach for new church discipleship. L.I.F.E. classes usually meet in a four-hour block or for one hour per week over a period of four weeks. Courses focus on specific aspects of the Christian life and the local church's ministry. Participants are encouraged to sign a covenant to practice the matters they have studied prior to the conclusion of each course.

101 and Beyond. The L.I.F.E. process of study begins with course 101, which focuses on salvation, the Lord's Supper, and baptism. Affiliated churches will also explain their denominational connection. The class ends with a discussion of congregational vision, direction, future, and central values.

As a membership type class, this is also the time to be sure people are clear on the content and application of the gospel itself. Regarding new member classes, in a study of new churches, Chuck Lawless states: "This study showed us that a membership class can be used effectively for evangelism... These churches invited non-members to attend their class, and they often found these guests open to the Gospel. Some churches even told us that it is highly unusual to hold a membership class without someone becoming a believer in the process. Wise church leaders will look at ways to use their membership class in a similar way."[3]

Disciplines of 201. The second class, course 201, focuses on the basic disciplines of Bible study, prayer, small-group koinonia, and tithing. At the close of 201, participants respond to a covenant opportunity to read the Bible regularly, to pray daily, to gather weekly with a small group of believers, and to begin tithing.

301: Disciples Taking Shape. L.I.F.E. course 301 emphasizes each participant's calling to confirm his or her spiritual giftedness and to identify a ministry interest (calling) within the congregation. Most churches using L.I.F.E. classes use the Saddleback Church's gifts-assessment tool, S.H.A.P.E., an acronym that stands for:

- Spiritual gifts
- Heart passion
- Abilities
- Personality type
- Experiences in life

Since every believer has qualities identifiable in the S.H.A.P.E. profile, this tool enables new churches to determine the best place of ministry for each participant.

401: My Mission. The final 401 L.I.F.E. class focuses on evangelism and missions. Participants explore God's expectations—the implications of living their personal faith in the larger world outside the church. As a result of this study and the discovery of their personal S.H.A.P.E. during course 301, members articulate their personal mission statements.

These L.I.F.E. classes center on four fundamentals: personal faith and church values, basic disciplines of the Christian life and small-group involvement, self-discovery of spiritual giftedness and ministry calling, and the development of a personal mission statement. Most churches modify them for their particular situation.

The Next Stage of Training. Beyond these fundamental areas, every individual needs more individualized training. In one of my church plants, we continued to use the college course numbering system for this variety of discipleship studies and training opportunities. Since the 201 course emphasized Christian spiritual disciplines, *Experiencing God*,[4] which provided greater focus on these disciplines, was offered as another 200s course. Since we related 301 to discovering one's ministry, courses such as "How to Teach the Bible" fit into that same family and received a 300s course number.

Examples of the L.I.F.E. classes from several churches can be found at www.newchurches.com/examples.

First the new church should equip all members with the fundamentals in the four L.I.F.E. classes. Next the church will need to offer a balance of other training opportunities based on members' perceived and actual needs. Progressive, creative planning throughout the disciple-making process will keep members motivated and excited and will reinforce the climate for church discipleship and disciple-making.

Discipleship by Environment

Some churches in a postmodern age are moving away from linear discipleship models. Instead, they're emphasizing opportunities for discipleship that are offered simultaneously or in a random order.

North Point Community Church[5] in Alpharetta, Georgia invites attendees to participate in three "environments." These environments include: the foyer—an entry-level service where guests experience the church for the first time (e.g. the worship service, Xtreme middle school service, Rush Hour high school service, and Kidstuf); the living room—social events where people interact and relationships are built; and the kitchen—small groups of six to eight people who meet together for Bible study and ongoing discipleship.

Pastor Andy Stanley explained to me, "Life is not sequential... People need to be in all three environments."[6] The church provides places of connection to people on their timetable.

Nonsequential Discipleship

New Horizons Fellowship[7] in Apex, North Carolina, defines its purposes and assimilation strategy with an atom:

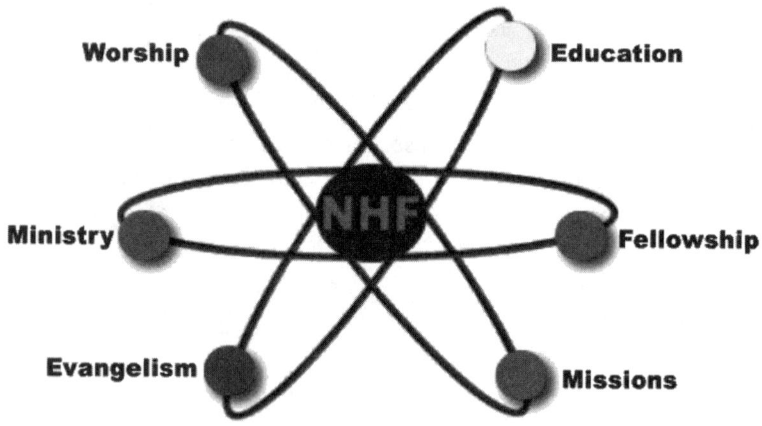

Instead of encouraging members to go through a sequential process, Pastor Ray Wickham tells church attendees they can start anywhere in the process. A church attendee might begin with a mission project such as helping to build a Habitat for Humanity house. Or they might start fellowshipping in a small group or begin at a discipleship class. Any point can be an entry point. The church does encourage all attendees to work all the way "around" the atom.

At New Horizons "we encourage believers to make sure that they have balance in their spiritual lives. Balance involves making sure that you're 'doing' the six purposes of the Christian life. . . . We believe that if you just emphasize one or two of these, it's like eating just chocolate or meat and not all the elements of the food pyramid! It's essential to have balance for spiritual health and growth."[8] We have used an approach more like this at Lake Ridge Church.

Create a Culture of Discipleship

Whatever approach the church chooses for disciple development, the pastor and other leaders must cultivate a congregational culture of intentional discipleship. The pastor should decide before beginning the new work what disciple-development plan the congregation will follow. But, without an intentional developmental approach, the church is likely to become "a mile wide and an inch deep."

Great Expectations. Entrepreneurial planters, especially gifted teachers, may be able to design discipleship materials for a new church. "Franchisees" probably will be wise to adapt someone else's materials for their new church's needs.

Whichever approach for materials the church follows, the planter should set clear standards for all members in their personal discipleship. These great expectations should appear in church literature. The planter-pastor should announce these expectations in meeting settings, in teaching, and in proclamation. This intentionality will help create a "congregational disciple-making culture" that will endure throughout the life of the church.

A Culture and a Ministry. Discipling as a personal ministry is different from discipleship as a design for the congregation's life. Although the two are intertwined, the church planter, while encouraging the entire congregation to become mature disciples, can personally disciple only a handful of leaders. Disciple-making is both a culture for the congregation and a personal ministry for the church planter.

What's the Difference? Discipling is a process of spiritual mentoring performed by the pastor for only a few individuals. Discipleship is a process in which all church members grow in faith, assisted by congregational programming. The church must provide discipleship curriculum as part of a discipleship culture designed to train all members. The planter-pastor mentors (disciples) only a few of those members personally. These functions are intertwined, and both are important.

Whom to Disciple? It's important to develop a leadership training methodology, but what's even more crucial is answering the question, Who should become the planter's disciples?

The planter should mentor a few handpicked individuals—three to five disciples—at any one time. They don't need to function in high levels of leadership, but they should be people of great potential. The church planter should invest disciple-making time almost exclusively in leaders or potential leaders for the long-range well-being of the congregation.

Biblical Principles. The Holy Spirit must grant discernment to the planter in the selection of people to mentor. Human beings are highly susceptible to temptation; God doesn't choose leaders based on outward appearances but on the purity of heart (1 Sam. 16:7). Our discernment must be tempered by prayer in order to be sound. Although we readily affirm this instruction, we practice it too seldom. The Son of God spent all night in prayer before choosing his closest companions in ministry (Luke 6:12–13). Each of those twelve failed at some point. But because of his training—and the power of the Spirit—his disciples ultimately grew to replicate much that Jesus had done—as he had promised they would.

Expecting the Best from Believers

Great expectations disciple-making is one component of a larger pattern found in healthy congregations. Such congregations expect great sacrifices and commitments from their members. Some church starters believe that if they require too much of people, members won't commit.

Some People *Will* Leave. Some unconvinced people will not participate, some because they don't like the commitment involved and some because they have already come a long way on the Christian journey before they came to your church. Some sincere and committed people may also leave because they aren't convinced of the strategy.

This will happen more than you think. If you target unchurched people, you may think that Christians won't come. They will and you want them. And many of them already know a lot about the Christian life. To tell them that they have to go through some classes on the "basics" can be a little hard to hear. But, mature believers can also understand that you went through the class, your family went through the class, and everybody else went through the class. It is not the only way, but it is the way you do things at your new church. By sharing your plan, you can win most people over. But remember that the Bible teaches to treat older men and women with respect. Share your reasons, don't change your plan, but ask them to be a part and have a compelling reason to do so.

Like Attracts Like. Some prospects, and even members, may become offended by such high expectations. Planters should remember that like attracts like. The greater the number of people interested in deep levels of commitment, the higher the spiritual intensity of the church will become. (Remember that even highly committed persons can become swallowed and pulled down by the mediocrity of the many whereas rarely do the high standards of a few lift the standards of the masses.)

Demand Evokes Commitment. When a church planter articulates high expectations and describes the vision of the congregation, members will respond positively. High expectations summon surprising commitments. High-expectation churches evoke serious commitments because human beings want to commit themselves to something bigger than themselves. High-expectation churches attract and affirm members who commit themselves to high standards of performance and discipleship.

Statistical research also demonstrates that the presence of high membership standards seemed to have a positive correlation in several samples. Each time a membership requirement was included, an increase in mean attendance was noticeable. Churches that expect more from their members are larger than those that do not. If you have high expectations for people, they will rise to meet them; but if you consistently have low expectations of involvement, your people will rarely rise above them.

Not in Words, but in Principle. Some people may question why a church imposes high standards for membership and discipleship, especially if the Bible records no specific mandate for those demands.

The first answer is that while the specific words may not appear in Scripture, the underlying principles do appear. Second, and perhaps more practical, the church's practice reflects the congregation's values in practicing its commitments. There is nothing wrong with a positive mind-set.

Help sincere but uncomfortable believers find a comfortable place. Disagreement by members or prospects about such policies does not mean that they are unspiritual because of their views. Nor does it mean that the congregation is too zealous when it sets requirements. Some people simply need a different type of church home. Helping these people see their need for a different church home is an important part of the planter's task of shepherding the entire flock.

Spiritual Infants

God entrusts churches with incredible gifts, unbelieving persons who come to relationship with Jesus Christ. As "foster parents," stewards of those spiritual infants, congregations must take the task of discipling new believers seriously. Following God's path for our lives must not be taken lightly.

Sunday worship, no matter how effective and spiritual, cannot provide sufficient spiritual nourishment for a new believer. The church needs to provide more support and instruction than one hour on Sunday mornings. Whatever the curriculum and delivery system, the church must provide instruction in Christian fundamentals. Beyond this basic instruction, the congregation should plan, provide for, and monitor the effectiveness of discipleship instruction through which the entire congregation finds resources to continue growing in their faith.

Although many persons teach and enable disciple-making in the congregation, the central role remains with the planter-pastor. The church planter is the person who must select and mentor the church's first generation of leaders. The church planter must choose the initial framework and system for disciple-making. The pastor must also take the initiative in modeling and communicating the importance of ongoing discipleship. If the planter performs these functions properly, the new congregation should mature, develop young believers, and honor God through the lives of many persons that will impact the new congregation over the course of its lifetime.

Assimilating Guests into the Fellowship

Assimilation is the process of enabling and encouraging prospects and visitors to become members and active participants in the church. Many guests attend for a week or two and then stop coming. Some will attend only sporadically. The object of assimilation is to encourage attendees to become fruit-bearing disciples.

New Believers; Unique Challenges. Although churches frequently do not recognize these needs, new believers present unique challenges. New churches must discern the needs of new believers in order to assimilate them. The church must identify goals for a follow-up program and design a system that enables the church to retain new believers.

Beyond Church as a Service. The congregation must move beyond the perception that "church" is a worship service that simply leads to more worship services. When the church allows itself to be perceived as a series of meetings, it deteriorates into nothing more than a gathering of people with unmet needs. A church needs a system to help people find stability that leads to long-term spiritual growth.

New Habits of Stability

The need for stability is fundamental to all human beings but most especially to new believers.[9] Most people come to Christ before the age of eighteen. If they come to Christ later, they often do so in the midst of a personal crisis. Since the years of youth are filled with upheaval, we may assume that crisis plays a major role in most decisions to accept Christ.

Crises usually do not disappear when a person becomes a Christian. Although the crisis of discovering one's need for a Savior can be resolved by a commitment to Christ, most unbelievers become Christians through other kinds of crises: a recent divorce, the death of a family member, the loss of a job, or some other catastrophic event that opens them to the saving work of the Holy Spirit.

The task of the church is to introduce Christ into people's lives when their stability is crumbling. Believers can help non-Christians understand that Christ alone is the way to experience lasting stability. Stability can take several different forms: biblical, relational, and functional.

Biblical Stability

Unchurched people cling to the idea that one can become a Christian without forsaking nonbiblical ideas. New believers may still read horoscopes or continue in unholy activities in which they participated before accepting Christ. The church cannot wait for the new believer to discover that such practices contradict biblical and doctrinal beliefs. We need to instruct new believers from the beginning. We should model behaviors which aid them in grounding their lives doctrinally and biblically in Christ.

Establishing Stability. The church that establishes new believers in the faith must provide help for young believers in a variety of areas: assurance of God's forgiveness, certainty of their salvation experience, and confidence that God hears their prayers. New believers need support as they develop a maturing understanding of God, Jesus Christ, and the church.

Stability Born of God's Word. New believers develop doctrinal stability in their lives when the church teaches and preaches God's Word as powerful, authoritative, and true. This area of stability is the easiest of the three to develop as long as new believers continue to attend church gatherings and pay attention to what they hear.

The Word as Daily Bread. The congregation should make every effort to teach young believers to rely on God's Word for insight (1 Pet. 2:2). If the church teaches new believers to study and search the Scriptures from the beginning of their relationship with Christ, they'll discover the need for the Word to become their daily bread and spiritual sustenance. As they study the Scriptures, new believers develop a habit that can transform their lives over the course of their lifetime.

Relational Stability

William Hendricks, in his book *Exit Interviews*, argues that new Christians are likely to leave the church within the first six months of faith if they don't develop seven significant relationships with the congregation in that time.[10]

These relationships pose an important challenge because the new church's strategy of assimilation must develop an atmosphere that encourages the relational stability that novice believers need. This atmosphere will develop as members model healthy relationships and as the church emphasizes relational accountability through small groups or Sunday school.

Unconditional Befriending. New believers need close Christian friends, especially disciple-makers who can accept them as they are while challenging them to mature. Many infant Christians make little effort to cultivate new friends because they feel comfortable with the friends they already have. New congregations must learn to accept the immaturity of new believers and make befriending them a priority. This attitude is the spirit of the hero of Acts, Barnabas. Without Barnabas, two young, aspiring leaders—Saul (later Paul) and John Mark (later the Gospel writer)—might not have become powerful, effective leaders in God's kingdom. If believers do not involve new converts in their circle of faith, they will likely never become mature believers.

The writer of Hebrews exhorted his readers to assemble with other believers for the purposes of fellowship and encouragement (Heb. 10:25). Leading new believers to regular participation in fellowship activities will not be simple. Such intimacy requires trust and an assurance of being accepted by others. This level of fellowship demands personal intimacy with God raised to a group level. Such intensity of fellowship can be intimidating to maturing believers and even more intimidating to younger Christians.

Small Groups. The church should encourage new members toward a small-group experience. Sometimes low-key events such as a meet-the-pastor luncheon or a *Survival Kit for Young Christians* study can encourage new people to get more involved in small-group fellowship opportunities.

Small-group ministry can nurture relational stability. Churches cannot assimilate people in crowds of a hundred or a thousand. Assimilation occurs individually and in small groups. These small groups should be a bonding place for new relationships. Small groups should not be used for an in-depth Bible study. Interaction between members should serve as the focus of small groups.

Functional Stability

New believers also long for functional stability. If they still wrestle with drug abuse, sexual immorality, and other concerns, they will be unable to focus on issues of spiritual maturity and discipleship until they settle these matters. New churches usually have few mechanisms for dealing with such high-demand issues.

We cannot assume that becoming a Christian will change new Christians' lives automatically. The church needs a way to expose new believers to systematic Bible teaching while also helping them overcome the moral or psychological baggage they bring from their pre-Christian life.

Recovery Ministries. Functional stability is the most difficult area to develop. A recovery ministry (something like a twelve-step program) is one example of a program for promoting functional stability in new believers.[11] Such ministries require the skills of trained leaders.

If the young congregation needs such a ministry but cannot find internal resources to staff and direct it, one option may be to ask the help of another church that already sponsors a recovery group. This sister congregation may be willing to provide counseling resources while the new church's people link with their support groups.

Crisis Ministries. Some people need resources for learning how to handle a personal crisis. Many may not need the church or the pastor to handle the crisis with them. Such resources may take the form of support from outside the church family or may include fee-based or sliding-scale fee counseling.

Nurturing Healthy Habits. Certain habits in the Christian believer nurture personal growth and speed up growth. The church cannot expect new believers to demonstrate good spiritual habits immediately. The church must help them take mini-steps of commitment that will eventually develop into habits displayed by mature believers.

Encouraging Church Attendance. Most churchgoers assume that sincere Christians attend church weekly. Such behavior is a big commitment for people who have not attended church in months or years—or ever. The new church must accept the fact that regular church attendance may be a difficult habit for a new believer to master.

The secret is to encourage baby Christians to make baby-step commitments that the church celebrates. Expecting too much of new believers can be a great discouragement to people who are new to the faith. The church should encourage them to make short-term commitments and allow them to see the benefit of developing new habits.

Mentoring and Discipling. New believers must perceive the importance of the Scriptures as soon as possible. The church must take the initiative to identify and address specific issues that new believers bring to their experience of faith. A well-designed one-on-one or small-group discipling program to foster meaningful assimilation of new believers can help with this need.

Iron Sharpening Iron. Many churches lose young believers because they never address the functional issues that plague almost everyone who is new to the faith. Some congregations find ways to help immature believers only in areas of biblical knowledge. Many churches succeed at the relational or doctrinal areas, but most churches miss the mark in helping new believers in areas of functional stability. Pastors and church planters do not have to counsel everyone personally, but congregations must take the responsibility for providing help in addressing issues of functional stability. God uses disciple-makers to sharpen and shape new disciples in Christ.

Resources for Further Reading

Arn, Win, and Charles Arn. *The Master's Plan for Making Disciples: Every Christian an Effective Witness through an Enabling Church.* Grand Rapids: Baker Books, 1998.

Barna, George. *Growing True Disciples.* Colorado Springs, Colo.: WaterBrook Press, 2001.

MasterLife, available through LifeWay Christian Stores, 800-458-2772.

Chapter 25

Growth in the New Church

Sometimes church planters invest so heavily in launch-day preparation that they flounder in the days following the birth of the new church, hampering the planter and the new church plant. This chapter is designed to prepare the starter for this letdown and to strengthen the planter to nurture the newborn church toward maturity.

Growth of the new church begins the first day after the launch, requiring a relationship list, developing an immediate follow-up process, designing an assimilation plan plus a small-group development strategy, and working toward legal recognition of the congregation.

Building a Relationship List

If the new church intends to follow up with people who visit church events, the church must, in some thorough fashion, record and organize the names of attendees to the first—and every—service. Not all churches decide to collect the names of guests. Some reason that it's better to allow people to attend without asking their names.

I think a better way to proceed is to encourage people to share their names and other pertinent information to the degree that they are comfortable. For example:

> Welcome to New Hope. We're glad you're here today. To the degree that you're comfortable, sing, pray, and participate with us. At the end of the service, each person in the church family fills out a card where they communicate with us prayer requests or other needs. If you're a guest and would like more information about the church, you can fill it out as well. No one will visit you unannounced. But if you write down your address, we will mail you information. If you include your phone number, I will call you. So please complete the card to the degree that you are comfortable.

This provides a low-key way for guests to indicate their interest. Asking only the guests to complete information cards singles them out. When guests have attended several times, they aren't likely to continue completing the cards unless everyone does.

The ideal, of course, is for everyone to complete response cards each time they attend. This process, especially as the church grows, can become unwieldy, but the benefits of having updated information outweigh the difficulties. An accurate database grows only from intentional and consistent encouragement of the congregation to complete these cards.

The Day after the Launch

The day after the congregation's first service is likely to be a day of rejoicing. Many churches meet their first-service attendance goal. Most consider their first service a success. But after several months of core development, advertising, and hard work, the big day passes quickly. Most church planters struggle with what steps to take in the days that follow the first service.

No one can fault the planter for being preoccupied with the launch day. The importance of that day cannot be overstated, but it must not prevent planning and preparing for follow-up and the second service.

Follow-up should begin immediately after the first service. The congregation could follow a definite schedule to follow up those wanting more information. Here's an example:

Sunday: Launch Day

- The follow-up team prepares a letter from the church outreach leader to guests. The outreach leader signs and transports the letters to the main post office.[1]
- The follow-up team makes brief phone calls to express welcome and gratitude to the guests who attended the service.

Monday

- The follow-up team completes their thank-you phone calls.

Tuesday

- Most follow-up letters arrive.
- The follow-up team submits the list of attendees to the pastor.
- The pastor prepares and sends his personal follow-up letter.

Wednesday

- The pastor and follow-up team prepare and mail postcard invitations to all prospects on the mailing list.

Thursday

- Most postcards arrive.

Friday and Saturday

- The pastor personally calls every family to invite them to return for the second service. The pastor may arrange a personal visit if the guests are responsive.

This system enables the new congregation to make five contacts with church guests who have given their names and information within the first week following launch Sunday. Three contacts arrive by mail. One comes through a personal call from the pastor and one from a church member.

Maintaining Direction and Growth

Maintaining direction and growth following the launch service is crucial. The planter is not the only one who invested heavily in the launch service, so keeping core group members and others motivated is important.

Losing the Core Group after Launch. Core-group members often leave the new start after launch day. In fact, the bigger and more successful the launch, the more likely it is that core-group members may withdraw. The group, which once had intimate, frequent contact with the planter, no longer experiences that intimacy. Suddenly the planter has become preoccupied with assimilating dozens or even hundreds of people who had not been present before launch day.

Prepare Them for the Problem. The first step in addressing this problem is to warn the core group of the typical difficulties of transition following the launch service. The best way to keep the core group is to keep them focused on the vision.

Burnout and Plateaued Growth. The church planter functions as a shepherd before the launch. The planter knows every member by name and stands ready to help and support the entire core group. This is simple when twenty people are involved. But when the church explodes to ten times that number, this shepherding becomes both impossible and unhealthy for the pastor. First, it pulls the planter toward burnout. Second, the impossibility of the planter's presence everywhere with everyone means that the church will quit growing unless the style of leadership changes.

Layers of Leaders. Lyle Schaller refers to this as a shift from "shepherd mode" to "rancher mode."[2] Schaller's metaphor explains that a shepherd is responsible to oversee and care for a flock of sheep. A rancher is different. A rancher oversees and equips shepherds for their caretaking role. Wise ranchers spend the majority of their effort training shepherds. The church planter actually shepherds leaders who, in turn, shepherd the remainder of the body.

Limitless Potential for Growth. When the rancher mode operates successfully, the potential numerical growth of a congregation has no limit. In this pyramid of influence and care, the pastor continues to shepherd the shepherds. As the congregation grows, each of those shepherds maximizes his or her care group. In this way the congregation forms a new layer of shepherd-leaders who begin to care for multiple families under their umbrella of responsibility. The church can create more layers of new leaders as the church grows in size.

Loss of Control. The core group will face not only a loss of intimacy but also a loss of control. Prior to the launch, the core group has supplied so much energy and input that they probably have come to "own" the church. But after the launch, a much larger congregation holds stock in the new church. These new members will not know about the prelaunch efforts of the core group, and they probably don't care about the personal costs to get the church started. These new people will present different ideas on how the church should be organized. The core group must learn to embrace these new members and new ideas.

Lost Hope for Realized Vision. The final thing for which core-group members must prepare is the possibility of failing to actualize their visions for the church's future. Core-group members usually appear to adopt the planter's vision, but often they adopt only part of that vision. Many core-group members develop their personal visions, thinking as a bride- or groom-to-be, "I will change things after we marry." After the church launches, some core-group members realize that the new direction is not the course for which they had hoped.

One common expression of this conflict occurs in reaching people. Many core groups really intend to reach unchurched persons, but when they realize the cost of succeeding—the changes that come with the addition of new people and their ideas—many balk. Suddenly they awaken to the "death of their vision." Their grief and anger become so compelling that they leave the congregation rather than stay and reinvest in the new church.

The departure of core-group members does not mean that they were dishonest about their commitments. More likely, they did not realize what it would take to reach new believers. Such discoveries can become so uncomfortable that many cannot continue.

Also, as the church continues to reach unbelievers, lost people who act in ungodly ways mingle with believers. "Church-cultured" members, many of whom were core-group members, may become offended and frightened by persons who have yet to adopt Christian lifestyles.

Vision Hijacking

Following the launch, when tensions begin to rise between the original core group and newcomers, a phenomenon called "vision hijacking" may occur. Vision hijacking is an attempt by church members, often highly invested core-group members, to redirect the church away from the planter's vision, especially when the original vision no longer seems workable. This usually happens at a low point in the life of the church.

Tom Nebel deals with this much more thoroughly in his coauthored book, *Church Planting Landmines*. He calls the phenomenon "Leadership Backlash" and illustrates through this graphic:

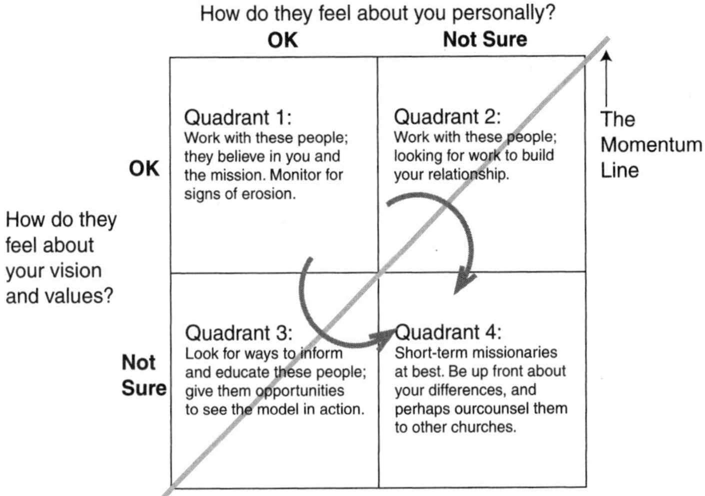

Certainly numerous dynamics contribute to leadership backlash, but two of the more compelling ones are how the leader is personally regarded by the others (i.e, do they "like" the leader's personality, style, and so on) and the direction that the leader is taking the organization. This diagram spells it out. We know what to do with people who both like the leader and the leader's vision. (Quadrant 1: work with these people!) We also know what to do with those who neither like the leader and the leader's vision. (Quadrant 4: outcounsel them!) But Quadrant's 2 and 3 are tricky, and they are temporary holding zones. Momentum is the key. If there is positive momentum in the organization, Quadrant 2 and 3 people slip into Quadrant 1. They may not have liked the leader or the leader's vision too much before, but they do now! But if there is negative momentum, 2s and 3s can slip into Quadrant 4. Then they become problematic and either move on or stick around until new leadership is in place. So the key to overcoming leadership backlash before it sneaks up on us is to build momentum whenever possible.[3]

Thwarting Attempts at Vision Hijacking. Churches and planters cannot avoid attempts at vision hijacking. The fact that new churches need strong core members in order to succeed also introduces the possibility that these members may try to redirect the church in a time of frustration. Every church planter I've known has experienced an attempted vision hijacking within the first three years of the church start. Although planters cannot avoid these attempts, certain steps can minimize their success.

The first step to avoid successful hijacking is to educate new members about the church's vision and direction. The pastor probably should be the teacher of these early classes because no other leader understands or can articulate the vision as well.

Second, the planter must recast the vision each month without exception. Listeners and followers have incredibly short memories. The leader must repeatedly and consistently recast the church's vision and values in order to cement members to the vision. Come up with new and creative ways to share this vision with the church. Telling it the same way repeatedly can get boring or dull; so look for different ways to do this to make it fun and keep your congregation more attentive.

A third step in averting the success of an attempted hijack is to prepare the core group for painful transitions that usually follow the church's launch. To be forewarned is to be forearmed.

Fourth, the pastor should involve every person in the church's mission and ministry. People who row the boat cannot easily rock the boat. New congregations always have at least one oar for every person; every member should pull an oar. As everyone gets involved and people begin to "own" the church and "own" a particular ministry within the church, the church will grow in health as well as in numbers.

Keeping Vision Before the People

By keeping the vision before the people, the planter reminds them of the direction for the new church. The planter must continually remind the entire congregation of the vision. People forget. Church members often lose track of the "main thing." The vision of the planter must be shared with the church—and not just once. Andy Stanley observes, "All God-ordained visions are shared visions. Nobody goes it alone. But God generally raises up a point person to paint a compelling verbal picture—a picture that captures the hearts and imaginations of those whom God is calling to embrace the task at hand."[4]

The planter should meet with key leaders at least monthly. Among the many details that must be addressed in that meeting, one central feature should be the recasting of vision. The planter must also make a weekly effort to place the vision before the entire group in order to keep everyone headed in the same direction. Although the planter may see such repetition as risky or boring, the people will benefit from a regular reminder of who they are and where they're going.

Vision is more than just a set of propositions, value statements, or truths; vision requires a mental image. It should touch people's hearts and motivate members to get involved in the purpose of the congregation. Vision should cry out, "This is something you long to be a part of, a purpose to which you want to make a major contribution." People must "in-vision" the core values of the congregation before they can become part of that vision.

Credibility and Vision

The power of the vision also requires a credible vision caster. If the church planter's attitudes, behaviors, and values suggest that he's not credible, the congregational vision suffers.

On the other hand, vision gains credibility with each success and with the anticipated likelihood of success. Each time the planter successfully casts a vision for the congregation or the core group, this experience prompts the followers of the congregation to believe more fully in the long-term vision.

In the same way that the planter's "credibility tank" fills with each success, failed efforts diminish credibility. Members and group leaders become energized and excited when anticipated successes lead to realized dreams. But underachievements or catastrophes strain the vision caster's credibility.

The Peak-to-Peek Principle

A successful mountaintop experience enables participants to adopt a greater vision and to work toward its achievement. The issue of credibility dovetails with the "peak-to-peek principle," which specifies that the time to cast a vision for the next endeavor is atop the peak of the current success.

This means casting a vision for the whole congregation by giving them a *peek* at what's ahead, beyond the *peak* they've just achieved.

At Millcreek Community Church, our staff envisioned an Easter service attendance of more than seven hundred, even though our normal attendance at that time was only 250. So, instead of casting the vision for seven hundred people, we rented the facilities of a local high school that would hold at least seven hundred, then we cast the vision for more than five hundred people. (Understand here that by "casting the vision," I mean what I announced as our goal.) We as the staff knew that the congregation was not yet ready to believe it could reach more than five hundred people, so we were careful to cast a credible vision.

On Easter morning, 750 people attended! On that day we cast the vision for our next endeavor. Here's how. Halfway through the service, I greeted our guests and members: "It's so great to see you today! We're so thankful for this record attendance of 750 people, which is about 250 more than we expected. Let me tell you what God will do through Millcreek Community Church this fall; we'll launch two daughter churches!" Sure enough, we started those churches six months after that Easter service.

The "peak-to-peek principle" means that the valley, which inevitably follows every peak experience, can be overcome by focusing the church on the next peak. The size of the current peak is not the major concern. Visioning from that peak is what's crucial, giving the people a "peek" at what's coming next.

So the church start with five persons prepares for the climb to ten. That success will set the stage for an immediate turn of the congregation's energies and attention to doubling again, or to some other worthy goal. Peak size in and of itself is not the concern. You want to pursue timing and consistency, "peeking" at the next "peak" from the middle of the current success.

Become a Vision-Caster

Established churches sometimes demonstrate no apparent need for vision-casting. This observation does not mean that such churches have no need for vision but that traditions and established patterns can project the appearance of vitality—for a period of time.

In a new church vision-casting is imperative. Asking people to make sacrifices—to attend a yet-to-be-established church, to wait until the new church is ready to launch, or to deny their kids an established children's ministry—is more sacrifice than many families can accept. Creating a vision for such families is indispensable in securing their confidence and involvement.

One of the ways a church planter can help people envision the future is to demonstrate where a similar vision is already functioning successfully. Even if this investigation means traveling some distance or viewing a high-quality videotape, both the planter's credibility and the core group's visioning capacity may benefit. Either of these options can enable core leaders to see what is still just an idea for them—just words. Afterwards, they will develop the ability to see the future and to commit themselves to that future.

Conclusion

Maintaining direction and growth is essential. Many new churches start and then fizzle out months later. They're unable to maintain momentum. They're distracted and often lose focus. Good planning and vision-casting from the start help avoid these obstacles.

Resources for Further Reading

Maxwell, John C. *Failing Forward.* Nashville: Thomas Nelson Publishers, 2000.

McIntosh, Gary L. *One Size Doesn't Fit All: Bringing Out the Best in Any Size Church.* Grand Rapids: Fleming H. Revell, 1999.

Minirth, Frank, et al. *What They Didn't Teach You in Seminary.* Nashville: Thomas Nelson Publishers, 1993.

Stanley, Andy. *Visioneering.* Sisters, Oreg.: Multnomah, 1999.

Chapter 26

Children in the New Church

One of the biggest challenges that a new church faces is children's ministry. If the children don't like the new church, the parents may not return. We must think beyond providing babysitting services for preschoolers while their parents go to church. Ministry to preschool children and their parents is real ministry.[1]

Sikes and Niles observe: "It's multifaceted. It's multidimensional. It's a multi-targeted ministry. Your church [child care] provides a mission field for those who are called to serve, a first impression for many new families, respite and training for parents, and most important, a child's first contact with the family of God outside his or her own home. It's a place where babies [and small children] can learn that the God who created them is Lord of all there is to know. And it's a place where we become even more awed by the wonder of God through [children]."[2]

New churches often neglect children's ministry because they focus on a myriad of other things. In some cases, this works for a time, particularly for some new churches reaching young adults without children. But it is generally not a long-term viable strategy.

Most new churches won't have a full children's ministry from the first service. People will understand that the church is just getting started. But the church planter must let the church know that a ministry for children is needed, and it's coming soon. The planter must continually remind the congregation of this vision, especially the parents. Once things have settled for the rest of the church and more people have been raised up to be leaders, more time and energy can be invested in children's ministries.

A growing minority of new churches are actually starting with a strong children's ministry. Perhaps influenced by Kidstuf at Northpoint Church, they are seeing children's ministry as the draw to start a new church. For example, Brian Jones (one of the church planters I coach) started The Pointe in Holly Spring, Georgia but for four months before worship they had a full children's program. Today it is still the most significant outreach program of the new church.

Bryan explained:

> We launched Kidstuf in October [2004] and followed with adult worship in January [2005]. This way we could launch twice—once with Kidstuf, then with adult worship later. We are reaching people who have not been active in any church, many who have not attended since childhood or have never been to church. Several families have come because the parents felt a need for their kids to be in church so they brought them to Kidstuf, also staying for worship. KidStuf allowed us to set a standard for excellence, so when we launched our adult worship, we had a quality goal to strive toward.[3]

Some churches—a small but growing number—are adopting a "family-integrated model"—adults and children of all ages actually worship together. This model is generally birthed out of the home-school movement. It has not yet made a major impact in culture, and most of these churches have not been able to impact lost people in a significant way. However, as emerging culture begins to discover the value of cross-generational community, this approach may begin to move beyond the homeschool / home birth / house church crowd. (See The National Center for Family Integrated Churches, http://www.visionforumministries.org/sections/ncfic/default.asp.)

For most new churches the children's ministry does not have to be functioning like a well-established church weekday program, but some important principles and key factors must be applied from the beginning.

Most new churches start with only a nursery or preschool. In North American culture today, most parents are comfortable with their children being elsewhere when the parents are trying to learn, but the nursery and preschool must be designed with security in mind. "Security means providing a worry-free environment where the child knows he is welcome, safe, and free from harm. . . . Guidance is direction given to help the child make choices . . . [and] a sense of accomplishment results from having been given opportunities to succeed."[4]

Provide security to parents by letting them know their children are well cared for in a safe environment. Many churches today use pager systems. Parents will sign in their child and receive a numbered vibrating pager. They must return the pager when they come back to the nursery or preschool to retrieve their child. This regulation will put parents at ease by demonstrating safety guards you've put into place. Using the pager system, parents know they can be contacted during worship if a problem occurs, and they know that no one can pick up their child except the person who has been issued the pager assigned to their child.

At Lake Ridge Church we use a pretty simple system. Since we are a new church in a school, we find it easier to check in children at their rooms rather than at a central desk. This eliminates one level of volunteers that a church plant may not yet have. At each room, there is a simple sign-in procedure that provides both parents and the church with needed information. Parents see an allergy-alert poster to let them know if the children are having a snack that day and what it is. The parent gives us the child's name and their contact information. This information is used to get in touch with the family in the following days to encourage them to visit the church again.

In terms of security system, we use a bracelet made of fibrous paper material that cannot be torn off (scissors must be used). The bracelet has two parts: one which attaches to the child with an adhesive patch at the end and a small tab that detaches from the bracelet which is kept by the parents. The tab also has an adhesive patch so it will not easily get away. Each bracelet has a separate four-digit number that is listed on the bracelet worn by the child and the tab kept by the parent. When it is time to pick up the child, the adult must have the tab with the matching number to the child they have come to pick up.

Recruiting and training children's workers is difficult when a church is new. A preschool worker should be a "Christian growing in relationship with Christ; a member of the church in which he or she serves; a person who is willing prayerfully to prepare and train; a person who loves preschoolers; a person who is punctual, flexible, and dependable; a person with a gentle, cooperative spirit; a person who demonstrates maturity, tact, and enthusiasm; and a committed Christian who will teach, visit, and reach out to preschoolers and their families."[5] If such a person does not yet exist in the new church, it may be necessary to get help from a nearby church.

Background Checks

All workers in a church nursery should fill out an application asking key questions. It should also include permission to do a criminal background check. *Every person regularly working with children needs to undergo a criminal background check—no exceptions.*

Without background checks, churches open themselves to serious liability. But that's not the most important reason. Without background checks, churches expose children to danger. A church should be a safe place, free from harm or scandal. Although it's sometimes difficult to do background checks with so much else going on, this step is essential.

> Sample applications can be found at www.newchurches.com/examples.

Worker Identification

All workers in church nurseries should have some sort of identification. This helps parents know who is working with their child. It also helps with security. Some churches have workers wear smocks or aprons with a monogram of the church name. The workers should also have name tags. Some churches print up photo ID badges for all workers.

Ministry to Parents

The first question most parents will ask their children after retrieving them is, "Did you have fun?" So it's important that children's activities be enjoyable and enthusiastic. When children have fun, they'll want to return and bring their parents.

The second question most parents will ask is, "What did you learn?" I have a three-year-old (Jaclyn), and she never remembers. But she'll often give me a sheet of paper with the lesson and say, "This!" So, as you teach preschoolers, be sure to give them something to take home to show their parents. This will demonstrate that they learned something, and the parents might even read it.

Vineyard Christian Fellowship[6] in Columbus, Ohio, is one of many congregations that considers ministry to children a good way to reach families. They send a large fluorescent postcard to the children of all guests. (It's large; it folds out to 17 x 24!) All it says is, "Thanks for coming to Vineyard." Ultimately, it's not the children who are reached by such a gesture; it's the parents.

Also, training parents and children is essential to growing churches. Our Research Team at NAMB recently surveyed more than three hundred churches with high rates of children's conversions. Of this effective churches reaching children, Phillip Connor, research missiologist at NAMB, explained: "Replication and regeneration appropriately describe successful children's evangelism. Not only do 50 percent of churches surveyed train parents to share Christ with their children, but approximately 75 percent of these same churches train the children of the church to share Christ with their friends."[7]

Conclusion

Clean nurseries, staffed with quality people who serve in a safe environment, are much more welcoming than "a place to keep kids" (a small, unpainted room with old donated cribs). New churches should pay close attention to what quality child care looks like in the churches in their area and emulate what they see. Then, they should train parents and children to be about the business of sharing the gospel in meaningful ways.

Provided by a friend of mine, here are some closing rules that should help every children's ministry.

Thou Shall Nots for Children's Ministry

1. Thou shall not leave children with children; children's workers should be over the age of eighteen.
2. Thou shall not have anyone work who has not undergone some form of criminal background check.
3. Thou shall not use unsafe or hand-me-down cribs, toys, sheets, and blankets.

4. Thou shall not give any child any food that has not been approved by the parents. Allergies can be deadly.
5. Thou shall not have an unclean room. All toys, cribs, and other things that little hands touch need to be washed with bleach.
6. Thou shall not have a child in the room without having the parents fill out a form with the child's name, allergies, and physical problems listed.
7. Thou shall not recruit people who are not called to children's ministry.
8. Thou shall not use people who are not trained in children's ministry and in child development.
9. Thou shall not see children's ministry as a necessary evil in order to attract their parents.
10. Thou shall not use the very short time given to just baby-sit. This is the time to teach children in the way they should go. Don't use videos to substitute for children's ministry.[8]

Resources for Further Reading

Beckwith, Ivy. *Postmodern Children's Ministry: Ministry to Children in the 21st Century.* Grand Rapids: Zondervan, 2004.

Capehart, Jody, with Lori Haynes Niles. *Touching Hearts, Changing Lives: Becoming a Treasured Teacher.* Loveland, Colo.: Group, 1999.

Children's Ministry magazine. Loveland, Colo.: Group.

Miller, Sue, with Davie Staal. *Making Your Children's Ministry the Best Hour of Every Kid's Week.* Grand Rapids, Mich.: Zondervan, 2004.

Sanders, Thomas, and Mary Ann Bradberry. *Teaching Preschoolers: First Steps Toward Faith.* Nashville: LifeWay Press, 2000, 17–18.

Wideman, Jim. *Children's Ministry Leadership: The You-Can-Do-It Guide.* Loveland, Colo.: Group, 2003.

Chapter 27

Congregational Formation

After planting a new church, the time for official congregational formation eventually arrives. This process moves the congregation from functioning as just a concept or even a worshipping group of people to becoming a legally and administratively recognizable unit. This, of course, only applies to churches that want to organize legally. Some may just want to covenant together, and that requires less organization. The information below is for churches wishing a more formal organization structure.

Milestones in the New Church's Life

A newborn human separates from his or her mother at birth but remains intimately dependent upon her. Likewise, new churches generally separate from the mother church but retain a degree of dependence for awhile. Within a reasonable period of time, if both congregations are healthy, their relationship becomes an expression of interdependence. The new church must complete certain tasks and pass milestones successfully to enable maturation and healthy interdependence between the two congregations.

Statement of Faith. The first major milestone is adoption of a confessional guide or beliefs statement. Denominational churches generally adopt the organization's statement of faith. Others may draw on the statements of churches they admire. Either way, the statement should address core issues and make clear the church's position on theological issues. The church needs to balance having a statement that is too inclusive (not detailed enough) which can lead to divisiveness inside the church with having a statement that is too narrow, leading to unnecessary divisiveness with other Christians and ministries.

Constitution. The constitution describes the new church. The congregation adopts the document as a written expression of the beliefs and principles around which it will organize its ministry. A constitution usually includes the congregation's articles of faith. Our church also included a section on church discipline to explain our values and systems. We required everyone who joined our church to read the constitution.

> At Lake Ridge Church, we used Church Planting Solutions (www.church-planter.org) to walk us through each step of this process, and Pat Furgerson and Beth Cygon from CPS helped me update this chapter. See http://church-planting4me.com/legalissues.htm..

A new church should not constitute at its launch service. Although great things happen on that day, the church has not matured in several crucial areas that need to be addressed before it's ready to pass the milestone of adopting its constitution. The congregation should have developed consistent giving and growth patterns and should have established a solid leadership core before taking this step. Andy Stanley often advises church planters he mentors: "Put off constituting as long as you can. . . . If you have a clear idea, make sure the people around you share it before you constitute."[1]

Before a church constitutes, it needs a reason to do so. It usually happens when the church is able to support itself. Larry Lewis believes the new congregation should have at least one hundred faithful resident members before constituting as an official congregation.[2] Although I would not assign an attendance limit, constituting is an event that establishes a separate and distinct identity for the church.

The constitution should be simple. Long constitutions that articulate every possible problem indicate mistrust rather than congregational health.

Collecting samples from other church plants helps move the process along. There are several examples of constitutions at www.newchurches.com.

Bylaws. These give more specific information about church operations than the constitution and define how the organization will govern itself. Bylaws are maintained by the church and do not require any outside (e.g. IRS or state) approvals. Most states require that a corporation (profit or nonprofit) have bylaws. Bylaws should address such areas as how church leaders will be elected, qualifications for leadership, membership, procedure to change bylaws, etc. Bylaws should be simpler to change than the articles of the constitution. If the congregation articulates them clearly in the beginning, the church's core values (found in the constitution) should rarely change.

Bylaws and operations manuals should be simple to change because they explain methodologies the church is using to incarnate and live out its core values. Changes in the constitution should be harder to do. Alterations in bylaws and operations manuals should be possible through decisions of the administrative team or the pastor/elders.

Following the spiritual connections, there are usually legal ones. It is important for churches to follow the law if they choose to create legal structures. The Bible teaches: "Let every person be in subjection to the governing authorities. For there is no authority except from God, and those which exist are established by God. . . . For because of this you also pay taxes, for rulers are servants of God, devoting themselves to this very thing. Render to all what is due them: tax to whom tax is due; custom to whom custom; fear to whom fear; honor to whom honor" (Rom. 13:1, 6–7 NASB). There are several steps that make this possible including an Employer Identification Number, IRS tax exemption, state tax exemption, post office nonprofit status, and insurance.

Employer Identification Number. This number is easy to obtain and necessary to open a checking account. If you don't have one by now, refer to chapter 18 for details.

Federal Tax Exemption. Churches are already tax exempt by nature of their existence. They do not need to prove their tax exemption in order to receive tax-exempt gifts. However, there are benefits to having a tax-exemption letter from the IRS. It makes getting a nonprofit bulk mail permit and state sales tax exemption easier. Additionally, having official 501(c)(3) status gives the church increased credibility with potential donors, particularly large foundations which may consider gifts to churches who serve the community. For those in denominations, the accounting office of their denomination or fellowship should have a letter that will suffice. Other churches that want the official letter will have to go through the entire process.

State Sales Tax Exemption. Some states do provide sales tax exemptions for churches. These differ from state to state. For instance, one state might provide a certificate to be presented to stores exempting them from paying sales tax at all where another state may allow a church to request reimbursement for taxes paid on a quarterly basis. An area church may be able to help you know the process, or call your local state representative who can guide you. Most states have their policy and any necessary applications posted on their Department of Revenue home page.

Nonprofit Bulk Mail Permit. Postage rates for nonprofit organizations are approximately 50 percent lower than for profit organizations. Because of that, it is in a church's best interest to get a nonprofit bulk mail permit before they do their first large mailing. Organizations apply for a bulk mail permit by submitting the applications and paying a fee for the permit. It is a good idea to establish a good rapport with the bulk mail point of contact at your local post office as they can help guide you through the application process as well as help you with future mailings.

In order to request nonprofit status on your bulk mail permit, the post office will want to see copies of your organizing instrument (e.g. articles of incorporation), examples of church activity (brochures, worship bulletins, newsletters, etc.), and your letter of exemption from the IRS. Many new churches won't have the letter of exemption from the IRS, and in that instance they can provide a copy of their application to the IRS or a financial statement. New churches cannot mail using the name of their mother church unless they use the name, address, and permit number of the mother church and indicate they are part of the mother church. If you plan to use your mother church's permit, you should speak with your local bulk mail agent at your local post office to ensure they will accept your mailing. Having a draft copy or sample of the piece you plan to mail can be useful.

Insurance. New churches will need several forms of insurance, including liability, workers compensation, auto/vehicle, if applicable, and malpractice/misconduct insurance. Understanding when you should begin insurance coverage and what types of coverage are best for you are important considerations. It's never too early to contact an insurance company to discuss your particular situation and to get a recommendation on types of coverage, level of coverage, and start date of coverage. Church Mutual Insurance (www.churchmutual.com) has a good plan for new church coverage.

Incorporation. Incorporation is the step that signals official legal recognition by government entities. It's a true milestone. In almost every state and in Canada, the congregation must be incorporated. This procedure protects the ministers and the officers of the church in the event that someone brings a lawsuit. Otherwise, they can be held personally liable for any problems if a church is not incorporated. Incorporation also signals that the congregation now stands on its own as a legal entity separate from the mother church. In order to incorporate, you will need a constitution and bylaws, so you can either create those before you publicly announce them to the church or incorporate after your constitution service.

The incorporation provides the state basic information about your church such as name, location, type of organization, purpose, etc. Each state has different incorporation requirements, and requirements for each state can generally be found on the Secretary of State's Web site for your particular state. Many states even provide an incorporation guide or instructions and a means to submit the request electronically. One important thing to note about incorporation is organizations, such as churches, that contemplate requesting 501(c)(3) status from the IRS should contact an attorney or a knowledgeable individual to ensure the appropriate language is used in their incorporation paperwork.

In most nonhierarchical denominations, once the church is incorporated, it becomes its own entity and needs to call a pastor. The new church should call the pastor and record that call in the official minutes of the church business for the pastor's role to be official. In most cases the church issues its call through a vote of the entire congregation.

No person can be a member of the new church until the congregation constitutes. At the time of constitution, charter membership is the first opportunity for a person to become a church member. The congregation should plan this opportunity as a major congregational and community event.

Many churches require charter members to attend the new members class, to sign a membership covenant and an original charter document, and to attend the chartering service.

Churches can obtain assistance from a lawyer, support ministry such as Church Planting Solutions, or even purchase incorporation kits from organizations like StartChurch (www.startchurch.com). Or, if the church prefers, and in particular if they have someone with good business sense, they can incorporate themselves by obtaining instructions from the Secretary of State for their state.

Conclusion

Church planters need to learn about and take care of details such as constitution and bylaws because they're vitally important. Not only do these documents encourage and protect the vision of the church, but they also safeguard the congregation from conflict.

Although the planter needs to take ultimate responsibility for these tasks, careful consideration should be given to delegating the details of this work to qualified laypeople in the congregation. For example, if you're blessed to have a lawyer or someone who works in the legal field, this person could take the lead. In addition, if you are affiliated with a denomination, a representative will have helpful checklists and advice. I recognize more and more the need for a good attorney in this process.

Resources for Further Reading

"Church Constitution Guide," available at www.newchurches.com.

"Church Planting System," www.church-planter.org.

Lewis, Larry. *The Church Planter's Handbook*. Nashville: Broadman Press, 1992.

McNamara, Roger N., and Ken Davis. *The Y.B.H. Handbook of Church Planting: A Practical Guide to Church Planting*. Longwood, Fla.: Xulon Press, 2005.

Chapter 28

Churches Planting Churches

Church planting should not end with the establishment of one church. The process can repeat itself when a new church matures to the point of becoming a sponsoring church. The kingdom is best advanced through multiplication and not just addition.

Many readers of this book will become church planters who will work hard at planting and growing their first church from inception to maturity. Then God will nudge them to plant another, and they may think: *It's taking everything in me to make this church plant work. I don't see how we can help start another church.* But a daughter church is the best way to expand on your zeal for church planting and to put into practice what you've learned from planting the mother church. Churches of all sizes and ages can take part in church planting.

I'm disappointed when gifted church planters have not, after three years, "mothered" a second church. I'm not disappointed in the church. I'm disappointed in the planter. Church planters need to be the best advocates and sponsors of next-generation churches. But it seems that if the church planter does not have in mind and heart to start another church early on, by the third year of the new church's existence, the planter has already forgotten how important church planting is to future expansion of the kingdom.

Casting the Vision

The planter is the person who develops and instills the vision to start new churches. From the first day of a new church plant, the planter should also strategize for reproducing that church and for advancing the kingdom of God by producing daughter churches. The common wisdom is that if you do not plant a daughter church within three years you never will.

The planter initiates a daughter church by casting a church-planting vision. This vision must come from the pulpit, from the heart and words of the pastor. It must come from the pastor because God has uniquely anointed the pastor to present his vision to the congregation.

Furthermore, the vision must come from the pulpit because presenting the vision through preaching signals to the church that, of all the many important matters the pastor could have preached, the church-planting vision has taken precedence. In other words, this vision shouldn't be mentioned casually like idle hallway conversation. It must be cast to the entire body.

Once the pastor has presented the vision, the people must catch that vision and then cast it among themselves. For the vision to survive, the church must catch it; for it to thrive, they must adopt and promote it as their own.

Another step toward planting is the church's appointment of a planting leadership team that's empowered to establish new congregations. When the pastor promotes the church from the pulpit and when the leaders of the congregation close ranks behind the pastor in the divine vision, the remainder of the church will join them in the important ministry of church planting.

In *The Ripple Church: Multiply Your Ministry by Parenting New Churches*, Phil Stevenson explains: "It is vital to assemble a team for creating a reproducing church. This parenting team is brought together for a purpose, then disbanded when the mission is accomplished. If a church parents regularly, a new team can be assembled for each new church plant. Doing so will involve more people in the process, and the more people that are involved, the greater will be the sense of ownership within the congregation."[1]

Teams for mission involvement allow churches to be involved at multiple levels. The Great Commission presents concentric circles through which to share the gospel (Acts 1:8): Jerusalem, Judea, Samaria, and the world. The center should be called the church's Jerusalem, the equivalent of a hometown or immediate area surrounding the congregation. The first circle from the center is Judea, which might be identified as one's association, county, or state. The Samaria circle describes a distinct ethnic or language group that lies a geographical distance or cultural distance from Jerusalem. The third and final concentric circle represents the world—every place where the name of Christ remains unproclaimed. All four echelons for evangelism also identify forums in which a church might strategize to start daughter congregations, and teams can help in each.

Reasons to Sponsor a Daughter Church

Becker and Williams have outlined several reasons existing churches should plant daughter churches.[2]

1. **To evangelize the unchurched.** Evangelistic effectiveness is one of several practical reasons to start new churches. The evangelist's longing to reach people soars to its zenith in church starting. Although every church, no matter its age, must strategize to evangelize, established churches make greater progress in kingdom evangelism by initiating new daughter churches. This commitment is necessary because evangelism occurs more rapidly in new churches than in longer established congregations.

2. **To develop new leaders.** One crucial imperative of new churches is leadership development. When new congregations demonstrate this capacity, leaders often arise at a more rapid pace than in older churches. The appearance of new leaders may actually outpace the new church's needs. As new leaders find fulfillment in their Spirit-anointed ministries, they often become dissatisfied with just occasional opportunities to serve.

If a new church develops several worship teams who alternate in leading, one team might receive the church's blessing in becoming leaders for a daughter church start. Each team—both those who leave and those who stay—would have the opportunity to lead worship more than occasionally during the month.

This type of situation allows leaders to continue to develop their abilities. Many pastors and planters testify that as their churches have commissioned leaders and sent them out, God has replaced those leaders and allowed even more people to become involved in the leadership core of the church.

3. **To grow the kingdom.** A maturing kingdom awareness is more important than a local church mentality. Church leaders need to look beyond their local churches. Leaders who are unwilling to make organizational sacrifices for the benefit of the kingdom are stunted in growth and immature in understanding God's larger purpose. When congregations initiate daughter churches, God accomplishes his purpose more effectively than when churches conserve resources in order to optimize local organizational strength and vitality.

4. **To transmit a lasting legacy.** Another reason for sponsoring new churches may be termed "the family legacy." Enduring families manifest a family heritage, a noble tradition passed from one generation to the next. This awareness of their family heritage creates excitement and energy for each new generation.

The same claim may be made for churches. Daughter churches can look with feelings of contentment upon their parentage in the faith. Their legacy lends strength to these churches, enabling them to feel more thoroughly rooted and grounded in history.

Sponsoring churches also become excited as they see God's people multiply and God's kingdom grow, because they're passing along their heritage to a new generation of churches. The excitement swells as these new-generation churches initiate their own daughter congregations. Sponsoring churches experience a kind of divine honor reserved for those who enable the success of their children, for they know that they played an important role in that success.

5. **To grow the denomination.** Although denominational growth often can model a kind of imperialism, there's clearly a difference between denominations that foster kingdom church plants—and grow because of those efforts—and denominations that initiate churches for sectarian reasons and for institutional survival.

It has been fascinating to watch the change in denominational emphasis over the last several years. The Assemblies of God fellowship has placed a renewed emphasis on churches planting churches through "Every Church a Parent or Partner" (www.parentorpartner.org). Denominations and fellowships are encouraging churches to get back into church planting for kingdom impact.

6. **To meet ethnic and language group needs.** At the beginning of the twenty-first century, urban centers of the United States and Canada have attracted ethnically diverse people groups. Today, as never before, North American believers can carry out international missions without leaving their own zip codes. Churches—whether new or long-established—face the opportunity to plant language and cross-cultural churches in North America, just as we plant congregations around the world among the same ethnic and language groups.

7. **To glorify God.** Although many people in a community may never attend your new church start, your presence represents the presence and the power of God to a community. God proclaims who he is as his people establish new churches. New churches are great testimony to a great God![3]

Becoming a Sponsoring Church

Leading a congregation to sponsor daughter churches presents its own set of challenges. In the 1970s, Jack Redford authored a practical study that addressed many challenges of church sponsorship. Redford gave nine sequential steps for planting a daughter church.[4]

1. **Select a missions committee.** A church-planting effort without a skilled, effective leadership-advisory team is like a ship without a rudder. The committee should be made up of missions-hearted persons who have the new church's best interest at heart. The committee may even be a church-planting team charged with the specific task of leading the new church start.

2. **Select the area.** This step may seem obvious, but a number of factors will influence the choice: size of the population, affinity of the planting team to the focus group, sociological congruity between the focus group and the sponsoring church, and other characteristics.

The presence of other churches can make a difference as well. If the sponsoring church takes the initiative in picking a location, the new work benefits greatly. The sponsoring church lends credibility to the start. If site location includes the sponsor's purchase of property, the advantages to the new congregation are considerable.

3. **Prepare the sponsoring congregation.** Preparation involves explaining to the proposed sponsoring church the events that must occur in order to plant a new church successfully. This explanation should include a

thorough list and an anticipated time line for coming events. Such explanations should include not only what will be done but also why it should be done. Laying out all of these factors in the beginning enables the sponsoring church to feel it has the adequate information to make an intelligent, responsible decision. If emergencies arise later, sponsoring church members can more easily accept such contingencies as a normal part of church planting.

4. **Cultivate the field.** The first reason for cultivating is to locate potential members and, especially, core group members. A second is to determine the community's needs that the new church may address. Third, cultivation stirs interest for the church that will emerge publicly in just a few months.

5. **Start home Bible studies.** Although this terminology describes Jack Redford's era and methods, the reader should understand this stage as the core group development phase described earlier in this book. After field cultivation comes the time for small group design. The planter or team should locate interested persons and then follow up immediately by involving them in a small group. Taking too much time between contact and involvement may squander good opportunities because some prospects may lose interest if not followed up quickly and appropriately.

6. **Establish the mission chapel.** With the successful initiation of one or more small groups, the sponsoring church should move toward establishing public worship. In Redford's day this did not involve a public "launch." Either way, this step means coalescing the small groups meeting at different locations into a larger group. This larger group is intended ultimately to be a church gathered publicly. It will gather publicly for worship as well as be scattered throughout the community.

7. **Plan finances.** The new mission should have a simple organization at this stage. The fellowship has not yet become a church. It probably collects no funds or, at best, limited financial gifts. Simplicity of organization will direct energies to stimulate vision development among core-group members. Simplicity will also maximize small group development. An overly sophisticated organization may impose unnecessary burdens on the new work. The sponsoring congregation probably should continue managing the mission's finances during this period.

8. **Secure facilities.** This involves finding a place in which the new church will meet. This step demands a particular wisdom. Ill-advised decisions can send wrong messages to the community if the sociological values

reflected in the facility are out of step with the tastes of the community. An extravagant meeting place can saddle the mission with unmanageable financial burdens. Too little space may hamper the development of the new congregation.

9. **Constitute the church.** The final step in the process from missions committee to a new church is the actual constitution of the new body. The sponsoring church will have transferred control and direction of the new church's finances to the fledgling congregation. The new church also should now take responsibility for all of its own administration and leadership.

Time-Honored Principles

Redford's terminology in the discussion above is a little dated, but the principles remain sound. Following this model will take some tweaking of terminology, but the idea is the same: your church needs to be organized and mobilized to get involved in church planting.

North America is filled with pastors and churches that aren't willing to sponsor daughter churches and to make the sacrifices necessary to support a new church start. It will require thousands of churches willing to sponsor church plants to reverse the self-destruction of North American culture.

Dino Senesi explained his church's practice to me as follows: "When I was pastor of a parent church we had a celebration of all congregations once a year. Most all of our churches were ethnic, which worked really well. They shared in the service and we fellowshipped over ethnic food afterwards. This was strategically placed before budget time in the mother church. Our people loved it and caught on. We had as many as six churches and missions and their pastors for the celebration. They sang, preached and testified. By far it was the most blessed and strategic thing that we ever did to encourage church planting through our congregation."[5]

When churches sponsor churches, they have the privilege of seeing lives changed because of their efforts.

Sponsorship and the Church Planter

Our discussion in this chapter has centered on the sponsoring church's responsibility. Ultimately, one person is primarily responsible for leadership in the new start. That person is the church planter. The sponsoring church must play a leading role in finding the church planter-pastor. In doing this the sponsoring church must address several concerns.

Theological Matters. The candidate's agreement with the theological convictions of the sponsoring church is important. The sponsoring church must decide what level of theological disagreement, if any, is acceptable. Churches vary widely on this matter. Some insist that the planter agree with the supporting church in every area of theology. Other congregations bend on some minor areas of theological understanding in view of the candidate's connection with the demographic focus group. The sponsoring church should define its expectations before beginning the search process.

Ministry Experience. Another issue that the sponsoring church should consider is its expectations of the candidate in regards to ministry experience. Must the candidate be a seasoned church planter? Has the candidate successfully ministered alongside other persons on a multiple-member church staff? Does this person demonstrate strong interpersonal skills and the ability to cooperate with others? Has this person shown responsible handling of authority? Can this person lead by modeling?

Behavioral Assessment. The sponsoring church may use a behavioral assessment[6] to aid in finding a planter. Such tools enable the sponsoring church to determine whether a candidate is just a strong leader or a strong leader *gifted for church planting*. The assessment can help locate individuals who have church-planting skills while also revealing those persons who, though strong in many areas, lack the essential giftedness for the planting task.

Supervisory Accountability. Other concerns worthy of consideration in calling a church planter are the issues of accountability, supervision, and mentoring. No matters are more important in the sponsor-church planter relationship. Supervisory accountabilities must be spelled out. Supervision, expectations about attending sponsoring church staff meetings, and detailed performance expectations must be agreed upon by the church and the candidate before his call to the new church field. The planter must understand the need for selecting a mentor or coach to assist in providing the emotional support that every new church planter needs.

Conclusion

The role of a sponsoring church is vital to the church-planting and church-reproduction process. Church planters should remember their divine calling not just to plant one church but also to continue planting churches long after their first church has been launched and developed. Pastors of established churches should use this information to create a tradition, a legacy of missions and church planting for their churches.

Resources for Further Reading

Allen, Roland. *Missionary Methods: St. Paul's or Ours?* Grand Rapids: Eerdmans, 1962; reprinted 2001.

Becker, Paul, and Mark Williams. *The Dynamic Daughter Church Planting Handbook*. Dynamic Church Planting International, 1999.

Coursey, Claylan. *How Churches Can Start Churches*. Nairobi, Kenya: Baptist Publications House, 1984.

Faircloth, Samuel D. *Church Planting for Reproduction*. Grand Rapids: Baker Book House, 1991.

Logan, Robert E., and Steve Ogne. *Churches Planting Churches*. St. Charles, Ill.: ChurchSmart Resources, 1995.

Stevenson, Phil. *The Ripple Church: Multiply Your Ministry by Parenting New Churches*. Indianapolis, Ind.: Wesleyan Publishing House, 2004.

Chapter 29

Breaking the Mold: Church-Planting Movements

Prayer, Jesus' purposes, and the Spirit's presence are at the heart of church planting. These three factors provide the focus of this concluding chapter. This book started with biblical, theological, and spiritual foundations. This is where it ends.

Foundations for Church Planting

Spiritual preparation is sometimes neglected when training church planters. This emphasis is crucial because church planting attracts energetic and entrepreneurial people who are generally more activity driven than contemplative and prayerful! Furthermore, training for church starting usually emphasizes practical areas and often neglects the spiritual. In the Master's business of planting his churches, there's no better place to begin than in gaining direction and purpose from him through prayer.

The Gospels record Jesus' use of the term "church" only two times. In the first he explained, in response to Peter's affirmation of faith, "I will build my church, and the gates of Hades will not overcome it" (Matt. 16:18). By these words Jesus indicated that He is the source of church growth. He did not advocate the centrality of methodology, but the centrality of deity: He promised that he would build his church.

In the second use of the term, Jesus focused on his protection and purification of the church. In Matthew 18:17, he explained how believers should react when their brothers and sisters refuse their admonitions: "If he refuses to listen to them, tell it to the church; and if he refuses to listen even to the church, treat him as you would a pagan or a tax collector."

Jesus will build; Jesus will purify his church. By definition, *church* refers to "ones who are called out." Clearly these tasks of building and purifying begin with and emanate from Jesus but are acted out through those he has called out. The spiritual foundations of church planting suggest that Jesus is the source of church growth and holiness. In order to know how to build and how to purify his church, we must remain in touch with the Lord of the church.

Church planting does not focus on advertising, organization, music, and worship. Planting does, of course, include all of these concerns, but it is not these things. Planting churches centers on touching, winning, and congregationalizing the lost. The wise church planter must remember to focus on what matters: the Lord and his purposes for the church.

A Personal Reflection

Some observers attributed the successful launch of Millcreek Community Church to effective advertising. Perhaps there's a degree of truth in that assessment. Advertising was important, but it was not the key. It was a useful methodology, but it was not the center of the church's successful launch.

On the night before our grand opening at Millcreek, I lost my voice. I felt deep frustration—even anger—at having spent a year in preparation only to become an "absentee father" at the moment the congregation was to be birthed. Our core group's prayers for my healing in order to preach on launch Sunday yielded no immediate results. Even my prayers on the morning of the launch, focusing all the faith I could muster, seemed of no avail.

Other problems also arose on that morning. Attendees trickled in to the service. As I stood in front of the stage, I experienced a crisis of faith. I prayed to God and said to myself at the same time, "God, I came here because I believed you wanted me to. I have invested my life in these people because I believe you called me. I'm now here to serve you by evangelizing this crowd, and I believe it to be your will. Please, God, in your grace let me have the privilege of sharing with these people your Word. You knew of my voice. You knew of the people who would attend. God, I'm sorry for trusting in myself. I want you to be glorified here today."

As I ended the prayer, I stepped on the stage. In that instant, my voice returned. By the beginning of the service, my concern was not about the number who attended but about God's activity in their midst that day. A total of 234 people visited the first service of Millcreek Community Church.

Immediately following the service, a television reporter covering our grand opening asked me: "Pastor, how do you account for such a great response to a new church where so many churches are declining?"

I suddenly found that my voice had again disappeared. I motioned for the reporter to talk to our designated spokesperson, and I walked to the side of the tent. With tears welling in my eyes, I prayed, "God, thank you. Thank you for showing me—though I could send out thousands of mailers, make more than fifty thousand phone calls, develop a core group, plan a service, and even create a facility—that, 'Unless the Lord builds the house, its builders labor in vain' (Ps. 127:1)." God showed me on that day that training is important, planning is essential, but, most important, God's Spirit is the only truly indispensable factor in church planting.

I would be grieved if a church planter were to read this book as just a tool kit of techniques for church starting. I hope it includes a great number of tools and techniques. But my greater intention is to move the reader to seek the Lord—the true Church Planter. I hope that, by reading these pages, the student will experience a taste of church starting—how awesome and humanly impossible it is. I want the reader to understand the centrality and indispensability of the One who founded and established the church—Jesus Christ, without whose presence the starter starts and the planter plants in vain.

When God is at work, a church is planted. It is always a miracle. When we allow ourselves to be used by God to plant churches that plant churches that plant churches, a church-planting movement can emerge.

Church-Planting Movements

Church-planting movements have caught the attention of missionaries in the international field. In a few places churches are exploding with entire people groups coming to Christ.

David Garrison has written an influential little book titled *Church Planting Movements*. It's available in its entirety at http://www. imb.org/CPM. The book describes and analyzes several church-planting movements. The following lengthy, edited quote describes the universal characteristics of such a movement:

> 1. **Prayer.** It is the vitality of prayer in the missionary's personal life that leads to its imitation in the life of the new church and its leaders. By revealing from the beginning the source of his power in prayer, the missionary effectively gives away the greatest resource he brings to the assignment.
>
> 2. **Abundant gospel sowing.** We have yet to see a church-planting movement emerge where evangelism is rare or absent. Every church-planting movement is accompanied by abundant sowing of the gospel.
>
> 3. **Intentional church planting.** In every church-planting movement, someone implemented a strategy of deliberate church planting before the movement got under way. There are several instances in which all the contextual elements were in place, but the missionaries lacked either the skill or the vision to lead a church-planting movement. However, once this ingredient was added to the mix, the results were remarkable.
>
> 4. **Scriptural authority.** Even among non-literate people groups, the Bible has been the guiding source for doctrine, church polity and life itself. . . . In every instance, scripture provided the rudder for the church's life, and its authority was unquestioned.
>
> 5. **Local leadership.** Missionaries involved in church-planting movements often speak of the self-discipline required to mentor church planters rather than do the job of church planting themselves. . . . Walking alongside local church planters is the first step in cultivating and establishing local leadership.

> 6. **Lay leadership.** Church-planting movements are driven by lay leaders. These lay leaders are typically bivocational and come from the general profile of the people group being reached. . . . Dependence upon seminary-trained—or in non-literate societies, even educated—pastoral leaders means that the work will always face a leadership deficit.
>
> 7. **Cell or house churches.** Church buildings do appear in church-planting movements. However, the vast majority of the churches continue to be small, reproducible cell churches.
>
> 8. **Churches planting churches.** In most church-planting movements, the first churches were planted by missionaries or by missionary-trained church planters. At some point, however, as the movements entered a multiplicative phase of reproduction, the churches themselves began planting new churches.
>
> 9. **Rapid reproduction.** Most church planters involved in these movements contend that rapid reproduction is vital to the movement itself. They report that when reproduction rates slow down, the church-planting movement falters. Rapid reproduction communicates the urgency and importance of coming to faith in Christ.
>
> 10. **Healthy churches.** Church growth experts have written extensively in recent years about the marks of a church. Most agree that healthy churches should carry out the following five purposes: (1) worship, (2) evangelistic and missionary outreach, (3) education and discipleship, (4) ministry, and (5) fellowship. In each of the church-planting movements we studied, these five core functions were evident.[1]

Church-planting movements have occurred before in North America. Baptists and Methodists on the western frontier planted thousands of churches in two decades. Calvary Chapel and Vineyard churches multiplied greatly in the 1970s and 1980s, and, though not church-planting movements in the technical sense, they were the closest thing to rapid church planting evidenced in the last century.

But there is no such movement today, and none is on the horizon in North America. Churches are being planted, but as of yet there's no movement. Some are trying to encourage systems that promote church-planting movements.

The most common system seeking to promote a church-planting movement is described in Kevin Mannoia's *Church Planting: The Next Generation*. This twenty-first-century church-planting system is the planting strategy of the Free Methodist Church. This book is a description of their strategy with a strong emphasis on application in denominational leadership structures. Although it specifically deals with the Free Methodist denominational structure (and often reads like an internal denominational document), its application is much broader.

The text provides more than just an example of the work of one denomination. The system described is an expansion and explanation of the system created by Bob Logan. (Logan wrote the foreword, and Mannoia calls him "the leading resource on church planting in America.") Due to the pervasive influence of Bob Logan, most denominationally based North American church planting has developed a similar structure.

The church multiplication system is described here as explained by Kevin Mannoia in his *Church Planting: The Next Generation* (Indianapolis, Ind.: Light and Life Communication, 1994). However, the system has also evolved since Mannoia's book. Subscribers to Bob Logan's *CoachNet* can see a more updated version of the described system at www.coachnet.org. Cultivating Church Multiplication Movements (C2M2) is a ten-part system that helps church-planting leaders develop a contextual strategy. Many denominations or agencies have adapted such systems to their own needs. The agency where I work, the North American Mission Board, uses a version developed for our context called the Church Planting Process. The CPP has greatly enhanced Southern Baptists' church-planting potential. My Ph.D. dissertation focused on the development, implementation, and results of this system.

The Church-Planting System

Mannoia divides the system into the following categories: Parent Church Network, Profile Assessment System, New Church Incubator, Recruitment Network, Pastor Factory, Church Planter's Summit, Maturing Church Cluster, Strategic Planning Network, Harvest 1000, and the Meta-Church Network.

The Parent Church Network is the development of a church-planting vision in a group of local or regional congregations. Mannoia includes this first because it requires no large commitment of staff or resources; just a commitment to explore the possibilities of planting. The Parent Church Network generally develops into a cluster of three to five churches interested in planting and multiplication.

The Profile Assessment System is designed to objectively measure "skills, performance, and personality profile in prospective planters." Mannoia believes that the assessment system is the most important aspect for short-term impact and that proper assessment leads to a 90 percent success rate for planters.

The New Church Incubator is a resource rooted in fellowship. Planters are provided an empowering environment to assist them in the development of new churches. The incubator generally meets once a month and is generally run by a trained facilitator. Between these monthly meetings a coach meets with each planter. This provides the emotional support needed for the planter and family.

The Pastor Factory is a resource to train laypeople to become founding pastors. This process generally is intended for the cell-based church. But any congregation with a leadership structure can use this system. This is generally divided into two categories: a leadership training system and a Pastor Factory network. They are divided by a sense of ministry call and the behavioral assessment mentioned earlier. Those who are called and assessed move from the leadership system to the factory network.

The Church Planter's Summit is a regular event, perhaps two or three days in length, to initiate new planter candidates. Candidates are generally invited to the event after they have completed the behavioral assessment and received a recommendation.

The Maturing Church Cluster is intended to provide new churches with needed support after the first year. The shift from year-old church to maturing church is significant, and the needs are significantly different. As the role of planter changes, the people must be included in the process in a different way.

The Strategic Planning Network is a network of pastors and lay leaders who want to avoid the pitfalls of institutionalization while focusing on the planting of new congregations. The intent is not to focus on new church planting exclusively but on the development of stronger established churches as well.

The Harvest 1000 is focused on the financial resources necessary for the creation of a church-planting movement. The goal is to raise funds specifically designated to new church plants. This task is one of the most difficult since there is no visible need—only a vision.

The Meta-Church Network is a cluster of churches committed to implementing the ideas of the metachurch. The term, coined by Carl George, refers to a church that changes people through small-group ministries.

Mannoia's book ends with resources for implementation. The flow-chart provides a visual picture that denominational leaders can understand and implement. The implementation time line for developing a comprehensive church-planting program is both realistic and challenging.

Many groups and denominations have adopted these systems, and they have helped raise church planting capacity. More churches are being started, and more of them are being successful

Conclusion

Perhaps as we combine the power of the Spirit and Spirit-led systems, church-planting movements can emerge in North America. My prayer, now that you've read this book, is that God will bless you as you begin this journey of planting his church. May God guide and empower you. In the words of Christian history's greatest church planter, "Now to him who is able to do immeasurably more than all we ask or imagine, according to his power that is at work within us, to him be glory in the church and in Christ Jesus throughout all generations, for ever and ever! Amen" (Eph. 3:20–21).

May God lead you to plant churches. There can be no greater task than evangelizing and congregationalizing North America. As we join God in this task, we become missional—*on mission* with God to see his kingdom expanded. We become participants in the *missio dei*. Who knows what God will do through us!

Resources for Further Reading

Akins, Thomas Wade. *Pioneer Evangelism*. Rio de Janeiro: Convenção Batista Brasileira, 1995.

Garrison, David. *Church Planting Movements*. Richmond, Va.: International Mission Board, 1999.

Mannoia, Kevin. *Church Planting: The Next Generation*. Indianapolis, Ind.: Light and Life Communication, 1994.

Nevius, John L. *Planting and Development of Missionary Churches*. Nutley, N.J.: Presbyterian & Reformed, 1958.

Patterson, George. *Church Multiplication Guide*. Pasadena, Calif.: William Carey Library, 1993.

Robb, John D. *Focus! The Power of People Group Thinking*. Pasadena, Calif.: MARC Publishing, 1989.

Notes

Chapter 1

1. Bill Easum, www.easumbandy.com/free resources.

2. http://www.rca.org/news/journals/eonline/0902strategies.html.

3. Aubrey Malphurs, *Planting Growing Churches for the Twenty-first Century* (Grand Rapids: Baker Book House, 1992), 44.

4. Tom Clegg and Warren Bird, *Lost in America: How You and Your Church Can Impact the World Next Door* (Loveland, Colo.: Group Publishers, 2001), 30; with additional information from an unpublished paper by Clegg, who is with Church Resource Ministries, www.crmnet.org.

5. Roland Allen, *Missionary Methods: Saint Paul's or Ours?* (Grand Rapids: Eerdmans, 1962), 106.

6. See Roger Fink and Rodney Stark, *The Churching of America, 1776–1990: Winners and Losers in Our Religious Economy* (New Brunswick, N.J.: Rutgers University Press, 1994).

7. Cited in Malphurs, *Planting Growing Churches*, 44.

8. Stuart Murray, *Church Planting: Laying Foundations* (Scottsdale, Pa.: Herald Press, 2001), 21.

9. Ibid., 25.

10. George Hunter, "The Rationale for a Culturally Relevant Worship Service," *Journal of the American Society for Church Growth, Worship and Growth* 7 (1996): 131.

11. Win Arn, cited in Malphurs, *Planting Growing Churches*, 32.

12. Win Arn, *The Pastor's Manual for Effective Ministry* (Monrovia, Calif.: Church Growth, 1988), 16.

13. http://www.christianitytoday.com/ct/2002/100/33.0.html.

14. http://www.barna.org/FlexPage.aspx?Page=BarnaUpdateNarrow&BarnaUpdateID=163.

15. http://www.gallup.com/poll/content/?ci=7759.

16. See book review at http://www.nimblespirit.com/html/spiritual_but_not_religious_re.htm.

Chapter 2

1. Craig Van Gelder, ed., *Confident Witness—Changing World* (Grand Rapids: Eerdmans, 1999), 1.

2. Wilbert R. Shenk, *Write the Vision* (Harrisburg, Pa.: Trinity Press International, 1995), 43.

3. Craig Van Gelder, *The Essence of the Church* (Grand Rapids: Baker Books, 2000), 98.

4. The Southern Baptist Convention plants the most churches of any evangelical denomination. The North American Mission Board, SBC, has set a goal of having 100,000 Southern Baptist churches by the year 2020, doubling the number of active SBC churches at the start of the twenty-first century. To achieve this, NAMB plans to help start sixty thousand churches, allowing ten thousand for attrition.

5. Richard J. Mouw, "The Missionary Location of the North American Churches," in *Confident Witness—Changing World,* ed. Craig Van Gelder (Grand Rapids, Mich.: Eerdmans, 1999), 4.

6. Douglas John Hall, "Metamorphosis: From Christendom to Diaspora," in *Confident Witness—Changing World,* ed. Craig Van Gelder (Grand Rapids, Mich.: Eerdmans, 1999), 69.

7. James V. Brownson, *Speaking the Truth in Love* (Harrisburg, Pa.: Trinity Press International, 1998), 4–5.

8. Douglas John Hall, *The End of Christendom and the Future of Christianity* (Harrisburg, Pa.: Trinity Press International, 1997), 66.

9. Charles Van Engen, *Mission on the Way* (Grand Rapids: Baker Books, 1996), 71.

10. Lesslie Newbigin, *A Word in Season* (Grand Rapids: Eerdmans, 1994), 67.

11. Van Engen, *Mission on the Way,* 164.

12. This scale was developed by Robert Don Hughes and is used here by permission.

13. Shenk, *Write the Vision,* 47.

14. George R. Hunsberger, "Sizing Up the Shape of the Church," *The Church Between Gospel and Culture,* eds. George R. Hunsberger and Craig Van Elder (Grand Rapids: Eerdmans, 1996), 338.

15. Hall, *The End of Christendom and the Future of Christianity,* 55.

16. Shenk, *Write the Vision,* 47.

17. George R. Hunsberger, "The Newbigin Gauntlet," in *The Church*

between Gospel and Culture, 5.

18. Aubrey Malphurs, *Planting Growing Churches for the Twenty-first Century* (Grand Rapids: Baker Book House, 1992), 27.

19. Craig Van Gelder, "Defining the Center—Finding the Boundaries," in *The Church between Gospel and Culture,* 45.

20. Paul McKaughan, Dellana O'Brien, and William O'Brien, *Choosing a Future for U.S. Missions* (Monrovia, Calif.: MARC, 1998), 22.

21. Hunsberger, "The Newbigin Gauntlet," 5.

22. Calvin Guy, "Theological Foundations," in Donald A. McGavran ed., *Church Growth and Christian Mission* (William Carey Library, 1976 reprint), 44.

23. Stuart Murray, *Church Planting: Laying Foundations* (Scottsdale, Pa.: Herald Press, 2001), 33.

24. Some have proposed that Paul's actions here are descriptive and not a good strategy. Since the Athenians "sneered," they reason that it proved to be an ill-advised strategy. This is a minority position. By connecting with the Athenian culture, he was able to connect with a resistant people.

25. Mouw, "The Missionary Location of the North American Churches," 8.

26. William J. Larkin, "Mission in Acts," in *Mission in the New Testament*, ed. William J. Larkin Jr. and Joel F. Williams (Maryknoll, N.Y.: Orbis Books, 1998), 180.

27. Daniel Montgomery, e-mailed to the author, November 9, 2005.

28. Martin Kähler as quoted in McKaughan, O'Brien, and O'Brien, *Choosing a Future for U.S. Missions*, 21.

29. James A. Scherer, "Key Issues to Be Considered in Global Mission Today: Crucial Questions about Mission Theology, Context, and Expectations," in *Mission at the Dawn of the 21st Century*, ed. Paul Varo Martinson (Minneapolis, Minn.: Kirk House Publishers, 1999), 12.

30. Wilburt Shenk, "The Culture of Modernity as a Missionary Challenge," in *The Church between Gospel and Culture*, 69–78.

31. Shenk, *Write the Vision*, 86.

32. Scherer, "Key Issues to Be Considered in Global Mission Today," 12.

33. Shenk, *Write the Vision,* 90.

34. Martin Erdmann, "Mission in John's Gospel and Letters," in *Mission in the New Testament*, ed. William J. Larkin Jr. and Joel F. Williams (Maryknoll, N.Y.: Orbis Books, 1998), 212.

35. Andreas J. Köstenberger and Peter T. O'Brien, *Salvation to the Ends of the Earth* (Downers Grove, Ill.: InterVarsity Press, 2001), 269.

36. International Missionary Council as quoted in James A. Scherer, "Mission Theology," in *Toward the Twenty-first Century in Christian Mission*, ed. James M. Phillips and Robert T. Coote (Grand Rapids: Eerdmans, 1993), 194–95.

37. Köstenberger and O'Brien, *Salvation to the Ends of the Earth*, 269.

38. Wilbert R. Shenk, "Mission Strategies," in *Toward the Twenty-first Century in Christian Mission*, ed. James M. Phillips and Robert T. Coote (Grand Rapids: Eerdmans, 1993), 221–23.

39. Shenk, "The Culture of Modernity as a Missionary Challenge," 71.

40. This was not an illegitimate mission, but it was an incomplete mission view.

41. Van Gelder, *The Essence of the Church*, 55.

42. Peter Beyerhaus, "Indigenous Churches," in *Concise Dictionary of Christian World Mission*, ed. Stephen Neil, Gerald H. Anderson, and John Goodwin (Nashville, Tenn.: Abingdon Press, 1971), 278.

43. Roland Allen, *Missionary Methods: Saint Paul's or Ours?* (Grand Rapids: Eerdmans, 1962), 98–99.

44. Mouw, "The Missionary Location of the North American Churches," 14.

45. International Missionary Council, "The Growing Church: The Madras Series," Papers Based on the Meeting of the International Missionary Council, at Tambaram, Madras, India, December 12–29, 1938. Vol. 2 (New York, International Missionary Council), 276, cited in Mark Terry, Ebbie Smith, and Justice Anderson, eds., *Missiology* (Nashville: Broadman & Holman, 1998), 311.

46. Donald R. Jacobs, "Contextualization in Mission," in *Toward the Twenty-first Century in Christian Mission,* ed. James M. Phillips and Robert T. Coote (Grand Rapids: Eerdmans, 1993), 240.

47. Shenk, "The Culture of Modernity as a Missionary Challenge," 72.

48. C. Peter Wagner, *Church Planting for a Greater Harvest* (Ventura, Calif.: Regal Books, 1990), 11.

49. Shenk, *Write the Vision*, 48.

50. Shenk, "The Culture of Modernity as a Missionary Challenge," 74.

51. John R. "Pete" Hendrick, "Congregations with Missions vs. Missionary Congregations," in *The Church between Gospel and Culture*, 304.

52. David J. Bosch, *Transforming Mission* (Maryknoll, N.Y.: Orbis Books, 1998), 21.

53. J. Andrew Kirk, *The Mission of Theology and Theology as Mission* (Valley Forge, Pa.: Trinity Press International, 1997), 39.

54. Dean S. Gilliand, "Contextual Theology as Incarnational Mission," in *The Word Among Us*, ed. Dean S. Gilliland (Dallas: Word Publishing, 1989), 10–11.

55. Van Gelder, *Confident Witness—Changing World*, 14–15.

56. Tom A. Steffen and David J. Hesselgrave, *Reconnecting God's Story to Ministry: Cross Cultural Storytelling at Home and Abroad* (La Habra, Calif.: Center for Organization & Ministry, 1997).

57. Bosch, *Transforming Mission*, 494.

58. Dean S. Gilliland, ed., *The Word Among Us* (Dallas: Word Publishing, 1989), vii.

Chapter 3

1. Talmadge R. Amberson, "The Foundations for Church Planting," in *The Birth of Churches*, ed. Talmadge R. Amberson (Nashville: Broadman Press, 1979), 45.

2. For a grid that helps in understanding components of each command, see Elmer Towns, *Getting a Church Started: A Student Manual for Theological Foundation and Practical Techniques of Planting a Church* (Lynchburg, Va.: Church Growth Institute, 1985), 8. This book is now available free at www.elmertowns.com. Towns includes Mark 16:15 in his list. However, the oldest and best Greek texts of Mark have not included this verse, suggesting that it is a later addition to the original text. Thus, I have included only four.

3. Outline created by John Worcester, http://www.churchplanting.net/resources/index.htm.

4. John Mark Terry, unpublished document.

5. http://www.redeemer2.com/rucpc/rucpc/index.cfm.

6. This meaning is exactly the reason for the eunuch's joy (Acts 8:39). He who loved the Jewish nation and the Jewish law could not, because of his emasculation, become part of the community and was denied baptism by the Jews. The gospel of Christ included even him and meant he could be baptized without first undergoing (an impossible) circumcision. See Frank Stagg, *The Book of Acts* (Nashville: Broadman Press, 1954), 106–9.

7. Eddie Gibbs, *ChurchNext: Quantum Changes in How We Do Ministry* (Downers Grove, Ill.: InterVarsity Press, 2000), 11.

8. Ibid., 33.

Chapter 4

1. Many biblical and historical examples here and in the rest of this chapter were researched and partly written for me by my former teaching assistant, J. D. Payne. Today he serves as a church planting professor. He also has written an excellent Ph.D. dissertation examining current church-planting practice in North America. He can be reached at jpayne@sbts.edu.

2. John B. Polhill, *Acts*, in the New American Commentary, vol. 26 (Nashville: Broadman Press, 1992), 319.

3. Justo L. Gonzalez, *The Story of Christianity: The Reformation to the Present Day,* vol. 2 (New York: HarperCollins Publishers, 1985), 246.

4. John Mark Terry, *Evangelism: A Concise History* (Nashville: Broadman & Holman Publishers, 1994), 128–29.

5. Robert E. Logan and Steven L. Ogne, *Churches Planting Churches: A Comprehensive Guide for Multiplying New Congregations* (Carol Stream, Ill.: ChurchSmart Resources, 1995), VHS tape, "Churches Planting Churches."

6. V. Simpson Turner Sr., "A History of African-American Evangelistic Activity," in Lee N. June, ed., *Evangelism and Discipleship in African-American Churches* (Grand Rapids: Zondervan Publishing House, 1999), 21.

7. Bob Gomez, e-mail to the author, November 10, 2005.

8. See http://homechurch.org/registry/index.html for a directory of house churches.

9. John Dee, "China Report 1999: A Visit with the Underground Church Now 85 Million Strong." See http://www.hccentral.com/magazine/china2.html.

10. Charles Brock, *Indigenous Church Planting: A Practical Journey* (Neosho, Mo.: Church Growth International, 1994), 262.

11. Brock, *Indigenous Church Planting*, 86.

12. Steve is the founder of the U.S. Center for Church Planting (www.churchplantingcenter.com).

13. Terry, *Evangelism*, 130.

14. C. Peter Wagner, *Church Planting for a Greater Harvest: A Comprehensive Guide* (Ventura, Calif.: Regal Books, 1990), 71–72.

15. www.wooddale.org.

16. Tom Correll, e-mail to the author, November 4, 2005.

17. See www.sainthadrews-lr.org/about/churchplanting.

18. Some may argue that Titus could also be an example of this paradigm, but this is not the case. An examination of the ministry of Titus reveals a similarity to that of the ministry of Paul. Titus 1:5 says, "For this reason I left you in Crete, that you might set in order what remains and appoint elders in every city as I directed you" (NASB). Titus was not confined to one location but rather was to minister across the island in the various cities. Timothy, on the other hand, was to concentrate on the church in Ephesus.

19. Michael Nicholls, "Missions, Yesterday and Today: Charles Haddon Spurgeon (1834–92), Church Planter," in *Five 'Til Midnight: Church Planting for A.D. 2000 and Beyond*, ed. Tony Cupit (Atlanta: Home Mission Board, 1994), 94.

20. Ibid., 94.

21. Ibid., 96.

22. Terry, *Evangelism*, 48.

23. See Loyd Childs, "Teams Multiply Churches in Malaysia/Singapore," *Urban Mission 2* (1985): 33–39; Ben A. Sawatsky, "A Church Planting Strategy for World Class Cities," *Urban Mission 3* (1985): 7–19; Roger S. Greenway, "The 'Team' Approach to Urban Church Planting," *Urban Mission* 4 (1987): 3–5.

24. James E. Westgate, "Church Planting Strategies for World-Class Cities," in ed. Harvie M. Conn, *Planting and Growing Urban Churches: From Dream to Reality* (Grand Rapids: Baker Books, 1997), 205.

25. Ibid., 204.

26. Ibid., 205.

27. From the author's Ph.D. dissertation, "The Impact of the Church Planting Process and Other Selected Factors on the Attendance of Southern Baptist Church Plants." Southern Baptist Theological Seminary, 2003.

Chapter 5

1. David J. Bosch, *Transforming Missions: Paradigm Shifts in Theology of Mission* (Maryknoll, N.Y.: Orbis Books, 2001), 132, citing W. H. Ollrog, *Paulus und seine Mitarbeiter* (Eukirchen-Vluyn: Neukirchener Verlag, 1979).

2. Richard N. Longenecker, *Acts,* The Expositor's Bible Commentary (Grand Rapids, Mich.: Zondervan, 1981), 284.

3. Craig Wurst, student paper, "Who Can Plant Churches?"

4. Daniel Sanchez, Curt Watke, Ebbie Smith, *Starting Reproducing Congregations* (Cumming, Ga.: Church Starting Network, 2001), 33–34.

5. Phil Stevenson, *The Ripple Church: Multiply Your Ministry by Parenting New Churches.* Indianapolis, Ind.: Wesleyan Publishing House, 2004.

6. From the author's Ph.D. dissertation, "The Impact of the Church Planting Process and Other Selected Factors on the Attendance of Southern Baptist Church Plants."

7. Kevin Maples, student paper, "Who Can Plant a Church?"

8. These categories describe thirteen qualities from chapter 2 of Charles Ridley's *How to Select Church Planters* (Pasadena, Calif.: Fuller Evangelistic Association, 1988), 7–11.

9. http://www.glcc.org/Programs/Adult/church_planting assessment_cente.htm.

10. http://www.churchplanting4me.org/approach.htm.

11. Joe Hernandez, e-mail to author, November 11, 2005.

12. http://www.acts29network.org/DF/PrintablePage.aspx?XslPath=\Content.xslt&ObjectTypeName=Simple%20Content&ObjectName=Assessment%20Process&Mode=Values.

13. http://www.pca-mna.org/planting%20ministries/assessment%20center.htm.

14. http://www.redeemer2.com/themovement/issues/2004/june/assessment.html.

15. http://www.covchurch.org/cov/news/item3542.html.

Chapter 6

1. Aubrey Malphurs, *Planting Growing Churches for the Twenty-first Century* (Grand Rapids: Baker Book House, 1992).

2. See Rick Warren, *The Purpose-Driven Church* (Grand Rapids: Zondervan, 1995) for helpful guidelines on organizing a church for growth.

Chapter 7

1. David Slagle, e-mail to author, October 1, 2005.

2. Roger N. McNamara and Ken Davis, *The Y.B.H. Handbook of Church Planting: A Practical Guide to Church Planting* (Longwood, Fla.: Xulon Press, 2005), 194.

3. Both of these graphs come from my Ph.D. dissertation. A summary of the study can be found at www.newchurches.com.

4. Ann Roth, *Study of Church Planting Effectiveness,* International Church of the Four Square Gospel, 2004 cited in Steve L. Ogne and Timothy D. Roehl, "Coaching: a New Paradigm for Empowering Missional Leaders for Ministry in a Changing World," unpublished D.Min. Dissertation, 2005, 119.

Chapter 8

1. We will consider vocational (full-time) church-planting teams at a later point.

2. Stephen J. Ro, www.redeemer2.com/themovement/issues/2004/june/first100.html.

3. See Bob Logan, *Church Planter Toolkit*, tape 7, "Getting Your Ministries Ready for Birth." Available from ChurchSmart resources (www.churchsmart.com).

4. www.riverside.org

5. Steve Sjogren and Rob Lewin, *Community of Kindness* (Ventura, Calif.: Regal/Gospel Light, 2003), 207. See also Steve Sjogren, "Growing Pastor [Past the] Temptation to Quit," online at http://www.plantthefuture.org/pdf/Growing_Past_the_Temptation_to_Quit__by_Steve_Sjogren.

Chapter 9

1. Adapted from Thom Rainer, *The Bridger Generation* (Nashville: Broadman & Holman, 1997) and census data. Much of the material in this chapter is analysis and insight based on census data.

2. Elmer Towns has provided helpful contrasts between the builders and boomers in his conference on "How to Reach the Baby Boomers." Much of my thinking on this topic is influenced by his work.

3. The writing and speaking of church-planting consultant John Worcester has greatly helped and influenced my research. Learn more about him by visiting www.churchplanting.net. I am also indebted to Jack Simms and others whose work can be found at http://webuildpeople.ag.org.

4. Joe S. Ratliff and Michael J. Cox, eds., *Church Planting in the African-American Community* (Nashville: Broadman Press, 1993), 72.

5. Hozell C. Francis, *Church Planting in the African-American Context* (Grand Rapids: Zondervan Publishing House, 2000), 45.

6. Oscar I. Romo, *American Mosaic: Church Planting in Ethnic America* (Nashville: Broadman Press, 1993), 41.

7. This data is from Richard Harris, *The Planter Update* (Alpharetta, Ga.: North American Mission Board, 2002).

8. Romo, *American Mosaic*, 90.

9. www.census.gov.

10. Craig Kennett Miller makes this observation in his article "Creating

New Faith Communities," *Partners in Discipleship*, May 2004.

Chapter 10

1. Stanley E. Grenz, *A Primer on Postmodernism* (Grand Rapids: Eerdmans, 1996), 174.

2. Richard J. Mouw, "The Missionary Location of the North American Churches," in *Confident Witness—Changing World*, ed. Craig Van Gelder (Grand Rapids: Eerdmans, 1999), 4.

3. Jimmy Long, *Generating Hope: A Strategy for Reaching the Postmodern Generation* (Downers Grove, Ill.: InterVarsity Press, 1997), 66.

4. Millard J. Erickson, *Postmodernizing the Faith: Evangelical Responses to the Challenge of Postmodernism* (Grand Rapids: Baker, 1998), 19.

5. Grenz, *A Primer on Postmodernism*, 12.

6. Jean-François Lyotard, *The Postmodern Condition: A Report on Knowledge*, trans. Geoff Bennington and Brian Massumi, Theory and History of Literature, vol. 10 (Minneapolis: University of Minnesota Press, 1984), xxiv.

7. Darrel L. Guder, *Missional Church* (Grand Rapids: Eerdmans, 1998), 39.

8. Leonard I. Sweet, *Soul Tsunami: Sink or Swim in New Millennium Culture* (Grand Rapids: Zondervan Publishing House, 1999), 18.

9. Eddie Gibbs, *ChurchNext: Quantum Changes in How We Do Ministry* (Downers Grove, Ill.: InterVarsity Press, 2000), 33.

10. Sweet, *Soul Tsunami*, 45.

11. Guder, *Missional Church*, 1.

12. Gibbs, *ChurchNext*, 10.

13. Ralph Greenwell contributed to the research and writing of this section as part of a study group, "Church Planting in a Postmodern Age."

14. Debbie Dornfeld contributed to the research and writing of this section as part of a study group, "Church Planting in a Postmodern Age."

15. Survey response from Downtown Community Fellowship, Athens, Georgia.

16. Sweet, *Soul Tsunami*, 307.

17. Sally Morgenthaler, *Worship Evangelism* (Grand Rapids: Zondervan, 1999), chapter 5.

18. Eugene Peterson, http://www.theooze.com/articles/read.cfm?ID=42&CATID=2.

19. Robert E. Webber, *Ancient-Future Faith: Rethinking Evangelicalism for a Postmodern World* (Grand Rapids: Baker, 1999), 91.

20. Gibbs, *ChurchNext*, 198.

Chapter 11

1. Donald A. McGavran, *Understanding Church Growth*, 3rd ed. (Grand Rapids: Eerdmans, 1990), 163–78.

2. http://www.redeemer2.com/themovement/issues/2003/dec/inthehood.html

3. Rick Warren, *The Purpose-Driven Church* (Grand Rapids: Zondervan Publishing House, 1995), 170.

4. Median is the "middle number." The median of 80 and 20 is 50. Note that demographic data may present averages that do not exist in reality. One way to protect against this fallacy is to construct a graph. Then the planter will have a visual representation of the data and will be able to identify possible false averages.

5. Tom A. Steffen and David J. Hesselgrave, *Reconnecting God's Story to Ministry: Cross Cultural Story Telling at Home and Abroad* (La Habra, Calif.: Center for Organization and Ministry), 1997.

6. McGavran, *Understanding Church Growth*, 163–78.

7. Larry L. Lewis, *Church Planter's Handbook* (Nashville: Broadman & Holman Publishers, 1992), 27.

Chapter 12

1. http://www.dawneurope.net/indexbody.htm.

2. George Barna, *Revolution* (Ventura, Calif.: Tyndale, 2005), 49.

3. Ibid.

4. Interview with Jennifer Campbell, *Leadership Network Advance*, May 2005.

5. Tim Keller and J. Allen Thompson, *Church Planting Manual* (New York: Redeemer Church Planting Center, 2005).

6. Glenn B. Smith, in lecture one, in *Urban Missiology in the Postmodern Metropolis*, discusses "Three Fundamental Questions" the urban practitioner should ask in developing an urban missiology. These are found in the *Interactive Learning Guide*, page 17, that coincides with the lecture.

Chapter 13

1. Michael Frost and Alan Hirsch, *The Shaping of the Things to Come: Innovation and Mission for the 21st-Century Church* (Peabody, Mass.: Hendrickson Publishers, 2003), 12.

2. Ibid.

Chapter 14

1. http://www.theooze.com/articles/article.cfm?id=1255.

2. http://www.nytimes.com/2001/04/29/national/29PRAY.html.

3. Donald R. Allen, *Barefoot in the Church: Sensing the Authentic Through the House Church* (Richmond: John Knox Press, 1972). Electronically reproduced at http://homechurch.org/miscellaneous/ allen2.html.

4. Wolfgang Simson, "Fifteen Theses Towards a Re-Incarnation of the Church," at http://www.house2house.tv/issues/wolfgang15theses.shtml.

5. Dick Scoggins, *Planting House Churches in Networks: A Manual from the Perspective of a Church Planting Team* (Fellowship of Church Planters).

6. Frank A. Viola, "Some Streams of the House Church," Present Testimony Ministry; 1405 Valley Place; Brandon, FL 33510; E-mail: Fviola3891@aol.com.

7. Wayne Grudem, *Systematic Theology: An Introduction to Biblical Doctrine* (Grand Rapids: Zondervan Publishing House, 1994), 857.

8. http://www.carolinaclassical.com/articles/luther_german_mass.pdf.

9. Nate Krupp, "Caution—Steps Toward Denominationalism," at http://www.radchr.net/stepstod.htm.

10. Charles Brock, *Indigenous Church Planting: A Practical Journey* (Neosho, Mo.: Church Growth International, 1994), chapter 2.

11. Ibid., chapter 4.

12. Roland Allen, *Missionary Methods: St Paul's or Ours?* (Grand Rapids: Eerdmans, 1962), 126.

13. Floyd Tidsmorth Jr., *Life Cycle of a New Congregation* (Nashville: Broadman Press, 1992), 91.

14. "The Church," at http://www.sbc.net/bfm/bfm2000.asp.

15. Westminster Confession of Faith, at http://www.pcanet.org/general/cof_chapxxi-xxv.htm#chapxxv.

Chapter 15

1. Personal interview with Chris Brewer, April 26, 2002.

2. Lunch meeting with Andy Stanley, August 25, 2002.

3. There are different versions of the Engel Scale. Malphurs describes a slightly different version than I have reproduced (Aubrey Malphurs, *Planting Growing Churches for the 21st Century* [Grand Rapids: Baker Book House, 1992], 275).

4. http://guide.gospelcom.net/resources/gray-matrix.php.

5. http://www.brigada.org/today/articles/gray-matrix.html.

6. Darrel L. Guder, *The Missional Church* (Grand Rapids: Eerdmans, 1998).

7. Mark Driscoll, *The Radical Reformission: Reaching Out without Selling Out* (Grand Rapids: Zondervan Publishers, 2004), 78.

8. Ibid, 68–69.

9. Robert Logan, *Church Planter Tool Kit*, audiotape 5.

10. LifeWay Prospect Services, 800-464-2799. This service sells lists

of new babies, new movers, new marriages, and lists of new families with children.

11. Herb Miller, *How to Build a Magnetic Church,* Creative Leadership Series, ed. Lyle Schaller (Nashville: Abingdon Press, 1987), 72–73.

Chapter 16

1. Bob Logan, *Church Planter Toolkit,* tape 7, "Getting Your Ministries Ready for Birth," available from ChurchSmart resources (www.churchsmart.com).

2. Aubrey Malphurs, *Planting Growing Churches for the 21st Century* (Grand Rapids: Baker Book House, 1992), 320.

3. Bob Roberts, e-mail to author, November 5, 2005.

4. John Worcester, e-mail to author, November 10, 2005.

5. http://www.highpointechurch.org/.

6. Roger N. McNamara and Ken Davis, *The Y.B.H. Handbook of Church Planting: A Practical Guide to Church Planting* (Longwood, Fla.: Xulon Press, 2005), 229.

7. The U.S. Postal Service requires a Qualifying Business Reply Mail (QBRM) account in order to receive business reply cards. Most post offices can explain the process of opening such an account. The permit costs US $205 and Canadian $465 at the time this was written. There is also a charge for each piece returned.

Chapter 17

1. Dale Galloway, *The Small Group Book* (Grand Rapids: Revell, 1995), 17.

2. Carl F. George, *Prepare Your Church for the Future* (Tarrytown, N.Y.: Revell, 1991).

3. "Meta" suggests the idea of change. Thus, "metachurch" is a "change" church, a church that changes or transforms in order to transform lives.

4. http://www.christthekinganglican.org.

5. http://www.christthekinganglican.org/docs/smgrps.htm.

Chapter 18

1. Adapted from Robert Logan and Steven L. Ogne, *Churches Planting Churches: A Comprehensive Guide for Multiplying New Congregations* (Carol Stream, Ill.: ChurchSmart Resources, 1995), 4, 10–11.

2. Ralph Moore, *Starting a New Church* (Ventura, Calif.: Gospel Light, 2002), 56.

3. Postage is always increasing.

4. Steve Allen, e-mail to author, November 10, 2005.

5. Tom Nebel and Gary Rohrmayer, *Church Planting Landmines: Mistakes to Avoid in Years 2 through 10* (St. Charles, Ill:. ChurchSmart Resources, 2005).

6. Steve Sjogren and Rob Lewin, *Community of Kindness* (Ventura, Calif.: Regal/Gospel Light, 2003), 172–74.

7. Dan Ramsey, *101 Best Weekend Businesses* (Career Press, 1996), as cited at http://www.plantingministries.org/chapt3.htm.

8. http://www2.churchplanting.com/churchplanting/hangin.html

Chapter 19

1. C. Peter Wagner, *Church Planting for a Greater Harvest* (Ventura, Calif.: Regal Books, 1990), 118. Italics in the original.

2. Elmer Towns, *Getting a Church Started: A Student Manual for Theological Foundation and Practical Techniques of Planting a Church* (Lynchburg, Va.: Church Growth Institute, 1985), available at www.elmertowns.com.

3. From "The Barometer of the Southern Baptist Faith in America," a PowerPoint presentation. This research was done for the North American Mission Board of the Southern Baptist Convention and presented at the NAMB summer meeting in 2001. Its research covers several groups.

4. http://www.churchmarketing.com.

5. http://www.churchmarketing.com/articles/robert.html.

6. Ed Stetzer and Eric Ramsey, *Strategic Outreach: A How-to Marketing Manual for Pastors and Church Leaders* (San Diego: Outreach, 2005), 97.

Chapter 20

1. Facilities for a growing new church will be discussed later.

2. http://www.nyjourney.com.

3. Portable Church Industries (PCI) can be contacted at 1260 Kempar Avenue, Madison Heights, MI 48071. Their phone number is 800-939-7722, and the Web site is www.portablechurch.com.

4. There is much litigation about churches using schools today. Since this may change, you can find up-to-date articles about U.S. and Canadian laws at www.newchurches.com/legal. You can also find a sample letter that explains the law to school administrators.

5. Ian Buntain, e-mail to author, January 9, 2003.

6. David Bryan, e-mail to author, November 6, 2005.

7. Keith W. Hinton, *Growing Churches Singapore Style* (Singapore: OMF, 1985), 196.

8. http://www.seminolechurch.com/ourstory.shtml.

9. http://www.lifeway.com

10. For ordering information, go to http://www.purposedriven.com/.

11. Oldham Little Church Foundation, 5177 Richmond, Suite 1068, Houston, Texas 77056.

Chapter 21

1. Aubrey Malphurs, *Planting Growing Churches for the Twenty-first Century* (Grand Rapids: Baker Book House, 1992), 335.

2. North American Mission Board church planters think tank, 24–26 August 2002, an invitation-only gathering to discuss how to improve training for church planting.

3. Examples of different types of church planting mailers can be found at www.newchurches.com/mailers. Church planters who want to share their own mailers may do so there.

4. www.tellstart.com.

5. http://www.easumbandy.com/resources/index.php?action=searchresults&pl_option[1]=5

6. http://users.characterlink.net/davebarba/press_on!_ministries011.htm

7. This percentage of positive respondents occurs primarily in the South and the Southeastern United States. Millcreek Community Church determined that getting 200 persons to attend the initial service required 55,000 phone calls (or dial-ups), a rate of 3.6 percent. I know of one church in Boston that used this approach and had a 4 percent response rate. This means it would take almost 80,000 calls to get 200 people at the first service. I am aware also of a church in Rhode Island that had higher than a 10 percent response rate. Response rates do vary.

8. http://www.bigskychurch.com.

Chapter 22

1. Darrell W. Robinson delineates this threefold purpose: exalting the Savior, equipping the saints, and evangelizing the sinner; see his *Total Church Life*, rev. ed. (Nashville: Broadman Press, 1993).

2. Sally Morgenthaler, *Worship Evangelism: Inviting Unbelievers into the Presence of God* (Grand Rapids: Zondervan Publishing House, 1995).

3. Bob Fitts, "The Lord Reigns," Integrity Music, 1989.

4. http://www.barna.org/FlexPage.aspx?Page=BarnaUpdateNarrow&BarnaUpdateID=199.

5. Aubrey Malphurs, *Planting Growing Churches for the Twenty-first Century* (Grand Rapids: Baker Book House, 1992), 187.

6. Though exaggerated, these problems were highlighted by James Michener's *Hawaii* (New York: Random House, 1959).

7. A theory of the source for this tune comes from Bill Moyers's PBS series on Genesis. There is little evidence that the tune comes from African slave ships. The American frontier was more likely the source of this hymn.

Chapter 23

1. http://www.nycradio.com/weblogs/mohler/1249963.aspx?view=print

2. Mark Driscoll, "What Gives Preaching Its Power?" *Leadership Journal*, Spring 2004, 32.

3. http://www.redeemer2.com/themovement/issues/2004/june/postmoderncity_1_p1.html.

4. http://marshill.fm.

5. http://marshill.fm/word/index.htm.

6. S. Greidanua, "Preaching from Paul Today" in *The Dictionary of Paul and His Letters*, eds. Gerald P. Hawthorne and Ralph P. Martin, eds. (Downers Grove, Ill., InterVarsity Press, 1993), 743.

7. Raymond Bailey, *Paul the Preacher* (Nashville: Broadman Press, 1991), 99.

8. Michael P. Green, "Sermon Illustrations," in *Leadership Handbooks of Practical Theology, Volume 1: Word and Worship*, gen. ed. James D. Berkley (Grand Rapids: Baker Book House, 1992), 11.

9. Bailey, 81.

10. http://www.ecclesiahouston.org.

11. Interview with Chris Seay, electronically published on disk by Sermon Resources Incorporated.

12. John R. Claypool, *The Preaching Event* (San Francisco: Harper Collins, 1989), 87.

13. Bailey, 28.

14. Larry Moyer, "Evangelistic Preaching," in *Leadership Handbooks of Practical Theology, Volume 1: Word and Worship,* James D. Berkley, gen. ed. (Grand Rapids: Baker Book House, 1992), 11.

15. Lloyd M. Perry, *Biblical Preaching for Today's World*, rev. ed, (Chicago: Moody Press, 1973, 1990), 143.

16. John R. W. Stott, *Between Two Worlds: The Challenge of Preaching Today* (Grand Rapids, Mich.: Wm. B. Eerdmans Publishing Co.), 201.

17. Calvin Miller, *Marketplace Preaching: How to Return the Sermon to Where It Belongs* (Grand Rapids: Baker Books, 1995), 142.

18. John Calvin, cited in Stott, *Between Two Worlds*, 128.

19. Ralph Moore, *Starting a New Church* (Ventura, Calif.: Gospel Light, 2002), 189.

20. John Mark Clifton, e-mail to the author, November 8, 2005.

Chapter 24

1. See Aubrey Malphurs, *Planting Growing Churches for the Twenty-first Century* (Grand Rapids: Baker Book House, 1992), 354–55.

2. Popularized by Saddleback Church; see www.purposedriven.com.

3. http://www.pastors.com/article.asp?ArtID=8667.

4. Available through LifeWay Christian Stores.

5. http://www.northpoint.org/.

6. Lunch meeting, 25 August 2002.

7. http://www.nhf.cc.

8. Ray Wickham, e-mail to author, October 19, 2002.

9. Dan Morgan, "Assimilating New Believers," unpublished paper.

10. Cited in Win Arn and Charles Arn, *The Master's Plan for Making Disciples: Every Christian an Effective Witness through an Enabling Church* (Grand Rapids: Baker Books, 1998), 156.

11. An excellent resource for an addiction-recovery ministry is Celebrate Recovery, http://www.celebraterecovery.com.

Chapter 25

1. Mailings should be taken personally by the outreach leader to ensure their timely arrival. This correspondence is so crucial that leaving it in the hands of subordinate team members may mean that mailings go out too late in the week or not at all. (I have witnessed this experience.) They should go to the main post office to ensure that letters are not misplaced or delayed by a satellite branch of the postal system.

2. Lyle E. Schaller, *Survival Tactics in the Parish* (Nashville: Abingdon, 1977), 52.

3. Tom Nebel, e-mail to the author, November 9, 2005, reproduced from Tom Nebel and Gary Rohrmayer, *Church Planting Landmines: Mistakes to Avoid in Years 2 through 10* (Charles, Ill.: ChurchSmart Resources).

4. Andy Stanley, *Visioneering* (Sisters, Oreg.: Multnomah, 1999), 85.

Chapter 26

1. Mandy Montgomery, my former student, helped research and write parts of this chapter.

2. Kim Sikes and Lori Haynes Niles, *The Warm and Wonderful Church Nursery* (Loveland, Colo.: Group, 1999), 5.

3. Brian Jones, e-mail to the author, November 9, 2005.

4. Thomas Sanders and Mary Ann Bradberry, *Teaching Preschoolers: First Steps toward Faith* (Nashville: LifeWay Press, 2000), 17–18.

5. Cos Davis, *Breakthrough: Preschool Sunday School Work* (Nashville: Convention Press, 1990), 78.

6. http://www.vineyardcolumbus.org.

7. Phillip Connor, e-mail to the author, November 9, 2005; see www.namb.net/reserach for more information.

8. Jeff Clark, e-mail to author, October 24, 2002.

Chapter 27

1. Lunch meeting, August 25, 2002.

2. Larry Lewis, *The Church Planter's Handbook* (Nashville: Broadman Press, 1992), 133.

Chapter 28

1. Phil Stevenson, *The Ripple Church: Multiply Your Ministry by Parenting New Churches* (Indianapolis, Ind.: Wesleyan Publishing House, 2004), 121.

2. These ideas emerge from Paul Becker and Mark Williams, *The Dynamic Daughter Church Planting Handbook* (Oceanside, Calif.: Dynamic Church Planting International, 1999), 11–15. It is available from Dynamic Church Planting International, http://www.dcpi.org.

3. Dino Senesi, e-mail to author, September 24, 2002.

4. Jack Redford, *Planting New Churches* (Nashville: Broadman Press, 1978).

5. Dino Senesi, e-mail correspondence, 4 September 2002.

6. A number of tools are available for this purpose. Among the better known are the Myers-Briggs Type Inventory, DISC, and LIF-O. The church planter assessment mentioned earlier is standard.

Chapter 29

1. http://www.imb.org/CPM/Chapter3.htm.

Annotated North American Church-Planting Bibliography

Updated November 2005

"I like reading sailing books by people who have circumnavigated the globe; I prefer history from the pen of eyewitnesses who participated when the tide turned for a nation; and I want to read church planting books by people who have been down the alley-ways of neopagan Western society and know what it means to call together a new body of believers in Jesus Christ." –J. Nelson Kraybill, from the Foreword to *Church Planting: Laying Foundations.*

Allen, Roland. *Missionary Methods, St. Paul's or Ours?* Grand Rapids, Mich.: William B. Eerdmans Publishing Company, 1962.

Though not directly related to North American church planting, this is a seminal book in missiology. Allen posits that the key to evangelizing the world is the adoption of "Paul's strategy." Paul relied on trained lay leadership as pastors and elders. Allen's prescriptions can be applied to the North American scene with the development of lay church planting strategies. His focus on the Holy Spirit's role is also key to fostering church-planting movements today.

Amstutz, Harold E. *Church Planter's Manual.* Cherry Hill, N.J.: Association of Baptists for World Evangelism, Inc., 1985.

This book starts as a standard manual with forms, procedures, policies, and the like. The second part of the book then provides five examples of planting situations. Each of these examples is taken from international fields but have application to North American contexts.

Becker, Paul. *Dynamic Church Planting*. Vista, Calif.: Multiplication Ministries, 1992.

DCP is a three-ring binder/workbook (not a paperback or hardback). It is intended as a guide for a church planter to move through the planting process sequentially. It includes a large section of checklists for the plant. It is a helpful resource for church planters looking for a step-by-step guide.

Becker, Paul. *Dynamic Daughter Church Planting*. Vista, Calif.: Multiplication Ministries, 1996.

This is the only book of its kind and is much needed. It provides church planting churches with the step-by-step guide that they need to reproduce themselves. If you are planting a daughter church, you need this resource.

Brock, Charles. *Indigenous Church Planting:* Nashville: Broadman Press, 1981.

Brock's resources are time-tested and valuable. However, they do reflect a paradigm used more frequently in decades past. His ideas often come from his years of church planting in the Philippines among tribal people. As such, they will often relate well in a lower socio-economic bracket in North America, but not to all contexts. The greatest value will be for indigenous lay persons seeking to plant churches in center cities or rural North America.

Bunch, David, Jarvey Kneisel, and Barbara Oden. *Multihousing Congregations: How to Start and Grow Christian Congregations in Multihousing Communities*. Atlanta, Ga.: Smith Publishing, 1991.

This resource is the only widely published resource available on planting churches in multi-housing congregations (in apartment buildings, trailer parks, etc). Since the vast majority of residents will only be reached by a ministry based inside the multi-housing facility, this is an essential resource. Although multi-housing ministry has declined in visibility in the last decade, the ministry remains essential since 60 percent of unchurched North America lives in multi-housing settings.

Chaney, Charles L. *Church Planting at the End of the Twentieth Century.* Wheaton, Ill.: Tyndale House Publishers, Inc., 1993.

In the early nineties, Chaney's book was the best available resource on the topic of North American church planting. Since it is out of print, it has been largely replaced by Malphur's church-planting book. The most recent revision adds contemporary methods like the "big start." This is one of the five best books specifically related to planting.

Cheyney, Tom, J. David Putman, and Van Sanders, eds. Seven Steps for Planting Churches. Alpharetta, Ga.: North American Mission Board, SBC, 2003.

This resource is a small book that contains a seven-step process for planting a church. The steps are principle-driven ("enlist a team" rather than "start a cell group," etc.) It answers, in a simple and practical way, "how" to get started. Since I am constantly asked by prospective planters, "If I want to start a church, how would I do it?" this book is a good starter resource for them. The authors are clear that it is only intended as an introductory piece and they offer suggestions of where to go deeper. This book can be downloaded free from www.churchplantingvillage.net.

Conn, Harvie M., ed., *Planting and Growing Urban Churches: From Dream to Reality*. Grand Rapids, Mich.: Baker Book House, 1996.

Conn's book is not a "how-to" resource for urban planting. It is an advocacy book, not a practitioner's book. If taken as advocacy, it does well. Conn points out the importance of having an urban strategy to reach the burgeoning inner cities of the world.

Dale, Felicity. *Getting Started: A Practical Guide to House Church Planting*. Karis Publishing, Inc., 2003.

There are many house church books out there. (I list many of them in the house church section of www.newchurches.com.*) This one is unique in that is provides a clear and reproducible (dare I say "simple") method for planting churches that meet in homes. As Felicity describes it, anyone can do it, which is sort of her point!*

Faircloth, Samuel D. *Church Planting for Reproduction*. Grand Rapids, Mich.: Baker Book House, 1991.

Faircloth's book starts as a survey oriented textbook, but quickly becomes a systematic church-planting strategy. It is not geared toward North American planting, but this is not a shortcoming. This is one of the few principle-oriented books available that relate to North American planting. In this case, Faircloth calls his system PERT (a system of Program Evaluation and Review Technique). Regardless of the terminology, this is an important missiological resource for discerning North American planters.

Francis, Hozell C. *Church Planting in the African American Context*. Grand Rapids, Mich.: Zondervan Publishing House, 2000.

Hozell's book is one of the most recent texts published in church planting. It is a valuable resource in a field with limited literature. Unlike the other texts dealing with African-American church planting, Hozell actually focuses less on the mechanics of planting and more on the sociology of the African-American church (preaching, ministry, leadership, etc.). These are helpful materials, but further study of "how to" plant in the African-American context would add to the strength of the book.

Galloway, Dale, and Warren Bird. *Starting a New Church: How to Plant a High-Impact Church*. Kansas City, Mo.: Beacon Hill Press, 2003.

Galloway and Bird are veterans to church growth. Their new resource is about planting "large" churches using contemporary methodologies. It comes as a manual with a CD, but it is a little pricey (about $100). If I were planning on using *contemporary outreach methods like direct mail, seeker-sensitive worship, and contemporary worship, I would invest in the resource before I invested thousands more in an outreach campaign.*

Harris, Richard H., compiler. *Reaching a Nation through Church Planting*. Alpharetta, Ga.: North American Mission Board, SBC, 2002.

Richard Harris is the Vice President of Church Planting for the North American Mission Board (Southern Baptist). For this book, he assembled several high profile leaders and several church-planting experts and asked them to "write what they know." Thus, the book covers a broad landscape from town and country planting, to postmodern, to being a mother church, to mentoring planters. Since the authors are so diverse, they bring a great spread of knowledge and experience. This was not intended as a "how-to book," but rather is a "why we should" book that does a good job answering that question in a multitude of contexts. The book is also available for download from www.churchplantingvillage.net.

Herron, Fred. *Expanding God's Kingdom through Church Planting*. Lincoln, Neb.: iUniverse, 2003.

Herron is from a Vineyard background and that is reflected in his writing. The Vineyard folks have done a great job in church planting, and Herron demonstrates why with this effective book. He lays out a thorough church- planting strategy with lots of detail and helpful suggestions.

Hesselgrave, David J. *Planting Churches Cross-Culturally: North America and Beyond*, 2nd ed. Grand Rapids, Mich.: Baker Book House, 2000.

Hesselgrave's book is a step-by-step guide to planting a church in a culture different from one's own. Though systematic, it avoids being simplistic. Instead, each step is explained in practice and in theory. This is the most valuable resource available for cross-cultural planting.

Hiebert, Paul G., and Eloise Hiebert Meneses. *Incarnational Ministry: Planting Churches in Band, Tribal, Peasant, and Urban Societies*. Grand Rapids, Mich.: Baker Publishing House, 1995.

On the surface, this book would have little to do with North American church planting. Understandably, its primary focus is planting in the developing world. However, it is not a book about methods or biblical underpinnings. It is about the sociological structures that make up a society. Since the book's primary focus is urban societies, it provides great discernment for inner-city planters seeking to understand the urban context.

Hurn, Raymond W. *The Rising Tide: New Churches for the New Millennium*. Kansas City, Mo.: Beacon Hill Press, 1997.

Hurn is former superintendent of the Nazarene denomination, and this text is geared toward Nazarenes. One strength of the book is the historical overview of Nazarene church planting. The book is primarily an advocacy work.

Jackson, John. *High Impact Church Planting: You Can Lead a Harvest-Directed Ministry.* Visionquest Ministries, 2000.

I had mixed feelings about High Impact Church Planting. The book was self-published and has too many errors in it (for example, Gallup never said there were 195 million unchurched, etc) and lacks the proper footnotes (no reference on many stats), and I disagree with several parts (you don't need $100-200K to start a high-impact church). However, it is a good primer to help church planters who want to plant churches that start with over 200 (Jackson's idea of a high-impact church plant). It is short (95 pages) and includes a large number of appendices (examples from the author's church).

Jones, Ezra E. *Strategies for New Churches.* New York: Harper and Row, 1976.

Jones writes about church planting from a mainline denominational perspective. The book was ahead of its time, particularly in its attempts to quantify personality characteristics in effective planters (as Ridley has done today). Unfortunately, it is not up to date with today's technologies and methods.

Jones, Tom, ed. *Church Planting from the Ground Up.* Joplin, Mo.: College Press, 2004.

First, full disclosure: at the editor's request, I wrote the foreword to his book. Second, my review: I don't usually like multiple authors—they tend to say the same things over and over. However, I like this book—a lot. I think I appreciate it because it is not a group of theorists giving their opinions. Instead, it is a series of church planters writing on well-defined themes. This is an excellent new resource for church planters.

Keller, Tim, and J. Allen Thompson. *Church Planting Manual.* Redeemer Church Planting Center, New York, 2002.

Keller and Thompson. What more can you say? Thompson was writing on church-planting movements when I was in grade school. Keller is helping lead a movement of church planting and city transformation. This is an excellent resource. It is a workbook, not the typical book, so it has projects and assignments to work though. It also has an urban focus that is appropriate for their passion.

King, Fred G. *The Church Planter's Training Manual.* Camp Hill, Pa.: Christian Publications, 1992.

This is a manual / book primarily geared at church planters in the Christian and Missionary Alliance Church with a small amount of universally applicable material. It consists of articles, forms, and examples. It will not be of great value to the non-CMA planter.

Lewis, Larry L. *The Church Planter's Handbook.* Nashville: Broadman Press, 1993.

Lewis is former president of the SBC Home Mission Board and now involved in the Mission America project. He is an experienced planter. Though the book is out of date technologically and methodologically, it provides excellent resources related to time management and the priority of evangelism in church planting.

Logan, Robert E. *Beyond Church Growth.* Old Tappan, N.J.: Fleming H. Revell Co., 1989.

Though the title can be misleading, the book is a great resource for church planting. It provides resources for all churches, but is a great supplement for Logan's "Church Planter's Toolkit" available from www.churchsmart.com *(the best widely-available resource). Bob Logan is the most significant church- planting leader in the last 50 years, and every church planter needs to be aware of his writings and his toolkit (see below).*

Logan, Robert E., and Steven L. Ogne. *Church Planter's Toolkit.* Pasadena, Calif.: ChurchSmart Resources (www.churchsmart.com), 1995.

The Toolkit is the most widely known resource in North American church planting today. It is a twelve-tape series that provides guidance through each step of planting a high-impact North American church. It is widely known because there is no other resource as effective for practical preparation. Its two disadvantages are that it is only available in tape format and Logan is a bit dry in his presentation (though the content makes up for that).

MacNair, Donald J. *The Birth, Care and Feeding of a Local Church.* Grand Rapids, Mich.: Baker Book House, 1976.

As can be guessed from the publishing date, this book is out of date. Redford's book is equally dated, but it provides the same resource information with more clarity. The section on "Locating Seed Families" is probably the only part of the book that would be helpful for planting today.

McNamara, Roger N. *A Practical Guide to Church Planting.* Cleveland, Ohio: Baptist Mid-Missions, 1985.

McNamara is writing from the perspective of starting an independent Baptist church in the fundamentalist tradition. The book is very detailed and provides example constitutions, services, etc. It will be of limited use to others.

McNamara, Roger N., and Ken Davis, *The Y.B.H. Handbook of Church Planting: A Practical Guide to Church Planting.* Xulon Press, 2005.

McNamara is back and with a vengeance (and a cowriter, Ken Davis). After reading The YBH Handbook, *I felt guilty that my church-planting book was only 365 pages. This book is 656 (not a typo) pages. When Ken Davis wrote me and told me about the book, I was unsure it would be helpful to planters outside of their tradition. I was wrong. The book is filled with helpful information with tremendous detail. Yes, it can have too much detail like when it explains that a planter should "shave, shower, and complete your devotions so you can be ready for breakfast by seven o'clock" (554), but you also won't find a more detailed resource on the mechanics of church planting.*

Malphurs, Aubrey. *Planting Growing Churches for the Twenty-first Century: A Comprehensive Guide for New Churches and Those Desiring Renewal,* 3rd ed. Grand Rapids, Mich.: Baker Book House, 2004.

Malphurs's book is a church planting text used in academia. The book is often accused of being too focused on large church planting with large mother churches. However, this is one of the best resources available. (I am a little biased since I wrote a study guide on the book, available at www.seminaryextension.org.)

Mannoia, Kevin. *Church Planting: The Next Generation.* Indianapolis, Ind: Light and Life Communication, 1994.

Mannoia provides a "systems" book. He describes the system of his denomination (Free Methodist) which mirrors that used by many others (and created by Bob Logan, see above). Mannoia divides the system into the following categories: Parent Church Network, Profile Assessment System, New Church Incubator, Recruitment Network, Pastor Factory, Church Planter's Summit, Maturing Church Cluster, Strategic Planning Network, Harvest 1000, and the Meta-Church Network. This will be a particularly helpful resource for groups and denominations that do not have a church-planting system.

Moore, Ralph. *Starting a New Church: The Church Planter's Guide to Success.* Ventura, Calif.: Regal Books, 2002.

Ralph is the founder of the Hope Chapel movement and currently pastors a Hope Chapel in Hawaii. The book is filled with good ideas and practical advice. He writes as a seasoned church planter dispensing advice to new church planters. I particularly like the chapters on relationships. Also, the section on teaching and preaching is a necessary corrective to some trends in church planting today. This is a great book.

Moorhouse, Carl W. *Growing New Churches: Step-by-Step Procedures in New Church Planting.* Chicago: Standard Publishing Company, 1975.

Moorhouse provides a workbook-like text that is primarily made up of example forms, publications, and brochures. It is out of date.

Murray, Stuart. *Church Planting: Laying Foundations.* Scottsdale, Pa.: Herald Press, 2001.

The author explains, "This book is not a training manual. It does not engage with all the practicalities of church planting. But it is written for practitioners rather than hearers." This is an excellent work that, I hope, will help prompt others to think missiologically and theologically about church planting. The book was originally (1998) available only in Great Britain but now has a North American version. The book is one of the few books that analyzes the criticisms of church planting and gives solid answers (not just refutations). There are some excellent references to postmodern church planting without the typical obsession with "nifty" ideas and methods. The theology is off in several ways (see Timmons below) but it is a helpful resource.

Nebel, Tom. *Big Dreams in Small Places: Church Planting in Smaller Communities*. St. Charles, Ill.: ChurchSmart Resources, 2002.

Most church-planting books tell the story of church planting in suburban areas. A few address urban contexts. This is the first that address rural areas, and it does it well. The book points out some of the unique challenges and opportunities in rural church planting and provides several helpful principles for successful ministry.

Nebel, Tom, and Gary Rohmayer. *Church Planting Landmines: Mistakes to Avoid in Years 2 through 10.* Saint Charles, Ill.: ChurchSmart Resources, 2005.

Tom and Gary will help a lot of church planters avoid the most common mistakes. They have clearly identified the problems that repeat themselves in plant after plant. This book is a great gift to church planters.

Nevius, John L. *Planting and Development of Missionary Churches.* Nutley, N.J.: Presbyterian and Reformed Publishing Company, 1958.

Nevius is not well known in North American church planting for good reason. His influence is primarily found in Korea. However, his ideas influence North American planting. His emphasis on indigenous ministry (three-selfs) helped spark the remarkable growth of the Korean church.

Ratliff, Joe S., and Michael J. Cox. *Church Planting in the African-American Community.* Nashville: Broadman Press, 1993.

Church planting is always difficult, but (according to Ratliff and Cox) it is even more so in the African-American community. In the African-American context, church planting is often perceived as an insult to the established church and its pastor. This work is intended for Southern Baptists, but is widely applicable in other situations. It provides advocacy, examples, and practical suggestions.

Reddin, Opal. *Planting Churches that Grow.* Springfield, Mo.: Central Bible College Press, 1990.

One of few women (or Pentecostals) writing on the topic of church planting, Redding provides an excellent resource. First, she provides insight into some of the growth in the Pentecostal movement by emphasizing spiritual gifts and the power of the Spirit. Second, she provides some interesting insights into planting churches targeted at cults and new-agers.

Redford, Jack. *Planting New Churches*. Nashville: Broadman Press, 1978.

Redford's book was, at one time, the most influential book on Southern Baptist church planting. His "Nine Steps" were the paradigm adopted by the Home Mission Board of the Southern Baptist Convention. Though dated, the book is still a valuable resource today for the mother church seeking to start a daughter congregation. Its "steps" should not be followed by the pioneer pastor. Instead, they are intended to be followed by the involved mother church starting a daughter congregation.

Ridley, Charles R. *How to Select Church Planters*. Pasadena: Fuller Evangelistic Association, 1988.

Ridley's writing and training have become the standard used in North America to evaluate potential church planters. This book, though difficult to find, is the standard writing and should be required reading for everyone who selects church planters.

Romo, Oscar I. *American Mosaic: Church Planting in Ethnic America*. Nashville: Broadman Press, 1993.

Romo describes the current ethnic church-planting system in place among Southern Baptists. This system includes ethnic fellowships and intentional ethnic planting and training. He does advocate the need for planting by describing an increasingly pluralistic society. He then provides suggestions and worksheets to develop an ethnic planting strategy.

Sanchez, Daniel R., Ebbie C. Smith, and Curtis E. Watke. *Reproducing Congregations: A Guidebook for Contextual New Church Development*. Cumming, Ga.: Church Starting Network, 2001.

This book is a textbook and has great value for academic use. The authors show a strong grasp of the available literature, and it is heavily footnoted. I am a big fan of Dr. Sanchez, and his thorough approach comes through. Because it is geared toward an academic setting, it may be too detailed for the average North American church planter. The book covers all of church planting, not just the North American side, so it moves from starting one church, to catalytic roles, to other topics. Honestly, I wish it were two books with more information in each. Dr. Sanchez tells me that they also have PowerPoints and accompanying notebook.

Schaller, Lyle E. *Forty-four Questions for Church Planters*. Nashville: Abingdon, 1991.

In Schaller's typical 44-question format, he addresses many surprisingly contemporary issues related to church planting. (The book was published in 1991.) Unlike many how-to books, Schaller uses his question format to explore in-depth the background of many issues.

Scoggins, Dick. ***Handbook for House Churches.*** **Online, accessed 1 December 1999, http://genesis.acu.edu/cplant/archive/contr036; Internet.**

Dick Scoggins and the Rhode Island house churches are the best known home-based church-planting movement in North America. The book describes the indigenous church-planting methods of Fellowship of Church Planters, a network of house churches in Rhode Island and southern New England. It is the only resource this reviewer knows of that deals with indigenous house churches from a North American perspective.

Shenk, David W., and Ervin R. Stutzman. ***Creating Communities of the Kingdom: New Testament Models of Church Planting.*** **Scottsdale, Pa.: Herald Press, 1988.**

Shenk and Stutzman consistently look to the same place as they explain their model: the Scriptures. This resource is the best in dealing with scriptural issues and application in church planting. The model is thoroughly biblical while remaining practical. It is among the best five books available on church planting.

Sjogren, Steve, and Rob Lewin. ***Community of Kindness: A Relational Approach to Planting and Growing a Church.*** **Ventura, Calif.: Regal Books, 2003.**

Steve Sjogren is probably better known for his Servant Evangelism strategies as described in Conspiracy of Kindness. However, Steve is an experienced church planter and church-planting mentor. The approach is dialogical—with 106 thought-provoking individual ideas (like small chapters). The authors say that the book might be subtitled, Church Planting Through Servant Evangelism.

Steffan, Tom. ***Passing the Baton: Church Planting that Empowers.*** **La Habra, Calif.: Center for Organizational & Ministry Development, 1997.**

This book can fool you. It is "about" international church planting, but it is very applicable to U.S. planting, particularly in the inner-city. (Steffan does training for World Impact, a pace setter in planting indigenous churches among the urban poor.) His emphasis on empowerment is an important addition to the training of every urban church planter.

Stetzer, Edward. ***How to Plant a Church, A Seminary Extension Study Course.*** **Nashville: Seminary Extension, 2001.**

It would be a little odd to review my own book, but it might be helpful to be aware of it as a resource for church planters. This is a study course for church planters published by our denominational agency that provides external education. It can be taken as part of a certificate program or transferred to an accredited college for credit through their system. I used Malphurs's Planting Growing Churches *as the textbook, and that book would be necessary to take the course.*

Stetzer, Edward J. *Planting New Churches in a Postmodern Age.* Nashville: Broadman and Holman Publishers, 2003.

Again, it is a little strange to review my own work. Instead, let me tell you what it covers. The book basically addresses two issues: the nuts and bolts of how to plant a church in North America and what many new churches are doing to reach postmoderns. It includes materials from a survey of several hundred church planters. The companion web site is www.newchurches.com.

Stevenson, Phil. *The Ripple Church.* Indianapolis, Ind.: The Weslayan Press, 2004.

Phil has done a great job writing a book for sponsor churches seeking to multiply themselves through church planting. As one of the few of its kind, the book is a helpful resource. It will give or clarify a God-honoring church planting vision.

Sullivan, Bill M. *Starting Strong New Churches.* Kansas City, Mo.: New Start, 1997.

The book is a smaller text that provides some basic church planting information. It is intended primarily as an advocacy book geared toward Nazarenes. The strength of the book is the chapter that deals with objections to planting.

Suarez, Gustavo V. *Connections: Linking People and Principles for Dynamic Church Multiplication.* Friendswood, Tex.: Baxter Press, 2004.

Gus is a friend of mine who is the state director of missions for the New Mexico Baptist Convention. His book is available in both Spanish and English and is a worthwhile read. The title is very descriptive—it is about making the right connections for church multiplication. As such, it has a lot of direction about how to involve partners in the work (the strength of the book). It is primarily geared toward Southern Baptists, but not exclusively so.

Sylvia, Ron. *Starting High Definition Churches.* Ocala, Fla.: High Definition Resources, 2004.

When I asked Ron how he planted his church, he said "by the book." He was not referring to Scripture (though he is deeply committed to such), but to The Purpose Driven Church. *His book is about how to plant purpose-driven churches that make a high impact. Ron draws heavily on his own experience (growing to 2000 in 10 years!), Rick Warren, Andy Stanley, and Ed Young, Jr. The book's title is very descriptive—this is a great resource to know how to plant large distinct churches that reach the lost. Ron is a leader whom we will hear more from in the coming years, and this is a great contribution.*

Thomasson, George. *The Church Blueprint: Practical Helps for Building the Body.* Columbus, Ga.: Brentwood Christian Press, 2002.

This book is a compilation of resources that will assist the new church in the effective establishment of its ministry program. It takes a church from inception through the first three years of early development. The book includes contributions from 15 different authors, all of whom are Southern Baptist and relating to the SBC context. A strength of the book is the included practical worksheets for implementing the steps in the book. The book can be ordered by e-mailing blueprint@bellsouth.net.

Tidsworth, Floyd, Jr. *Life Cycle of a New Congregation.* Nashville: Broadman Press, 1992.

Tidsworth, former director of the Home Mission Board's church-planting department, has provided a planting handbook. The title is misleading since the text deals little with the actual life cycle. Instead, it primarily focuses on the birth of a new church and then its reproduction—with little about the life cycle in the middle.

Timmis, Stephen, ed. *Multiplying Churches: Reaching Communities through Church Planting.* Hearn, Rossshire, England: Christian Focus Publications, 2000.

This book is an advocacy, rather than a "how-to," book. The authors are quite clear about their intent: "(T)his is not a 'how-to' book… What the book is trying to do is to move church planting up the church agenda, and focus upon the principles rather than the practice." I believe they accomplished the former, but I am not sure about the latter. Their book is strong on encouraging people toward church planting but it is really too small (128 pages) to address the principles. The chapter on ecclesiology is excellent as is Timmis's closing chapter. It includes much review of Murray (see above) and correctly points out and corrects some of his theological issues.

Tinsley, William C. *Upon This Rock: Dimensions of Church Planting.* Atlanta, Ga.: Baptist Home Mission Board, 1985.

Tinsley's book is an advocacy book for Southern Baptists. Long before other denominations began to promote planting, Tinsley (and Redford) promoted planting among SBC churches. The book is out of date, but was a genuine forerunner that still contains some helpful principles.

Tinsley, William C. *Breaking the Mold: Church Planting in the Twenty-first Century.* Dallas: Creative Church Consultations, Inc., 1996.

This book is more up to date than Upon This Rock (and a better book, I believe). Tinsley displays a strong grasp of church-planting principles but also deals with some of the new issues that began to emerge in the late 90s. Tinsley is unique in that he has not just written church-planting books, but has also ventured into some good devotional material as well (see his publishing house, http://www.veritaspublish.com/). Tinsley has planted churches and has spent his life in mission service. He is director of a new missions agency, WorldConnex.

Towns, Elmer L. *Getting A Church Started: A Student Manual for the Theological Foundation and Practical Techniques of Planting a Church*. Lynchburg, Va.: Church Growth Institute, 1985.

Towns's book has been published in various forms. (The latest is a workbook that contains the full text of his book and tapes presented at a recent church growth conference.) The book remains the same. It is geared toward the independent Baptist. It is highly sequential and provides an effective list of tasks that will provide the planter direction.

Towns, Elmer L., and Douglas Porter. *Churches that Multiply*. Kansas City: Beacon Hill Press, 2003.

This book is a little different than many others listed... and that may be its strength. It is a series of Bible studies written in the down-to-earth style of Elmer Towns. It is not a "how-to" book. Instead, it is a series of Bible studies geared toward laypeople in the church. Dr. Towns showed me an early version that was entitled "Our Church Planting a Church." That describes the book well.

Wagner, C. Peter. *Church Planting for a Greater Harvest*. Ventura, Calif.: Regal Books, 1990.

Wagner's book is an advocacy book. It is an excellent resource for the person seeking to convince a church or denominational leader why church planting is important. It has limited methodology, but contains a good amount of denominational research.

The opinions expressed are mine alone and may not reflect the opinions of the schools where I teach or the mission agencies I serve.

Send additional suggestions for review to mail@newchurches.com

Index